COURTS AND CABINETS

BOOK
PRODUCTION
WAR ECONOMY
STANDARD

THE TYPOGRAPHY AND BINDING OF THIS BOOK CONFORM TO THE
AUTHORIZED ECONOMY STANDARDS

By the Same Author

STUDIES IN DIPLOMACY
AND STATECRAFT

BEFORE THE WAR
STUDIES IN DIPLOMACY
   Vol. I. The Grouping of the Powers
   Vol. II. The Coming of the Storm

RECENT REVELATIONS OF
EUROPEAN DIPLOMACY
   4th Edition, Revised and Enlarged

COURTS
AND
CABINETS

BY

G. P. GOOCH, D.Litt., F.B.A.

AUTHOR OF "HISTORY OF MODERN EUROPE, 1878-1919"
"STUDIES IN DIPLOMACY AND STATECRAFT," ETC.

LONGMANS, GREEN AND CO.
LONDON ∾ NEW YORK ∾ TORONTO

LONGMANS, GREEN AND CO. LTD.
OF PATERNOSTER ROW
43 ALBERT DRIVE, LONDON, S.W.19
NICOL ROAD, BOMBAY
17 CHITTARANJAN AVENUE, CALCUTTA
36A MOUNT ROAD, MADRAS

LONGMANS, GREEN AND CO.
55 FIFTH AVENUE, NEW YORK

LONGMANS, GREEN AND CO.
215 VICTORIA STREET, TORONTO

First Published 1944
Second Impression 1944

CODE NUMBER: 17715

PREFACE

A WORK by the present writer entitled *Studies in Diplomacy and Statecraft*, published in 1942, contained an essay on Political Autobiography which surveyed the apologias of some makers of history during the last four centuries. The present volume deals with writers whose testimony is of value less for what they did than what they saw and heard. That their records have to be microscopically examined in the light of their opportunities of observation, their principles and prejudices, the interval between the events described and the date of composition, and other considerations has been a commonplace since the appearance of Ranke's first book in 1824. Such contributions to knowledge are no longer taken at their face value. It has been the task of generations of editors and critics to assess the significance of each work as a whole and of the various parts, often written at different times, which compose it. These learned labours have established that historical memoirs of this class, when cautiously read, are indispensable to the study not only of the foreground of men and events but of the background of habit and atmosphere.

The thirteen authors selected for treatment in the present volume are of varying merit and celebrity, but none of them can be ignored. That eight are French, four are English, and only one is German illustrates the familiar fact that in this field of historical composition France occupies the first place, England the second, and Germany the third. No country in modern Europe can compare with France in the glitter of courts and the variety of political thrills; and nowhere has there been such a demand for historical memoirs, an appetite so gross that it has often been fed by the marketing of spurious material. The English members of the present team cannot compare with the countrymen of Dumas in colour and romance, but their historical content is in no way inferior. Wilhelmina, the sister of Frederick the Great, represents a country which has never been greatly attracted either to historical memoirs or historical novels; and her narrative, readable though it be, is less trustworthy than any of the other works included in the present survey.

The thirteen studies, seven of which have appeared in the *Contemporary Review*, possess many common features. As he turns the pages the reader continually murmurs, '*Plus ça change, plus c'est la même chose.*' 'All the world's a stage, and all the men and women merely players.' Revolutions, we are told, change everything except the human heart. Whatever the country or the century, the picture of human nature in the dramas

5

here briefly described is strikingly similar. There are the same glaring contrasts of good and evil types, the same hectic scramble for power and place, the same jealousies and backbiting, the same repulsive greed. The sub-title of this book might well be *Studies in Human Nature*. The great ones of the earth live in glass houses where we watch them in dress and undress, at work and at play. Viewed as a whole it is not a pretty picture, and the cynic may smile grimly as the blemishes emerge. But we should beware of identifying Whitehall or Windsor with England, Versailles or the Tuileries with France, Potsdam with Germany. While kings, queens and princesses, emperors and ministers, mighty soldiers and scheming *arrivistes*, were at their card-tables or busy with love and war, ordinary men and women were performing their unrecorded tasks and creating the wealth which their superiors felt themselves entitled to waste.

These studies are designed for readers without time or inclination for the originals or who lack access to large libraries, and for this reason copious quotations in French or English, abridged or unabridged, are given. Yet their purpose is rather to stimulate than to satisfy healthy appetites, and some, it may be hoped, will follow up the clues. Brief summaries and characterisations of works in several volumes—de Boislisle's incomparable edition of Saint-Simon is in forty-one—can serve merely as signposts to territory of inexhaustible human and historical interest. For the professional student there is the added attraction of attempting to discover how far these celebrated recorders and portrait-painters are to be trusted—a task which involves the patient exploration both of documentary collections and of the world of monographs in which the results of the critical scholarship of the last hundred years are mainly enshrined. The writer is indebted to the Directors of the *Contemporary Review* for permission to reprint.

G. P. G.

January 1944.

CONTENTS

CHAPTER I

MME DE MOTTEVILLE AND ANNE OF AUSTRIA

THE *Memoirs* of Mme de Motteville, published in 1723, put Anne of Austria on the map. The sister of Philip IV of Spain, the wife of Louis XIII, and the mother of Louis XIV, was hardly one of the dominating figures in French history, nor was her career lit up by the garish colours of tragedy or romance. She had more character than personality, and few queens have felt less desire to rule; yet her share in the making of the Absolute Monarchy is not to be despised. When her unloving husband died in 1643 she dedicated herself to preparing her four-year-old son for the throne, while striving courageously, if not always wisely, to maintain the royal prerogative intact. The best method, it seemed to her, was to retain the services of Mazarin, whom Richelieu had trained as his successor and whom Louis XIII had appointed when the mighty Cardinal passed away. That the Spanish princess was not a mere cipher, that she took her political duties seriously, that she made up in tenacity and clearness of purpose for her indolence and lack of brains, that she was every inch a queen, we learn from all the memoirs of the time, but from none so authoritatively and in such convincing detail as from those of her lady-in-waiting. Though Mme de Motteville was no politician her unrivalled opportunities of observation place her in the front rank of witnesses. A less finished artist than the incomparable de Retz, she had less reason to lie than the Queen's most damaging critic. Her four stout volumes record with an attractive simplicity what she saw and heard in an age of storm and stress. She knew too little of Mazarin's secrets to do full justice to the crafty Italian, but the portrait of her beloved mistress is a masterpiece of interpretation.

Françoise Bertaut, born in 1621, was the daughter of a middle-class Gentleman of the King's Chamber. Her mother, who was connected with a noble Spanish family and spent part of her youth in Spain, was favoured by Anne of Austria on her arrival in France, and, being bilingual, was employed to conduct the private correspondence with Madrid. Married at fourteen to a shy French lad of the same age, Anne felt very homesick, for of the Spanish ladies who had accompanied her only the one who had brought her up was allowed to remain. Neglected by her husband, whose passion was the chase, she took pleasure merely in what reminded her of Spain, and the sympathetic secretary became the trusted friend. When Richelieu, in pursuance of his policy of severing her contacts with her native land, ordered Mme Bertaut and her child Françoise to leave the Court, the Queen gave the latter, now ten years old, an

allowance of 600 livres.   After receiving a good education she was
married at eighteen to Langlois de Motteville, First President of
the Chambre des Comptes in Normandy, a rich, childless octogenarian.   Unsuitable as was the union, which lasted only two
years, it was not unhappy.   'J'y trouvai de la douceur avec une
abondance de toutes choses.   Si j'avois voulu profiter de l'amitié
qu'il avoit pour moi, je me serois trouvée riche après sa mort.'   In
the year of her marriage she visited the Queen, who received her
kindly and increased her allowance to 2000 livres.   On the death
of her husband and parents, Mme de Motteville returned to Paris
with her sister, and the longed-for death of the Cardinal when she
was twenty-one reopened the doors of the Court.   She never
remarried, and there is as little trace of passionate emotions in her
writings as in her life.   This serene, affectionate, cheerful, intelligent, good-natured, and unambitious woman proved a restful
and understanding companion to the sovereign whom she served
with utter devotion to the end.

The detailed narrative begins with her return to Court in 1643,
but some preliminary chapters sketch the background of events.
A brief preface asserts that kings are praised to their face, blamed
behind their back, and never told the truth.   Hence the author's
resolve to write 'in my idle hours for my own amusement what I
know of the life, character, and tastes of the Queen, and to repay
the honour she has done me in admitting me to intimacy.   I cannot
praise her in everything, but I can do her justice as future historians
who have not known her virtue and kindness cannot do.'   She
recorded events and impressions while the other ladies of the Court
were out walking or playing cards.

Mme de Motteville painted an elaborate portrait of her mistress
in 1658 which fills nine pages and is printed at the beginning of the
book.   Even a brief summary brings Anne of Austria to life, for it
embodies the intimate experience of fifteen years of sunshine and
storm.   'Nature has given her good inclinations, her sentiments
are all noble, her soul is full of sweetness and firmness.   Though it
is not my wish to exaggerate, I can say that she possesses qualities
which rank her with the greatest queens of old.   She is tall and
well built.   Her expression, gentle and majestic, always inspires
love and respect.   She has been one of the great beauties of the
century and she still puts young aspirants in the shade.   Her
large eyes are perfectly beautiful, a blend of sweetness and gravity.
Her little mouth has been the innocent accomplice of her eyes.
Her smile can win a thousand hearts, and even her enemies cannot
resist her charm.'   Her white hands were the talk of Europe.
Spectators were always delighted at the sight of her dressing or
at table.   Though she dressed well she was not the slave of fashion,
and many Parisiennes spent more on their clothes.

Her virtues, continues Mme de Motteville, particularly her generosity, ripened with her years. She was a frequent communicant, and certain persons curried favour by their show of piety. Her character was solid and she gave herself no airs. She was modest without being offended by innocent gaiety. She did not listen to evil talk, and when once she believed in people it was difficult to destroy her confidence. She was gentle, affable, and familiar with all who had the honour to serve her. She talked well and rejoiced in delicate and witty converse. She was indolent and had read little, but she made up by personal contacts. Charlemagne meant nothing to her, but she knew the history of her own time. She often visited the theatre with her son. She spent hours daily at the card-table, but those who had the honour to play with her said she displayed neither excitement nor desire for gain. She was indifferent to grandeur and admiration, loved few people but those dearly. As Regent she had been obliged to bestow her friendship on someone (Mazarin) whose ability could sustain her, and in whom she could find counsel and fidelity, service and the sweetness of confidence. Her heart was incapable of weakness or change when once she was persuaded that she was doing right. The love which her husband did not require was given to her children, especially the eldest, whom she adored. Her good treatment of her attendants was rewarded by their fidelity and gratitude. Kindness took the place of tenderness, but she was sympathetic and discreet with those who confided in her. She hated her enemies and by nature she would have liked revenge, but reason and conscience restrained her. She was seldom angry, and never deeply stirred except by the interests of the Crown. In danger she was brave and calm. When informed that her *femme de chambre* was writing her memoirs she modestly desired that she would not be praised beyond her deserts.

A very different portrait is painted in one of the most celebrated passages of the *Memoirs* of de Retz: 'La Reine avoit, plus que personne que j'aie jamais vu, de cette sorte d'esprit qui lui étoit nécessaire pour ne pas paraître sotte à ceux qui ne la connoissoient pas. Elle avoit plus d'aigreur que de hauteur, plus de hauteur que de grandeur, plus de manières que de fond, plus d'inapplication à l'argent que de libéralité, plus de libéralité que d'intérêt, plus d'intérêt que de désintéressement, plus d'attachement que de passion, plus de dureté que de fierté, plus de mémoire des injures que des bienfaits, plus d'intention de piété que de piété, plus d'opiniâtreté que de fermeté, et plus d'incapacité que de tout ce que dessus.' In weighing this elaborate indictment we must remember that it is the work of an embittered exile whose dreams of power had been shattered by his notorious failings and by her devotion and loyalty to the Minister of her choice. The *Memoirs* of La Rochefoucauld, another distinguished *frondèur*, are scarcely less critical. But neither the Cardinal nor the Duke knew her or understood her half so well as her lady-in-waiting.

The introductory chapters describe the reign of Louis XIII as seen through the eyes of the Queen, who often talked of her past trials. Neglected by her husband, bullied by Richelieu—she was haunted by the fear that he would send her back to Spain—excluded from politics, deprived of her intimate friends, it was natural that the heart of the childless woman should turn with longing to the land of her birth. The stage is dominated by the towering figure of Richelieu, who banished or executed all his enemies from Marie de Médici and Cinq-Mars downwards, and of whom Mme de Motteville always speaks with a sort of shuddering awe. Louis XIII appears as a colourless and lonely creature, unable to live happily either with or without the terrible Cardinal. The belated birth of her two sons gave the Queen something to live for, but the King's tenderness during the period of pregnancy did not last, and he had to be urged to embrace her when her child was born. The expectation that she would now take her place on the Council was unfulfilled, and she never strove for power. Starved for love, she had attracted the passionate Buckingham, who had come to conduct Henrietta Maria to England, but her heart was never touched. That she talked freely to Mme de Motteville about such intimate experiences proves that the *femme de chambre* was also the trusted friend.

Richelieu passed away in December 1642. When the priest urged him to pardon his enemies he replied, in a famous phrase, that he had had none except those of the state. That is what every dictator affects to believe, yet France was longing for a gentler hand. Richelieu, in the celebrated phrase of de Retz, 'avait foudroyé plutôt que gouverné les hommes.' Louis XIII, himself a dying man, had no time to show what he could do. In placing Mazarin at the helm he followed Richelieu's advice; but the release of prisoners from the Bastille and the recall of exiles hinted that the Cardinal's cruelties had not been to his taste. Serenity returned to the faces of the courtiers, and the throng in the Queen's antechamber indicated the relief that her power had increased; but she received no greater consideration from the King. He expressed regret that he had kept his mother in exile and had not made peace with Spain, but there was no contrition for the treatment of his wife. When told that he was dying he remarked that he had never felt so much joy in his life as at the news that he was about to leave it. The Queen surprised Mme de Motteville by confessing that she felt real grief at the loss of her husband, as if her heart had been torn out. The intentions of Louis le Juste had been excellent, and it was generally considered the fault of the Cardinal that his good qualities had never found scope.

The full narrative begins when Anne of Austria became Regent in May 1643 and within fairly broad limits could do what she liked. Mme de Motteville was never dazzled by the splendours of Court life, and she confesses that some of its incidents were as good as a comedy. Having neither ambitions nor fears she was happy enough, but she testifies that a Court is not a happy place. 'We have now reached the Queen's regency, and shall see, as in a picture, the revolutions of fortune's wheel; the climate of that country which is called the Court, the measure of its corruption, the good luck of those who are fated to live there. For no one is the air mild or serene. Those who seem entirely happy and are adored like gods are most menaced by the storm. The thunder never ceases. It is a windy region, dark and subject to continual tempests. Its inmates are chronic sufferers from the contagious malady ambition which deprives them of repose, ravages their hearts, and affects their reason. This malady also generates a distaste for the best things. They are ignorant of the price of equity, justice, and kindness. The sweetness of life, the innocent pleasures, everything which the sages of antiquity declared to be good, seem to them ridiculous. They are incapable of knowing virtue and obeying its maxims unless chance removes them from this sphere. Then, if they can cure themselves of this malady, they become wise and see the light. No one should be such a good Christian or philosopher as a courtier cured of his delusions.' The *Memoirs* may be described as a commentary on this pungent text, though the sky is rarely so dark as it suggests.

The Queen received the plaudits of the people as she drove back to Paris from Saint-Germain where Louis XIII had died. 'La Reine,' writes de Retz, 'étoit adorée beaucoup plus par ses disgrâces que par sou mérite. L'on ne l'avoit vue que persécatée, et la souffrances, aux personnes de ce rang, tient lieu d'une grande vertu. L'on se vouloit imaginer que elle avoit eu de la patience, qui est très-souvent figurée par indolence. On donnoit tout, on ne refusoit rien.' Never did a Regency open under such happy auspices, testifies Mme de Motteville, and never did a queen of France possess so much authority and glory. Her first task was to recall her banished friends—Mme de Senecé, her *dame d'honneur*, Mlle de Hautefort, who had so nearly won the tepid heart of Louis XIII, Mme de Chevreuse, the inveterate intriguer, once the superintendent of her household. She needed no encouragement to become the effective ruler by annulling the will of the late King which limited her power by the nomination of a council. No monarch had the right to bind his successor, and the Parlement of Paris, that august corporation of lawyers which longed to recover the authority it had lost under the Cardinal, was delighted to co-operate. Orleans was appointed Lieutenant-General, and Condé his deputy, while Mazarin continued to carry on the business of the State.

Anne of Austria, we are repeatedly informed, was indolent by nature, and she soon found the burden of rule almost intolerable. There was such a throng of petitioners with complaints of Richelieu and demands for redress that she sometimes kept in her room. 'Chacun lui demandait des grâces, et chacun se faisoit un mérite auprès d'elle des choses passées.' A buffer was needed, and Mazarin was there. Mme de Motteville never liked, never greatly disliked, never really knew, and never fully understood that supple and complicated personage. She realised that her mistress had no choice, for he was a born diplomatist and held all the threads of foreign policy in his hands. 'Je vous remets mon ouvrage entre les mains,' wrote the dying Richelieu, 'pour le conduire à sa perfection.' The Cardinal chose well, for no member of the Bourbon clan, legitimate or otherwise, was equal to the task. The Queen had asked a friend what he was like, and received the reassuring reply, 'the exact opposite of Richelieu.' He won over the two most influential men in France, the head of the House of Condé and Gaston, Duke of Orleans, brother of the late King, commonly known as Monsieur; and the conquest of the Queen's favour was only a matter of days. He quickly mastered the Council and began the long evening talks with the Regent which, on her side at any rate, ripened into love. He disarmed rivals and antagonists by 'sa manière douce et humble, sous laquelle il cachoit son ambition et ses desseins.' If Richelieu was the lion, Mazarin was the cat: there was something a little feline in the movements of this master of *finesse*. 'Le fort de M. le Cardinal Mazarin,' testifies his bitter enemy, de Retz, 'était proprement de donner à entendre, de faire espérer; de jeter des lueurs, de les retirer; de donner les vues, de les brouiller. Il s'érigea en Richelieu, mais il n'en eut que l'impudence de l'imitation. Il ne fut ni doux ni cruel, parce qu'il ne se ressouvenoit ni des bienfaits ni des injures. Il avait de l'esprit, de l'insinuation, de l'enjouement, des manières, mais le vilain cœur paroissoit toujours au travers. Il avoit beaucoup d'esprit mais n'avoit point d'âme.' Mme de Motteville pays homage to his extraordinary skill and the mildness of his rule. 'Never did a man with so much power and so many enemies pardon so easily or imprison so few.' He was envied, hated, and despised, but not greatly feared, for he never shed blood. Olivier d'Ormesson, his antagonist in the Parlement, speaks of 'un grand douceur dans le visage.' His worst fault was his shameless avarice.

A year after her husband's death the Queen Regent moved from

the Louvre to the Palais Royal, which Richelieu had left to
Louis XIII, and it is here that most of the scenes so vividly
described were enacted. Mazarin bought a house close by, and a
door was made in the garden wall so that he could enter more or
less unobserved. A year later the Queen Regent announced to
the Council that the Cardinal, who was unwell, had been assigned
a room in the palace so that he could discuss affairs of state with
her at any time. Tongues began to wag and the stream of
Mazarinades to flow. Anne hated causing people pain, particularly
when they were old friends, and a sharp attack of jaundice was
attributed by her doctors to worry; but there were limits to her
tolerance. The criticisms and admonitions of Mlle de Hautefort
became so intolerable that she had to leave the Court. When
Mme de Motteville pleaded for her, the Regent was cool, and to a
request for permission to visit her replied coldly 'Do as you like.'
A much more formidable personage, the Duchesse de Chevreuse,
was also dismissed, for the incorrigible intriguer had joined the
ranks of Mazarin's foes. The observant *femme de chambre* saw a
good deal of the quarrels of the Court, and the Queen told her
more. She does not spare her sex. 'Les dames sont d'ordinaire
les premières causes des plus grand renversements des États;
et les guerres, qui ruinent les royaumes et les empires, ne procédent
presque jamais que des effets que produisent ou leur beauté ou
leur malice.' There was no country, she added, where tongues
wagged more unrestrainedly and people were more inclined to
misjudge and calumniate their sovereigns.

Graver problems had to be faced than the quarrels of pretty
women, for France felt the lack of a master hand. Richelieu had
laid the foundations of Absolute Monarchy, but the completion of
the proud structure awaited the coming of Louis XIV. Though
Mazarin possessed the Queen's confidence and won her heart, he
had no party behind him, and he was disliked as a foreigner to the
end. The victories of the Duc d'Enghien in the Spanish wars,
welcome though they were, cost money, and the crushing burden
of taxation led to riots in the provinces from 1643 onwards.
Mazarin, like Richelieu, had no understanding of finance, which
he left to Emery, 'l'esprit le plus corrompu de son siècle,' as
de Retz calls him; and every new impost raised angry protests.
The Duc de Beaufort, the frivolous son of the Duc de Vendôme,
a bastard of Henri IV, won the title of Le Roi des Halles and
captained the little group of political critics known as Les
Importants; but his seditious activities were interrupted by
imprisonment at Vincennes. When the Regent visited the Parlement in state in 1648, accompanied by her son, Monsieur, and
Condé, she was treated to an outspoken discourse by Omer Talon
on the burdens of the people and the power of favourites. The

warning was in vain. So anxious was she to exalt Mazarin's power that she wished everything, above all favours, to appear as his decision. Mme de Motteville, though the soul of loyalty, felt that he was given too much power, and in 1646, after three years of his undisputed rule, her position at Court was threatened for the first time. Mlle de Beaumont, one of the Queen's ladies, was so frank in her criticisms that the Minister persuaded the Queen to dismiss her. Since Mme de Motteville was her friend, though she never approved her audacious sallies, he wished for her dismissal as well. For once he was refused. 'La Reine qui me connoissoit dès mon enfance, et qui savoit que j'avois des intentions droites, ne pouvait douter de ma fidélité. Elle fut assez bonne de répondre de moi à son ministre, et de l'assurer de la netteté de mon procédé, sans en être instruite par moi; tout il est vrai qu'en toutes occasions il faut bien faire et de ne se vanter jamais. Comme le Cardinal Mazarin n'avait pas fortement déterminé ma perte, il se laissa aisément persuader par elle; et je me sauvai de cette sorte d'un châtiment que je n'avois pas mérité, et d'un péril que je n'aperçus qu'après qu'il fût passé.'

Mazarin's suspicions remained, for some of her acquaintances were no friends of his, and one day he took her severely to task: 'Comme il ne connaissait pas mes intentions, et qu'il jugeoit de moi sur l'opinion qu'il avoit de la corruption universelle du monde, il ne pouvait s'empêcher de me soupçonner de me mêler de beaucoup de choses contraires à son interét. Il me dit un jour qu'il étoit persuadé de cela, parce que je ne lui disois jamais rien des autres, que j'écoutois parler les mécontens, que j'étois dans leur confidence, et que par ma manière d'agir je faisois voir clairement le peu d'affection que j'avais pour le service de la Reine: ajoutant que mes amis me faisoient tort en publiant que j'étois une honnête personne, sûre et généreuse, parce que cela vouloit dire qu'on pouvoit murmurer avec moi sans crainte.' It was the most disagreeable interview in her life, but she retained her poise. It was not her habit, she replied, to tell tales. Since she had always been faithful to the Queen and felt no hostility to the Minister, she discharged her duty in defending the truth against the grumblers, some of whom were her friends. Her watchword was to be faithful to all and to seek no reward beyond the approval of her conscience. Those who spread reports should be the objects of his greatest distrust, while those who did no harm to anyone could never fail in their duty. Mazarin took no further steps, but she realised that his favour had not been regained, and her comment on this incident is unusually severe. His reproaches, she declares, showed 'combien nous étions malheureuses de vivre sous la puissance d'un homme qui aimait la friponnerie, et avec qui la probité avoit si peu de valeur qu'il en faisoit un crime.'

Mme de Motteville never dreamed of going into opposition to the Minister whom she continued to regard as the only possible ruler of France. Here is a more balanced portrait, painted in 1647, a year before the Fronde. 'The greatness of his genius set him above his fellows not only by good fortune but by his intellectual superiority. None of his entourage had influence with him except when it was necessary for his designs. He had great experience in foreign affairs and he was capable of the loftiest enterprises. He was a great worker. His policy was subtle; he was a master of intrigue; he reached his goal by *détours* and *finesse* which were almost impossible to follow. He was neither malicious nor cruel. He had no unmeasured ambition at first, dispensing with the big establishment which all other favourites had possessed. He had taken no posts, dignities, or charges. His avarice was not yet fully revealed. Several who paid court to him owed him great favours, and many of them were richer than he. He was pleasant enough, and, despite his faults, he will doubtless be spoken of as an extraordinary man. His prodigious power will astonish every one. He shared the destiny of great men both in his good and evil fortune. I doubt if all the centuries will be able to provide a greater reputation.' Yet it would have been better for France had the Regent possessed more ability or self-confidence, for his knowledge that he was indispensable rendered him less considerate to everyone else. Doing everything himself, he was difficult to see, and there were murmurs among the persons of quality who thronged his antechamber. Anticipating Frederick the Great, he used to say that he was content to let them talk so long as they let him act. Mme de Motteville tired of these criticisms, not only because they were sometimes unjust but because they were futile. He rode with a light rein, preferring warnings to punishments. He could please when he liked, and it was impossible not to feel the charm of his blandishments; but when the favourable expectations were unfulfilled they were replaced by disgust.

During the first five years—le temps de la bonne Régence, to quote Saint-Evremond—Mazarin's power was unassailable. The prestige of the monarchy stood high, the royal favour seemed a sure defence, military victories strengthened his hands, and he was not a man of blood. Little by little, however, his adopted country became conscious of his faults, some of which were attributed to his foreign origin. People complained that he was ignorant of French customs and did not trouble to learn them; that he failed to govern in accordance with the ancient laws; that justice was not administered. These criticisms are dismissed by Mme de Motteville as not very serious. His temperament, in her view, disposed him less to do evil than to neglect to do good.

2

He seemed neither to esteem any virtue nor to hate any vice. He made profession neither of piety nor the reverse, though he indulged in occasional raillery. He gave ecclesiastical preferment without troubling about the virtue of the nominee. By nature he was distrustful. He professed to fear nothing and to despise advice to take care of himself, though in reality his personal safety was always in his mind. Despite the swelling chorus of criticism the favourite was still a person to cultivate. 'Lorsqu'il monta en carrosse pour s'en aller, toute la Cour du Palais Royal était pleine de cordons bleus, de grand seigneurs, de gens de qualité qui par leur empressement paroissoient s'estimer trop heureux de l'avoir pu regarder de loin. Tous les hommes sont naturellement esclaves de la fortune, et je puis dire n'avoir guère vu de personne à la Cour qui ne fût flatteur, les uns plus, les autres moins.' The author of this pungent passage stood aloof from the flattering throng.

Mazarin was safe enough so long as the two most powerful men in the state were not his foes. Gaston, Duke of Orleans, appears in the pages of Mme de Motteville as the cowardly weathercock that he was—'le dernier des hommes,' as the Queen contemptuously described him. He was good-looking and intelligent, talked well and was widely read. He was rather too proud of his rank. He would keep ladies of quality standing, and, unlike his brother, did not bid the men put on their hats when the weather was bad. He was said to be timid and lazy, and no one desired to see him in command of the troops. This is letting off lightly a man neither respected nor loved, of whom de Retz truthfully declared that fear soiled the whole course of his life, and that he was the most uncertain man in the world. Very different was the young Duc d'Enghien, the bravest of the brave, the victor of Rocroy, of whose military genius all Europe was beginning to talk. When he succeeded his father in 1646 as head of the House of Condé and the first nobleman in the land, he began to attend the Council and to develop political ambitions. At the moment the Queen was too popular, Monsieur too loyal, the Cardinal insufficiently hated to take risks; but Mme de Motteville watched the growth of his fame with apprehension. Sooner or later, she felt, the young hero was likely to fish in troubled waters.

The return to Paris in 1647 of his beautiful sister increased Condé's influence, for Mme de Longueville shared both his ability and his thirst for power. Every one hoped to win her favour and she quickly dominated the life of the Court. 'Il étoit impossible de la voir sans l'aimer et sans désirer de lui plaire. Elle devint l'objet de tous les désires; sa ruelle devint le centre de toutes les intrigues, et ceux qu'elle aimoit devinrent aussitôt les mignons de la fortune. Ses courtisans furent révérés du ministre; et dans peu de temps nous allons la voir la cause de toutes nos révolutions et de toutes les brouilleries qui ont pensé perdre la France. Enfin on peut dire qu'alors toute la grandeur, toute la gloire, toute la galanterie étoient renfermées dans cette famille de Bourbon, dont M. le Prince étoit le chef, et que le bonheur n'étoit plus estimé un bien s'il ne venoit de leurs mains.' Next to her brilliant brother no one held such a high place in her circle and in her heart as the Duc de la Rochefoucauld, author of the celebrated *Maxims* which enshrine the polished cynicism of the era of the Fronde.

With the opening of 1648 we reach the most detailed, the most exciting, and the most valuable portion of the *Memoirs*. We are fortunate in possessing a story of the Fronde by an inmate of the Court as thrilling and elaborate as those of de Retz and La Grande Mademoiselle, the brain and the Amazon of the Opposition. It was an unhappy time for the author, for she hated turmoil and made no pretence to courage. Like Anne of Austria, she could conceive no other system than the personal rule of kings; yet she was never a blind royalist, for she detested cruelty and injustice. Though she realised that neither her mistress nor Mazarin was a heaven-sent pilot, she thought them a better team than the lawyers, the princes, and the mob with whom they had to contend. The perils of this miniature French Revolution bound the Queen Regent and her faithful friend closer than ever.

The storm which had been brewing broke in January 1648, when the Parlement of Paris—the most important of the ten Parlements of France—emerged as the temporary champion of popular rights. Anything less like the English Parliament it is impossible to imagine, for it possessed no vestige of representative character and lacked political experience. It was a Court of Appeal, not a legislature. Divided into four sections, it appointed its own members, some of whom had bought their posts, while others possessed what may be described as hereditary fiefs. Some of them, like Mathieu Molé and Olivier d'Ormesson, were good lawyers and men of excellent character, but they formed a caste. Never before had they had such a chance of making history as in the interregnum between the death of Richelieu and the majority of Louis XIV, for the States-General had ceased to meet and fiscal abuses cried aloud for remedy. Though they possessed no direct political authority, they had claimed and exercised the right since the fifteenth century to make humble remonstrances to the King, and royal edicts were solemnly registered at a *Lit de Justice*. In 1641 Richelieu had compelled them to register a declaration forbidding the discussion of administrative matters, but their prestige revived in 1643 when they cancelled the limitations on the Regent imposed by the will of Louis XIII. Combining with other discontented elements in the state they were able for a brief space to challenge the authority not only of the Spanish Regent and the Italian Cardinal, but of the Crown. Mazarin learned from the *Mazarinades* which poured from the press in hundreds that he was hated, and that the country desired the Regent to rule; but this was impossible, for she was obviously unequal to the task. If the deeper cause of the First Fronde was the weakness of the Government, its occasion was the heavy cost of the war. Risings had occurred in 1643 and 1644. The kind heart of the Queen was touched by the terrible poverty of the people, but there was little she could do, and at times she complained that her Minister was *trop bon*. That his mildness was taken for timidity was true enough, and the collapse of the Stuart throne was not without psychological effect in the turbulent capital of France. Mazarin fully understood that he could not go too far.

When Henrietta Maria left England, after the defeat of Charles I, she returned broken and almost penniless to the land of her birth, where she was welcomed and succoured by her sister-in-law. Her account of the civil war, fully reproduced by Mme de Motteville, aroused sympathy rather than apprehension, for at that time the Regent did not believe that such things could happen in France. 'She had a great contempt for the lawyers, and could not imagine that this section of the King's subjects might upset her affairs. She was ignorant of the great events which from small beginnings have overturned the most powerful kingdoms and ruined the strongest empires. Thus knowing only her own grandeur, and the external display by which royalty is surrounded, she was unable to conceive that her regency, which she saw accompanied by so much glory, could be exposed to revolution. That is why she proposed punishment as a remedy to nip revolt in the bud, and this sentiment was shared by the cleverest heads at Court. She often told her intimates that she would never consent to *cette canaille* (the lawyers) attacking the authority of her son; so much so that her Minister, who had never believed that their audacity would reach a point at which he would be compelled to yield, ended by regretting that he had excited her against the Parlement. This princess, so gentle and kind, had nevertheless an incomparable firmness. If she had found support she would have pursued a policy of severity and vigour in this encounter, where it was a question of punishing the subjects who wished to oppose the King's authority.' When stirred to anger, as we learn from de Retz, an unfriendly critic, her voice rose to a high falsetto. Mazarin remarked that she possessed the courage of a valiant soldier unaware of the extent of the danger.

The first open challenge to the Government came from the Parlement at the *Lit de Justice* of January 15, 1648, held to register seven new taxes. 'Il importe à votre Majesté,' declared the Avocat-Général, Omer Talon, in addressing the little King and his mother, 'que nous soyons des hommes libres et non des esclaves.' For the last ten years, he continued, the countryside had been ruined. The peasants were reduced to sleeping on the straw in order to supply the extravagances of Paris, and the only property they possessed was their souls. The Queen Regent was implored to reflect on the public misery, 'ce soir dans la solitude de votre oratoire,' and to give the people peace and bread. Five months later, on June 30, delegates of various official corporations joined with the Parlement in drawing up a programme of financial and administrative reforms, including the abolition of Richelieu's officials, the Intendants, and the hated *lettres de cachet*. Mazarin bowed to the storm, accepted most of the demands, cancelled the new taxes, and dismissed Emery, the Minister of Finance.

The Government had lost the first round, and the gravity of the situation was no longer in doubt. The people, testifies Mme de Motteville, were crushed by taxation; the kingdom impoverished by the long war; everyone complained. The courtiers detested the Minister. Everyone wished for a change, though rather from confusion of thought than on rational grounds. The Minister being despised, every man felt at liberty to follow his own caprice. All sections, though from different motives, combined to condemn the Queen and her favourite, forgetting the injustice of allowing the Parlement to reform the state as it liked, a course which would lead to the destruction of the monarchy. If the Parlements had the power to correct the errors of kings and ministers, they might commit greater errors themselves, and substitute vice for virtue on the throne. In a word, the ambitions and passions of the many might be much more dangerous than those of a single individual. The Parlement should have realised from the docility of the Cardinal, and the offers already made, that if they had discovered some disorder in the finances and modestly requested reform it would have been granted, and they would have deserved the reputation of irreproachable subjects and magistrates. Since this was not their attitude, the Minister was driven to dissimulation in the promised royal reply. The Queen, it declared, had such a good opinion of their fidelity that she could not believe their meetings could be deliberately prejudicial to the service of the King, and therefore she allowed them to be held. Mazarin was so shaken by the tempest that he begged Mme de Senecé, who was looking after his nieces, to educate them 'en simples demoiselles,' since he did not know what would become of them or of himself.

The dismissal of Emery, himself an Italian and a friend of Mazarin, encouraged the Parlement to further demands. Every councillor, writes Mme de Motteville sarcastically, seemed to the people an angel descended from heaven to save them from the pretended tyranny of the Cardinal. Monsieur attempted to mediate, but the Queen's monarchical pride was deeply hurt. After one of her usual complaints of his mildness Mazarin humbly replied: 'Enfin, madame, je vois bien que j'ai déplu à Votre Majesté. J'ai très mal réussi dans le dessein que j'ai toujours eu de la bien servir. Il est juste que ma tête en réponde. Sur quoi la Reine, qui étoit douce et qui avait de la bonté pour lui, persuadée de ses bonnes intentions et de son désintéressement, lui dit qu'elle ne le puniroit pas de son malheur, et qu'il devoit être assuré qu'il ne perdroit jamais par là ni son affection ni sa confiance.' That is how these little scenes always ended, for her admiration and gratitude had grown into love. The royal romance was the theme of many scurrilous *Mazarinades*. Were they secretly married, as some authorities believe? We cannot tell. She neither affirmed nor denied it. Mme de Motteville says nothing about it, but her silence may be due to discretion. Even with such a friend at her side the Queen was sometimes depressed. When he remarked that she was not looking well, and bade her take care of herself, she gloomily replied that in view of the evil state of her affairs she did not worry about death. The little King, aged ten, heard the words and began to cry quietly.

At this stage of the preliminary skirmishing Mme de Motteville interrupts her narrative to expound her own simple creed. The Parlements possessed the right of making remonstrances to their kings and telling them the truth frankly and respectfully: next to the States-General they were the most useful outlets for popular discontents. Fortunately they were living in a century when, thanks to the virtues of the Queen, there was no need of drastic change. 'Elle vouloit que sous son règne tous pussent jouir d'une douce tranquillité et ne fussent occupés qu'à servir Dieu et le Roi.' Protests were unjust and unnecessary since she had followed the moderating advice of her Minister. Almost all the rebellions in French history, she argues, had been unjustifiable. 'Our kings, scions of the greatest race in the world, and in comparison with whom the Cæsars and most of the princes who have ruled over many nations are only commoners (*roturiers*), have provided saints of the royal blood. None of them deserves the name of very wicked, such as we find in other monarchies, who have been the execration of their peoples and are still the object of anger and horror. It is unjust and contrary to reason that subjects command where they should obey. A state in which the head lacks power, and to whom the subjects refuse the obedience which is his due, is a ship without a pilot.' The evil example of revolt set by Paris was followed by the provincial Parlements. 'Ainsi toutes choses, au dedans de la France, étaient en mauvais état.' Such was the sombre prospect in 1648 as seen through the windows of the Palais Royal.

The faithful *femme de chambre* was moved to admiration by the steadfast courage of her mistress. 'Everywhere there was a horrible spate of curses against the government, a mad licence in the insults to the Minister. The Queen, who was openly attacked, was hated on account of the man whose greatness she upheld. In their blindness and ignorance the truth was overwhelmed; for the Cardinal did not deserve such hatred nor the Queen so much blame.' Regarding herself as the source of the authority she conferred on him, she thought she could easily recover it and could not diminish it by handing him a share, since it was given only to enable him to serve her better. She was mistaken, and her line of policy earned contempt and blame from those who envied his omnipotence. Yet in believing it to be her duty to support him, she was primarily concerned with the glory of the Crown, and the attacks of the Parlement strengthened her desire to resist. She did not believe that he was the real cause of its revolt. Though she often thought him too weak, she could not as a Christian blame his desire to win over his opponents, and she realised that if he had been dealing with reasonable beings he would have met with the desired response. Though aware of all the inventions of popular malice against her motives and character, her knowledge of her own heart helped her to bear them and her faith led her to hope for divine protection. She knew that, whatever she did, she would never escape the evil interpretations usually placed on the actions of princes nor the hatred which nations are accustomed to feel for their ministers. This is finely said, but to the end of her days Mme de Motteville never quite realised the measure of the Queen's devotion to the Cardinal nor the strength she derived from this partnership of head and heart.

CHAPTER II

MME DE MOTTEVILLE AND THE FRONDE

THE Fronde took its name from the sling used by boys to hurl stones, and the word suggests irresponsibility. The drama of the First Fronde—a conflict between the Parlement and people of Paris and the Crown—opened on August 26, 1648, with the arrest of Broussel, a respected old magistrate who had won popularity by perpetually crying '*Moins d'impôts, pas d'impôts.*' Other officials were arrested at the same time, but Broussel was the hero of the day. The Government had decided to strike at its critics when on August 22 the news arrived of Condé's victory over the Spaniards at Lens. Paris hit back with the cry '*Aux Armes!*' and the erection of barricades across the narrow streets. De Retz, the Coadjutor of his uncle the Archbishop of Paris, thirsting for power and popularity, and desiring to supplant Mazarin as the First Minister and favourite of the Queen, describes how he came to the Palais Royal to warn the Court of its peril. 'Rendez Broussel au peuple, ou vous risquerez gros. Vour êtes assiégés, et un contre mille.' 'J'étranglerais plutôt leur Broussel de ces mains,' cried the angry Queen, whose Hapsburg pride was deeply hurt. Her face, even more than her words, told the visitor what she thought of him as she contemptuously exclaimed: 'Allez, Monsieur, allez vous reposer: vous avez bien travaillé.' The snub was never forgiven by the Catiline of the Church, as he has been called, henceforth one of the most dangerous enemies of the Crown, though he always pretended to be its friend. After this encounter the stout-hearted Queen smilingly inquired if Mme de Motteville had not been scared. She had always teased her about her 'poltronnerie.' 'J'avois pensé mourir d'étonnement quand on me vint dire que Paris était en armes: ne croyant pas que jamais dans ce Paris, le séjour des délices et des douceurs, on pût voir la guerre ou les barricades que dans l'histoire et la vie d'Henri III. Enfin cette plaisanterie dura tout le soir; et comme j'étois la moins vaillante de la compagnie, toute la honte de cette journée tomba sur moi.'

On the following day, August 27, a deputation of the magistrates, with Molé at their head, came to the Palais Royal to demand the release of the prisoner. The First President, declares de Retz, was as intrepid as Gustavus Adolphus or Condé himself, caring only for the good of the state. They were sharply lectured by the Queen, who warned them that the King, her son, would punish them some day. It was a blank cartridge, for the boy was only nine, and the spokesman advised her to avert the unpleasantness of a forced surrender by a voluntary act. It was impossible, she replied, to accept this blow to the royal authority and to leave unpunished a man who had attacked it with such insolence. They could see by the mildness of her Regency what were her intentions. She was quite disposed to pardon Broussel, but they knew that kings were obliged to exercise a certain severity for the sake of order. When she left the room the First President ran after her and implored her to think again. Let them do their duty, she replied, and let them show more respect for the wishes of the King, in which case she would grant all the favours they could justly expect. The Chancellor explained that the prisoners would be released if the Parlement ceased to discuss affairs of state.

On their way back from the Palais Royal the magistrates were held up at the barricades in the Rue Saint-Honoré by an excited crowd. The First President, with a pistol at his head, was told that they would kill him unless Broussel was freed and that he must at once return to the Palace. The conflict between the Parlement and the Crown had entered on a new phase, for henceforth the mob took a hand in the game. Mme de Motteville watched the magistrates filing back into the Palace, where, as they had eaten nothing all day, the kind-hearted Queen ordered a meal. This time she did not appear, and there was less disposition to exchange reproaches than to find a way out. The Chancellor presided, Monsieur was present, and Mazarin made a brief speech. Recognising that the Parlement, like the Queen, had good intentions, he declared that agreement should be easy. Mme de Motteville was told by an eye-witness that he repeated these words several times in a confused manner, so that they produced merriment instead of making an impression. On emerging from the Council his face was serene, and indeed he was always gentler, more human, and more easy of approach in misfortune than when the sun shone. This gentleness, she explains, was only skin deep, for his promises were rarely fulfilled, and petitioners owed his favours rather to his weakness than to kindness of heart.

After the meeting the magistrates were received by the Queen and a compromise was reached, for the violence in the street had complicated the situation. She grudgingly consented to release Broussel next day, and the Parlement promised to confine itself to its legal functions for the next few months. It was a victory over the Crown, declares Mme de Motteville, who complains that, though the misfortunes of her mistress were great, the number of sympathisers was small. 'Voici donc le prisonnier Broussel que la Reine est contrainte de rendre: le Parlement est victorieux, et lui et le peuple sont les maîtres.' The mob was in an ugly mood, threatening to sack the Palais Royal and expel the Cardinal if they were tricked. The cry was heard: '*Vive le Roi tout seul et M. de Broussel!*' That night even the Queen was anxious and her timid *femme de chambre* did not go to bed. On his release next morning 'le pauvre petit homme, qui n'avoit rien recommendable que d'être entêté du bien public et de la haine des impôts,' received a triumph worthy of a Roman Emperor. During this brief crisis, when there were rumours that the young King might be carried off to the Hôtel de Ville, his mother sustained the courage of the whole Court. 'Ne craignez point,' she said; 'Dieu n'abandonnera pas l'innocence du Roi; il faut se confier en lui.' Mazarin, now thoroughly alarmed, kept his horses saddled and bridled throughout the night.

The crisis in Paris, though soon over, left trouble behind. Monsieur, hitherto friendly, demanded more power from the Government whose weakness had been exposed. Having failed to obtain a cardinal's hat for a *protégé*, he publicly denounced the ingratitude of the Queen and exclaimed that her Minister was a rogue. Though some influential malcontents rallied to his standard, his record was not that of a man of action, and Condé assured the Queen that he would guarantee the safety of the Court. Mazarin, as usual, preferred negotiation to a fight. The Palais Royal and the Luxembourg, testifies Mme de Motteville, were afraid of one another, and the former, where the kidnapping of the young King was a nightmare, was guarded by troops. In September the Queen and her son left Paris; but after a month of negotiations Mazarin persuaded her to sign the Declaration of Saint-Germain suppressing the new taxes, and the Court returned. The Opposition was not satisfied with its victory, for Mazarin was still at the helm, and de Retz was mobilising his enemies. The Court was weary of useless concessions, and on January 6, 1649, accompanied by the young King and Mazarin, Monsieur and Condé, the Queen fled to Saint-Germain, where nothing was ready for their reception. The secret had been well kept, and Mme de Motteville, who had spent the evening with her mistress as usual before retiring to her home near the Palais Royal, had no suspicions. At the last moment she was invited by a friend in the service of Mazarin to follow her mistress, but she declined for various reasons 'qui toutes regardoient ma commodité et mon repos.' What they were she does not explain. When the news spread in the early morning there was consternation in the capital. Some, moved by duty or calculation, hastened to Saint-Germain, while others sought refuge in their country homes.

Fearing bloodshed the terrified *femme de chambre* decided to make for her old haunts in Normandy. She was not drawn to Saint-Germain, where even the grandees were living in discomfort. 'D'autre côté, je n'étois pas assez vaillante pour demeurer dans une ville assiégée où je me verrais, peut-être, reduite à beaucoup de souffrances et à faire malgré moi des vœux contre les armes du roi.' The Parlement endeavoured to rebuild the bridges, but the Queen had lost faith in soft words. Seeing that there was no retreat, it armed the citizens and proclaimed Mazarin an enemy of the state. Friends of the Court were now exposed to such threats and insults that Mme de Motteville, accompanied by her sister and a friend and wearing a mask, attempted to escape. Set upon by the mob in the Rue Saint-Honoré she took refuge in the church of Saint-Roch where High Mass was in progress. She knelt before the altar; but a woman, more horrible than a Fury, tore off her mask, denounced her as a Mazarine and cried that she ought to be torn in pieces. The mob poured into the church, shouting for the blood of the fugitives. The Curé, who happened to be her confessor, pleaded with the crowd, and some friends, hearing of her plight, came to her rescue and escorted her home. It was the narrowest escape of her life. Not till the exiled Henrietta Maria kindly took her into her apartments in the Louvre a few days later did she feel herself safe, though even then the nights were made hideous by the cry ' *Aux Armes !*' The city was blockaded by the royal troops under the command of Condé, who had resisted the appeal of de Retz to join the Opposition, and the citizens were confronted by the spectre of semi-starvation.

Mme de Longueville had declined the invitation to accompany the Court to Saint-Germain, and the Queen of the Fronde took up her quarters in the Hôtel de Ville. Conti, her younger brother, described by de Retz as *un zéro*, also stayed in Paris, and her lover La Rochefoucauld was at her side. Condé denounced the apostasy of his family, but Monsieur, who had been on friendly terms with the Parlement, strove in a half-hearted way for peace. The Queen longed for reconciliation, but, as she explained to her friends, she would not commit the mistake of Charles I in throwing Strafford to the wolves. Mazarin, however, was no Strafford, for he never favoured a fight to a finish. After an almost bloodless civil war peace was concluded in May with the abolition of *lettres de cachet* and the recognition of the claim of the Parlement to financial and administrative supervision. It was only a truce, for the Queen grudged concessions to men who, she said, had wished to dethrone her son. Mazarin, though equally chagrined, recommended the compromise in the belief that he would ultimately regain the lost ground. Most of the Frondeurs came to pay their respects at Saint-Germain, but the interviews were chilly enough. De Retz visited the Queen but not the Cardinal. The Duc de Longueville, who turned pale and blushed, said not a word. When Mme de Longueville was received in private audience the *femme de chambre* broke the embarrassing silence by asking what time she had left Paris. It was so obvious that no restoration of confidence had occurred that this inveterate intriguer strove to detach her brother Condé from the Court.

A brief visit to Paris convinced Mme de Motteville that rebellion was still in the air. One need not be an astrologer, she remarks, to foretell a speedy renewal of the strife. She paints a depressing picture of France in the summer of 1649. The taxes were in arrears, the peasants groaned, the soldiers were unpaid, the Court ill served, and some of the Crown jewels were in pawn. 'This monarchy, so great and opulent, with a Court admired by all Europe, was quickly reduced to utter misery.' When the Court returned in August, after an absence of seven months, the Queen was surprised by the acclamations of the crowd, and for the moment she seemed to have the ball at her feet. She received the Parlement, the merchants and other official bodies, all outwardly very subdued. The turbulent Mme de Chevreuse, weary of exile, asked and received pardon. De Retz, recognising that discretion was the better part of valour, came at the head of the Paris clergy to pay their respects. Mme de Motteville noticed that he turned pale and his lips trembled while speaking. 'Sa honte me fait plaisir,' remarked the Queen; 'et si j'avois de la vanité, je pourrois dire même qu'elle me donne de la gloire.' He cut the Cardinal, but next day he had to humble his pride and paid him a visit. Mazarin, the least vindictive of men, was polite, and a superficial reconciliation was staged. De Retz, however, continued to malign him; Conti was unreconciled, and, worst of all, Condé began to sulk.

M. le Prince, as he was always styled, had long felt jealous of Mazarin, and a refusal of his request for a high appointment for his brother-in-law, the Duc de Longueville, wounded his pride. After an interview in which the Cardinal explained that he must defend the interest of the state, Condé ironically remarked 'Adieu, Mars!'—a *mot* which he repeated with gusto to his friends. He had a legitimate grievance, for Mazarin had promised the place. The Queen, who had imposed her veto, gave way, and the concession revived the hopes of the Frondeurs. The real source of trouble, comments Mme de Motteville, was Mme de Longueville. She was wrong, for Condé's ambition burned like a flame. His dissatisfaction waxed when the Queen removed from the Court a *protégé* of his who had rashly aspired to her affections. When Condé complained of this decision, the most placable of rulers remarked to her *femme de chambre* that she was growing tired of his pretensions, in which she and Mazarin detected a danger to the state.

In January 1649 the Government had discomfited its foes by the flight from Paris; in January 1650 it played an even bolder

game. The detailed account of the arrest of Condé, his brother,
and his brother-in-law, the Duc de Longueville, the Governor of
Normandy, is one of the most dramatic passages in the *Memoirs*.
The secret was well kept, and the unsuspecting Princes were
arrested at the Palais Royal without any fuss. When informed
of the Queen's order Condé exclaimed: 'Moi, vous m'arrêtez!
Au nom de Dieu, retournez à la Reine, et dites-lui que je la supplie
que je lui puisse parler.' The request was refused, and the
prisoners were driven off to Vincennes. The road was so bad
that the carriage overturned in the open country and Condé
darted away, only to be caught a moment later. 'They have
taken a lion, a monkey, and a fox,' exclaimed Monsieur, who,
like everyone else, resented the growing arrogance of the eagle of
Rocroy. The second, more formidable, and more discreditable
civil war—the struggle between the Princes and the Crown,
between the sword of Condé and the wits of Mazarin—had begun.

On the evening of this eventful day the Queen spoke of M. le
Prince with great moderation. In view of his birth and his
services she was sorry to have had to arrest him, but it was
necessary for the tranquillity of the state and the interests of the
King. To the effusive congratulations of one of her ladies she
replied coolly that she could not feel joy at such an event; she
would have been happy if he had not forced her to act. Mme de
Motteville, delighted by such magnanimity, kissed her hand in
gratitude. 'This illustrious prisoner was nothing to me. But I
confess that the fate of such a great man excited my pity, and I
was incensed to see his enemies triumphing over his misfortune,
men who had sinned against the Queen a thousand times more
than he.' Parisians rejoiced at the fate of the famous commander
who had blockaded their city. He was not, however, without
influential friends, for Turenne fled to raise an army of deliverance,
and Mme de Longueville strove to rally Normandy. The
Frondeurs of 1649 swarmed to the Court, declaring that they
would defend the Queen, and earning the amused contempt of
Mme de Motteville for 'leur orgueil ridicule et leurs fanfaronnades
un peu trop fortes.' No one knew better than the Queen and
Mazarin how little their hearts had changed. She and her son
paid a brief visit to Rouen in order to counteract the Longueville
influence, while Mme de Longueville, Turenne, and La Rochefoucauld were declared guilty of *lèse-majesté*. Their disloyal retort
was to conclude a treaty with Spain. Condé's wife, preferring
gentler methods, obtained an interview with the Queen, and,
holding her little son by the hand, threw herself on her knees
amid sobs. The defeat of Turenne strengthened the hands of the
Court, but at the end of 1650 the Parlement demanded the liberation of the Princes, and Monsieur, incorrigibly jealous of the

Cardinal, began to sulk. De Retz, always playing for his own hand and obsessed by his ambition for a cardinal's hat, manœuvred with such agility that no one trusted him or knew exactly where he stood.

At the opening of 1651 Monsieur, now so hostile that he declined to attend the Council, persuaded the Parlement to demand the liberation of the Princes and the dismissal of Mazarin. The latter resolved to liberate the prisoners, who had been removed from Vincennes to Havre. On the evening of February 6, the date chosen for his departure, the Queen conversed with him in presence of everybody, in the belief that she would probably not see him again. 'We who were present could detect no change in her face. She remained grave. Her heart, doubtless touched by anger, hate, pity, grief, and resentment, betrayed none of these feelings; I never saw her more tranquil.' Next day, kissing her hand, Mme de Motteville asked her mistress how she was. 'You can judge for yourself,' was the reply. Then taking her faithful friend into her oratory she asked: 'What do you say to my situation?' 'Fearful,' was the reply; 'you need the special grace of God and extreme sagacity to extricate yourself. They are forcing you to part with a Minister. It is a sign of weakness, and if you yield this violence may destroy your authority altogether. But, Madame, forgive me for saying (thinking solely of your interests) that the Cardinal, in the opinion of the wisest men, having failed in many things, those who are faithful to you regret to see you suffering for his errors or misfortune. Perhaps a man of your own choice, detached from all the cabals which are so odious to you, might be more useful in times like these, when you are in such need of advice.' Though the Cardinal had always treated her ill, she added, she would do her utmost in the service of her mistress.

Never had Mme de Motteville spoken so frankly, but the Queen listened attentively and without taking offence. 'You are right in all you say; but it is not easy to find the disinterested person who belongs to no cabal and can give me suitable advice. I think myself obliged to defend a minister of whom they are trying to deprive me by force. I hope God will take pity on the King and not make him suffer for the misfortunes of the Cardinal and myself. I agree that he has failings and has made many mistakes. I know also that he has excellent intentions towards the King and myself; that he has conducted affairs splendidly when allowed to do so; that the first five years of my Regency were happy; and that his betrayal by those whom he has benefited increases my compassion.' After a short silence she added: 'I cannot talk further about this matter, for I fear my weakness. As for you, I confess that the Cardinal has not been kind. But I am most grateful to you for acting thus. It is a mark of your goodness of heart, which I have always gladly recognised, and you deserve more than you have got.' In the evening, with the room full of people, the anxious Queen whispered: 'I wish it was always night; for though I cannot sleep, I like the silence and solitude, because during the day I only see people who betray me.'

Mazarin's departure set all tongues wagging. Was he going to open the doors of Condé's prison? Had he at last given up the struggle against his many foes? Monsieur, now in almost open opposition and coached by de Retz, declined pressing invitations to the Council and the Court until he was promised the liberation of the Princes and the banishment of the Cardinal. He had always aspired to the first place, and now he believed that his hour had come. He advised the Queen to promise the permanent elimination of the Cardinal and to pretend that it was her own idea. When she feigned consent, the Parlement issued a decree of banishment from France. Knowing that she was playing for time and fearing that she would once again leave the capital, Monsieur, now a mere puppet of de Retz, ordered the people to arm and the gates to be watched. She believed that he was planning to seize the young King, and though her ladies trembled at the thought of dangers ahead she displayed her usual courage. It was nothing, she declared, merely a crazy popular excitement which would pass, and she had no desire to leave home. For a month she and her son were virtually prisoners in the Palais Royal, while Monsieur behaved as if he were the ruler of France. Though only a boy at the time, Louis XIV was never to forget these days of humiliation.

Mazarin proceeded to Havre, where he informed the Princes of their unconditional release. The Queen, he declared, begged Condé to love the state, the King, and herself. Condé, embracing him, replied that he was grateful for the justice done to him, and that he would always be the good servant of the King and Queen, adding 'et de vous aussi, Monsieur.' The Cardinal was invited to dinner, but the Prince was in no yielding mood. He had won a resounding victory with the aid of Monsieur, who went to meet him at Saint-Denis. The same evening the Princes paid their respects to the Queen. Since Condé and Monsieur were now in control of the situation, Mazarin crossed the German frontier, and settled at Brühl, near Cologne, keeping in touch with the Queen through an active correspondence and waiting for the tide to turn. All declarations against the Frondeurs were annulled, but Condé is criticised by his supporter La Rochefoucauld for missing his chance. Now was the moment, he argues, to transfer the Regency to Orleans and with it the person of the King. All parties would have consented, so great was the consternation of

the Cardinal's friends owing to his flight, and he could never have
returned.

During this agitating period Mme de Motteville was a real
comfort to the Queen 'qui me faisoit cet honneur de prendre
quelque confiance en moi.' The Opposition had been united in
the demand for the eviction of Mazarin, but after its victory it
broke up into fragments fighting each other for power. Some,
believing that the supple Cardinal might ultimately return,
established contact with him and asked his advice. The Queen's
tactics were to give his enemies rope enough to hang themselves.
There was even talk of re-arresting the Princes, who, fearing for
their liberty and even their lives, took flight. To a message from
the Queen that he had nothing to fear Condé roughly replied that
he could no longer trust her word, and that he would never appear
at Court so long as valets of the Cardinal were in favour. When
the ministers whom he disliked were removed he returned to
Paris, but his restless spirit was never satisfied for long. The
Coadjutor, equally selfish but rather more adroit, tried to curry
favour at Court, and was bought by the Cardinal's hat on which
he had set his heart. These dissensions strengthened the hands
of the Queen, whose self-confidence waxed as her promising son
grew towards manhood. In September 1651, at the age of
thirteen, in accordance with a royal ordonnance, Louis XIV
attained his majority. The Regency came to an end in name
though not in fact, for Mazarin remained at the helm.

Condé, a bungling amateur on the political stage and goaded
into civil war by his intransigent sister, asked help from Spain.
The Queen took up the challenge, left Paris with her sons, and
summoned Mazarin to return. The Parlement placed a price on
the Minister's head, and the second and much more serious civil
war began. If a case could be made for the first Fronde, the
second was without excuse and it brought nothing but disaster to
France. Condé won the opening rounds of the civil war and was
received with plaudits by the fickle citizens. He and Monsieur
assured the Parlement that if Mazarin and his adherents left the
Court they would lay down their arms, for they always pretended
that they were not fighting against the King.

During the desperate battle of July 2, 1652, in the Faubourg
Saint-Antoine—the only major struggle of the campaign—the
Queen, with Mme de Motteville at her side, spent most of her
time before the altar of the Carmelite Convent at Saint-Denis,
where news of the fighting and the casualties were brought to her.
Condé as usual was in the thick of the fight. That lusty Amazon
La Grande Mademoiselle, the daughter of Monsieur, watching the
scene from the roof of the Bastille and fearing the defeat of her
hero, ordered the guns of the fortress to fire on the royal troops.

A nephew of Mazarin lost his life, La Rochefoucauld an eye. Wounded and dying men were brought to Saint-Denis, where they were tended by the Queen. On the following day Mme de Motteville passed through the great hall where the wounded were lying and crying out for food.

Condé was in no mood for peace, but on July 4 the rebel cause was lost when the Hôtel de Ville was set on fire and pillaged by the mob. The spectre of anarchy terrified the citizens, who had had enough of civil strife. Condé and Monsieur left Paris, and the Court returned in October 1652 amid the acclamations of the crowd. The young King forbade the Parlements to meddle with the affairs of state, exiled a number of leading Frondeurs, and took up his residence in the Louvre. When the slippery de Retz came by invitation to pay his belated respects in December, he was arrested and sent to Vincennes. 'Thus ended the Fronde,' comments Mme de Motteville. 'He had been the chief and the source, and he was the last to be overthrown.' Mazarin described him as 'un monstre,' and explained 'Le repos et l'obédience envers le roi ne peuvent s'ajuster avec le séjour du Cardinal de Retz à Paris.' It was the last scene of the brief political career of the brilliant adventurer who had betrayed every one in turn. Yet his loss is our gain, for there was nothing left for him, as for La Rochefoucauld, but to write his *Memoirs*.

Mazarin had won the game, for the storm which began in 1648 had blown itself out. The bourgeoisie realised at last that the Princes cared only for themselves. The Court, the Parlement, and the whole of France, records Mme de Motteville, lined up under his power. People had learned by bitter experience that his domination was preferable to the sham liberty they had craved. Those who had despised him began to fear him; and growing respect was accompanied by a disposition to pardon his failings in view of his good qualities and his luck. Condé had joined his old enemies the Spaniards in Flanders, Conti was glad to marry a niece of the Cardinal, the penitent Mme de Longueville retired to a convent, and de Retz escaped to Rome. Neither the Regent nor Mazarin desired revenge, and no blood was shed. Though no one was more delighted than Mme de Motteville, she continued to mix praise of the Cardinal with blame. He would have been the finest man in the world if he had been content to abase his enemies and to enjoy the greatness lavished on him by fortune without wishing to destroy the legitimate power of the woman who had supported him so loftily. For he assumed the authority both of mother and son, becoming rather the tyrant than the master of their wills. The sole idol of the courtiers, he desired that petitioners for favours should address themselves exclusively to him, and removed from the King's entourage all who had been placed there by his mother. Henceforth his avarice had full rein, and he kept the young King so short of money that he could give nothing to the poor soldiers when he visited the army.

From the end of the Second Fronde till the death of her mistress in 1666 the main theme of Mme de Motteville's *Memoirs* is the emergence of the young King. Mother and son were devoted to each other, but when the inflammable boy fell in love with Mazarin's niece, Marie de Mancini, the first difficulties arose. She had set her heart on the match with her niece which was ultimately arranged as a vital element in the restoration of peace with Spain, and in any case the proud woman would have frowned on a partner not of royal blood. Her apprehensions were increased by the apparent readiness of the Cardinal to further the ambitions of his niece, and for once she stood up to him. 'Je ne crois pas, M. le Cardinal, que le Roi soit capable de cette lâcheté, mais s'il étoit possible qu'il en eût la pensée, je vous avertis que toute la France se revolteroit contre vous and contre lui, que moi-même je me mettrois à la tête des révoltés, et que j'y engagerois mon fils.' Mazarin, adds Mme de Motteville, hid his resentment from the world but carried it in his heart to the end; yet he was too much of a statesman to pursue the project and wisely removed the temptress from Paris. The King bowed to necessity, and after an hour's painful talk his mother whispered: 'Le Roi me fait pitié, il est tendre et raisonnable tout ensemble; mais je viens de lui dire que je suis assurée qu'il me remerciera un jour du mal que je lui fais, et selon ce que je vois en lui, je n'en doute pas.' A day or two later she received a letter which brought tears to her eyes. 'Le Roi est bon,' she remarked; 'je vous assure, le Roi est bon.'

The reconciliation was more welcome at a time when she seemed to fret under the yoke of the master of France. Her wishes as expressed to the other ministers were not always obeyed, and if she pressed her point they often replied that they must consult the Cardinal. One day she went so far as to confess that he was becoming so difficult and avaricious that she did not know if she could bear it. Mme de Motteville, never a Mazarine, was a sympathetic listener, and when she suggested that the Cardinal should have shown more consideration to the sovereign who had given him power, she blushed and exclaimed 'Vous avez raison.' It is difficult to reconcile this reported conversation with the emotional correspondence of which the *femme de chambre* knew nothing and which was only revealed two centuries later in the famous *Carnets* of Mazarin. Despite occasional friction it was a union of hearts and minds which only death could break. Perhaps she was following his advice at the end of the First Fronde—'aussi faut-il que la reine se souvienne de se plaindre de moi.'

The Minister had no competitor, and the conclusion of peace with Spain in 1660, symbolised by the marriage of the King to the Infanta Maria Theresa, was the summit of his career. The proud Condé, whose cause was pleaded by Spain, bowed the knee and asked for forgiveness. At last the wily Italian could say *Nunc dimittis*, and a year later he was dead. Had he lived there must soon have been a contest of wills in which the King was certain to win. The Queen bore the blow with apparent composure, and the nation heaved a sigh of relief. He had become a multi-millionaire and had dreamed of the Papacy. He had served France without loving her, and France had never given him her love. Had he ever really loved anyone except himself? Mme de Motteville's parting comments on his avarice and thirst for power indicate that she too was glad to see him go. She had particularly resented the attempts which she believed him to have made to diminish the affection and reverence of the King for his mother.

When a dauphin was born in 1661 Anne of Austria declared that God had granted all her desires, and that she asked nothing more except her own salvation. Though her love for the King was undiminished, she realised that he needed her no longer, and she talked of retiring from the Court. He had loved her tenderly, but her influence now steadily declined, for he resented every suggestion of restraint. When, for instance, she desired her faithful *femme de chambre* to become the *gouvernante* of the children of her younger son, her advice was ignored. For the first time, confesses Mme de Motteville, she had aspired to promotion, and her disappointment was keen. 'I saw myself exposed to the misfortune of losing my tranquillity or failing to obtain a coveted honour. The latter occurred, and I suffered painfully from the blows of my enemies. By an astonishing contrariety of our passions and desires, I felt hurt at missing a post which would have flattered my *amour-propre*, yet at the same time I felt consoled by the hope of enjoying a future of peace. Wishing to cure myself entirely of ambition, I resolved no longer to aspire to distinctions at Court but to remain there solely to fulfil my duties to the Queen Mother. In this I followed the promptings of my heart, which had long felt disgust at the creatures, the trifles and the disagreeable things which had occupied me.' Here is her final verdict on a quarter of a century of Court life: 'La maison des rois est comme un grand marché où il faut aller nécessairement trafiquer pour le soutien de la vie et pour les intérêts de ceux à qui nous sommes attachés par devoir ou par amitié.'

After enjoying robust health throughout life Anne of Austria developed cancer and died in 1666 after terrible sufferings bravely borne. No one mourned her more than Mme de Motteville, whose

unchanging devotion was rewarded by a legacy of 30,000 livres.
' Je n'ai de ma vie connu une personne moins avide de gloire ni
d'applaudissement.   Son humilité a été cause que la bonté de son
esprit et la bonté de son jugement n'ont pas eu tout l'éclat et toute
l'éstime qu'elle aurait pu en recevoir du public.'   That we know
the shining qualities of this kind-hearted woman is due to the
lucky accident that her *femme de chambre* had the urge and the
capacity to write.   That the portrait painted with such wealth of
detail was broadly true to life is suggested by the affection and
gratitude of the son whose throne she had pluckily and successfully
striven to save.   Of the remaining years of Mme de Motteville's
life we know little, but we may assume that her chief occupation
was the revision of her delightful narrative.   When she died in
1689 at the age of sixty-eight her masterpiece was complete.

Bibliographical Note.—The best edition is by Riaux, 4 vols., to which Saint-
Beuve's admirable essay, reprinted from *Causeries du Lundi*, vol. 5, serves as
Introduction.   An abridged English translation was published in 1902 in
3 vols.   The best detailed history of the period is by Chéruel, *La Minorité de
Louis XIV*, 4 vols., and *La France sous Mazarin*, 3 vols.   The best brief
surveys are in *Histoire de France*, ed. Lavisse, vol. 7, and Ranke, *Französische
Geschichte*, vol. 3.   Hassall, *Mazarin*, and Marcel Boulenger, *Mazarin*, are
useful sketches.   Among the biographies of the leaders of the Fronde, Batiffol,
Cardinal de Retz and *La Duchesse de Chevreuse*, Arvède Barine, *La Grande
Mademoiselle et la Fronde*, Cousin, *Mme de Longueville*, Bourdeau, *La Roche-
foucauld*, Duc d'Aumale, *Histoire des Princes de Condé*, are recommended.

CHAPTER III

LA GRANDE MADEMOISELLE AND THE FRONDE

No two books on the same period could be more different than the *Memoirs* of Mme de Motteville and of Marie Louise of Orleans, Duchesse de Montpensier, usually called La Grande Mademoiselle. While the gentle and timid lady-in-waiting to Anne of Austria was quite content to be a recorder of events, the daughter of Gaston, Duc d'Anjou and later Duc d'Orléans, the granddaughter of Henri IV and the first cousin of Louis XIV, thirsted for action and fame. Arvède Barine, the best of her biographers, salutes her as an authentic heroine from the pages of Corneille. She was called La Grande Mademoiselle on account of her tall stature, and contemporaries emphasise her masculine appearance. That she was not a beauty did not trouble her for a moment. No Bourbon princess was ever prouder of her royal blood or more tenacious of her rights. The dawn was brilliant, and she seemed to have the ball at her feet. For a brief hour during the Second Fronde her ambition was gratified and she plunged headlong into the fray; the sound of drums and trumpets was music to her ears. But she paid the penalty for choosing the weaker side, and the latter half of her life was a grotesque anti-climax. The glittering matrimonial visions of the richest heiress in Europe faded away one by one, and her belated union with Lauzun proved a humiliating fiasco. The whole drama might be entitled 'Mademoiselle in Search of a Husband.' Like many other fallen idols she found consolation in her pen, and her reminiscences are indispensable for the history of seventeenth-century France. The mannish yet not unsympathetic heroine of the story is herself, but the full-length portraits of her father and Condé are almost as good as the masterpieces of de Retz. Published in 1735, nearly half a century after her death, they won immediate popularity and kept their place amid the swelling flood of competitors.

Mlle de Montpensier, born in the Louvre in 1627, was of Bourbon blood on both sides of the family, and until the marriage of Louis XIV, more than thirty years later, she was the second lady in the land. Her mother, the daughter of Henri de Bourbon, Duc de Montpensier, died a week after the birth of her only child, who thus became sole heir to her enormous estates. The baby was transferred to the adjoining Tuileries, where she lived till she was evicted by the King after the collapse of the Second Fronde. An independent establishment with about three hundred attendants was no substitute for the disciplined care of a home. Monsieur, as her frivolous father was called, lived in the stately Luxembourg, dreaming of the great deeds which he lacked the will to accomplish. He married again, quarrelled with his brother, Louis XIII, and left France for Flanders after the banishment of his mother. Marie de Medici was devoted to the daughter of her favourite son, but she was banished by Richelieu when the child was three and died abroad. Thus Mademoiselle grew up without love. Though emotionally starved she was not unhappy, for she was too robust and superficial in the earlier part of her life to suffer deeply or long. Her governess, the Marquise de Saint-Georges, chosen by Marie de Medici, was a well-meaning mediocrity and had little influence or authority. 'If I possess some good qualities,' she writes, 'they are natural and not due to my education, good though it was, for I never had to fear the slightest punishment. I heard so much about my high birth and great possessions that I was vain till reason taught me that it is not enough.' Her education, far from being good, was so neglected that she never learned either grammar or spelling, and her letters would disgrace an elementary school. The childless King and Queen, whom she called *mon petit papa* and *ma petite mamman*, were kind to her. Commissioners were appointed to look after her estates, but she had no playfellows and no real friends.

Her earliest political impression was her hatred of Richelieu, the enemy of her father, who wished him to make his peace with the King, to cancel his marriage with Marguerite of Lorraine, and to marry his niece. In her wrath the little girl, a rebel from her cradle, chanted all the songs against the terrible Cardinal that she knew by heart. Monsieur returned to France when his daughter was seven, and their relations were happy until she was old enough to discover how selfish and cowardly he was. In the year before her birth he had encouraged his friends to compromise themselves in the so-called Chalais conspiracy, had abandoned them when he saw the danger-signal, and had revealed the whole story to the Government. While Chalais was beheaded and other conspirators were exiled, he was rewarded for his treachery by the duchies of Orleans and Chartres, the county of Blois, and a sum of money. That he was neither loved nor respected was nothing to him, and these dark shadows were hidden from the child who saw in him the charming playfellow only nineteen years older than herself. At the age of ten she toured the châteaux of the Loire, romping up and down the famous double staircase at Chambord, glimpsing but not catching her father on the other side. At Richelieu she marvelled at the splendid palace of the dictator; at Chenonceaux she visited her cousin, the Duc de Beaufort, the future Frondeur, the son of Vendôme, a bastard of Henri IV; at Fontevrault she was welcomed by the Abbess, another bastard of her adored grandfather. That her father was *persona ingrata* at Court was

no handicap, and she was treated with unvarying kindness. She
acted as youthful chaperon to the King in his Platonic advances
to Mlle de Hautefort, the monarch and his lady returning from the
hunt in her carriage. While her father was a dilettante intellectual, taking part in the activities of a discussion circle, she was
bored by books till she blasted her own career. She had too little
patience to read the long-winded novels which fascinated her
contemporaries, but she loved the dramas of Corneille with their
pæans to the heroic life.

The birth of Louis XIV at Saint-Germain in 1638, after twenty-
three years of a childless marriage, diminished the status of the
King's brother, hitherto heir to the throne, but opened up possi-
bilities for his daughter. Mademoiselle, now a girl of eleven, was
delighted with the baby, whom she used to call *mon petit mari*.
Though it was only a child's fancy, it annoyed Richelieu, who
ordered her to leave Saint-Germain and summoned her to her
first political interview. She was too old, he declared, to use such
terms. She was reduced to tears and left him with anger in her
heart. The reprimand was a tactical blunder, for it made her
think seriously of a match with the future ruler of France. The
Queen, who had protested in vain against the eviction of her niece
from Saint-Germain, shared her detestation of the dictator and
consoled her as best she could. 'It is true that my son is too
young,' she remarked, 'but you shall marry my brother.' The
brother in question was Cardinal Archbishop of Toledo, a layman,
and Commander-in-Chief of the Spanish armies in Flanders. The
girl was not impressed, for at this time, she explains, she was more
interested in dances than in matrimony. The potential suitor
died when she was fourteen, and she was soon to fly at higher
game. Feeling herself not only the richest heiress but the greatest
princess in Europe, she expected to find herself within a few years
seated upon a throne, possibly an empress, almost certainly a
queen. She confesses to a quick temper, and liked to have her
own way: 'Je suis fort méchante ennemie, étant fort colère et
fort emportée.' That verdict does her less than justice, for she
was a kind-hearted Amazon, not a virago, and she never committed
an act of cruelty in her life. A regular tomboy, bursting with
animal spirits, fearless and frank, she would have made a popular
ruler and brought a blast of fresh air into the stuffy chambers of
the most ceremonial court. She professed to despise the tender
passion, and the matrimonial projects which increasingly occupied
her thoughts were without a tinge of emotion or romance. Visions
of loving comradeship and a happy home never crossed her mind
till she was a middle-aged woman. Strictly moral herself, she
made no fettering conditions: what mattered was the rank of the
suitor, not his character, intelligence, or looks. Yet this craving

for the highest place was generated, not by any overmastering desire to rule, but by the accident of her royal birth. She preferred pageantry to power, for she lacked application and had no sustained interest in matters of state.

The first shock of her life was the execution of Cinq-Mars for treason and the revelation of her father's failings which it brought. Louis XIII, to use Richelieu's expression, always needed a *jou-jou* or plaything. The tragedy of the King's favourite is dismissed in a few lines on the ground that it was too painful a theme: some people, she admitted, believed that Monsieur's evidence was the determining cause of his death. Richelieu would in any case have destroyed the ambitious young man who had engaged in treasonable negotiations with Spain, but Monsieur broke his own record. As an enemy of the Cardinal he had had dealings with Cinq-Mars, but when the King wearied of his worthless favourite and apologised to the dictator, Gaston betrayed his friends without a qualm. Mademoiselle expresses no opinion on his conduct in this crisis, for she was only fifteen, but she was horrified by his gaiety on his first visit after the heads of the Grand Ecuyer and his friend de Thou had fallen at Lyons. They were Richelieu's last victims, for he was a dying man. Mademoiselle shared the relief of France, but the melancholy King only survived his terrible Minister by a few months. Visiting her uncle during his long illness at Saint-Germain, she helped to secure her father's return to Paris and the reconciliation of the brothers. His wife was now allowed to re-enter France on condition that a new marriage ceremony took place. The chilly nature of the meeting between Monsieur and Madame after a parting of years surprised observers who were unaware that Gaston loved nobody but himself. Mademoiselle gave her stepmother useful advice, for she was a stranger to the ways of the Court; but the newcomer, a *malade imaginaire* who rarely left her rooms, described by the observant Tallemant as 'une pauvre idiote,' was too dull and impersonal to kindle affection. Monsieur was more interested in securing the future of his daughters by the second marriage than in the happiness of his wife. The Luxembourg was never in any sense a home to the masculine lady in the Tuileries.

Mademoiselle confirms the evidence of Mme de Motteville and other witnesses that the first phase of the Regency was a happy and hopeful time. 'It was nothing but perpetual rejoicings everywhere. Hardly a day passed without serenades in the Tuileries and the Palais Royal. The disgrace in which the Queen had lived during her husband's life had touched everybody's heart and earned her affection. Everyone looked forward to the fruits of the goodness she had shown herself to possess.' The author joined in the chorus of thanksgiving, for she had received nothing but kindness from Anne of Austria, but her satisfaction, like that of France, was short-lived. The Queen has received rather too much praise from Mme de Motteville, too little from de Retz. She was ignorant and lazy, and she never swerved from the narrow authoritarianism of the Spanish Court; but she possessed a kindly heart and cruelty was foreign to her nature. 'One could hardly have believed that she who had such painful experience of the danger of leaving all authority to a single minister, clever though he was, would have been capable of abandoning it completely to the most unskilful and unworthy man in the world. It was soon discovered that the death of the King had been a great loss, and her conduct was thought by everyone to acquit him of the blame he had incurred for having despised her and allowed her no political influence.' It is one of the few bitter passages in the *Memoirs*. Mademoiselle was never a good hater, and we must bear in mind that this part of her book was written in the chill shades of exile from the Court. That Mazarin had critics in plenty we learn from the *Mazarinades*, but no one except Mademoiselle accused that consummate diplomatist of being *malhabile*.

Royalties marry early, and the search for a husband began before the girl was out of her teens. When her aunt, the Queen of Spain, died in 1644, tongues began to wag despite the fact that the countries were at war. 'People thought that the widower (Philip IV) was a suitable match for me, and the Queen told me that she longed for it. Cardinal Mazarin talked to me in the same strain, adding that he had learned it was desired in Spain. He and the Queen talked to Monsieur and me about it for some time, and with spurious good will dangled this honour before our eyes, though they had no such intention of obliging us. Yet such was our good faith that we did not realise their lack of it, and thus it was easy for them to wriggle out of it, as they did, by dropping the subject. I should not have liked it, for with my temperament I should not care to be Queen at the price of unhappiness.' This was not a case of sour grapes, for she was only seventeen. Three years later, in 1647, when the wife of Ferdinand III and the sister of Anne of Austria died, the Abbé de la Rivière, her father's factotum, told Mademoiselle that she ought to marry the Emperor. He corrected himself, and said that it should be his brother, the Archduke Leopold. 'I replied that I should prefer the Emperor; but though we discussed it at length the conversation had no results.'

At this stage a new claimant appeared in the person of her first cousin, the Prince of Wales. Charles I had sent him to join Henrietta Maria in order to be out of harm's way. The royal family, including Mademoiselle, was at Fontainebleau. 'He was only sixteen or seventeen, but tall for his age, with a good head, black hair, dark complexion, and passably agreeable in his person. It was a drawback that he neither spoke nor understood French properly. During his three days at Fontainebleau he paid visits to all the princesses. From this moment I realised that the Queen of England wished me to believe that he was in love with me, was constantly talking of me, and would have come to my room at any hour had she not intervened, found me very much to his taste, and was in despair at the death of the Empress, greatly fearing that I might be married to the Emperor. I listened to all this as in duty bound, but I did not take it so seriously as perhaps she wished.' She might have been more impressed if the young man had spoken for himself instead of through third parties. She confesses, however, that at this time she was thinking so much of the Emperor that she felt no interest in her English cousin. When her father reminded her that Ferdinand was older than herself she proudly replied that she cared more for the position than the individual. The self-assurance of this girl of nineteen was colossal, and her craving for a crown would have been a little repulsive had it been less naïve. On the occasion of a ball of unusual magnificence at the Palais Royal a throne with three steps was erected at one end of the hall. 'Neither the King (aged 8) nor the Prince of Wales (aged 16) cared to occupy it. So there I sat, alone, with the two princes and all the princesses at my feet. I did not feel in the least embarrassed. Everyone told me that I had never appeared more at my ease and that, as I was qualified by birth to occupy a throne, I should stay longer and possess more freedom when I had one of my own.'

A curious phase of her campaign for the Imperial Crown is described with her usual frankness. 'The desire to be Empress, which was never out of my mind, suggested the adoption of habits suitable to the Emperor's mood. I had been told that he was devout, and I followed his example with such success that after having feigned the mood for some time I now for one week had a real urge to become a Carmelite nun. I told nobody. I was so obsessed that I neither ate nor slept, and I was so worked up that they feared I might fall dangerously ill. Whenever the Queen went to convents, which she often did, I remained alone in the church, and, thinking of all the people who were fond of me and would regret my retreat, I began to cry. I can only say that during that week the Empire was nothing to me. I felt a certain vanity in the idea of leaving the world at such a time. I mean that it was only my perfect knowledge of that world which made me abandon it, despite the hope of such a great and satisfying situation; for I could not be charged with having taken this resolution as a result of disappointment.' When she asked her father's consent he replied that her mood was caused by the lack of zeal in high quarters for her marriage to the Emperor. That was impossible, she replied, for she no longer coveted the post: she would rather serve God than wear all the crowns in the world. This sort of talk was too much for the worldly Monsieur, who knew his daughter better than she knew herself. 'It is Mme de Brienne and these bigots who put these ideas into your head. Don't talk to them and I shall beg the Queen not to take you with her to convents.' His cold *douche* produced the desired result, and the idea was dropped. Three days later she confesses it had passed out of her mind, and when the Court teased her about the rumours of retirement she laughed with the rest and denied that she had ever given it a thought. Yet a trace of this mood remained for a short time in abandoning her make-up and reading the *Life of St Theresa*. The glamour of the Austrian marriage returned, for though the Emperor had married again it was always possible that the new Empress might die in childbed. An officer named Saujon, brother of one of her ladies, attempted to further her interests in this quarter, and Mademoiselle was sharply lectured by the Queen and her father when his activities were discovered. She proudly disclaimed all knowledge of the affair and left the Palais Royal with anger in her heart.

A new chapter opened in 1648 with the First Fronde. Though she was now twenty, she had taken singularly little interest in public affairs; it had been enough for her to dream of a throne and to have a good time. Since however a husband seemed as far off as ever, and balls had lost their novelty, she was conscious of a void. Lacking public duties and intellectual interests, lovers and intimate friends, she was often bored and pined for some outlet for her energies. That she should turn to politics was not surprising in an age unique in French history on account of the number and influence of beautiful, clever, high-born, and dissolute ladies on the public stage. The Duchesse de Chevreuse, *née* Rohan, the eldest and ablest of them all, had defied Richelieu at the height of his power and had returned to France after his death only to find Mazarin in command. She belonged to the category of people who instinctively oppose any government of which they are not in name or in fact the head. 'Voilà le diable,' exclaimed Louis XIII on his death-bed; and Mazarin declared that France was only tranquil when she was not there. Anne de Gonzague, Princess Palatine and sister-in-law of Prince Rupert, belonged to the same class of Amazons—able, ambitious, beautiful, riding about the country as a gay cavalier. More beautiful and far more unpolitical was Condé's only sister, who was married to the Duc de Longueville, a man twice her age. Swept into the vortex of the Fronde by her lover, the Duc de la Rochefoucauld, author of the cynical *Maxims*, she used to murmur in her gentle voice, 'Je n'aime

pas les plaisirs innocents.' Among lesser stars were the Duchesse
de Châtillon, Condé's mistress, and Mme de Montbazon, stepmother of Mme de Chevreuse, the most dissolute of them all.

In this brilliant throng Mademoiselle occupies a place apart, for
her morals were beyond reproach, and she lacked beauty, charm,
and political talents. She craved for physical activity and excitement, and boasted that she was never tired. She confessed to a
lack of tenderness. That she could to some extent influence
events if she were to throw her energies and her wealth into the
fray was hardly in doubt, but her indifference to public affairs
left it an open question which side she would join. Like the
Queen she was surprised by the revolt. She sensed the unpopularity of the Cardinal and was vaguely aware of the gathering
discontent, but she had no notion of the growing sufferings which
touched the gentle heart of Vincent de Paul. The burden of the
long war with Spain was increased by vicious financial expedients.
Mazarin was no financier, but to oppose the Minister was to oppose
the Court. As her matrimonial projects one after the other
collapsed she was led to think increasingly of the King, now a
promising lad of ten: to be Queen of France was an even more
alluring prospect than a throne in Whitehall, Vienna, or Madrid.
Moreover her pride of birth and her royalist principles indicated
support of the Bourbon monarch. Thus at the outset the balance
tilted to the side of the Court, though she was never more than a
lukewarm champion of the cause identified with the Cardinal's
rule.

Mademoiselle's narrative of the First Fronde is relatively brief,
for she played a very minor part in the drama. She shared the
Queen's contempt for *cette canaille*, which looked to England for a
model and audaciously desired to limit the authority of the
Crown. On the other hand, she realised that some reforms were
necessary and she resented the Cardinal's monopoly of power.
That she was not a whole-hearted supporter of the Court was
sensed by the people of Paris, and the discovery of her popularity
encouraged her to dream of a political *rôle*. On receiving the news
of the erection of barricades after the arrest of Broussel, she set
out for the Luxembourg. After crossing the Pont Neuf she found
the street barred by chains, but a joyful surprise was in store for
her. 'The people of Paris has always loved me because I was
born and brought up there. That has won me a respect and
favour greater than they usually feel towards persons of my
quality, and in consequence when they saw my servants they
lifted the chains.' After a brief visit to her father she drove to
the Palais Royal. French history, she remarks, was full of such
scenes. 'But for me, who had never witnessed them and was too
young to think, all the novelties were a delight; and as I was not

particularly pleased with the Queen and Monsieur at that time, it was a great pleasure to see them embarrassed. So long as an incident, whatever its importance, served as a diversion, I thought of nothing else all the evening. During the following days I amused myself in watching all the people with swords who were not used to them and carried them awkwardly. That is what amused me while all France trembled, though I had a great interest in her preservation.' One of the charms of the *Memoirs* is the frankness and naïveté of the author. The sight of wounded men from her window was a new but less pleasant experience. 'The ensuing misfortunes accustomed me to the sight of dead and wounded men without eradicating my first feelings of pity.'

Mademoiselle was present at the Palais Royal when some leading members of the Parlement came to demand the release of their colleagues. When they had got their way they filed out proudly, and one of them spoke to her in a very free vein. 'That was the origin of the troubles which ensued and of the attacks on the authority of the King. It should teach kings, when they are old enough to rule, and, when they are not, those in authority, that they must weigh carefully everything, even the smallest matters, and consider the consequences. Too much clemency at one time is as bad as too much rigour at another.' How this maxim was to be applied she left to cleverer people than herself. The concessions extorted from the Crown went much too far for her taste, particularly the right to be examined within twenty-four hours of arrest and to be set at liberty if innocent. 'This was a terrible limitation of the King's authority. Though justice must be done to everybody, there are crimes which, though not deserving death, require imprisonment without assigning reasons. Since he is responsible for his actions to God alone, it was hard to make him responsible to the Parlement. My birth predisposes me to disapprove this declaration, and for the same reason those of humbler origin will probably approve it. To me it seems that the authority of a single ruler is so modelled on the divine pattern that one should freely submit to it with joy and respect if God has not assigned us our position in that sphere. For my part I realise that if I were born in a republic I should be quite ready for revolt if I could, even if it were not for my benefit—so highly do I esteem monarchy.' When she wrote this confession of political faith she could not foresee that her cousin would one day break her heart by the exercise of his royal authority against the only man she ever loved.

The withdrawal of the Court to Rueil on September 12 and later to Saint-Germain was a gesture of dissatisfaction, not a declaration of war, and the need of cleaning the Palais Royal served as a pretext. Mademoiselle, like her father, remained in

Paris, but she went twice or thrice a week to pay her respects and finally followed suit. After six weeks of absence the Court returned to the capital, where the claims and authority of the Parlement continually increased. Neither side was in a mood to yield, and early in the morning of January 6, 1640, the royal family stole away to Saint-Germain, accompanied by Monsieur and Condé. Mademoiselle only learned of the project on the previous evening when she supped at the Luxembourg. Between three and four in the morning she heard a loud knock at her door, and a messenger from the Palais Royal arrived. The King, Queen and Monsieur, she was informed, were expecting her. Monsieur had sent her a letter. Putting it under her pillow she replied that the orders of the King and Queen were enough. Pressed to read it, she found that it was merely an exhortation to obedience. 'The Queen had desired that Monsieur should give me this command, believing that I should not obey hers and that I should have been only too happy to stay behind in Paris and join her opponents; for I never met anyone who avowed himself an enemy of the King.' For once obedience was something more than a duty. 'While M. de Comminges was talking to me I was enraptured to see the blunder they were making and to be a spectator of the miseries it would cause them. This was a partial revenge for the persecutions I had suffered. I did not then foresee that I should find myself a member of a considerable party in which I could do my duty and revenge myself at the same time. However in taking this sort of vengeance, one inflicts damage on oneself.' The persecutions of which she speaks were imaginary, for except the arrest of Saujon she had no grievance against the Court.

Mademoiselle took her place in the carriage of the Queen, who was in excellent spirits. 'I never saw anyone so gay. If she had won a battle, taken Paris, and hanged all who had incurred her displeasure, she could not have been more so.' Nothing was ready for them at Saint-Germain, for the Court always had to bring what it needed when it moved. The food, she complains, was bad, but Monsieur congratulated her on her equanimity. 'I am a person whom nothing troubles,' she adds complacently, 'and am far above trifles.' When Saujon was at last released, she admits that she had no further complaint. Her self-satisfaction was increased by fresh evidence of her popularity in the streets, for her household requirements were forwarded without demur while those of the King and Queen were held up. In these circumstances the Queen begged her to send her own carriages for the most urgent requirements. 'They lacked everything, and I had all I desired. Permits were given for everything I asked for, and I was overwhelmed with civilities.' One of her pages described in the presence of the King, Queen and Cardinal how he had been

received by the Parlement. He had been told that she had only
to express her desires and she would always meet with becoming
respect. Despite these satisfactions to her pride she was terribly
bored at Saint-Germain, and when the Queen lingered in her
oratory she went to sleep, 'not being a lady with a taste for long
prayers and meditations.' With her usual engaging naïveté she
confesses how little she concerned herself with the troubles of
France. She only thought of her diversions, knowing little of the
public weal, 'car quoique l'on soit née y ayant assez d'intérêt,
quand l'on est fort jeune et fort inappliquée, l'on n'a pour but
que les plaisirs de son âge.' Like humbler mortals she had to
learn in the school of adversity.

The feud between Court and Parlement was inconvenient to
both sides. The army, divided into two forces under Condé and
Monsieur, was too small to storm the capital, but large enough
to prevent an adequate supply of food. All Paris flocked to the
receptions of Mme de Longueville, Queen of the Fronde, at the
Hôtel de Ville, but the contemplation of her beauty was no lasting
compensation for soaring prices and empty stomachs. The
conflict, in which little blood had been shed, ended with the treaty
of Rueil in March. Mademoiselle was the first of the royal
family to return to Paris, where she was warmly welcomed, for
everyone knew that she was no friend of the Cardinal. The King
and Queen remained till August at Saint-Germain, whither penitent
or calculating Frondeurs hastened to make their peace. Paris was
glad to see them back, but there was thunder in the air. The
sword of Condé had smitten the First Fronde, and his arrogance
disgusted both the Court and the capital. The crafty Mazarin,
with his ear to the ground, saw his chance of winning over the
Parlement and forming a broad front against the overweening
soldier who behaved as if he were the master of France.

With the opposing forces so evenly balanced the importance of
Monsieur naturally increased. A prince with more backbone
might have come out strongly on the side of the Court, as his wife
and daughter pressed him to do; but it was his instinct to avoid
committing himself in critical situations. ' Foible, timide, léger,' is
the verdict of La Rochefoucauld. De Retz describes him as trembling with fear, and a popular satire held him up to ridicule. When
France supplicates him to defend her against Condé he replies:

> . . . Je veux dormir.
> Je naquis en dormant. J'y veux passer ma vie.
> Jamais de m'éveiller il ne me prît envie.
> Toi, ma femme et ma fille, y perdez vos efforts,
> Je dors.

Exasperated like everyone else, Mademoiselle visited the Luxembourg on January 18, 1650, and reproached him for his undignified

passivity in regard to Condé. 'Vous le devriez faire arrêter; on a bien fait arrêter son père.' 'Patience,' he replied, 'vous aurez bientôt contentement.' Concluding that something was afoot she hurried to the Palais Royal, at the entrance of which she found retainers of Conti, the younger brother of the great soldier, in obvious alarm, though they knew as little as she. She found the doors locked and two armed soldiers outside the Queen's chamber.

When the Council was over and the arrest of Condé, Conti, and the Duc de Longueville, all of whom had been invited to the palace, had taken place, Mademoiselle was admitted and heard the story from the Queen's own lips. For once the hearts of the two proud women beat in harmony. 'Nous nous entretin mes commes des gens ravis de se voir vengés des personnes qui ne nous aimoient pas. Il n'y avoit rien de plus injuste que l'aversion que j'avois pour M. le Prince; elle a bien changé depuis.' Condé's wife was ordered to leave Paris, and Mme de Longueville escaped to Normandy, of which her husband was Governor, and thence to Holland.

The capital, like the Court, breathed a sigh of relief when the foremost soldier of France, as contemptible in politics as he was incomparable in war, was under lock and key at Vincennes, whence he was shortly removed to Havre. Mademoiselle accompanied the Court in its tour through the south, where Condé's influence was strong; but she was never happy for long away from Paris. The siege of rebellious Bordeaux was a passing excitement, and after its surrender she rejoiced to find herself, not the Queen, the popular favourite. 'No one visited the Queen and no one took any notice of her when she passed through the streets. I do not know if she was very pleased to hear people say that I had a large Court.' The cause of this flattering differentiation was clear enough. The Queen, though never personally unpopular, was politically identified with Mazarin, who had hardly another trusty friend in France.

Well aware of the aversion of Mademoiselle for her favourite, the Queen complained that she was becoming *furieusement Frondeuse*. That was an exaggeration, yet it was true that she was changing her attitude. Monsieur, who had always been jealous of the fame and popularity of Condé, now resolved to join the Parlement in demanding his release. When he declared that he would not go to the Palais Royal while Mazarin was there, his daughter rejoiced, though she doubted whether he would keep his word. At last she found herself in a position of importance. An agent of the Cardinal begged her to disarm Monsieur's hostility in return for a free hand in all that concerned himself and his family. On the same day an emissary from the Queen arrived on a similar errand: Mademoiselle was reminded of their old friendship of which she intended to give new evidence. She stiffly replied that she was the humble servant of the Queen, but that Monsieur had long been on very bad terms with the Cardinal and found it difficult to bear the contempt displayed by him on every occasion.

She reported the conversation to her father at the Luxembourg, now besieged by 'les frondeurs de toutes professions,' who advised him to send a message through her to the Palais Royal.

THE QUEEN. Well, are you not surprised to see your father wishing to persecute and evict the Cardinal who loved him so much?

MADEMOISELLE. Monsieur does not hate the Cardinal, but he loves the King and the State as in duty bound, and, being convinced of our evil plight, he believes that he is not rendering good service to the King. That is why he desires his removal.

THE QUEEN. Why did he not say so sooner?

MADEMOISELLE. His respect for Your Majesty made him bear it as long as possible in the hope that he would profit by his advice, but since it was ignored he felt bound to make a public declaration to the Parlement this morning.

Mazarin, who understood to perfection the art of *reculer pour mieux sauter*, left on February 7 for Havre, liberated the Princes without conditions, and crossed the French frontier. Condé hurried to Paris, where the fickle citizens welcomed him as heartily as they had applauded his arrest. The Queen received him with frigid courtesy, but Mademoiselle swung round from enmity to ardent support. The reconciliation took place in a frank talk at supper at the Luxembourg on the evening of his return.

'Nous nous avouâmes l'aversion que nous avions eue l'un pour l'autre. Il me confessa avoir été ravi, lorsque j'avois eu la petite vérole, avoir souhaité avec passion que j'en fusse marquée, et qu'il m'en restât quelque difformité, et qu'enfin rien ne se pouvait ajouter à la haine qu'il avoit pour moi. Je lui avouai n'avoir jamais eu joie pareille à celle de sa prison; que j'avois fort souhaité que cela arrivât, et que je ne pouvois songer à lui que pour souhaiter du mal. Cette éclaircissement dura fort longtemps, réjouit fort la compagnie, et finit par beaucoup d'assurances d'amitié de part et d'autre.'

The conversation is characteristic of the woman who loved plain speaking, and the new partnership was to make history in the Second Fronde. When shortly afterwards Condé's wife was dangerously ill, many people foretold that Mademoiselle might be her successor. She discussed the notion with her trusted steward, summarising the points in its favour. Her father was now on friendly terms with M. le Prince; they were of the same royal

4

blood, and the aversion of the Queen for Monsieur barred his daughter's marriage with the King. The chief argument on the other side was that the Court would scarcely consent to the union of the two most powerful families in France. The critical stage of the illness was over in three days, and the match with Condé passed out of her mind though the new political partnership remained intact.

At this moment Charles II revisited Paris after his defeat at the battle of Worcester. They danced together and Mademoiselle found him improved, though his French was still poor. Henrietta Maria renewed her plea, explaining that in view of his present misfortunes her son could not approach Monsieur without knowing if his suit was acceptable. Mademoiselle replied that her present situation was so happy that she had no thought of marriage; that she was satisfied with her rank and possessions; that she received the proposal with all respect but begged time for consideration. Jermyn, the secretary and future husband of the widowed Queen, added his arguments but gained no ground. She appealed to Monsieur, who replied that his daughter belonged not to him, but to the state and the King, whose consent would be required. When at last the young Prince pleaded his own cause he was bluntly told that he ought to be trying to regain his throne instead of dancing at Paris. Mademoiselle had visions of her money being used up in an unsuccessful campaign, and she was far too proud to covet a throne without a kingdom.

CHAPTER IV

LA GRANDE MADEMOISELLE, CONDÉ, AND LOUIS XIV

IN 1652 Mademoiselle for a brief space made history, as she had always longed to do. The stage was set for a final trial of strength between the Court party, guided by Mazarin, and the various Opposition groups under the selfish leadership of Condé. The Cardinal, who had never lost touch with the Queen, returned to France in December 1651, despite the fact that 50,000 crowns were set on his head and that Monsieur and Condé had covenanted to continue the struggle till he was expelled. The wily Italian, however, had strong cards in his hand, above all the unchanging devotion of the Queen and the custody of the King, an attractive boy of thirteen. Turenne's antagonism having been bought off by promises, he was appointed to the command of the royal troops, and the dangerous enmity of de Retz was neutralised by a promise of the long-coveted Cardinal's hat. Mazarin had also the luck to be dealing with two political amateurs, for Monsieur was a coward and Condé plunged gaily into treasonable association with Spain.

Monsieur was pressed to go to Orleans, the city from which he derived his title, and to gain or hold it for the Fronde. He yielded reluctantly, for his policy was to evict the Minister without burning his boats. Mademoiselle remarked to her steward: 'Je gagerois que j'irai à Orléans'; for her youthful illusions about her father were gone. Moreover he had told her that the citizens of Orleans had begged him to send his daughter if he could not come himself. She dutifully replied that he well knew that she was always ready to obey him. She explained to her steward that it was precisely what she desired, since it was the darling wish of Condé and would earn the gratitude of her new friends. Next day she found Monsieur in a pitiable state of nerves. He was persecuted by the friends of Condé to go to Orleans, he declared, but he had decided against it, since all would be lost if he left Paris. Mademoiselle was disgusted but in no way surprised. 'Toutes les conversations que l'on avoit avec lui, lorsqu'il n'étoit pas satisfait des gens que le vouloient faire agir, finissoient toujours par des souhaits d'être en repos à Blois, et par le bonheur des gens qui ne se mêlent de rien. À dire le vrai, cela ne me plaisoit point. Je jugeois par là qu'à la suite du temps cette affaire iroit à rien, et qu'on se verroit réduit, comme on a été, chacun chez soi. Ce qui ne convient guere aux gens de notre qualité, et convenoit encore moins à avancer ma fortune; de manière que ces sortes de discours me faisoient toujours verser

des larmes et me causoient beaucoup de chagrin. Je demeurai
assez tard chez Monsieur; tout le monde me venoit dire: Vous
irez assurément à Orleans.'

Mademoiselle embarked in high spirits on the most joyous
adventure of her life. She rode part of the way when her carriage
broke down, and the troops were delighted when she began to
give orders. She laughed when summoned to a Council of War,
but she found her feet and was rewarded by the assurance that
nothing should be done without her commands. After fruitless
demands for the opening of the gates she was allowed to enter
Orleans without her troops, for the city fathers were disinclined
to commit themselves too far to either side. The people cried:
'Vive le Roi, les Princes, et point de Mazarin!' She was called
La Maréchale and made her first speech at the Hôtel de Ville.
She was commissioned by her father, she declared, to protect the
citizens against the evil designs of Cardinal Mazarin or to die
with them. They were not against the young King, who should
be guided by Monsieur and Condé. Their party was that of the
King, and all the trouble arose from his being in the hands of a
foreigner who thought only of his own interests. She was congratulated on her spirited oration, which she reproduces, and
which, doubtless a little touched up, reads well enough. 'Vous
m'avez sauvé Orléans et assuré Paris,' wrote her father ecstatic-
ally; 'c'est une joie publique, et tout le monde dit que votre
action est digne de la petite-fille de Henri le Grand. Je vous
dirai encore que je suis ravi de ce que vous avez fait.' Even more
welcome were the flatteries of Condé, who compared her to
Gustavus Adolphus. She admits that his services to France at
this time were not of the same order as his victories at Rocroy
and Fribourg, Nordlingen and Lens; 'mais il faut que les intentions
des grands soient comme les mystères de la Foi. Il n'appartient
pas aux hommes d'y pénétrer; on les doit révérer, et croire
qu'elles ne sont jamais que pour le bien et le salut de la patrie.
L'on doit juger ainsi de celles de M. le Prince, puisque c'est
l'homme du monde des plus raisonnable.' This confession of faith
is at once the most celebrated as well as the most revealing passage
in the book.

Monsieur sent his daughter a *plein pouvoir*, but received no
thanks. 'J'eus assez de vanité pour croire que cela choquoit
l'autorité de ma naissance d'écrire qu'un morceau de parchemin
m'en fût donner.' She changed her tune when the cautious
citizens opposed the desire of Condé to visit her unless they
received the Duke's permission. The document was produced,
but Mademoiselle gave the burghers a piece of her mind. To
an audacious critic who declared that the name of M. le Prince
was odious in the city of Orleans she replied: 'Il n'appartient pas

à des bourgeois d'Orléans, ni à qui que ce soit en France, de parler ainsi des princes du sang; on les doit respecter comme des gens qui peuvent être les maîtres des autres.' It never occurred to her that her estimate of 'les grands' as above criticism and entitled to unquestioned obedience might not be generally shared. The charm of novelty soon wore off, and the bored princess yearned for the familiar delights of the capital.

On May 4 Mademoiselle, accompanied by Condé, returned to Paris, where she was loudly acclaimed. So cordial had their relations become that he sketched out a dazzling future for them both. 'There was nothing he desired so passionately as to see me Queen of France; nothing would be more to his advantage in view of the favour I had for him; he was confident that I should always consider him above all other men as depending on me; there was nothing he would not do to ensure the success of this affair; I had only to command, and he would obey me in everything as a most faithful and zealous servant. We exchanged many protestations of friendship, with great sincerity on my side and I believe on his as well.' No one even in that amorous age fell in love with Mademoiselle, who confesses that she had always had a great aversion for love, even when legitimate; 'toute cette passion me paroissoit indigne d'une âme bien faite.' We may therefore assume that the exuberance of the profligate Condé was a tribute to her political significance rather than to her personal charms. This was in no way distasteful to her, for though she preferred male to female company she was never a flirt.

Among her many visitors was Henrietta Maria, who compared her to Joan of Arc. It was the happiest time of her life. 'Monsieur et M. le Prince venoient tous les jours en mon logis, et tout ce qu'il y avoit de personnes considerables dans le parti, tant hommes que femmes, de sorte que la cour étoit chez moi, et j'étois comme la reine de Paris, Madame [her stepmother] aimant aussi peu à voir le monde qu'il aimoit peu à aller chez elle. Je passois fort bien mon temps; j'étois honorée au dernier point et en grande considération. Je ne sais si c'étoit par la mienne propre ou parce que l'on croyoit que j'avois beaucoup de part aux affaires. C'étoit une chose assez vraisemblable que j'y en devais avoir; mais une très véritable et malaisée à croire, c'est que je n'y en avois pas, Monsieur ne m'ayant jamais fait l'honneur d'avoir de confiance en moi. Cet aveu m'est rude à faire, mais beaucoup plus pour l'amour de lui que pour l'amour de moi; car quiconque m'aura connue jugera que je l'ai assez méritée, et ceux qui auront lu ces *Mémoires*, et ne me connoîtront que par là, jugeront aisément que je méritois cet honneur. Pour M. le Prince, il n'en faisoit pas de même, car il ne savoit rien dont il ne me fît part.' We shall scarcely be doing injustice to Monsieur if we suggest that his reticence was less the result of distrust than of jealousy of her popular appeal.

Condé was now her authentic hero, and on July 2, 1652, the most memorable day of her life, she saved him from destruction. At 6 A.M. there was a knock at her door. He had sent an urgent appeal to Monsieur, saying that he had been attacked at dawn that morning near Montmartre; that he had been refused entry into the city at the Porte Saint-Denis; that he was continuing his march since he could not remain where he was. Monsieur had replied that he was ill. The messenger added that Condé had also charged him to beg the aid of Mademoiselle. Rising to the occasion she hurried to the Luxembourg, where she was disgusted to find her cowardly father at the top of the stairs.

MADEMOISELLE. Je croyais vous trouver au lit; le Comte de Fiesque m'avoit dit que vous vous trouviez mal.

MONSIEUR. Je ne suis pas assez malade pour y être, mais je le suis assez pour ne pas sortir.

After vainly exhorting her father to ride to the help of Condé she advised him to make his subterfuge a little more plausible by going to bed. She wept with anxiety as she thought of the situation of Condé and the brave officers among her father's troops. Her anguish was increased by the sight of some of his attendants in high spirits at the thought that the hero would perish. 'Ils disoient: Dans des occasions comme celles-ci, se sauve qui peut. Its étoient amis du Cardinal de Retz, et c'étoit lui qui les faisoit parler ainsi.' She could not understand how he could be so tranquil, she remarked acidly to her father. Was he about to make a treaty with the Court sacrificing Condé to the Cardinal? He did not reply. Her visit had lasted an hour, during which, she sadly reflected, all her friends might have been killed. Finally she obtained a letter from Monsieur authorising her to inform the city authorities of his wishes.

Hurrying to the Hôtel de Ville she made a speech to the Governor of Paris and his colleagues, explaining that her father was slightly unwell, and conveying his desire that a force of 2000 should be sent to Condé's relief. The promise was given. She then declared her conviction that her hearers would be delighted to extricate M. le Prince from his perilous situation; that his person ought to be dear to all good Frenchmen; and that she believed that there was not one who would not risk his life to save him. Reserving her chief request till the last, she begged that the hard-pressed troops might be admitted to the city. When the city fathers looked questioningly at each other she impatiently exclaimed: 'It seems to me that there is no need for deliberation. Monsieur has always shown such favour to the city of Paris that it is only right in their situation, when the safety of both is at stake, that you should display your gratitude.' If Condé were defeated, Mazarin's vengeance would fall upon them. 'It is for us to avert this fate by our efforts; and we could render no greater service to the King than to retain for him the largest and finest city in his kingdom, which has always been the most faithful in his service.' Her compliment to the city which had so recently staged the First Fronde was undeserved, and a cold douche was administered by Marshal de l'Hôpital, the Governor of Paris. 'You know, Mademoiselle, that if your troops had not approached the city, those of the King would not have come, for the latter were only sent to drive them away.' She was in no mood for further discussion. 'Mais songez, Messieurs, que pendant que l'on s'amuse à disputer sur les choses inutiles, M. de Prince est en péril dans vos faubourgs, et quelle douleur et quelle honte ce serait pour jamais à Paris s'il y périssait faute de secours! Vous pouvez lui en donner, faites-le-donc vitement.' While they withdrew to discuss the request she prayed at a window, and in a few minutes they returned to inform her that the troops should be admitted into the city.

Mademoiselle dispatched the joyful tidings to her hero and hastened to the scene of the struggle. In the Rue Saint-Antoine she met a sorry cavalcade of dead and wounded men, among them La Rochefoucauld, his face covered with blood. She spoke to him, but he was unable to reply. When the gates of the Porte Saint-Antoine were opened, Condé was among the first to enter. 'He was in a pitiable condition. His face was thick with dust, his collar and shirt covered with blood, though he was not wounded; his cuirass full of dents. His sword was in his hand, but he had lost the scabbard. He said to me: "You see a man in despair; I have lost all my friends." Throwing himself on to a chair in the house where the meeting occurred he wept and begged pardon for giving way to grief.' 'Et après cela,' comments Mademoiselle, 'que l'on dise qu'il n'aime rien! Pour moi, je l'ai toujours connu tendre pour ce qu'il aime.' Distressing as were the sights of battle she rejoiced in her power, imagining herself back in Orleans, commanding and being obeyed. Quickly recovering his self-control, Condé plunged back into the fray. He had only 5000 men against 11,000 under Turenne, but he was a host in himself. 'It étoit partout. Les ennemis ont dit qu'à moins d'être un démon, il ne pouvait pas humainement faire tout ce qu'il avoit fait: il était à toutes les attaques. Enfin il fit des choses qui passent l'imagination, tant que par sa grande valeur que par la prudence avec laquelle il agit et un sang-froid que tout le monde admira.'

Such a hero of romance it was a privilege to serve, and Mademoiselle threw the last remnants of discretion to the winds. She

had secured permission to open the gates, but she now took a
step on her own responsibility for which she could hardly expect
to be forgiven. The Governor of the Bastille informed her of his
readiness to do the bidding of Monsieur if a written order was
produced. The message was promptly forwarded to the Luxembourg, and the order duly arrived with a promise that the writer
would follow. She sent the welcome news to Condé, who hurried
to the *rendez-vous*. He seemed quite changed since the morning,
with a smiling face and an air of gaiety. He began with a
thousand compliments and expressions of gratitude. 'I have a
favour to ask,' said Mademoiselle, 'namely that you do not refer
to the injury he has done you.' 'I have only to thank him,'
replied Condé diplomatically; 'without him I should not be here.'
Mademoiselle laughed as she replied: 'A truce to raillery. I
know you have causes of complaint. They drive me to despair,
but for love of me do not mention them.' He promised, pretending to believe in Monsieur's friendship for him, and to be convinced
that it was the friends of de Retz who had prevented him from
doing what he desired. A moment later Monsieur arrived,
embraced the hero with a smiling face, as if he had worthily
played his part, and asked for an account of the combat. Condé
confessed that he had never been in such peril, and Monsieur went
on to the Hôtel de Ville to thank the authorities.

When they were gone Mademoiselle entered the Bastille, which
she had never visited, and paced up and down on the ramparts.
She ordered the cannon, which pointed to the heart of the city,
to be swung round so as to face Saint-Antoine. Through a tele-
scope she discerned a crowd of people and carriages on the heights
of Charenton and concluded that it was the King—a supposition
which she subsequently verified. Seeing the enemy cavalry in
motion, she sent word to Condé, who was also scanning the
horizon from a neighbouring belfry. 'The troops sent by Marshals
Turenne and La Ferté to press ours back came close up to the
city, but two or three volleys were fired from the Bastille, as I had
ordered when I left.' Such is her version of the most celebrated
exploit in her life. Most of her contemporaries, on the other
hand, testify that she herself fired the cannon against the King's
troops. To Mme de Motteville she afterwards declared that she
had given no such order, but the statement in her *Memoirs* is more
likely to be correct. The grateful Condé promised his utmost
help to procure her a suitable marriage, but her activities on July 2
destroyed any slight possibility of her becoming Queen of France.

Two days later, on July 4, she took part in the last political
action of her life. A meeting was arranged at the Hôtel de Ville
to unite the Parlement, Monsieur, and Condé. Monsieur was to
be Lieutenant-General of the State, with power to give orders on

every subject and wielding the authority of the King so long as
the boy was a prisoner in the hands of the Cardinal.   The latter
was to be declared an enemy of the state, a criminal, and the
disturber of the public peace, by declarations of all the Parlements,
and to be banished for life.   Condé was to be Generalissimo of
the King's armies.   While the Parlement was deliberating on
these high matters, Mademoiselle took a walk in the streets and
was greeted with the cry of 'Vivent le roi, les princes, et point de
Mazarin!'   At this point, when the Opposition appeared to be in
unchallenged control of the capital, news was brought to the
Luxembourg that the Hôtel de Ville was on fire and shooting had
occurred.   She volunteered to go and restore order, but her first
attempt to reach the scene of action failed.   When she arrived
during the night the streets and the building were almost deserted.
The riot sealed the fate of the Second Fronde, for the citizens had
had their fill of civil war, mob violence, and privations, and the
revolt collapsed.

Two months later, in October 1652, Condé and his little army,
failing to secure satisfactory terms, withdrew from Paris.   The
Court returned, and Mademoiselle received a letter from the young
King instructing her to vacate the Tuileries in order to make
room for his brother.   Her father was furious but he realised that
the game was up.   Would she be driven out? she asked.   He
replied coldly that he could not mix himself up in her affairs, for
she had behaved so badly to the Court and had not followed his
advice.   This characteristic *volte-face* was too much for his high-
spirited daughter, who reminded him that she had gone to Orleans
by his order and received his thanks.   'And the affair of Saint-
Antoine?' he rejoined; 'do you not believe that it has greatly
damaged you at Court?   You were so eager to play the heroine,
to be told that you were of our party and twice saved it, that,
whatever happens to you, you will find consolation in recalling all
the praises you have received.'   Her request to live in the Luxembourg or to join him at Blois, whither he now retired, was roughly
declined.   His unfeeling and sarcastic phrases were the last straw,
and she decided to give up the hopeless fight.   'I was tired of the
war.'   When Condé left Paris she had wept, but now, when he
urged her to join him, she declined.   For her the Second Fronde
had been an adventure, an escape from the demon of boredom,
not a crusade.   At the age of twenty-five the political career of
the Amazon was over.   She can hardly be blamed for resenting
the dictatorship of Mazarin, but it was madness and treason for the
granddaughter of Henri IV to take up arms against the King.
It was also a miscalculation, for the Second Fronde was the last
kick of dying feudalism against the Absolute Monarchy which the
distracted nation was at last willing to accept.   On the day after

his return and the flight of Mademoiselle the King held a *Lit de
Justice* and forbade the Parlement to meddle with 'general affairs.'
A second ceremony declared Condé and his adherents guilty of
treason. In December de Retz was arrested; January 1653
witnessed Turenne's victories over Condé, and in February
Mazarin returned in triumph. Henceforth not a hand was lifted
against the throne till the French Revolution.

Mademoiselle fled in disguise from Paris to her small manor of
Saint-Fargeau, which was to be her home for the next five years.
The King wrote approving her choice, and assuring her that she
could reside there in liberty and safety. She proudly replied that
she had no fears since she had nothing on her conscience, being
incapable of any action unworthy of her birth or patriotism.
Despite this parade of injured innocence, her spirits sank when
she arrived at two in the morning. The bridge over the moat was
broken and the grass in the courtyard was up to her knees. 'Fear,
horror and grief gripped me to such an extent that I wept. Now
I was away from the Court I pitied myself for not having a better
home.' Her nerves were overstrained, and when the curtains of
her four-poster opened mysteriously at night she summoned one
of her ladies to share her bed. Her health and spirits quickly
returned, and before long Saint-Fargeau was transformed into a
comfortable residence. Her misfortune is our gain, for it is to
her years of disfavour that we owe the earlier and most important
part of the *Memoirs*. 'I used to wonder how a person used to
Court life and of high rank could occupy herself, since for grandees
to be away from the Court is to be in complete solitude, despite
the number of their domestics and their visitors. Yet now I am
in retirement I am glad to find that the writing of reminiscences
is an agreeable occupation. One has time for it, and God has
given me a good memory.' Aided by her steward, Préfontaine,
who had shared many of her experiences and corrected her spelling,
she wrote rapidly and with increasing zest the story of her life up
to her flight from Paris in 1652. She who had read nothing but
the *Gazette* now discovered the charm of books, particularly
history and novels, which were read to her while she worked at her
tapestry. She enjoyed the society of Segrais, a minor poet and
member of the Académie Française who accepted a position in
her household; she was visited by travelling actors who played
her beloved Corneille; and she corresponded on politics with
Condé and on less dangerous topics with Mme de Sévigné.

Since she could travel wherever she liked except to Paris,
Mademoiselle often took the waters at Forges, visited Port Royal,
where she was impressed by the piety of the inmates, met the
eccentric Christina of Sweden, and kept in touch with her father
by occasional journeys to Touraine. The affectionate intimacy

of the years of childhood was over. She had lost all respect for his character, and he resented her indifference to his daughters. Desiring to secure their future, he tricked her into paying a large sum to meet his debts. The chapters on her eclipse are the least interesting portion of the book. Her ladies were troublesome, and she was not an easy mistress. 'She would have been the happiest princess in the world had she wished,' records Segrais. 'She used to say: Mon Dieu, pourquoi m'avez vous fait de l'humeur dont je suis?' As the years passed she became bored and gloomy. She realised that her prestige was gone. That there were no more suitors told its own tale. Though she still dreamed of Condé, they were no longer in unison; for he had joined the Spaniards, who were at war with his country, and she longed for reconciliation with the Court if it could be accomplished without loss of face. When she read of festivities at Paris her nostalgia became acute. Monsieur was restored to favour in 1656, and proceeded to negotiate with Mazarin for her pardon. The Cardinal, never vindictive, declared that the word of Mademoiselle could be trusted, for she was 'une princesse de bonne foi.' The compliment pleased her, but she had no intention of making herself too cheap. When she was advised to see Fouquet, the factotum of Mazarin, she haughtily replied: 'Je suis d'une qualité à ne pas chercher les ministres subalternes.'

The return of the lost sheep to the fold took place in 1657 at Sedan, where the good-natured Queen made things easy. When their carriages met Mademoiselle descended and kissed her hands and dress. The Queen embraced her, remarking that she was pleased to see her, that she had always loved her, that at times she had been incensed, that she bore her no grudge for the affair at Orleans, but that for her conduct at the Porte Saint-Antoine she would have strangled her had she had a chance. Mademoiselle meekly rejoined that she deserved such a fate for incurring her displeasure; it was her misfortune to be mixed up with people who had talked her into actions where her duty obliged her to do what she had done. 'I wished to talk of that first,' rejoined the Queen, 'and to tell you all that is in my heart, but I have forgotten everything, and there is no need to recur to it. Be assured that I will love you more than ever.' Once again Mademoiselle kissed her hands and was embraced. 'I do not find you at all changed,' remarked the Queen, 'though it is six years since we met. You are fatter and your complexion is improved.' 'Has not Your Majesty heard that I have grey hair? As I do not wish to deceive Your Majesty in any way I have used no powder to-day so as to show it to you.' When the Queen looked at her hair and expressed astonishment, Mademoiselle explained that it was in the family. The Queen overwhelmed her with kindness, though her strictures on Monsieur were severe. 'How many promises to me has he made and broken! I should find it very difficult to trust him again.' Such words were painful to a daughter's ears, but she knew they were justified.

The King, now nineteen, arrived a day or two later, and received his repentant cousin with smiles. 'Voici une demoiselle que je vous présente,' said his mother, 'et qui est bien fâchée d'avoir été méchante; elle sera bien sage à l'avenir.' He laughed good-humouredly. Shortly afterwards his brother arrived, embraced his cousin, and complimented her on her improvement in looks. It only remained to make peace with the Cardinal. She bowed, remarking to the Queen: 'Il me semble, Madame, qu'il seroit bien à propos que Votre Majesté nous fît embrasser, après tout ce qui s'est passé. Pour moi, ce sera de bon cœur.' When Mazarin knelt to her she raised and embraced him. It was the greatest delight to see her again, he declared, and he had long desired it, but there were obstacles which could not be overcome. He added his congratulations on her looks. That evening she joined the family supper and dance. Next day she invited the Cardinal into her carriage.

MAZARIN. Qui vous auroit dit en 1652 que le Mazarin auroit été en portière avec vous, vous ne l'auriez pas cru, et si le voilà lui-même ce Mazarin qui faisait tout de mal.

MADEMOISELLE (*laughing*). Pour moi, je ne l'ai pas cru si méchant, et j'ai toujours jugé que les choses en viendroient où elles sont.

MAZARIN. Vous l'avez dit même, car je sais que M. le Prince et vous riiez souvent de tous les emportements de Son Altesse royale contre moi, et que vous disiez ensemble: Il reviendra; il est bon homme. Pour moi, j'en serai bien aise, pourvu qu'il nous traite bien et que nous y trouvions notre compte. N'est il pas vrai que vous avez dit cela?

They talked freely of the Fronde, particularly of Condé and de Retz. The latter, declared Mazarin, had a black soul, could not be trusted, and owed his Cardinal's hat to the Queen alone. Condé, on the contrary, was good at bottom, and reconciliation with him would be an easy task. The Cardinal could now afford to be magnanimous, for he knew he had won. His combination of firmness and subtlety had saved France from anarchy, and, though never popular, he remained in unchallenged control till the day of his death. 'He speaks to the Queen like a chamber-maid,' testifies Montglat, 'and scolds the King like a schoolboy.' Mademoiselle had never been really dangerous, and now she fed out of his hand. He presented her with a pretty little dog, which she introduced to her friends with the words, 'C'est M. le Cardinal qui me l'a donné.'

Mademoiselle settled into the Luxembourg and returned to the usual round of balls, dinners, and entertainments in which her youth had been spent, but she knew that she had ceased to count. Her faint hope of marrying Monsieur, the younger brother of the King, ended with his marriage to Henrietta, the favourite sister of Charles II. Her father, cured of his ambitions and universally despised, preferred Blois to Paris, where he realised that he too, once the first man in France, had no longer a part to play. Every evening during a brief visit to the capital he came to his daughter's room and lamented his fate. 'Je suis dans un ennui terrible de me voir ici; j'ai la dernière impatience de m'en retourner; le monde m'ennuie; je n'y suis plus propre. Si je demeurois ici longtemps, je serais malade de la fatigue que j'y ai.' Mademoiselle scolded him for giving way to such gloom, but in vain. He dreamed of marrying one of his daughters to the King, but no one believed in such a possibility except himself. 'Monsieur me fait pitié de croire que je voulusse que mon fils épousât votre sœur,' remarked the outspoken Queen; 'c'est assez d'être fille de Madame pour que cela ne soit jamais: sa personne, son humeur et ses manières me sont odieuses, et je noierois plutôt mon fils.' 'Madame,' protested Mademoiselle, 'elle est fille de mon père.' 'Cela ne fait rien; elle l'est de votre belle-mère, ce qui gâte tout.' This was a shrewd thrust, for Mademoiselle confesses that her stepmother was unattractive and that she had no desire to see her half-sister occupying a position at Court superior to her own. Of this there was no fear, for Mazarin and his mother had other plans for Louis XIV. The long conflict with Spain came to an end, and the marriage of the King to his cousin Marie Thérèse was to set the seal on the reconciliation.

The royal family, including Mademoiselle, set out on its leisurely journey to the Pyrenees in 1659. Taking Blois on the way they found Monsieur failing and depressed. 'I am old and worn out, so I may die during your absence. If I do, I recommend your sisters to you. I know you do not love Madame, and that she has not treated you as she should have done. That is not the fault of my children; for love of me take care of them. They will need you, for Madame will not be much help.' Both were in a tender mood. 'Il m'embrassa trois ou quatre fois. Je reçus cela avec beaucoup de tendresse, car j'ai le cœur bon.' His apprehensions were fulfilled, for he died in the following year at the age of fifty-two. When the news reached her she wept, but he had long ceased to count in her life.

On paying his visit of condolence the Cardinal declared that his obligations to her father outweighed the harm he had received; he bore him no ill-will, since he had been badly advised. He would devote more thought than ever to her fortunes; it was his business and she need not worry. He would also look after her sisters, to whom she must be a mother since their mother ruined everything she touched. Mazarin was as celebrated for his promises as for the facility with which he forgot them, and a year later he was dead. The King, who was equally sympathetic, promised that he would be a father to her. The return of Condé, whose pardon was stipulated in the Treaty of the Pyrenees, gave her particular pleasure, for he was as friendly as when they had parted seven years before. He had never forgotten his obligations, he declared, and would always study her interests. He resumed his place at Court without embarrassment on either side, for Le Roi Soleil, henceforth the undisputed master of France, could afford to be magnanimous.

After the marriage of the King to the virtuous but boring Marie Thérèse Mademoiselle played no great part at Court. She shared the Luxembourg with her unloved stepmother and endeavoured to revive the literary glories of the Hôtel de Rambouillet. No cards were allowed, for she had always disliked the games of chance in which Anne of Austria delighted, and gallantry was discouraged, for she had never approved of the tender passion. Though in no way an intellectual, her interests had widened with adversity, and in addition to Segrais and the learned Huet her salon could boast of La Rochefoucauld, Mme de Sévigné, and Mme Lafayette. The craving for a throne had vanished, and when Henrietta Maria once more pressed the claims of her son, on the ground that the Restoration had taken place, she knocked at a closed door. 'Le Roi et la Reine,' was her reply, 'me font trop d'honneur de vouloir de moi; je ne le mérite pas, les ayant refusés pendant leur disgrâce; et c'est par cette même raison que je le refuse encore, parce que je ne crois pas le mériter. Il auroit toujours cela sur le cœur et je l'aurois sur le mien et cela nous empêcheroit d'être heureux. Qu'il jouisse de sa bonne fortune avec quelqu'un qui lui ait obligation. Pour moi je ne voudrois pas qu'il eût rien à me reprocher, voulant être heureuse. Je ne sais point ce que Dieu me garde; mais j'attendrai l'accomplissement de ses volontés sur moi avec tranquillité et sans aucune impatience de me marier.' Segrais describes her refusal as a great mistake, but our knowledge of the Merry Monarch suggests that she had a lucky escape.

Charles II married Catherine of Braganza in 1662, and in the same year Mademoiselle refused her last offer of a throne.

Turenne (*a cousin on her mother's side*). Je veux vous marier.

Mademoiselle. Cela n'est pas facile; je suis contente de ma condition.

Turenne. Je veux vous faire reine de Portugal.

Mademoiselle. Fi! je n'en veux point.

TURENNE. Les filles de votre qualité n'ont point de volonté; elle doit être celle du roi.

MADEMOISELLE. Est ce de la part du roi que vous me venez parler?

TURENNE. Non, c'est de moi.

MADEMOISELLE. Il fait bon d'être Mademoiselle en France avec cinq cent mille livres de rente, faisant honneur à la cour, ne lui rien demander, honorée par ma personne comme par ma qualité. Quand l'on est ainsi, on y demeure. Si l'on s'ennuie à la cour, l'on ira à la campagne, à ses maisons, où l'on a une cour. On y fait bâtir; on s'y divertit. Enfin quand l'on est maîtresse de ses volontés, l'on est heureuse car l'on fait ce que l'on veut.

TURENNE. Mais quand l'on est Mademoiselle, on est sujette du roi. Il veut ce qu'il veut. Quand on ne le veut pas, il gronde; il passe souvent plus loin: il chasse les gens. Quelquefois il met en prison dans sa propre maison, envoie dans un couvent, et après tout cela il faut obéir, et l'on fait par force ce que l'on auroit fait de bonne grâce, après avoir beaucoup souffert. Qu'est-ce qu'il y a à repondre à cela?

MADEMOISELLE. Que les gens comme vous ne menacent point ceux comme moi; que je sais ce que j'ai à faire; que si le roi m'en disoit autant, je verrois ce que j'aurois à lui répondre.

Though she rightly guessed that Turenne was speaking in the name of Louis XIV, and that the threats were not mere bluff, she was determined to have nothing to do with the most physically and morally repulsive of all her actual or potential suitors. When she told her cousin that she would be ready to marry the Duke of Savoy she received an angry snub: 'Je songerai à vous quand cela me conviendra et je vous marierai où il sera utile pour mon service.' This clash was followed by an order to withdraw to Saint-Fargeau till further notice. 'I have never seen the King so incensed as he is against my niece,' was the comment of the Queen Mother; but this time Mademoiselle accepted her fate calmly. After eighteen months of silence she wrote to congratulate the King on a new pregnancy of the Queen, adding her regret at being deprived of the honour of paying her respects. Her letter brought a friendly reply, and in 1664 she was welcomed back. 'Il faut oublier le passé,' said the King; 'je suis content de vous, ne parlons plus de rien.' When she tried to kiss his hand he embraced her. 'Confess that you were very bored,' said he. To which she replied: 'Not for a moment.' He was in excellent spirits and promised to work for her marriage to the Duke of Savoy. Despite her restoration to favour she no longer enjoyed Court life so much as formerly. Though she was on friendly terms not only with the Queen but with the La Vallière and the Montespan, she had no intimate friends and there was no warmth in her life.

In 1670, at the age of forty-three, Mademoiselle astonished the world by falling in love with the Comte, later Duc, de Lauzun. The days of her ambition were over, and she asked for nothing more than domestic happiness. 'L'ennui de ma condition, quoique heureuse, me prit et l'envie de me marier. Je raisonnois en moi-même (car je n'en parlai à personne) et je me disois: Ce n'est point une pensée vague; il faut qu'elle ait quelque objet; et je ne trouvai point qui c'étoit. Je cherchois, je songeois et je ne le trouvois point. Enfin, après m'être inquiétée quelques jours, je m'aperçus que c'étoit M. de Lauzun que j'aimois, qui s'étoit glissé dans mon cœur. Je le regardois comme le plus honnête homme du monde, le plus agréable, et que rien me manquoit à mon bonheur que d'avoir un mari fait comme lui, que j'aimerois fort et qui m'aimeroit aussi; que jamais personne ne m'avoit témoigné d'amitié, qu'il falloit une fois en sa vie goûter la douceur de la vie aimée de quelqu'un qui valût la peine que l'on l'aimait. Il me parut que je trouvois plus de plaisir à le voir et l'entretenir qu'à l'ordinaire; que les jours que je ne le voyois point il m'ennuyoit. Je crus que la même pensée lui était venue; qu'il n'osait me le dire; mais que les soins qu'il avoit de venir chez la reine, de se rencontrer dans la cour, quand elle sortoit, dans les galeries, enfin partout où l'on se trouvait voir par hasard, me le faisoient assez connoitre.' The middle-aged princess had more heart than in the days of her pride she had cared to admit.

The object of her belated affections was a cadet of an old and impoverished Gascon family who, like d'Artagnan, had come to Paris as a boy to seek his fortunes, had entered the army, and in 1669, at the age of thirty-six, climbed to the high office of Capitaine des Gardes. Mademoiselle had always admired dashing soldiers, and the prowess of Lauzun had earned the praises of his cousin Turenne. Intelligent, vivacious, adroit, and a clever talker, he was highly attractive to women. He read his latest admirer like a book, accepting the rôle of confidential adviser which she designed as a preliminary stage of her courtship: 'Il serait bien glorieux d'être chef de votre conseil.' That his heart was engaged nobody but Mademoiselle ever believed, but she was the richest heiress in France. 'You could make a man equal to sovereigns,' he remarked insinuatingly, 'but where is he?' Having no reason to make himself too cheap, he drew her on by his calculated reserve. When Henrietta, sister of Charles II, known as Madame, the wife of Monsieur, died, he urged Mademoiselle to take her place. 'Le roi veut que vous épousiez Monsieur; il lui faut obéir.' She replied that she had formed other plans for her happiness. At last she decided to inform him of her choice, writing 'C'est vous' on a piece of paper which she carried for days in her pocket and finally put into his hands.

LAUZUN. Je vois bien que vous vous moquez de moi.

MADEMOISELLE. Rien n'est plus sérieux ni plus résolu.

Her will prevailed, and she wrote to the King to beg his permission. The Captain of his Guards, she explained, was not unworthy of her. He was surprised, was the reply; she should think it well over; he loved her and would not constrain her. He repeated the words in an interview, adding that Lauzun had many enemies. 'Sire, si Votre Majesté est pour nous, personne ne nous sauroit nuire.' When she tried to kiss his hands he embraced her. She confided her secret to the Queen, whose reaction was less sympathetic.

THE QUEEN. Je désapprouve fort cela, ma cousine, et le roi ne l'approuvera jamais.

MADEMOISELLE. Il l'approuve, madame, et c'est une chose résolue.

They resolved to marry at once, for there was an outcry when the news became known. Louis XIV, bombarded by his wife, his brother, Condé, Gaston's widow, and Louvois, bowed to the storm and withdrew his consent.

THE KING. Je suis au désespoir de ce que j'ai à vous dire. On m'a dit que l'on disoit dans le monde que je vous sacrifiois pour faire la fortune de M. de Lauzun. Cela me nuiroit dans les pays étrangers, et je ne devois point souffrir que cette affaire achevât. Vous avez raison de vous plaindre de moi; battez-moi si vous voulez.

MADEMOISELLE. Ah! sire, que me dites-vous? Quelle cruauté! Quand j'ai dit la chose à Votre Majesté, si elle me l'eût défendue, jamais ne n'y aurois songé; mais l'affaire ayant été au point où cette est venue, la rompre, quelle apparence! Que deviendrai-je?

She was already on her knees. He joined her. 'Nous fûmes trois quarts d'heure embrassés, sa joue contre la mienne; il pleuroit plus fort que moi.'

THE KING. Ah! pourquoi avez-vous donné le temps à faire des réflexions? Que ne vous hâtiez-vous?

MADEMOISELLE. Hélas, sire, qui seroit méfié de la parole de Votre Majesté? Vous n'en avez jamais manqué à personne, et vous commencez par moi et M. de Lauzun! Je mourrai, et je serai trop heureuse de mourir. Je n'avois jamais rien aimé de ma vie; j'aime et aime passionnément le plus honnête homme de votre royaume. Je faisois mon plaisir et la joie de ma vie de son élévation. Vous me l'aviez donné; vous me l'ôtez; c'est m'arracher le cœur.

THE KING. Les rois doivent satisfaire le public.

While Lauzun accepted the royal veto with dignified resignation, Mademoiselle cried her eyes out. Her friends, with the exception of Mme de Sévigné and a few others, turned against her and she

5

seemed to be wasting away. 'Je suis plus fâché que vous de vous voir en l'état où vous êtes,' said the King. 'Je vois bien que c'est moi qui vous cause tous ces pleurs, et ils sont si raisonnables que je ne sais que vous dire.' She cried so much that Lauzun treated her like a child. 'Le moyen me voir, c'est de ne plus pleurer.' Many of her contemporaries and some of her biographers believe that a secret marriage took place with the King's consent, but no evidence had been produced. A second shattering blow quickly fell, for Lauzun was arrested and imprisoned in the fortress of Pignerol, where Fouquet and the mysterious Man in the Iron Mask were interned. No reason was assigned, but Louvois resented his influence with the King, and the Montespan doubtless had a hand in it; for Lauzun regarded her as the chief author of the King's veto and had denounced her in no measured terms. The shock was all the greater since he had stood exceptionally high in the royal favour and his genuine devotion to the King was the best feature of his character. Mademoiselle dared not ask her cousin for an explanation, but it was clear that he was punished, not for anything he had done but for what he had said. For the next ten years she lived in the thought of the loved one pining behind the bars of his sunless prison, elaborated schemes for his release, and dreamed of future happiness together.

She laid down her pen for the second time in 1676, five years after the arrest and five years before the liberation of Lauzun. When she resumed her narrative in 1689 or 1690 the scene had changed out of all recognition. He was discharged in 1681 on grounds of health, but without being restored to favour. A secret union probably took place, and in the middle of the eighteenth century we hear of an old woman who resembled Mademoiselle, received a pension, and believed herself to be her daughter. The Princess had been chilled by his coldness when they met after ten years, and closer acquaintance revealed his many failings— his avarice, his selfishness, his bad temper, his sharp tongue, his infidelities. His brother-in-law, Saint-Simon, speaks of his smile, 'qui démontrait la profondeur de sa fausseté.' He had no use for a plain woman of fifty-five except to squander her wealth, and there were plenty of younger beauties available. After two years of growing friction the inevitable break occurred.

LAUZUN. Je m'en vais et je vous dis adieu pour ne vous voir de ma vie.

MADEMOISELLE. Elle auroit été bien heureuse si je ne vous avois jamais vu; mais il vaut mieux tard que jamais.

LAUZUN. Vous avez ruiné ma fortune, vous m'avez coupé la gorge; vous êtes cause que je ne vais point avec le roi; vous l'en avez prié.

MADEMOISELLE. Oh! pour celui-là, cela est faux; il peut dire lui-même ec qui en est.

Lauzun lost his temper but she kept hers in control. 'Adieu donc,' said she, as she left the room. Returning a little later and finding him still there she said: 'C'est trop; tenez votre résolution; allez-vous-en.' He tried to return to her, but she had had enough. On her death-bed she refused to see him, and his name is not mentioned in her will.

The closing years of her life were sad, and her *Memoirs* break off in the middle of a sentence in 1688. The removal of the Court to Versailles diminished the social importance of the capital, and though she occasionally appeared at balls such diversions had lost their savour. She lived long enough to witness Lauzun's restoration to favour, to hear of his conspicuous services in piloting Mary of Modena, the wife of James II, and her baby to France in the crisis of 1688, and to follow his military misadventures in the campaign in Ireland which culminated in the battle of the Boyne. She died unregretted in 1693 at the age of sixty-six, the last survivor of the almost legendary epoch of the Fronde. In the words of Gourville, 'les jeunes, n'en ayant eu connaissance que du temps où le roi a établi son autorité, prendraient ceci pour des rêveries.' Her brief and futile political career had ended forty years earlier, and it was time to go. Like many other failures she lacked judgment and was her own worst enemy. Yet in the age of *Le Roi Soleil* it is refreshing to find a woman of unblemished character who scorned servility, loved open dealing, and never stooped to a dishonourable act.

Bibliographical Note.—The *Memoirs* should be read in Chéruel's edition, 4 vols. Arvède Barine's biography (vol. 1. *La Grande Mademoiselle et la Fronde*; vol. 2. *Louis XIV et la Grande Mademoiselle*) is a masterpiece. Ducasse, *La Grande Mademoiselle*, Meriel Buchanan, *The Great Mademoiselle*, which comes down to 1660, and Eleanor Price, *A Princess of the Old World*, are readable sketches. Sainte-Beuve's essay is in *Causeries du Lundi*, vol. 3. The best biography of Lauzun, whose mother was a La Force, is by the Duc de La Force. Mary Sandars, *Lauzun, Courtier and Adventurer*, contains new material on his later life.

CHAPTER V

BURNET AND THE STUART KINGS

BURNET's *History of My Own Time* is no less indispensable to the study of England in the seventeenth century than Clarendon's *History of the Rebellion*. The Bishop was a smaller man, and his book has not exerted such far-reaching influence as that of the founder of the Tory party. But for half a century he stood close to the heart of events, and in his first-hand account of the Glorious Revolution, when he helped to make history, we hang on his lips. Though few works of the kind have been so bitterly attacked, its merits have been increasingly recognised as the passions of the age cooled down. Macaulay justly remarked that other writers of the Stuart era would have been convicted of no less bias and inaccuracy if their works had been subjected to the same searching scrutiny. That his testimony is not all of equal value, that he sometimes accepted gossip as fact, that his pages are crowded with errors, that he is often unjust, is true enough. 'I do not believe that Burnet intentionally lies,' declares Dr Johnson, 'but he was so much prejudiced that he took no pains to find out the truth. He was like a man who resolves to regulate his time by a certain watch, but will not inquire whether the watch is right or wrong.' Here the stout old Tory, who was much more of a party man than Burnet, was decidedly unfair, for experts of a later age pronounce a relatively favourable verdict. In the critical analysis appended to the sixth volume of his *History of England Principally in the Seventeenth Century* Ranke concludes that, though he was credulous and uncritical, his mistakes are rarely vital. Airy, the learned editor of the volumes on Charles II, assures us that his comparative freedom from grave error, certainly from wilful misrepresentation, is remarkable. His worst fault, declares Firth, was his want of discrimination. The man who believed that Charles II committed incest with his sister Henrietta could believe anything.

When we pass from the value of the testimony to the character of the witness we are on firmer ground. 'The faults of his understanding and temper,' writes Macaulay in the course of a masterly characterisation, 'lie on the surface and cannot be missed. His high animal spirits, his boastfulness, his undissembled vanity, his propensity to blunder, his provoking indiscretion, his unabashed audacity, afforded inexhaustible subjects of ridicule. Yet Burnet, though open in many respects to ridicule and even to serious censure, was no contemptible man. In his moral character, as in his intellect, great blemishes were more than compensated by great excellence. Though often misled by prejudice, he was emphatically an honest man. His nature was kind, generous, grateful, forgiving.' Ranke regards him as a worthy prelate and a well-meaning man. Lecky pronounces him vain, pushing, boisterous, indiscreet, inquisitive. 'Yet his faults were much more than balanced by great virtues and splendid acquirements. He was honest and indomitable, courageous, kind, generous and affectionate, a man of fervent piety, wide sympathies and rare tolerance.' His accomplished biographer, Miss Foxcroft, pictures him as a person of immense vitality, genial, humane, religious without fanaticism, tactless and self-complacent but fundamentally independent. Even the Tory Swift, one of his sharpest critics, admits that he was a man of generosity and good nature. We may add that he was well aware of some of his own failings.

The Preface dated 1702 explains the nature and purpose of the book. 'I am now beginning to review and write over again the History of my own time which I first undertook twenty years ago, and have been continuing it from year to year ever since. For above thirty years I have lived in such intimacy with all who have had the chief conduct of affairs, and have been so much trusted and on so many important occasions employed by them, that I have been able to penetrate far into the true secrets of counsels and designs. . . . I writ with a design to make both myself and my readers wiser and better, and to lay open the good and bad of all sides and parties, as clearly and impartially as I myself understood it, concealing nothing that I thought fit to be known, and representing them in their natural colours without art or disguise, without any regard to kindred or friends, to parties or interests. For I do solemnly say this to the world, that I tell the truth on all occasions as fully and freely as I upon my best inquiry have been able to find it out. I have given the characters of men very impartially and copiously, for nothing guides one's judgment more truly in a relation of matters of fact than the knowing the tempers and principles of the chief actors. I reckon a lie in history to be as much a greater sin than a lie in common discourse, as the one is like to be more lasting and more generally known than the other. I find that the long experience I have had of the baseness, the malice, and the falsehood of mankind has inclined me to be apt to think generally the worst both of men and of parties. And indeed the peevishness, the ill nature, and the ambition of many hot clergymen has sharpened my spirit perhaps too much against them; so I warn my readers to take all I say on these heads with some grains of allowance, though I have watched over myself and my pen so carefully that I hope there is no great occasion for this apology.' He stands midway between the historians and the writers of memoirs, and he explains that he leaves all common transactions to ordinary books.

Burnet was born in Edinburgh in 1643, and passed the first thirty years of his life in Scotland. The portion of the *Original Memoirs* relating to Scotland before the Restoration is lost, but there is plenty of biographical material on the early period in the brief *Autobiography* written in 1710 and published by Miss Foxcroft, and in Book I of the *History*. His father, whom he loved and revered, was a distinguished lawyer, a steady royalist, a tolerant Erastian with a preference for Episcopacy. His mother was a fiery Presbyterian. Gilbert was a precocious boy, reading omnivorously and eagerly gathering information from his elders. 'Now I began to be known to great men,' we read in a revealing passage in the *Original Memoirs,* 'and I have ever since been much in their company, which has brought much envy and censure on me from other clergymen who fancied that I used odd arts to compass it. But I can give no other account of that matter than this: I never sought the acquaintance of a great man in my whole life, but have often declined it. Many loved me for my father's sake, and I had a facetiousness and easiness in conversation that was entertaining. I had read a variety of things and could dress them in easy words, so that many liked my company. I never imposed it on any, but I do not deny that I had great vanity in finding my company so much desired. I talked much, and was in many things very foolish and very faulty; yet I began eagerly to set myself to serve all people that were low or in affliction.'

Burnet adopted his father's attitude of moderate royalism, but he broke away from the religious allegiance of the majority of his countrymen. He did not hold with Charles II that Presbyterianism was not a religion for gentlemen; yet he was disgusted by what he calls its rough sourness and narrowness of soul, and he was convinced that it was incompatible with good order and discipline in the Church. After studying theology at Aberdeen he shocked his mother by deciding to become an Episcopalian minister. Though he found much to criticise in the church of his adoption he never regretted his choice, and the Latitudinarian strove unceasingly by tongue and pen to reconcile the body which he had left with that which he had joined. The first of his three wives was a Presbyterian. Even his enemies admit that he was a man of genuine piety. As a young parish priest at Saltoun, and later as Professor of Divinity at Glasgow, he quickly won a reputation for learning and zeal. He was one of the best preachers of his time, and an unceasing stream of publications poured from his pen. He was soon a marked man, and he declined a bishopric before he was thirty. Though we usually think of him as a Whig, he would be best described in the first half of his life as a moderate

Conservative. He speaks with horror of 'the murder' of Charles I and with a rare detachment of Cromwell. 'The enthusiast and the dissembler were mixed so equally that it was not easy to tell which was the prevailing character. He was indeed both. When his own design did not lead him out of the way, he was a lover of justice and virtue and even of learning.'

Burnet divides his survey of the reign of Charles II at 1673, on the ground that up to that point he knew Scottish affairs well, but only possessed such a general knowledge of England as he could pick up at a distance. His account of Scotland in the Restoration era is of enduring value, for he enjoyed the confidence of several of its leading figures. Lauderdale could have said *L'état c'est moi* with better reason than any of its rulers except Dundas a century later, and his early experiences had made him a believer in autocracy. He was called the King of Scotland, and for some years Burnet was his intimate friend. 'He made a very ill appearance: he was very big; his hair was red, hanging oddly about him; his tongue was too big for his mouth, which made him bedew all that he talked to: and his whole manner was rough and boisterous, and very unfit for a court. He was very learned, not only in Latin, in which he was a master, but in Greek and Hebrew. He had read a great deal in divinity, and almost all the historians ancient and modern: so that he had great materials. He was haughty beyond expression; abject to those he saw he must stoop to, but imperious and insolent and brutal to all others. He had a violence of passion that carried him often to fits like madness, in which he had no temper. He was the coldest friend and violentest enemy I ever knew. He at first seemed to despise wealth, but he delivered himself afterwards to luxury and sensuality; and by that means he ran into a vast expense and stuck at nothing that was necessary to support it. In his long imprisonment he had great impressions of religion on his mind, but he wore these out so entirely that scarce any trace of them was left. His great experience in affairs, his ready compliance with everything that he thought would please the king, and his bold offering of the most desperate counsels, gained him such an interest in the king that no attempt against him nor complaint of him could ever strike it till a decay of strength and understanding forced him to let go his hold. He was in his principles much against popery and arbitrary government; and yet by a fatal train of passions and interests, he made way for the former and had almost established the latter.' This darkly shaded portrait, needless to say, was painted after their rupture. Clarendon's verdict is even more severe, but the saintly Richard Baxter expressed his respect. He was a complicated character and there can be no doubt as to his moral deterioration in later life. Burnet's character studies lack the majesty of Clarendon, but he was a close observer.

The main problem for the rulers of Scotland was the retention or abandonment of Presbyterianism as the official system. Lauderdale, himself a Presbyterian, advised the King to keep the people friendly by leaving it alone, but he was overborne by Archbishop Sharp, a narrow-minded time-server, who deserves the invective that Burnet hurls at his head. The King, we are told, hated Presbyterianism, and when Clarendon and Ormond advised the substitution of Episcopacy the issue was settled. The ministers were ejected, and many of their successors are described as dregs and refuse. Burnet witnessed these proceedings with grief, finding his chief consolation in the society of Bishop Leighton, afterwards Archbishop of Glasgow, a convert from Presbyterianism like himself. It says much for him that he won and retained the friendship of this saintly scholar, the undaunted champion of tolerance in an intolerant age.

Burnet first crossed the Border in 1663 at the age of twenty, and in the following year he visited the Continent. 'From Holland, where everything was free, I went to France, where nothing was free.' 'I was as inquisitive as I could possibly be,' he confesses. In England he cultivated the Latitudinarians and the Cambridge Platonists, in Holland the tolerant Arminians. He prefaces his account of England, where 'all was joy and rapture,' with a series of character studies beginning with Charles II. 'He had a very good understanding: he knew well the state of affairs both at home and abroad. He had a softness of temper that charmed all who came near him, till they found how little they could depend on his good looks, kind words and fair promises, in which he was liberal to excess because he intended nothing by them but to get rid of importunity. He seemed to have no sense of religion. He said once to myself that he could not think God would make a man miserable for taking a little pleasure out of the way. He disguised his popery to the last: but when he talked freely he could not help letting himself out against the liberty that under the Reformation all men took of inquiring into matters, for from their inquiring into matters of religion they carried the humour further, to inquire into matters of state. He was affable and easy, and loved to be made so by all about him. The great art of keeping him long was the being easy and the making everything easy to him. He had great compass of knowledge, though he was never capable of great application or study. He had a very ill opinion both of men and women, and did not think there was either sincerity or chastity in the world out of principle. He thought that nobody served him out of love, and loved others as little as he thought they loved him. He hated business and could not be easily brought to mind any; but when it was necessary, and he was set to it, he would stay as long as his ministers had work for him. The ruin of his reign and of all his affairs was occasioned chiefly by his delivering himself up at his first coming over to a mad range of pleasure. The Duchess of Cleveland was a woman of great beauty, but most enormously vicious and ravenous, foolish but imperious, ever uneasy to the King and always carrying on intrigues with other men while she pretended she was jealous of him.' In the *Original Memoirs* Burnet declares roundly that the Court was full of pimps and bawds, and that all matters in which one desired to succeed must be put in their hands. 'He thinks to be wicked and to design mischief is the only thing that God hates, and has said to me often that he was sure he was not guilty of that.'

The description of James written in 1683 for the *Original Memoirs* is fuller and more interesting than that composed for the *History* twenty years later. 'He has naturally a candour and a justice in his temper very great, and is a firm friend but a heavy enemy, and will keep things long in his mind and wait for a fit opportunity. He has a strange notion of government, that everything is to be carried on in a high way and that no regard is to be had to the pleasing the people; and he has an ill opinion of any that proposes soft methods and thinks that is popularity; but at the same time he always talks of law and justice. He thinks that all who oppose the King in Parliament are rebels. He is a prince of great courage and very serene in action. He abhors drunkenness, and neither swears nor talks irreligiously. He has pursued many secret pleasures, but never with an open avowing them, and he does condemn himself for it; but he is ever going from one intrigue to another, though it is generally thought that these have been very fatal to him, and that the death of so many of his children is owing to that. He is a zealous and hearty papist. I took the freedom to object to him that the rest of his life was not so exact that so high a zeal as he has shewed in his religion could be believed to flow from an inward sense of his duty to God, otherwise that would appear in other things. His answer was that a man might have a persuasion of his duty to God so as to restrain him from dissembling with God and man in professing himself to be of another religion than that which he believed was true, though it did not restrain all his appetites. He was so far from being displeased with me for the freedom of speaking to him upon so tender a point, that he not only seemed to take it well from me but he has spoken very kindly of me to many others upon that very account.' When this was written the breach had already taken place, but the aversion revealed in the *History* was still to come.

Shaftesbury is also painted in vivid colours. 'I knew him for many years and in a very particular manner. He had a wonderful facility for speaking to a popular assembly. He had a particular talent of making others trust to his judgment and depend on it; and he brought over so many to a submission to his opinion that I never knew any man equal to him in the art of governing parties and of making himself the head of them. He was, as to religion, a deist at best. He had a dotage of astrology in him to a high degree. He fancied that after death our souls lived in stars. He had a wonderful faculty at opposing and running things down, but had not the like force in building up. He had such an extravagant vanity in setting himself out that it was very disagreeable. He pretended that Cromwell offered to make him king. His strength lay in the knowledge of England and of all the considerable men in it. He understood well the size of their understandings and their tempers; and he knew how to apply himself to them so dexterously that, though by his changing sides so often it was very visible how little he was to be depended on, yet he was to the last much trusted by all the discontented party. He had no sort of virtue, for he was both a lewd and corrupt man, and had no regard either to truth or justice.' That is certainly not the whole story of the founder of the Country Party. Neither ambition nor vanity, declares his latest biographer, provides the key to his political career, but the desire to preserve the old landmarks of his country against autocracy, Romanism, and French dictation.

Burnet was not easy to please, and there is far more blame than praise in his book. There are indeed only a few people in whom he finds no blemish, above all his father, Archbishop Leighton, Robert Boyle the chemist, 'an angel of purity,' Lord and Lady William Russell, and Queen Mary. He admired Clarendon, 'a true Englishman and a sincere Protestant,' and lamented his fall. 'The Court was delivered of a great man, whom they did not love and who, they knew, did not love them.' The King, we are told, had grown weary of his imposing way, and Lady Castlemaine, whom the Chancellor, a stern moralist, had always pointedly ignored, worked eagerly for his overthrow. Burnet detested loose living as much as cruelty, religious intolerance, and political vindictiveness.

A new chapter opened in 1673. He had made friends with the Hamiltons while he was professor at Glasgow, and was invited to edit the family papers of the Civil War period. His first book, *Memoirs of the Dukes of Hamilton*, was soon ready, and Lauderdale, who had read the manuscript and supplied information, introduced him to the King, whose consent was needed before it could be published. Charles read portions, praised it, and gave the desired permission; he heard him preach, liked the sermon, made him a chaplain, and gave him a long private audience. It was the first of his many interviews with royalties. 'I took all the freedoms with him that I thought became my profession.' Having talked of Church matters the fearless divine proceeded to scold him for his course of life. 'He bore it all very well and thanked me for it. Some things he freely condemned, such as living with another man's wife; other things he excused, and thought God would not damn a man for a little irregular pleasure. He seemed to take all I had said very kindly, and during my stay at Court he used me in so particular a manner that I was considered as a man growing into a high degree of favour.'

Burnet's success in London led to a breach with his patron. 'The Duke of Lauderdale had kept the Scotch nation in such a dependence on himself that he was not pleased with any of them that made any acquaintance in England, and least of all in the Court. So he looked on the favour I had got into with a very jealous eye, and his Duchess questioned me about it. I told her, what was very true as to the Duke (of York) that my conversation with him was about religion, and that with the King I had talked of the life he led.' It was all in vain, for Lauderdale had lost confidence in his *protégé*, and when Burnet's friend, the Duke of Hamilton, led an attack on his administration of Scotland, suspicion turned into hatred. Lauderdale even believed that the journey to London had been arranged by his enemies, and proceeded to ruin Burnet's newly won position at Court. 'He told the King that I had boasted to his wife of the freedom I had used with him upon his course of life. With this the King was highly offended, or at least he made much use of it to justify many hard things that he said of me; and for many years he allowed himself a very free scope in talking of me. I was certainly to blame for the freedom I had used with the Duchess of Lauderdale; but I was surprised by her question and I could not frame myself to tell a lie.'

On his next visit to London Burnet was received with great kindness by the Duke of York. 'He told me the King was highly incensed against me, and was made believe that I was the chief spring of all that had happened. He himself believed me more innocent; and said he would endeavour to set me right with him, and he carried me to the King who received me coldly. Some days after, the Lord Chamberlain told me he had orders to strike my name out of the list of the chaplains, and that the King forbid me the Court and expected I should go back to Scotland.' James intervened with his brother, who allowed his critic to come and defend himself. 'He said he was afraid I had been too busy, and wished me to go home to Scotland and be more quiet. The Duke upon this told me that if I went home without reconciling myself

to Duke Lauderdale, I would be certainly shut up in a close prison,
where I might perhaps lie too long. So I resigned my employment
(in Glasgow University) and resolved to stay in England. The
Duke brought Duke Lauderdale and me once together, to have
made us friends; but nothing would do unless I would forsake all
my friends and discover secrets. I said I knew no wicked ones,
and I could not break with persons with whom I had lived long in
great friendship.'

The breach became final in 1675 when Burnet, acting under
protest, obeyed the command to relate at the bar of the House of
Commons what he knew about Lauderdale. 'I said I, as well as
others, had heard him say he wished the Presbyterians in Scotland
would rebel, that he might bring over the Irish papists to cut
their throats. I was next examined concerning the design of
bringing a Scottish army to England. I said nothing had passed
that was high treason. I said further, I knew Duke Lauderdale
was apt to say things in a heat which he did not intend to do.'
Burnet was a vain man, but he is quite ready to admit mistakes,
and here was a gross breach of confidence. 'I was much blamed
for what I had done. Some, to make it look the worse, added
that I had been his chaplain, which was false; and that I had
been much obliged by him, though I had never received any real
obligation from him, but had done him great services, for which
I had been very unworthily requited by him. Yet the thing had
an ill appearance as the disclosing of what had passed in confidence.
The truth is, I had been for above a year in a perpetual agitation,
and was not calm or cool enough to reflect on my conduct as I
ought to have done. This broke me quite with the Court, and in
that respect proved a great blessing to me. It brought me out of
many temptations, the greatest of all being the kindness that was
growing on me to the Duke, which might have involved me in
great difficulties, as it did expose me to much censure.'

For the next few years Burnet devoted himself to his congenial
duties as Preacher at the Rolls Chapel and to the composition of
the first two volumes of his monumental *History of the Reformation*,
which won him a European reputation and for which he received
the thanks of the House of Commons. He kept aloof from politics,
having lost the favour of the Court and feeling no inclination to
join the Opposition. The Popish Plot, however, brought him back
to the political arena in 1678, and a letter to the King, warning
him that a militia bill passed by both Houses might be turned to
dangerous use, renewed his contacts with Whitehall. 'He rejected
the bill and thanked me for the advice I sent him. I waited often
on him all the month of December. He came to me to Chiffinch's,
a page of the backstairs, and kept the time assigned to me to a
minute. He was alone and talked much and very freely with me.

We agreed in one thing, that the greatest part of the evidence was a contrivance. He fancied there was a design of a rebellion on foot. I assured him I saw no appearances of it. I told him there was a report that he intended to legitimate the Duke of Monmouth. He answered quick that, well as he loved him, he had rather see him hanged. He spoke much to me concerning Oates's accusing the Queen. He said she was a weak woman and had some disagreeable humours, but was not capable of a wicked thing, and, considering his faultiness towards her in other things, he thought it a horrid thing to abandon her. He said he looked on falsehood and cruelty as the greatest of crimes in the sight of God. He knew he had led a bad life, but he was breaking himself of all his faults, and he would never do a false or wicked thing. I spoke on all these subjects what I thought became me, which he took well. This favour of mine lasted all the month of December 1678.'

The passionate emotions revealed by the Popish Plot made the position of the Duke of York the problem of the hour. That an ardent Catholic should rule in a Protestant country was a nightmare. But should the peril be averted by his exclusion from the throne or by limitation of his powers? Shaftesbury argued for the first alternative, Halifax, his nephew and at first his disciple, for the second. No one in England had a greater horror of Rome than Burnet, but he distrusted Shaftesbury and feared that his championship of Monmouth might provoke civil war. The Trimmer, however, is censured for doing the right thing in the wrong way. 'The truth is, Lord Halifax's hatred of the Earl of Shaftesbury, and his vanity in desiring to have his own notion preferred, sharpened him at that time to much indecency and fury in his whole deportment. I got many meetings appointed between Lord Halifax and some leading men, in which as he tried to divert them from the exclusion, so they studied to persuade him to it, both without effect.' Burnet attempted to mediate on the basis that a Protestant Protector, preferably the Prince of Orange, should exercise the royal power during the reign of a Catholic king; but the plan was naturally unacceptable in both camps. When the Exclusion Bill was rejected by the Lords, the policy of limitation was dropped for lack of support. The opposition melted away, and the spectre of civil war stampeded the country into the King's camp.

Hating violent courses and having emancipated himself from the doctrine of passive obedience, Burnet was ideologically attracted to Halifax, and for twenty years the Trimmer played an important part in his life. His elaborate portrait of the most brilliant figure on the political stage reflects the cooling of the friendship and is indeed a good deal less than just. 'He was a man of a great and ready wit, full of life and very pleasant, much turned to satire.

He let his wit run much on matters of religion, so that he passed for a bold and determined atheist; though he often protested to me he was not one and said he believed there was not one in the world. He confessed he could not swallow down everything that divines imposed on the world. He was always talking of morality and friendship. He was punctual in all payments and just in all his private dealings; but with relation to the public he went backwards and forwards and changed sides so often that in conclusion no one trusted him. He seemed full of commonwealth notions, yet he went into the worst part of King Charles' reign. He was out of measure vain and ambitious. The liveliness of his imagination was always too hard for his judgment. For when after much discourse a point was settled, if he could find a new jest to make even that which was suggested by himself seem ridiculous, he could not hold, but would study to raise the credit of his wit, though it made others call his judgment in question.' A fragment of the *Original Memoirs*, written on his death in 1695, is even more severe. 'His spirit was restless, and in spite of all his pretences to philosophy he could not bear to be out of business. He stuck up, as all discontented men do, to be a patriot, but he discovered too manifestly what lay at bottom.'

Halifax made fun of friend and foe, yet he respected Burnet's abilities and zeal. 'He pressed me vehemently to accept preferment at Court, and said if I would give him leave to make any promises in my name, he could obtain for me any employment I pleased; but I would enter into no engagements. I was contented with the condition I was in, which was above necessity though below envy. The Mastership of the Temple was like to fall, and I liked that better than anything else. So both Lord Halifax and Lord Clarendon moved the King in it, who promised I should have it; upon which Lord Halifax carried me to the King.' He did not expect a very friendly reception owing to an incident which had occurred a year before. 'Mrs Roberts, whom he had kept for some time, sent for me when she was a-dying. I saw her often for some weeks, and among other things I desired her to write a letter to the King, expressing the sense she had of her past life; and at her desire I drew such a letter as might be fit for her to write, but she never had strength enough to write it. So upon that I resolved to write a very plain letter to the King. I set before him his past ill life, and the effects it had on the nation, with the judgments of God that lay on him, and that was but a small part of the punishment that he might look for. I pressed him upon that earnestly to change the whole course of his life. I carried this letter to Chiffinch on January 29, and told the King in the letter that I hoped the reflections on what had befallen his father on the thirtieth of January might move him to consider these things more carefully.' The King read the letter twice and threw it into the fire without a word.

Whatever the feelings of Charles, he received Burnet in a friendly spirit. 'Lord Halifax introduced me with a very extraordinary compliment, that he did not bring me to the King to put me in his good opinion so much as to put the King in my good opinion; and added that he hoped the King would not only take me into his favour but into his heart. The King had a peculiar faculty of saying obliging things with a very good grace. Among other things he said, he knew that if I pleased I could serve him very considerably, and that he desired no service from me longer than he continued true to the church and the law. The discourse lasted half an hour, very hearty and free; I was in favour again, but I could not hold it. I was told I kept ill company; but I said I would upon no consideration give over conversing with my friends, and so I was where I was before.'

That the triumph of the Court had not extinguished discontent but merely driven it underground was revealed by the Rye House Plot and its ramifications. Burnet was slowly moving from his youthful moorings towards the common-sense doctrine that, if a ruler attacks the foundations of the national life, it is a duty to resist. Believing as he did that this had not yet occurred, he disapproved not only all projects of assassination but even talk of organised resistance. Yet, though still not a Whig, he was the friend of leaders of the Country Party, whose opposition to the Court was notorious. For the first and last time in his life he lost his nerve. Shattered by the death sentence on Lord William Russell he dispatched an abject letter to the King, which, needless to say, is not mentioned in his book. Though he was in no way concerned in the plot, he promised to have nothing more to do with anyone in opposition to the Court. If Lord Russell desired his ministration, he added, he could not refuse. Next day the expected summons arrived, and he found himself face to face with one of the noblest of men. This time it was the victim who steadied the divine, for his conscience was clear. He had had no designs on the King's life, and he was not ashamed of the political convictions which his visitor was before long to adopt.

'Lord Russell from the time of his imprisonment looked on himself as a dead man and turned his thoughts wholly to another world. He read much in the Scriptures, particularly in the Psalms, and read Baxter's dying thoughts. He was as serene and calm as if he had been in no danger at all. His behaviour during the trial was decent and composed, so that he seemed very little concerned in the issue of the matter. He then composed himself to die with great seriousness. He said he was sure the day of his trial was more uneasy than that of his execution would be. All possible methods were used to have saved his life; money was offered to Lady Portsmouth, and to all that had credit,. and that without measure. He was pressed to send petitions and submissions to the King and the Duke; but he left it to his friends to consider how far these might go, and how they were to be worded. All he was brought to was to offer to live beyond the sea in any place that the King should name, and never meddle any more in English affairs. But it was all in vain; both King and Duke were fixed in their resolutions.

'The last week of his life he was shut up all the mornings, as he himself desired; and about noon I came to him and stayed with him till night. All the while he expressed a very Christian temper, without sharpness or resentment, vanity or affectation. His whole behaviour looked like a triumph over death. He said sins of his youth lay heavy upon his mind; but he hoped God had forgiven them, for he was sure he had forsaken them, and many years he had walked before God with a sincere heart. He was still of opinion that the King was limited by law, and that when he broke through those limits his subjects might defend themselves and restrain him. He said he felt none of those transports that some people felt; but he had a full calm in his mind, no palpitation at heart, no trembling at the thought of death. The day before his death he received the sacrament from Tillotson with much devotion; and I preached two short sermons to him, which he heard with great affection; and we were shut up till towards the evening. Then he suffered his children, that were very young, and some few of his friends, to take leave of him, in which he maintained his constancy of temper, though he was a very fond father. He also parted with his lady with a composed silence; and as soon as she was gone he said to me: The bitterness of death is past. For he loved and esteemed her beyond expression, as she well deserved it in all respects; and she had the command of herself so much that at parting she gave him no disturbance.' Swift grumbled that he had never read so ill a style, but here Burnet rises above himself.

Within an hour of the execution in Lincoln's Inn Fields the declaration prepared by Russell was selling briskly in the streets. Burnet had helped him with the form though not the substance, but it was widely assumed that it was his work. The Court shared the belief and he was summoned before the Cabinet Council. At the King's command he read the journal of the victim's last days which he had prepared for the widow. Charles was silent, but his brother's hostility was unconcealed. It was the last time that he saw the Stuart princes. He lost his appointment at the Rolls Chapel, and was violently attacked in many of the pamphlets which poured from the Press. So insecure did he feel that he decided to go abroad, but before his plans were fixed Charles II died.   He concludes his survey of the reign with a further character sketch.   He had great vices, we are told, and scarcely any virtues. He was dissolute and ungrateful, gentle in manner though without tenderness in his nature, and in his later years he became cruel. He deliberately corrupted young men of quality both in religion and morality, and he left England much worse than he had found it.

CHAPTER VI

BURNET AND WILLIAM III

THE volume on James II is the most valuable and the most dramatic portion of Burnet's *History of My Own Time*. 'A great King with strong armies and mighty fleets, a vast treasure and powerful allies fell all at once: and his whole strength, like a spider's web, was so irretrievably broken with a touch that he was never able to retrieve what for want both of judgment and heart he threw up in a day. The sad fate of this unfortunate prince will make me the more tender in not aggravating the errors of his reign. I will remember how much I was once in his favour, and how highly I was obliged to him.' Permission to pay his duty to the new ruler was refused, but he was allowed to go abroad. He discovered the preparations for Monmouth's rebellion, and warned Lady William Russell against mixing herself up in the plot; but he was shocked by its savage repression. To avoid the compromising society of exiles and outlaws in Holland, he went first to France, where he witnessed the Dragonnades. On reaching Rome he was offered an audience by the Pope but declined, knowing the noise it would make. He returned through France, Switzerland, and Germany, carrying away an abiding impression of horror at the cruelties inflicted on the Huguenots and a deepened resolve to defend English Protestants against the assaults of a Catholic King. 'Here was such a real argument of the cruel and persecuting spirit of popery, wheresoever it prevailed, that few could resist the conviction. So that all men confessed that the French persecution came very seasonably to awaken the nation and open men's eyes in so critical a conjuncture.' Burnet rightly judged systems and institutions by their fruits. 'I love all men that love God and that live well. I have very large notions of the goodness of that God of love whose mercies I could never limit to any one form or party of religion; and so I am none of those that damn all Papists, for I have known many good and religious men among them. The chief ground of my abhorrence of that Church is that carnal, designing, ambitious, crafty, perfidious and above all cruel spirit that reigns among them, chiefly among the Religious Orders and most eminently among the Jesuits, who are the pests of society and the reproach of the Christian religion.'

The most important chapter in Burnet's life opened with his return to Holland in 1686 after a ramble, as he calls it, of more than a year. Halifax and Lady William Russell had prepared the ground for him. He was promptly invited to Court, where his memorable association with William and Mary began. 'I found

they had received such characters of me from England that they
resolved to treat me with great confidence, for at my first being
with them they entered into much free discourse with me concerning the affairs of England. The Prince, though naturally cold and
reserved, yet laid aside a great deal of that with me.' The voluble
and cheerful divine was struck by his gravity and complete indifference to danger. 'I fancied his belief in predestination made
him more adventurous than was necessary. But he said as to
that he firmly believed in a providence; for if he should let that
go, all his religion would be much shaken, and he did not see how
providence could be certain if all things did not arise out of the
absolute will of God. The Prince had been much neglected in his
education, for all his life he hated constraint. He spoke little.
He put on some appearance of application, but he hated business
of all sorts. Yet he hated talking and all house games more.
This put him on a perpetual course of hunting, to which he seemed
to give himself up beyond any man I ever knew; but I looked on
that always as flying from company and business. The depression
of France was the governing passion of his whole life. He had
no vice but of one sort, in which he was very cautious and secret.
He had a way that was affable and obliging to the Dutch. But he
could not bring himself to comply enough with the temper of the
English, his coldness and slowness being very contrary to the
genius of the nation.' No Englishman ever loved William of
Orange, but Burnet held him in high respect.

The portrait of Mary, 'the most wonderful person I ever knew,'
is painted in much warmer colours. 'The Princess possessed all
that conversed with her with admiration. Her person was majestic
and created respect. She had great knowledge, with a true understanding and a noble expression. There was a sweetness in her
deportment that charmed, and an exactness in piety and of virtue
that made her a pattern to all that saw her. She managed her
privy purse so well that she became eminent in her charities. She
knew little of our affairs till I was admitted to wait on her. And
I began to lay before her the state of our Court and the intrigues
in it ever since the Restoration, which she received with great
satisfaction and showed true judgment and a good mind in all the
reflections that she made.' The friendship thus auspiciously begun
was to last unbroken till the end.

Burnet's first task was to satisfy himself about the Prince's
notions on constitutional government and the Church of England.
The response in both cases was satisfactory. Only a constitution,
declared William, could long resist a powerful aggressor or raise
the money needed for a great war. He liked the government and
ritual of the Church, but blamed the condemnation of foreign
churches by some English divines. Burnet explained that they were

not all of that mind, and his own championship of toleration led William to declare that it was all he asked. He regretted some of the ceremonies, such as the surplice, the cross in baptism and the bowing to the altar, but he would never try to introduce Calvinism. This exploratory conversation took place in the presence of Mary and lasted for several hours. 'Great notice came to be taken of the free access and long conferences I had with them,' and James II began to prick up his ears. He complained to his daughter, who showed his letters to Burnet and consulted him about her replies. He had outgrown his notions of passive obedience, and he advised William to put the fleet in order; but he did not share the impatience of the Opposition. 'I said that I did not think every error in government would warrant a breach. If the foundations were struck at, that would vary the case, but illegal acts in particular instances could not justify such a conclusion. The Prince seemed surprised at this, for the King made me pass for a rebel in my heart, and he now saw how far I was from it. I continued on this ground to the last.' He was, indeed, always a moderate in Church and State.

Burnet's greatest achievement was to remove a misunderstanding between William and Mary. He asked her what she intended her husband to be if she came to the throne. She had never thought about the matter, believing that whatever accrued to her would come to him by right of marriage. When told she was mistaken, she asked him to propose a remedy. The remedy, he replied, was to promise that she would give him the real authority as soon as it came into her hands, and try to get it legally vested in him during his life. This would lay the greatest obligation on him possible and lay the foundation for a perfect union between them, which had been of late a little embroiled. Burnet asked pardon for his presumption in dealing with such an intimate matter, explaining that no one had suggested it or should ever know without her leave. 'I hoped she would consider well of it, for, if she once declared her mind, I hoped she would never go back or retract it. I desired her therefore to take time to think of it. She presently answered me she would take no time to consider of any thing by which she could express her regard and affection to the Prince, and ordered me to give him an account of all that I had laid before her, and to bring him to her, and I should hear what she should say upon it.'

William was out hunting, but next day Burnet reported the conversation and went with him to the Princess. 'She in a very frank manner told him that she did not know that the laws of England were so contrary to the laws of God as I had informed her; she did not think that the husband was ever to be obedient to the wife; she promised him he should always bear rule; and she asked only that he would obey the command, Husbands love your wives, as she should do that, Wives be obedient to your husbands in all things. From this lively introduction we entered into a long discourse of the affairs of England. Both seemed well pleased with me and with all that I had suggested. But such was the Prince's cold way that he said not one word to me upon it that looked like acknowledgment. Yet he spoke of it to some about him in another strain. He said he had been nine years married and had never had the confidence to press this matter on the Queen which I had now brought about easily in a day. Ever after that he seemed to trust me entirely.'

Henceforth Burnet was numbered among the unofficial advisers of the Court. He drew up the instructions for Dykvelt, who was sent to study the situation in England and to dissipate suspicions of the Prince. He argued with Penn, 'a talking vain man,' who was employed by James to urge William to support his tactical measures of toleration. The King now realised that the Scottish divine was a formidable enemy, and Dryden assailed him in *The Hind and Panther*. The publication at Amsterdam of a volume of letters on his recent travels, 'in which my chief design was to expose both popery and tyranny,' aroused anger, but though its sale in England was forbidden it circulated none the less. 'My continuing at The Hague made him conclude that I was managing designs against him.' James rightly believed him to be the author of some anonymous attacks on his proceedings; described him as a pernicious man; and, hearing that the exile was about to marry a Dutch subject of British descent, decided to act. On learning that a prosecution had been ordered, Burnet successfully petitioned the States-General for naturalisation in view of his intended marriage. The angry monarch retaliated by a charge of high treason for the transfer of allegiance; a sentence of outlawry was passed, and the offender was threatened with kidnapping if the States refused extradition. The States backed him up, explaining that naturalisation was a sacred thing and that the honour of a country was concerned in its observance. James described the reply as an affront and a just cause of war, and Burnet learned that an order had been seen in the Secretariat for £3000 to an unnamed person to seize or murder him. 'It had no other effect on me but that I thought it fit to stay more within doors and to use a little more than ordinary caution. I thank God I was very little concerned at it. I resigned up my life very freely to God. I knew my own innocence.' So strong was the pressure from London that he did not see the Prince and Princess for eighteen months, though he corresponded with them through Bentinck and continued to reside at The Hague. There was now a danger from Versailles as well as from Whitehall; for Louis XIV, angered by

his championship of the tortured Huguenots, promised facilities
to any kidnapper who might desire to bring him to England
through France.

At the close of 1687 Burnet inserted a remarkable prophecy in
his *Original Memoirs*, which reveals how closely he had studied
the Prince of Orange. 'His martial inclination will naturally
carry him, when he comes to the crown of England, to bear down
the greatness of France; and if he but hits the nature of the
English nation right at first he will be able to give laws to all
Europe. But if the Prince does not in many things change his
way, he will hardly gain the hearts of the nation. His coldness
will look like contempt, and that the English cannot bear; they
are too impatient to digest that slowness that is almost become
natural to him in the most inconsiderable things, and his silent
way will pass for superciliousness. But that which is more important, he will be both the King of England and Stadtholder.
The Dutch will perhaps think a King of England too great to be
their Stadtholder, and the English will hardly be brought to trust
a prince that has an army of 30,000 men at his command so near
them. If this matter is not settled upon the first opening his
succession to the Crown of England, there will arise a train of
jealousies upon it that, being fomented as they will certainly be
from France, may throw us into a mistrust that will perhaps never
be healed. This and another particular, that is too tender to be
put in writing [probably the *liaison* with Elizabeth Villiers], are
the only things that can hinder him from being the greatest King
that has been for many ages.'

At the opening of 1688 it was widely felt by Tories no less than
Whigs that the attack on the Constitution and the Church must
be resisted, and Admiral Russell came over to discover William's
plans. The Prince replied that if he were invited by men of high
standing to come and rescue the nation and the religion, he believed
he could be ready by the end of September. At this critical
moment the news that the Queen was expecting her confinement
came like a thunderclap, and Burnet enlarges on the suspicious
circumstances of the occasion. 'All coffee-house chat!' wrote
Swift in one of his bitter notes, and the historian has been sharply
attacked for his credulity. Yet the story as he tells it was enough
to arouse suspicion. Mary of Modena had buried all her children
soon after they were born; nobody expected her to bear a healthy
child, and symptoms unusual during pregnancy occurred. 'It was
soon observed that all things about her person were managed with
a mysterious secrecy, into which none were admitted but a few
papists. She was not dressed or undressed with the usual
ceremony.' That a warming-pan brought in during her labour
was not opened gave rise to the legend of a suppositious child.

'No cries were heard from the child, nor was it showed to those in the room. The under-dresser went out with the child, or somewhat else in her arms, to a dressing-room.' Burnet based his story mainly on the information reaching William and Mary, and he learned more after his return to England. 'What truth may be in these, this is certain, that the method in which this matter was conducted from first to last was very unaccountable. If an imposture had been intended, it would not have been otherwise managed.' He does not pronounce a final verdict and perhaps he could never quite make up his mind, but he believed James II capable of anything in the furtherance of his unconstitutional designs.

In Burnet's opinion the time to act had come at last, for the cup was full. He had helped to draft the Prince's declaration to the English people, and his offer to accompany William as his chaplain was accepted. 'Being fully satisfied in my conscience that the undertaking was lawful and just, and having had a considerable hand in advising the whole progress of it, I thought it would have been an unbecoming fear in me to have taken care of my own person when the Prince was venturing his, and the whole was now to be put to the hazard. It is true, I being a Scottish man by birth had reason to expect that, if I had fallen into the enemy's hands, I should have been sent to Scotland and put to the torture there.' In a farewell conversation with Mary he found her with a great load on her spirits, but satisfied of the lawfulness of the design: it was the first time he had seen her for two years. 'After much other discourse I said that, if we got safe to England, I made no doubt of our success in all other things. I only begged her pardon to tell her that, if there should happen to be at any time any disjointing between the Prince and her, that would ruin all. She answered that I need fear no such thing; if any person should attempt that, she would treat them so as to discourage all others from venturing on it for the future.'

On October 3, on the eve of his departure from The Hague, Burnet confided his thoughts to his *Original Memoirs*. 'The design is as just as it is great, and the Prince, as far as it is possible to see into a man's heart, goes into it with great and noble intentions. He seems to be marked out by Providence for the doing of wonders, and as his first essay was the saving of this state, when it was almost quite overrun by the French, so he now seems to be led by Providence to a much nobler undertaking, in which, if God bless him with success, and if he manages the English as dexterously as he hath hitherto done the Dutch, he will be the arbiter of all Europe, and will very quickly bring Louis the Great to a much humbler posture, and will acquire a much juster right to the title of Great than the other has ever done.' What Burnet called Providence Professor Trevelyan, in his admirable little book, *The English Revolution, 1688-9*, rightly calls luck. 'In the affair of the Revolution the element of chance, of sheer good luck, was dominant. It was only the accident of James II that gave our ancestors the opportunity to right themselves. At the end of Charles II's reign nothing seemed less probable than that England would soon become either a powerful state or a free and peaceful land. The violence of her factions for half a century past had reduced her to prostration before a royal despotism in the pay of France. Nothing could really have saved England except the apparently impossible—a reconciliation of Tory and Whig, Church and Dissent. That miracle was wrought by the advent of James II, who united against himself the old antagonists. The eleventh-hour chance thus given to our ancestors was neither missed nor abused. It was the victory of moderation, a victory not of Whig or Tory passions, but of the spirit and mentality of Halifax, the Trimmer. The settlement of 1689 was in its essence the chaining up of fanaticism alike in politics and religion.' Burnet's conversion to the policy of resistance helps to render the Revolution of 1688 intelligible, for he was never prone to extreme courses.

Despite the delay imposed by storms and a contrary wind, William retained his usual tranquillity of spirit. At last the desired east wind blew the Dutch fleet down the Channel, but it swept them past the intended place of disembarkation, and it seemed that they would have to land in Plymouth. At this moment it turned south, and the whole fleet sailed happily into Torbay. On landing the Prince took Burnet heartily by the hand and asked if he did not now believe in predestination. 'I told him I would never forget that providence of God, which had appeared so signally on this occasion. He was cheerfuller than ordinary, yet he returned soon to his usual gravity.' When a dead calm had allowed the safe landing of the horses, a great storm from the west shattered the King's fleet as it was advancing down Channel to the attack. 'Now, by the immediate hand of Heaven, we were masters of the sea without a blow. I never found a disposition to superstition in my temper. I was rather inclined to be philosophical on all occasions. Yet I must confess that this strange ordering of the winds and seasons, just to change as our affairs required it, could not but make deep impressions on me as well as on all that observed it.' He had no lack of material when he preached a thanksgiving sermon a few days later in Exeter cathedral.

As the Prince marched towards London his distracted uncle sent Commissioners to discuss the situation with him at Hungerford. The cautious Halifax had declined to join in the invitation to William, but the Trimmer had no love for James and at this

moment he played a useful part. 'He took occasion to ask me,
so as nobody observed it, if we had a mind to have the King in
our hands. I said, by no means, for we would not hurt his person.
He asked next what if he had a mind to go away. I said nothing
was so much to be wished for.' The Prince approved both replies,
and the King fled in disguise from his capital, flinging the Great
Seal into the river. Burnet was instructed to take care of the
papists and to secure them from all violence. 'These orders I
executed with so much zeal and care that I saw all the complaints
that were brought me fully redressed. When we came to London,
I procured passports for all that desired to go beyond sea.'

In the agitated discussions about the new form of government
Burnet's knowledge of Mary's views enabled him to speak with
authority. He had promised never to reveal their historic conversation at The Hague except with her permission. In her
absence he consulted the Prince, who gave him a free hand, and
when Mary arrived she approved what he had done. Her gaiety
when she reached Whitehall struck observers as lacking in consideration for her father. 'I confess I was one of those that censured
this in my thoughts. I had never seen the least indecency in any
part of her deportment before; which made this appear so extraordinary that some days after I took the liberty to ask her how it
came that what she saw in so sad a revolution, as to her father's
person, made not a greater impression on her. She took the
freedom with her usual goodness. She assured me she felt the
sense of it very lively upon her thoughts. But she told me that
the letters which had been sent to her had obliged her to put on
a cheerfulness in which she might perhaps go too far, because she
was obeying directions and acting a part which was not very
natural to her.' The more he knew of this noble woman, the
more she won his affectionate regard. The members of the royal
family knew as well as the man in the street that James II was
impossible. In the last conversation between William and
Charles II the latter had foretold that, if his brother came to the
throne, he would not hold it four years.

Burnet's eminent services were rewarded by his appointment as
Royal Chaplain, Clerk of the Royal Closet, Chancellor of the
Garter, and Bishop of Salisbury. It was the first vacancy to be
filled, and his zeal in the discharge of his diocesan duties was
beyond praise. Hating bloodshed and turmoil as he did, the
peaceful revolution filled him with satisfaction, and on the first
Sunday in London he preached before William in St James's
Chapel on the text 'It is the Lord's doing.' Protestantism and
liberty, the twin causes nearest to his heart, had been saved from
imminent peril, for behind James II had stood Louis XIV, the
deadly enemy of both. Henceforth it was his dream to reconcile

the clergy to the new régime. That William was chilly and un-
sociable with his subjects was a drawback, and his wretched health
caused anxiety. He missed his hunting, and the lack of exercise
made him peevish. 'The gaiety and the diversions of the Court
disappeared. And though the Queen set herself to make up what
was wanting in the King by a great vivacity and cheerfulness, yet,
when it appeared that she meddled not in business, few found
their account in making their court to her; though she gave a
wonderful content to all that came near her, yet few came.' That
the King made Hampton Court his principal home and spent large
sums on its renovation increased the prevailing discontent.
Influential politicians renewed relations with James, High Church-
men sulked, and the Whigs seemed determined to clip his wings.
It is not surprising that he remarked acidly to Burnet that, while
a commonwealth and monarchy were both good, the worst form
of government was a King without treasure or power. Unable to
trust either party, he played with the idea of returning to Holland,
leaving the government in the hands of the Queen, whom the
Tories would probably support. Burnet learned of the project
from Shrewsbury, who had secured its abandonment. 'The Queen
knew nothing of it till she had it from me; so reserved was the
King to her even in a matter that concerned her so nearly.' The
Revolution was a happy event but was not the prelude to a happy
reign. Why, asked the King of Burnet, should they be so jealous
of him who came to save their religion and liberties? That it was
partly his own fault he never understood.

Burnet was never overawed by royalty, and soon after the
establishment of the new régime he went a little too far, though
doubtless in a good cause. 'I was set on by many to speak to him
to change his cold way,' he writes in his *Autobiography*; 'but he
cut me when I entered upon a freedom with him so that I could
not go through with it.' A man with a thinner skin would have
dropped the subject, but the Bishop wrote him 'a very plain letter
to let him see the turn the nation was making from him. This
offended him so that for some months I was not admitted to speak
to him.' Shortly afterwards Halifax told Burnet that he had
never heard the King say a kind word of him. This, however, was
only a passing phase, for at critical moments he turned to the man
whose fidelity was never in doubt.

On the day before he set out for the Irish campaign which was
to end with the victory of the Boyne, the King called Burnet into
his closet. 'He seemed to have a great weight upon his spirits
from the state of his affairs, which was then very cloudy. He said
for his own part he trusted in God, and would either go through
with his business or perish in it. He only pitied the poor Queen,
repeating it twice, and wished that those who loved him would

wait much on her and assist her. He lamented much the factions and the heats that were among us, and that the bishops and clergy, instead of allaying them, did rather foment and inflame them; but he was pleased to make an exception of myself. He said the going to a campaign was naturally no unpleasant thing to him; he was sure he understood that better than how to govern England. He added that, though he had no doubt nor mistrust of the cause he went on, yet the going against King James in person was hard upon him, since it would be a vast trouble to himself and to the Queen if he should be either killed or taken prisoner. He desired my prayers and dismissed me, very deeply affected by all he had said.' Never before had he shown Burnet his deepest feelings. Mary was new to the task of government, but, as the Bishop expected, she rose to the occasion. 'The Queen balanced all things with an extraordinary temper, and became universally beloved and admired by all about her.' While her husband was away he saw her once a week and declares that her behaviour was in all respects heroic. It was an anxious time, for the ruler never spared himself on the battlefield.

The death of Mary from smallpox in 1694 was the most poignant affliction of Burnet's public life, and once again the King poured out his heart. 'He called me into his closet and gave a free vent to a most tender passion. He burst into tears and cried out that there was no hope of the Queen, and that from being the happiest he was now going to be the miserablest creature on earth. He said during the whole course of their marriage he had never known one single fault in her. There was a worth in her that nobody knew besides himself, though he added that I might know as much of her as any other person did.' The sufferer was quite ready to go. 'She seemed to desire death rather than life, and she continued to the last minute in that calm and resigned state. She was almost perpetually in prayer. The day before she died, she received the sacrament, all the bishops who were attending her being admitted to receive it with her. We were, God knows, a sorrowful company, for we were losing her who was our chief hope and glory on earth.' Burnet was surprised by the uncontrollable grief of the King. 'His affliction for her death was as great as it was just; it was greater than those who knew him best thought his temper capable of. He went beyond all bounds in it: during her sickness he was in an agony that amazed us all, fainting often and breaking into most violent lamentations. When she died, his spirits sunk so low that there was great reason to apprehend that he was following her; for some weeks after he was so little master of himself that he was not capable of minding business or of seeing company. He turned much to the meditations of religion and to secret prayer. The Archbishop was often and long with him.

He entered upon solemn and serious resolutions of becoming in all things an exact and an exemplary Christian.' Shortly afterwards the Bishop paid final homage in *An Essay on the Memory of the late Queen*, which was widely read and translated into French and Dutch.

When Mary was gone Burnet rarely appeared at Court, and his summary of the sole reign of William III is almost devoid of interest. On one occasion he braved the wrath of the King, who had made large grants from the Irish forfeitures to his Dutch favourites and his former mistress Elizabeth Villiers. When William remonstrated, Burnet sturdily replied that he would risk his displeasure rather than please him in what he feared would be the ruin of his government. He was with him at the end, however, and the vivid description of the deathbed is followed by the finest of his portraits. After dwelling on his personal appearance and his feeble health he depicts him as above all a soldier. 'His behaviour was solemn and serious, seldom cheerful and but with a few; he spoke little and very slowly, and most commonly with a disgusting dryness which was his character at all times except in a day of battle, for then he was all fire though without passion; he was then everywhere and looked to everything.' Though he received little education he spoke Dutch, French, English, and German equally well, and understood Latin, Spanish, and Italian. 'He had a memory that amazed all about him, for it never failed him. He was an exact observer of men and things. His designs were always great and good, but it was thought he trusted too much to that, and that he did not descend enough to the humours of his people to make himself and his notions more acceptable to them. This, in a government that has so much of freedom in it as ours, was more necessary than he was inclined to believe. His reservedness grew on him so that it disgusted most of those who served him, but he had observed the errors of too much talking more than of too cold a silence. His genius lay chiefly in war. He knew all foreign affairs well, understood the state of every court in Europe very particularly. He instructed his own Ministers himself, but he did not apply enough to affairs at home. He loved the Dutch and was much beloved among them; but the ill returns he met from the English nation, their jealousies of him and their perverseness towards him, had too much soured his mind. Few men had the art of concealing and governing passion more than he had, yet few men had stronger passions.'

Burnet concludes his tribute on a more personal note. 'I had occasion to know him well, having observed him very carefully in a course of sixteen years. I had a large measure of his favour, and a free access to him all the while, though not at all times to the same degree. The freedom that I used with him was not always acceptable, but he saw that I served him faithfully, so, after some intervals of coldness, he always returned to a good measure of confidence in me. I was in many great instances much obliged by him, but that was not my chief bias to him. I considered him as a person raised up by God to resist the power of France and the progress of tyranny and persecution. The series of the five Princes of Orange that was now ended in him was the noblest succession of heroes that we find in any history. After all the abatements that may be allowed for his errors and his faults, he ought still to be reckoned among the greatest princes that our history or indeed any other can afford.' Two centuries later there is little to be added to this masterly analysis.

With the death of William III Burnet's political influence waned still further. He preached the first sermon before the new sovereign, and he was mainly responsible for her decision to augment poor livings by the surrender of revenues known as Queen Anne's Bounty. He gave valuable assistance in the passage of the Act of Union with Scotland through the House of Lords, but he only records two conversations with the Queen. The popularity of the notorious Dr Sacheverell revealed the growing strength of the extreme Tories and filled the Whigs with apprehension. 'During this winter (1710) I was encouraged by the Queen to speak more freely to her of her affairs than I had ever ventured to do formerly. I told her what reports were secretly spread of her through the nation, as if she favoured the design of bringing the Pretender to succeed to the crown, upon a bargain that she should hold it during her life. I said, if she was capable of making such a bargain for herself, by which her people were to be delivered up and sacrificed after her death, as it would darken all the glory of her reign, so it must set all her people to consider of the most proper ways of securing themselves, by bringing over the Protestant successors, in which, I told her plainly, I would concur if she did not take effectual means to extinguish these jealousies. Her ministers had served her with that fidelity and such success that her making a change among them would amaze the world.' The Queen heard him patiently, though almost in silence. 'Yet, by what she said, she seemed desirous to make me think she agreed to what I laid before her. But I learned afterwards it had no effect upon her. Yet I had great quiet in my own mind, since I had with an honest freedom made the best use I could to her.'

Marlborough and Godolphin were replaced by Harley and St John, and the Tories, supported by Anne, strove to end the long struggle with France. Burnet, who could never forget the atrocious persecution of the Huguenots, advocated a fight to a finish. 'Before the opening of the session pains were taken on

many persons to persuade them to agree to the measures the
Court were in.   The Duke of Marlborough, upon his coming over,
spoke very plainly to the Queen against the steps that were already
made.   But he found her so possessed that what he said made no
impression, so he desired to be excused from coming to council,
since he must oppose every step that was made in that affair.
Among others the Queen spoke to myself.   She said she hoped
the Bishops would not be against peace.   I said a good peace was
what we prayed daily for.   But the preliminaries offered by France
gave no great hopes of such an one, and the trusting to the King
of France's faith after all that had passed would seem a strange
thing.   She said we were not to regard the preliminaries; we should
have a peace upon such a bottom that we should not at all rely
on the King of France's word; but we ought to suspend our
opinions till she acquainted us with the whole matter.   I asked
leave to speak my mind plainly, which she granted.   I said any
treaty by which Spain and the West Indies were left to King
Philip must in a little while deliver up all Europe into the hands
of France, and if any such peace should be made, she was betrayed,
and we were all ruined; in less than three years' time she would be
murdered and the fires would be again raised in Smithfield.   I
pursued this long, till I saw she grew uneasy; so I withdrew.'
The good Bishop's emotions were too much for him, and such
extravagant language defeated his purpose.   'I long for peace,'
declared the Queen to a French diplomatist; 'I hate this dreadful
work of blood.'   Burnet lived just long enough to preach before
George I and to dedicate to him the Elizabethan volume of the
History of the Reformation, which completed a work begun forty
years before.   Protestantism and constitutional liberty in England
were safe, and the stout old warrior could die happy.

The celebrated Conclusion written in 1708 was defined by Burnet
as a sort of testament.   His intention throughout the work, he
explains, had been not so much to tell a fine tale and to amuse
his readers with a revelation of secrets and intrigues, but to make
the next age wiser by exposing the errors in government and the
follies of parties.   His thoughts, he begins, had always run most
and dwelt longest on the concerns of the Church and religion.   He
had always had a true zeal for the Church of England, had lived
in its communion with great joy, and had pursued its true interests
with an unfeigned affection.   There were, however, many things
which he wished to alter, particularly with a view to bringing back
dissenters.   It had been his lifelong conviction that Protestants
should stand together against their common foe.   'Popery is a
mass of impostures, supported by men who manage them with
great advantages, and impose them with inexpressible severities on
those who dare call anything in question that they dictate to them.'

Turning from the Church to the laity, the historian describes the body of the people as much the happiest and best of any nation he had seen. The gentry, on the other hand, were the most ignorant, and far less educated than the Scots. The universities, with their high Toryism, were largely to blame. Plutarch's *Lives* ought to be given to men of property at an early age. More care should be taken for the education of the nobility, particularly in the field of history. The commercial classes were the best element in the community. Political life, he complains, was poisoned by the feud between Whigs and Tories, each party attributing to the other extreme opinions held only by a small group. To heal this breach, which had rent the nation from top to bottom, he recommends frequent meetings of good men in both camps. Among urgently needed reforms are mentioned the codification of the law and the tightening up of poor relief. Writing with the authority of a man who had known five sovereigns he concludes his message with some plain words to rulers. 'There is not anything more certain and more evident than that princes are made for the people, and not the people for them. And perhaps there is no nation under heaven that is more entirely possessed with this notion of princes than the English in this age; so that they will soon be uneasy to a prince who does not govern himself by this maxim, and in time grow very unkind to him.' That is Burnet at his best, and that was the lesson of the Revolution of 1688, the supreme event in his busy life.

Bibliographical Note.—*The History of My Own Time*, published by his son in two massive folios in 1724 and 1734, is not the work which Burnet first planned. His *Original Memoirs*, which he called *The Secret History*, begun in 1683 at the age of forty, were far more autobiographical. The manuscript is lost, but substantial fragments covering 1660–64, 1679–96, and 1708–13 survive in a copy with corrections in his hand preserved in the Harleian Collection in the British Museum. They have been edited, with other material, by Miss Foxcroft in a volume entitled *Supplement to Burnet's History of My Own Time*. The work was seen by friends at the time, and it was used by Macaulay and Ranke. The publication of Clarendon's masterpiece in 1702 suggested the transformation of his reminiscences into a narrative of wider scope. The differences in the early part are great, in the middle considerable, in the later portions slight. He omitted unfulfilled prophecies, reflections falsified by events, censures calculated to wound the feelings of families or friends; there is less colour and less invective. Some changes, on the other hand, are due to more interested motives, such as the partial concealment of his early intimacy with Lauderdale, the toning down of his utterances on passive obedience, and the omission of attacks on Marlborough. *The Life of Gilbert Burnet*, by Clarke and Foxcroft, is one of the best biographies of the period. Firth's masterly Introduction is reprinted in his *Studies Historical and Literary*. The survey of Burnet's writings by Sir A. W. Ward in *The Cambridge History of English Literature*, vol. ix, ch. 7, reaches much the same conclusions. Macaulay's *History of England* should be studied in the light of Firth, *A Commentary on Macaulay's History of*

England. The best short survey of the time is by G. N. Clark, *The Later Stuarts.* Ogg, *England in the Reign of Charles II*; Trevelyan, *The Revolution of 1688–9* and *England under Queen Anne*; Keith Feiling, *History of the Tory Party*; Foxcroft, *Life of Halifax*; Mackenzie, *Life of Lauderdale*; Louise Fargo Brown, *The First Earl of Shaftesbury*, are useful. Ranke's *History of England, principally in the Seventeenth Century*, retains its value, particularly in the field of foreign affairs.

CHAPTER VII

Saint-Simon and Louis XIV

In the ranks of the recorders Saint-Simon occupies a place apart. Like Pepys among the diarists, it is not a case of *primus inter pares* but of unchallengeable superiority. His *Memoirs* are unique in their vast bulk, their Venetian colouring, their Tacitean pungency, their power to bring a dead world to life. To his contemporaries Pepys was known merely as a hard-working official at the Admiralty, and the Duc de Saint-Simon was almost lost among the throng of courtiers in the gilded galleries of Versailles during the closing decades of Le Roi Soleil; yet both of them have their place among the Immortals. Like Goethe, who occupied himself with *Faust* for sixty years, Saint-Simon began his masterpiece before he came of age, and finished it on the eve of his death at the age of eighty.

Only specialists are expected to read every page of a narrative cumbered with details of forgotten persons and events. The road from fountain to fountain, as Macaulay complained, lies through a very dry desert. Yet we must be careful how we skip; for at any moment we may stumble across some revealing portrait, some flashing phrase, such as the famous picture of Fénelon—'des yeux dont le feu et l'esprit sortaient comme un torrent,' or the description of the Duchesse de Berry, daughter of the Regent, as 'un modèle de tous les vices.' In the glittering pageant of French literature his achievement ranks with the comedies of Molière, the tragedies of Racine, and the essays of Montaigne. Readers who lack time or inclination for intensive study may select volume 1 (for the author's background) in de Boislisle's edition; volume 21 (for the dazzling picture of the Court when the news arrived that the Dauphin was dying and the courtiers surged forward to his son the Duc de Bourgogne); volumes 26–27 (for the full-length portrait of the Duke of Orleans, the man of the future, when the new Dauphin was struck down); volume 28 (a panoramic survey of the reign, character, and court of Louis XIV on the occasion of his death); volume 35 (describing in vivid detail the longed-for degradation of the bastards), and volumes 38–39 (reporting on the author's ceremonial mission to Madrid in 1721). If his prose lacks the majesty of Bossuet and the limpid charm of Mme de Sévigné, it grips the reader by its rapid flow, its sparkle, its unexpected turns. His eager personality is stamped on every page. One can say of him, writes Sainte-Beuve, in one of the best of his essays, what Buffon says of the earth in spring, 'Tout fourmille de vie.' His work is not a book but a world.

With Saint-Simon, as with Pepys and Greville, the world had to wait a long time for a complete edition. Soon after his death in 1755 the 173 folio volumes were taken from the family by Choiseul and placed in the Foreign Office on the ground that they contained secrets of state. A few privileged individuals were permitted to see them, and extracts were published during the next half-century; but the full significance of the work was only recognised when it appeared in twenty-one volumes in 1829–30 under the auspices of Général de Saint-Simon, great-nephew of the author, to whom the precious manuscript was restored by Louis XVIII. The complete text was published by Chéruel in 1856–58, with a masterly Introduction by Sainte-Beuve. At the end of the century the definitive edition in forty-one volumes, one of the glories of French scholarship, was begun by de Boislisle. Though the handwriting is well formed and the text is neat enough, the letters are small and not always easy to read, abbreviations are frequent, and the syntax sometimes suffers from excess of compression. The editorial notes, which claim as much space as the text, are not only indispensable to the study of a classic but a mine of information on French and in a lesser degree on European history in the seventeenth and eighteenth centuries.

The *Memoirs* in their final form are the work of an old man. Saint-Simon felt the urge to write in boyhood, and we possess a lively description of a Court funeral composed at the age of fifteen. He began to record his experiences during the ample leisure of a campaign in Germany in 1694, when he was nineteen. By 1700 he had kept a journal for six years, something fuller than a mere diary but far less detailed than the version we possess. For the next thirty years he accumulated an enormous mass of material which he carefully guarded from prying eyes. ' Je me suis toujours trouvé instruit journellement de toutes choses par les canaux purs, directs et certains.' Valuable information was gathered from the King's confessor, the chief doctor, and other sources, though he learned little about state affairs. When his political career ended with the death of the Regent in 1723 he left the Court, which he only revisited at long intervals. His *Memoirs* became his sole occupation, but a fortunate accident was needed to brace him to the effort of putting his testimony into final shape.

In 1729 a copy of Dangeau's *Journal*, briefly recording the events of each day at Court from 1684 to 1720, was lent him by his friend the Duc de Luynes, grandson of the diarist, and himself author of a similar compilation on the early years of Louis XV. Readers who dip into the seventeen volumes published during the Second Empire will agree with Saint-Simon's strictures on the dryness of the entries and the total absence of colour and atmosphere—'ce tableau extérieur de la Cour, un esprit au-dessous du médiocre, très futile, très incapable en tout genre, si plat, si fade, si grand admirateur de riens; une fadeur à faire vomir.' Here is a typical extract, dated Monday, September 11, 1684: 'Le roi alla tirer dans son parc; Mme la Dauphine se fit saigner et garda le lit tout le jour. Monseigneur prit médecine.' Comings and goings, events great and small, are noted without comment. It is a work to be consulted, not to be read, a discreet Court circular, simple, dreary, impersonal; yet it is unjust to ask more from the good old Marquis than he has to give. Saint-Simon himself mixes praise with blame. The diary, he admits, was filled with facts which did not get into the papers; Dangeau was 'honnête et très bon homme.' He never attacked anybody and he had no axe to grind. He excelled at the various card games which counted for so much in the boredom of Court life, making money at gaming tables without cheating, an honourable distinction at such a time. The soldier, courtier, minor poet, and Member of the Académie Française was a good deal more than 'le vieux valet de chambre imbécile' of Voltaire, who published an annotated volume of extracts. Mme de Maintenon described him as a man 'qui ne veut rien blâmer'; and Mme de Montespan remarked that nobody could help loving and laughing at him. Saint-Simon had a complete copy made for himself, to which in the course of ten years he added a vast number of annotations, some very brief, others expanding into elaborate memoranda. These precious additions are reproduced in full in every volume of de Boislisle's edition, in which they fill many hundred pages. Some of them, in particular the panoramic survey of the reign, were composed with so much care that they were incorporated with little alteration in the final text. They are indeed of superior evidential value, since the interval between the events described and the composition of the notes is less by a decade or even more. When this task was completed, the author turned in 1739 to the composition of the work as we have it to-day. He laid down his busy pen in 1751 at the age of seventy-six.

In the Considérations Préliminaires, written in 1743 and prefixed to the first volume, Saint-Simon describes the aims and methods of his work. 'Ecrire l'histoire de son pays et de son temps, c'est repasser dans son esprit avec beaucoup de réflexion tout ce qu'on a vu. . . . Son ouvrage doit mûrir sous la clef et les plus sures serrures, passer ainsi à ses héritiers, qui feront sagement de laisser couler plus d'une génération ou deux, et de ne laisser paraître l'ouvrage que lorsque le temps l'aura mis à l'abri des ressentiments. La vérité la plus pure et la plus exacte sera mon guide unique et ma maîtresse.' That he believed himself a truthful historian is beyond doubt, for he was a man of high principles and unblemished character; yet it is impossible to accept him at his own valuation. One need not be an expert to discover that he is a passionate partisan, stuffed with prejudices, narrow in his outlook, implacable

in his hatreds, a voluble witness, not a judge on the bench.   The
first scholar to approach the problem of his veracity was Lémontey,
who was charged by Napoleon in 1808 to write the history of the
eighteenth century with the aid of the archives of the Foreign
Office.   The author of *Histoire de la Régence* pointed out that the
Memoirs were the work of an embittered old man with a limited
knowledge of state affairs, writing long after most of the scenes
he described.   Not till the appearance of the fifth volume of
Ranke's *Französische Geschichte* and of Chéruel's massive volume
Saint-Simon considéré comme historien de Louis XIV was the
historical value determined by masters of the craft.   Readers,
remarks the latter, are at first charmed and impressed; but when
we compare his picture of persons and events with other contemporary authorities we realise how his passions and prejudices
obscured his vision.   He allowed his inflamed imagination to run
riot, and some of his most finished portraits, such as Mme de
Maintenon, Louvois, Villars, Vendôme, and the Duc du Maine, are
mere caricatures.

Saint-Simon was in a special sense his father's son, for his
heritage of convictions coloured his *Memoirs* and governed his life.
The first Duke, who began as a royal page, owed the creation of
the family fortunes to the favour of Louis XIII.   The King was
devoted to the chase, and the young *écuyer* earned his gratitude by
ingeniously arranging that he could change his steed without
dismounting.   The author of the *Memoirs* boasts that his family
was descended from Charlemagne, but what he regarded as indubit-
able is dismissed by everyone else as a myth.   The Saint-Simons
were members of the lesser nobility, of whom no one had heard
much till Louis XIII made his favourite Duc et Pair, heaping gifts,
offices, and honours on his head.   The paternal gratitude was
inherited in full measure by his son.   A portrait of their patron
hung in every room in their old château near Chartres, and they
dutifully attended every year at the memorial service at Saint-
Denis.   The author of the *Memoirs* was present on fifty-two anni-
versaries, though, as he tells us, he was the only mourner.   He
always wore a ring with a portrait of Louis XIII mounted in
diamonds.   Despite the learned labours of Batiffol, Louis XIII
remains a shadowy figure, sandwiched in between his full-blooded
father and his majestic son; but to the Saint-Simons he remained
'le roi mon maître,' the model ruler, Louis le Juste, with a far
better claim to the title of le Grand than his overpraised successor.

The only child of a second marriage, born in 1675 when Claude,
the first Duke, was sixty-eight, the lad looked up to his father with
veneration and hung on his lips.   'Je suis né pour la lecture et
pour l'histoire,' he writes.   He adopted not only his father's
devotion to the half-forgotten monarch, but his fanatical hatred

of Mazarin, the low-born, greedy foreigner, and his systematic depreciation of Louis XIV. The old Duke, who had been a star performer in the earlier reign, quickly receded into the background and never forgave Louis XIV for making so little use of his services. The King and Queen attended the christening of the child, and in 1691, at the age of sixteen, he was presented at Versailles on entering the corps of Mousquetaires. The King embraced the old Duke, observing that the boy was very young. 'He will serve Your Majesty all the longer,' was the adroit reply. When Claude died two years later the King again showed much kindness. 'Continuez d'être sage et à bien faire,' he remarked in promising to take care of the young man.

No one was less of a soldier than the fastidious Saint-Simon. He was present at various sieges and at the battle of Neerwinden, but he was bored by the life. After a year in the Mousquetaires he entered the cavalry; but when he was passed over in a list of promotions he seized the opportunity of leaving the army on the plea of ill-health. The King was annoyed and showed his displeasure. 'Il ne me parla plus; ses regards ne tombaient sur moi que par hasard.' After the summer campaigns Saint-Simon, like other young officers, used to spend part of the winter at Court, but in 1702 he became a resident in the palace which was to be his real home for the next twenty-one years. He had recently married the daughter of Marshal Lorges and had three children. At first he lived as a guest of the brother of his adored wife, but in 1710, on her appointment as *dame d'honneur* to the Duchesse de Berry, the couple received a suite of their own. He paid brief visits to his château, and at Easter he made a retreat at La Trappe, where he inherited his father's friendship for the famous Abbé de Rancé. The King, who liked his courtiers to be always at hand even though they had no duties to perform, invariably noticed his absence and asked the reason. Saint-Simon was by temperament as little of a courtier as soldier. He was never overawed by the ruler whom most of the inhabitants of Versailles regarded as a demigod, for he rated the nobility to which he belonged above the office or the person of the King.

Though one-third of the work is devoted to the Regency, the most brilliant and familiar portion is that which portrays the last two decades of Louis XIV. The principal actor dominates the stage, and on his death the narrative is interrupted for a panoramic survey of the reign. One need not be an unreserved admirer of the Grand Monarque to feel that less than justice is done to the greatest reign in the history of France, above all to the glories of the earlier half. Dangeau is charged with servility and with admiring whatever the King did. Saint-Simon, on the other hand, found far less to praise than to blame. One cannot deny him

Scarron, we are asked to believe, made her sordid living by *liaisons* in the interval between the death of her husband and her selection by Mme de Montespan to look after her eldest bastard. That she loved the child, supported his fortunes, and thereby insulted the *noblesse* to which Saint-Simon belonged, is treated as a criminal offence. She is credited with plenty of brains, but they were used in the service of her selfish ambitions. She is accused of deliberately supplanting the Montespan, whose fall in reality was due to her own bad temper. The Maintenon was out for power and she got it, for she ruled the Kingdom through the King, cleverly coaching the ministers to push her projects. 'Tout sans exception en sa main, et le Roi et l'État ses victimes.' Thus she was mainly responsible for the miseries of his closing years. In one direction alone were her efforts without success. Her enemy professes to be in doubt whether she was in fact mistress or wife. He asserts that she strove to become a Queen, and that only the advice of Louvois, Bossuet, and Fénelon prevented the King from yielding to her demands.

Though living for many years under the same roof, Saint-Simon has produced an unrecognisable caricature of Mme de Maintenon. The key to her character is to be found in her voluminous correspondence, where she presents herself as a woman disliking pomp and ceremony, completely satisfied with her position, lacking the slightest desire to be mixed up in politics. 'Je ne sais point les affaires.' How far she influenced the King and how far she merely encouraged him in his decisions, such as the disastrous revocation of the Edict of Nantes, cannot be precisely determined. That she was hardly 'the most influential woman in French history,' to adopt the title of a famous study by Döllinger, is as clear as that she was happiest with her 'little girls' at Saint-Cyr. Saint-Simon's unscrupulous schemer was a woman of unblemished character, tact, and refinement, who by reforming the King's life rendered conspicuous service to the state. Dangeau rarely pronounces judgment, but in recording her death he for once lets himself go. 'Une femme de si grand mérite, qui avait tant fait de bien et tant empêché de mal pendant sa faveur qu'on n'en saurait rien dire de trop.' This tribute produces an explosion from Saint-Simon: 'Voilà bien froidement, salement et puamment mentir à pleine gorge.' Of the two witnesses Dangeau was in a far better position to judge. She was too cool and reserved to be very lovable, but the mud hurled by Saint-Simon and Liselotte at 'the old slut,' 'Mme Ordure,' does not stick.

As the King advanced in years the thoughts of the courtiers, who had little else to do, turned increasingly to the future. Monseigneur, his only legitimate child, lived close by at Meudon, rigidly excluded from political influence, caring for nothing but hunting and the pleasures of the table—'grand mangeur comme toute la maison royale. Un tissu de petitesses arrangeés qui formaient tout le tissu de sa vie, sans vice ni vertu.' In the vast portrait gallery there is no one so mindless, so colourless, so impersonal as this unworthy pupil of Bossuet, trembling before his formidable father and jealous of his gifted son. Though he was too mediocre to hate, Saint-Simon dreaded his accession, for he was surrounded by his enemies. The description of his death in 1711 is a masterpiece. The writer was paying a brief visit to his château when a courier from his wife brought the joyful news that the Dauphin was down with smallpox. If he were to die, his son, the Duc de Bourgogne, the gifted pupil of Fénelon, 'tout simple, tout saint, tout plein de ses devoirs,' would become heir to the throne. The prospect of sudden and unexpected deliverance from the nightmare of an unfriendly régime set up a tumult of emotions. Next day his wife's courier reported an improvement, and on the third, when he hurried back to Versailles, he learned that the patient was out of danger. The respite was brief, for the case was hopeless. Couriers from Meudon now arrived every quarter of an hour. The Duc de Bourgogne and his charming wife, the Rose of Savoy, held open court and were equally gracious to all comers. In Saint-Simon's glowing phrase it was like the coming of the dawn. Not only was the whole Court there, but 'tout Paris' and 'tout Meudon' flocked to worship the rising sun. During this drama of expectancy, which lasted five days, Liselotte visited Saint-Simon for a two hours' talk. 'We let ourselves go, not without some scruples, my wife endeavouring to moderate the tone of this strange talk.'

At last the decisive news of approaching death reached the palace late at night, when Mme de Saint-Simon was going to bed. Her husband rushed out and found 'tout Versailles' assembled or assembling, the women emerging from their beds or bedrooms just as they were. Only eyes were needed to distinguish the conflicting interests reflected in the faces. 'La joie perçoit à travers les reflexions momentanées de religion et d'humanité par lesquelles j'essayois de me rappeler. Ma délivrance particulière me semblait si grande et si inespérée qu'il me semblait que l'Etat gagnait tout en une telle perte. Parmi les pensées je sentois malgré moi un reste de crainte que le malade en rechappât et j'en avois une extrême honte.' Making his way to the apartments of the Duke of Orleans he was amazed to find him in tears. 'No wonder you are surprised—I am surprised at myself. But the spectacle touches me. He is a good man who treated me well when he was allowed.' The Duc de Bourgogne cried quietly, while the Duc de Berry, his younger brother, sobbed aloud.

For a brief space there was a breath of spring in the stuffy galleries of Versailles and an abounding hope in the heart of the little Duke. Here at last was the ruler of his dreams—a young man of high character, marked intelligence, and lofty ideals, ready to listen to the counsels which in talks behind locked doors he poured into his ear and set forth in memoranda designed to remove the abuses of the long reign. Saint-Simon noticed that for the first time the courtiers began to cultivate him. Alas, these brightly tinted dreams were doomed to disappointment. Less than a year after his father's death the Duc de Bourgogne, his wife, and eldest son died within ten days. As usual, when prominent people were suddenly struck down, there was talk of poison. Saint-Simon could love as well as hate, and this was the most poignant sorrow of his life. An unusual note of tenderness is heard. The Dauphin, he declares, was born for the happiness of France and of all Europe. 'C'était un bien dont nous n'étions pas dignes.' 'I wished to withdraw from the Court and the world, and it took all the wisdom and influence of my wife to prevent it. The truth is that I was in despair.' 'Vous venez d'enterrer la fortune de la France,' he wrote to his friend, the Duc de Beauvilliers, Governor to the late prince. The Duke of Orleans, now marked out as Regent for the little boy who was to become Louis XV, shared some of his views, but he never inspired the devotion and confidence which our author reposed in the young prince so cruelly snatched away.

The three remaining years of the reign were a gloomy time. The routine of Court life, the dancing, the gambling, the music, continued, but the sparkle had gone. The weary old ruler, like Francis Joseph two centuries later, went on with his work, but the joy was past. The Rose of Savoy, the flower of the Court, the only member of the royal family who gained his affection, was dead. Mme de Maintenon was nearing eighty. The victories of Villars, a *bête noire* of Saint-Simon, had revived for a moment the glory of French arms. The grandson of the monarch who said '*Il n'y a plus de Pyrénées*' retained the Spanish throne despite the triumphs of Marlborough and Prince Eugène. Yet the country was poor and depressed, exhausted by continual wars, and the old ruler knew that he was not beloved. He felt it was time to go, and in 1715 he passed away at the age of seventy-seven. The sun had set in a bank of dark clouds. Few shed tears, and Saint-Simon was not among them. His lifelong friend the Duke of Orleans stepped forward as Regent, and at the age of forty the author of the *Memoirs* began his brief political career.

CHAPTER VIII

SAINT-SIMON AND THE REGENCY

SAINT-SIMON was neither a statesman nor a political thinker, but he had ideas of his own on the governance of France. Mme de Maintenon described him as 'glorieux frondeur, et plein de vues.' The King was to remain the symbol of national unity and continuity, the ceremonial head of the state, the dispenser of patronage, but he was not to be omnipotent. One of the objections to the doctrine of Absolute Monarchy was that the ruler was rarely his own master. Louis XIV, for instance, was dominated by 'the old Sultana' and by his chief ministers, who are angrily denounced as *les cinq rois de France*. What made the system particularly odious to the vain little Duke was that these men, like Colbert, were often mere bourgeois. It had begun with the detestable Mazarin, and Le Grand Monarque was only too willing to accept the services of clever upstarts. The mind of Saint-Simon was continually occupied with the problem of administrative machinery, and towards the end of the long reign he was ready with a plan. The King, he felt, had too much power. While some reformers dreamed of a revival of the States-General, which had not met since 1614, he argued for government by departmental councils presided over by the dukes and peers. The country was to be run by the aristocracy. Such a far-reaching change had no chance unless it was approved by the *de jure* or *de facto* ruler of France. The Duc de Bourgogne was coached and converted, and he would have been the man to carry it out. When he was gone the would-be reformer fell back on his old friend the Duke of Orleans, the predestined Regent during the minority of Louis XV.

There is nothing more curious in the career of *le petit dévot sans génie*, as d'Argenson called him, than his lifelong friendship with the most dissolute figure of the time. Louis XIV, who was not squeamish, described his nephew as *un fanfaron de crimes*, and no portrait in the gallery is painted with such care. It is indeed his masterpiece. He only watched Louis XIV from afar, as we study the ways of an actor on the stage, but he knew Orleans as a friend. The later volumes of the first part of the *Memoirs* are increasingly concerned with the complex individual whom the writer regarded in some measure as a pupil. He had stood by him when the courtiers cut him, and when he was insulted by the mob at the funeral of the Duc de Bourgogne in the belief that he had poisoned the Dauphin. The Regent would not have the same authority as the King, but there might perhaps be time, if the plans were ready and due energy were displayed, for the new system to take root.

Orleans, we are told, was well aware what was wrong with the state. The friends talked a thousand times of the evils of government—the necessity to break with the system of Mazarin, 'a foreigner from the dregs of the people,' and to substitute the *noblesse* for the bourgeois (*gens de rien*) and the lawyers (*gens de robe*) who had climbed up the steps. Saint-Simon was furious that the Presidents of the Parlement did not uncover when they addressed the dukes and peers, as they did to the princes of the blood. The reader becomes heartily sick of hearing about 'l'usurpation énorme du bonnet'—the weighty question whether the President of the Parlement in addressing the peers should keep his cap on his head or put it on the table. Unfortunately the nobles had been kept so long in the background that many had become ignorant and frivolous, their vitality sapped.

'What post would you like?' asked the Duke. 'That is for you to decide,' replied Saint-Simon. When, however, the Ministry of Finance was offered him, he wisely declined on the ground of his complete ignorance of the subject. He proved unable to manage his own affairs, and his later years were clouded by financial anxieties. He also declined the post of governor of the boy King. Finally he accepted a place in the prospective Council of Regency consisting of fifteen members. His plan included the summons of the States-General after the death of Louis XIV, not in order to share in the burden of rule, but as a lightning conductor for the unpopularity of drastic financial reforms.

Everything, it was clear, would depend on the wisdom and steadfastness of the Regent, whose failings filled his friends as well as his enemies with apprehension. Though sociable enough, he was a lonely man. 'I was the only person with whom he could have heart-to-heart talks. He was gifted by nature, and his first instincts were usually right. He never gave himself airs. He had the weakness of believing himself to resemble Henri IV in everything. Like Henri IV he was naturally good, human, compassionate.' He wished no harm to anyone. He loved liberty, for others as well as for himself. In England, he used to say, there were no *lettres de cachet*. He had no ambition either to reign or to rule. No one was more expressly formed to secure the happiness of France. Unfortunately, he was badly educated. He had been ruined by his evil genius, the Abbé Dubois, whom his father in an unlucky hour had chosen as his tutor. Next to Mme de Maintenon no leading character is painted in such forbidding colours as this corrupter of youth. 'Tous les vices combattaient en lui à qui en demeurerait le maître.' Avarice, debauchery, and servility were his gods, perfidy, flattery, and servility his means. He excelled in low intrigues. 'Une fumée de fausseté sortait de tous ses pores.' His influence was the more fatal since his pupil was a weak nature, temperamentally drawn rather to art than to politics. He loved painting, was a minor composer, and, like Charles II, was interested in science. 'Il était né ennuyé,' seeking distraction from a loveless marriage and political impotence in shameless debauchery. The old King, knowing the difference of their outlook, kept him at arm's-length, and chose a Council of Regency in which he was only to be the nominal president, and power would be in the hands of the Duc du Maine. When his chance came at the age of forty he was too old to change. The later volumes of the *Memoirs* are the record of a disappointment which was not altogether a surprise.

The pages on the illness and death of Louis XIV are written in an unusually gentle vein, for the weary old man preserved his dignity to the last. The reader misses his imposing figure, and the second part is as inferior in interest to the first as the continuation of *Don Quixote* or *Paradise Regained*. For Saint-Simon, on the other hand, the next eight years were the most memorable of his life. The will of the late King was annulled, and Orleans, with the approval of the Parlement of Paris, was declared Regent with full powers. That the observer was a failure on the political stage, lacking a sense of proportion and intransigent about trifles, was better known to his friend than to himself. The two men remained on terms of intimacy, but his advice was rarely accepted and his appeals to the Regent to reform his life fell on deaf ears. Mme de Maintenon, he suggested, should retain all the pecuniary advantages secured to her by Louis XIV. 'There was nothing more to fear from this almost octogenarian fairy. Her powerful and pernicious wand had been broken; elle était devenue la vieille Scarron.' The suggestion that the gigantic deficit left by the war of the Spanish Succession should be met by a declaration of national bankruptcy was rejected without ceremony. The advice to summon the States-General every five years in order to make humble suggestions can hardly be described as a sign of constructive statesmanship, for his belief that they would feed out of the Regent's hand was unlikely to be realised. He had condemned the revocation of the Edict of Nantes; but when the tolerant Orleans proposed to allow the return of the Huguenots he opposed the plan on the ground that it would cause controversy and confusion. In money matters he was one of the most disinterested of men, and he refused to join in Law's bubble schemes.

In the field of foreign affairs Saint-Simon's arguments for a permanent alliance with Spain, on the ground that Austria and England were the enemies, was rejected in favour of partnership with England, the darling project of Dubois. That the old tutor and later the secretary of Orleans emerged as First Minister, Archbishop of Cambrai, and finally Cardinal was the greatest grievance of all. The Abbé was a greedy adventurer, but Saint-Simon presents us with a moral monster, and it was always an embarrassment when they met at the Palais Royal. The councils only lasted for three years, after which the more convenient system of individual ministers was restored. The influence of the Council of Regency was slight, for the chief decisions were taken elsewhere and a good deal of its time was spent on trifles. On one occasion Saint-Simon raised the hoary issue of the prerogatives of the dukes, but his prejudiced account of the discussion is contradicted by the testimony of other eye-witnesses. Here is another reminder that the *Memoirs*, however circumstantial, are the work of a man writing twenty or thirty years after the event and must be carefully checked.

In one quarter of the heavens alone was there a patch of blue sky. If the principal sorrow of Saint-Simon's life was the death of the Duc de Bourgogne, his keenest delight was the solemn degradation of the bastards in 1718. The story of the planning and execution of this *coup* fills a volume. When death wrought sudden havoc in the royal family the stock of the Duc du Maine rose rapidly, and when in 1714 the bastards were placed in the line of succession Saint-Simon felt that the cup of degradation was full. Orleans, like the other princes of the blood, was horrified, but none of them was filled with the fanatical resentment which burned in the neurotically sensitive bosom of the little Duke. The conflict between the *légitimes* and the *légitimés* was a veritable obsession, and when the Regent annulled the will of Louis XIV and took the helm with full powers it seemed to him that the time for action had come. It is characteristic of the irascible little man that he should have been *plus royaliste que le roi*, and that he should complain of the lack of zeal in the Palais Royal for the good cause. Orleans described his friend as 'l'homme qui aime le mieux les légitimes et qui hait le plus cordialement les bâtards.' And here is the author's description of himself. 'Ma passion la plus vive et la plus chère est celle de ma dignité et de mon rang; ma fortune ne va que bien loin après, et je la sacrifierois avec transport de joie pour quelque rétablissement de ma dignité.' We must remember that the Duchess of Orleans was the sister of the Duc du Maine, and that her husband had no desire to hurt her feelings. Dissolute though he was, he was neither hard nor ungenerous.

Saint-Simon could hardly be expected to do justice to the Duc du Maine, whom he describes as a rattlesnake and denounced to his face; but the chief bastard was not without ambition, and there were men who desired to use him for their own purposes. Some of them wished to substitute Philip V of Spain, the grandson of Louis XIV, for the Duke of Orleans as Regent, and the so-called Cellamare conspiracy (named after the Spanish Ambassador) was staged by Alberoni, the able and ambitious director of Spanish policy. The Duc du Maine, ever the rival of Orleans, and his clever wife, a Condé, were involved, and on its discovery the Regent at last determined to destroy his influence in the state.

The supreme moment came on August 26, 1718, when the Duc du Maine was solemnly deprived of his leading position in the life of the state. For once Saint-Simon was a maker as well as a recorder of history, for without this gadfly it is doubtful if the lethargic Regent would have taken the plunge. 'I was the oldest and most attached, the most outspoken of his servants, and he had entire confidence in me; but he was on guard against what he called my vivacity, my love for my dignity which was so challenged by the usurpations of the bastards and the enterprises of the Parlement.' After three years of the Regency he had almost lost hope and had ceased to press his point. When, however, Orleans complained of the Parlement of Paris (a legal, not a legislative body) he returned to the charge. The Regent, he argued, was losing all his authority, and it was time to assert himself. His decisions should be announced at a meeting of the Council of Regency, which would be immediately followed by a *Lit de Justice* at the Tuileries in the presence of the young King. An elaborate undated report, filling seventy large folio pages in Saint-Simon's hand, preserved in the Foreign Office, was incorporated in the *Memoirs* with only trifling changes. Every detail of the programme was worked out by three men—the Regent, Saint-Simon, and the Duc de Bourbon of the House of Condé. 'I am at the crisis of my Regency,' remarked Orleans, 'and I am resolved to strike a big blow at the Parlement.' In one respect he went further than his adviser, for he had decided to transfer the education of the young King from the Duc du Maine to the Duc de Bourbon.

Before the meeting the Regent assured his anxious friend that he would not flinch. The two ducal bastards, Maine and Toulouse, were present as members of the Council of Regency, but they walked out. While the documents were being read our chronicler scrutinised the faces with his trained eye. 'The Regent had an air of authority that was new to me.' For once he played his part to the entire satisfaction of his friend. The secret had been well kept, and the members of the Council had the surprise of their lives when a serene and determined voice announced that, in justice to the peers, *les légitimés* were deprived of the privileges accorded to them by the will of their father. The account would do credit to a twentieth-century Special Correspondent in a *cause célèbre*. 'Immobile, collé sur mon siège, pénétré de tout ce que la joie peut imprimer de plus sensible et de plus vif, du trouble le plus charmant, d'une jouissance la plus démesurément et la plus persévéramment souhaitée, je suois d'angoisse de la captivité de mon transport, et cette angoisse même était d'une volupté que je n'ai jamais ressentie ni devant ni depuis ce beau jour. Que les plaisirs des sens sont inférieurs à ceux de l'esprit!' Toulouse was excepted as Saint-Simon had proposed, since he stood aloof from his brother's political ambitions. The education of the King was taken from Maine and given to the Duc de Bourbon. Saint-Simon spoke briefly when each member of the Council was asked for his opinion. There was no overt opposition, but the faces of Villars, Villeroi and other survivors of the old régime told their own tale.

The second act of the drama began when the Parlement assembled, and the young King was fetched. Everyone stared at Saint-Simon, for his attitude and influence were well known. 'Je me mourois de joie; j'en étois à craindre la défaillance; mon cœur, dilaté à l'excès, ne trouvoit plus d'espace à s'étendre. La violence que je me faisois pour ne rien laisser échapper étoit infinie, et néanmoins ce tourment était délicieux. . . . Je triomphois, je me vengeois, je nageois dans ma vengeance; je jouissais du plein accomplissement des désirs les plus véhéments et les plus continus de toute ma vie.' He concentrated his fury on the First President. 'Je l'accablai à cent reprises de mes regards assénes et prolongés avec persévérance. L'insulte, le mêpris, le dédain, le triomphe, lui furent lancés de mes yeux jusqu'en ses moelles. Souvent il baissoit la vue quand il attrapoit mes regards; une fois ou deux il fixa le sien sur moi, et je me plus à l'outrager par les sourires dérobés, mais noirs, qui achevèrent de le confondre. Je me baignois dans sa rage et je me délectois à le lui faire sentir.'

When the ceremony was over Saint-Simon congratulated the principal performer on his firmness and dignity and went home for a meal. Before he sat down an urgent message arrived which turned his joy to anguish. Since the Regent felt he could not write to his wife, would his friend go to Saint-Cloud, where the Duchess lived, and break the news of her brother's fate? Quickly swallowing a little food, he hurried to the Palais Royal. 'I am the last person for the task,' he protested, 'for my hostility to the bastards is notorious.' 'No,' was the reply, 'she likes you and admires your frankness.' It was impossible to decline, and there was just a chance that she would refuse to see him. She had no love for her brothers, particularly the elder, but she was sensitive about her position, and her prestige in some measure depended on theirs. A vivid account follows of a painful interview. The neglected wife wept bitterly, but took it better than was expected and drove to Paris to see her husband. Our fiery author was not a tactful person, but on this occasion he seems to have discharged his distasteful mission with good feeling and success. Very different was the reception of the news by Liselotte, the mother of the Regent, who also lived at Saint-Cloud and who rejoiced at the downfall of the bastards.

Saint-Simon watched with angry disgust the ever-growing ascendancy of Dubois. The weakness of the Regent was the misfortune of France. He had been taken in by the financial humbug of Law and he could never shake off the influence of his old tutor. When the latter began scheming for a cardinal's hat Saint-Simon renewed his protests and appeals. 'This lively and all too veracious summary of the conduct of the Abbé Dubois impressed him as I never saw him impressed before. He put his elbows on the table, took his head in his hands and remained silent for some time, his nose almost touching the table, as was his habit when he was greatly upset. Then he jumped up, took a few turns and said, as if speaking to himself: Il faut chasser ce coquin. Mieux tard que jamais, replied his visitor, mais vous n'en ferez rien.' As the friends silently paced up and down the room, Saint-Simon read in his face the painful conflict between his reason and the mastery which he had allowed Dubois to establish over his will. 'Il faut l'ôter,' he repeated two or three times. The visitor withdrew, conscious of having done his duty but without much hope of success. His apprehensions were well founded, for the plausible minister quickly talked his master over. Three weeks later Saint-Simon found Orleans so chilly and embarrassed that he asked the reason. The Regent confessed that he was indeed greatly displeased and then let himself go. 'You want me to do whatever you wish, and you decline whatever you do not like.' The visitor recalled the offers and once again explained his reasons for declining them. Orleans admitted that it was all true and that it was Dubois who had poisoned his mind. 'If he can turn you against an old friend like myself,' rejoined Saint-Simon, 'nobody is safe if he wants to ruin him.' The penitent prince promised to tell Dubois not to discuss Saint-Simon again. The incident was closed, but the Regent became less open with him than of old, and the clever *arriviste* obtained his cardinal's hat.

Before the curtain fell on Saint-Simon's political career he was entrusted with a task which exactly suited his inclinations. After the so-called Cellamare conspiracy Dubois, in alliance with the Emperor, England, and Holland, declared war against Spain. The restoration of peace in 1720 was followed by a rapprochement. Having always advocated the closest co-operation with Spain, Saint-Simon welcomed the matrimonial arrangement by which the young King of France was to marry a Spanish Infanta, and the heir to the Spanish throne a daughter of the Regent. When the negotiations were completed it was decided to send a mission to Madrid for ceremonial purposes, and the leading French expert on Court etiquette was selected as its chief. It was the last ray of sunshine in his public career. An additional attraction was the prospect of securing honours for his two sons, whom he took in his large train. Spain, moreover, was the classic land of the grandees, so universally respected and so proudly conscious of their rights— such a contrast to 'ces insectes de cour, ces champignons de fortune, ces excrements de la nature humaine' at Versailles. The mission, lasting six months, is described in vivid detail in volumes 38 and 39 of the *Memoirs*, which are as indispensable for the Spain of Philip V as for the study of the author's character.

The secret had been well kept. One day in June 1721 Saint-Simon was greeted at the Palais Royal with the words: 'I must tell you something which I desired more than anything in the world, and which will delight you just as much; but you must keep it to yourself. If M. de Cambray' (Dubois), added the Regent with a laugh, 'knew I had told you, he would never forgive me.' Then he told me of his reconciliation with the King and Queen of Spain, the marriage of the King to the Infanta when she was of an age to marry, and of the Prince of Asturias to Mlle de Chartres. My astonishment was even greater than my joy. The Duke of Orleans embraced me. I asked how it was managed, particularly the marriage of his daughter. He replied that the Abbé Dubois was a magician when he was set on anything. Since Louis XV was only eleven and the Infanta only three, and since Europe dreaded the union of the crowns, Saint-Simon urged that the betrothal should remain a secret. The Regent agreed, but added that the King and Queen of Spain were most anxious for their daughter to be brought up in France. In that case, rejoined Saint-Simon, an embassy must be sent to Madrid to sign the contract. 'Un seigneur de marque et titre' was required, and he offered himself for the task. Perhaps, too, Orleans would ask Philip V to make his son a Grandee of Spain. Saint-Simon cared far more for titles than for money, and the mission, though it cost the state a large sum, left him a poorer man. To the Regent's delight he felt it his duty to visit Dubois, and an outward reconciliation was staged. The gulf, however, was too wide to bridge, and the Cardinal, while hiding his disapproval from the Regent and smothering the prospective envoy with attentions, determined to do him all the harm he could. This verdict on 'the venomous serpent,' pronounced long afterwards, is contradicted, so far as words go, by the contemporary correspondence of the envoy with the First Minister, thanking him for his frankness, friendship, and cordiality since their reconciliation. When the boy King was informed of his matrimonial destiny in the Council of Regency and asked for his concurrence, his eyes filled with tears, and he murmured *Oui* in an almost inaudible voice.

Saint-Simon was in his element at Madrid, comparing the

etiquette of the Court with that of Versailles, and studying the genealogies of the noble families of Spain. He was warmly welcomed, for the Spanish sovereigns rejoiced that their infant daughter was to become Queen of France. Catching smallpox he used the six weeks of his illness for a *Tableau de la Cour d'Espagne en 1722*, which he finished in the years after his return. The more important parts are printed as an appendix to volumes 39 and 40, and sections are reproduced in the *Memoirs*. The most interesting pages are those describing the King and Queen. The former was shy, colourless, silent, cold, suspicious, loving the chase and inclined to war. Though very ill-favoured by nature he was childishly vain, and one day after an audience he asked Saint-Simon if he did not think him very handsome, the handsomest man he had ever seen. His religion was merely habit, scruples, little observances, above all 'une grand peur du diable.' His most attractive quality was his love of France. The Queen, Elizabeth Farnese, 'the Termagant of Spain,' with the ravages of smallpox on her face, possessed the personality and the will-power that her husband lacked. She never allowed him out of her sight, attended all audiences, and saw all the dispatches. 'Ce tête à tête éternel que jour et nuit elle avait avec lui lui donnait tout lieu de le connoître et, pour ainsi dire, de le savoir par cœur.'

The envoy was liberally rewarded with compliments and honours for himself and his sons, undistinguished young men. 'Monsieur,' said the King, 'je suis si content de vous en toutes manières, et de celle en particulier dont vous vous êtes acquitté de votre ambassade auprès de moi, que je veux vous donner des marques de ma satisfaction, de mon estime et de mon amitié. Je vous fais grand d'Espagne de la première classe, et en même temps celui de vos deux fils que vous voudrez choisir pour être grand d'Espagne, et je fais votre fils aîné chevalier de la Toison d'or.' Saint-Simon was a happy man. He could not foresee that the Regent had but a short time to live and that Louis XV would marry not a Spanish but a Polish princess.

The envoy returned to find Dubois more than ever in control. 'His power over the mind of his master was without limits, and he took care that everyone should know it. But that did not make things go better. Everything stagnated, both abroad and at home. He gave little time or thought to affairs, and then only in order to keep all the threads in his hands. His narrow brain was incapable of taking in more than one thing at a time, and then only what directly concerned his personal interest.' He had reduced the Regent to such servitude that he dared not decide the merest trifles. 'It was no longer a question of the Duke of Orleans —whom not even the ministers dared to approach without the permission of the Cardinal, whose good pleasure, that is his interest or caprice, had become the sole motive force of the government. The Duke saw it and felt it: he was a paralytic who could only be set in motion by the Cardinal.' No one was so distressed, not only because of his old friendship, but because he saw there was no remedy. Dubois, he records, still feared him but avoided an open breach. The whole story of the Regency is presented as a duel between the disinterested friend and the unscrupulous adventurer in which 'la foiblesse incroyable' of the Regent made him the tool of his evil genius.

Not content with his *de facto* position as the real ruler of France, Dubois sought and obtained the title of Premier Ministre. To Saint-Simon's remonstrances the Regent replied with an appeal *ad misericordiam*. He was tired of work every day, was bored every evening, and was confronted by the importunity of Dubois every moment: he added that neither wine nor women gave him any more satisfaction. It was in vain that Saint-Simon foretold that Dubois would be a new Mazarin. The Regent listened patiently: then there was a long silence. His head, held between his hands, fell lower and lower. Then he rose, looked sadly at his visitor, and cast his eyes down as if in shame. Finally he remarked: 'Il faut finir cela; il n'y a qu'à le déclarer tout à l'heure.' Saint-Simon bowed and left the room. On the following day Dubois was declared Premier Ministre.

The Cardinal sent a messenger to thank Saint-Simon for his promotion and received the curt reply that it was due to his own unaided efforts. When they met at the Palais Royal the cynical Dubois effusively welcomed his chief antagonist, ascribing his promotion to his influence. 'Il me protesta qu'il voulait ne se conduire que par mes conseils, m'ouvrir tous les portfeuilles, ne me cacher rien, concerter tout avec moi. Je sentois tout ce que valoit ce langage d'un homme qui ne cherchoit qu'à se cacher sous mon manteau, et à jeter, s'il l'eût pu, tout l'odieux de sa promotion sur moi, comme l'ayant conseillée, poursuivie et procurée.' Sickened by this elaborate farce Saint-Simon went home, as he says, to breathe. 'J'avais le cœur navré de voir le Régent à la chaîne de son indigne ministre et n'osant rien sans lui ni que par lui, l'état en proie à l'intérêt, à l'avarice, à la folie de ce malheureux, sans qu'il y eût aucun remède. . . . Je n'approchois plus de ce pauvre prince à tant de grands et d'utiles talents enfouis qu'avec répugnance. En effet, qu'aurois-je eu à dire ou à discuter avec un régent qui ne l'étoit plus, pas même de soi, bien loin de l'être du royaume, où je voyais tout en désordre?' The Cardinal only enjoyed his triumph for a few months. His death was welcomed by the Regent with relief, and once again Saint-Simon poured out vials of his wrath on 'ce monstrueux personnage.' Dubois was an unscrupulous *arriviste*, but he was not quite such a political bungler as his critic suggests. The two old friends resumed their intimacy, but at the end of the same year 1723 the Regent died of a stroke. Saint-Simon's political career was over, and the last real champion of the French nobility decided to end his *Memoirs* at this point.

In the closing reflections, added shortly before his death, the author once more proclaims his devotion to truth. True memoirs are the only good ones, and they are only true when written by the man who has witnessed and taken part in the things he describes or derived them from people worthy of all confidence. The writer must sacrifice everything to truth, 'as I have done, to the detriment of my fortune.' Impartial he did not claim to be, but he was certainly just. He had always mentioned his authorities, and if he was not sure of his ground he had said so. 'I think I may say that no other work contains more detailed information about so many matters, nor forms a more curious and instructive whole. . . . If they are published I feel sure that they will produce a prodigious revolt.' His forecast was correct, for skirmishes still continue on various sectors of his vast battle-front, and the work forms the most significant contribution to the history of France ever made by a single individual.

Bibliographical Note.—The edition of the *Memoirs* by A. de Boislisle, in 42 vols., which supersedes that of Chéruel and reproduces the voluminous commentaries on Dangeau's *Journal*, is one of the glories of French scholarship. The first serious attempt to assess the value of the work was made by Ranke in his *Französische Geschichte*, vol. 5. Chéruel, *Saint-Simon, Historien de Louis XIV*, provides the fullest analysis of the first and larger half of the work. The best introductions to the man and the writer are by Gaston Boissier, in the *Grands Écrivains Français*, and by René Doumic. Clifton Collins, *Saint-Simon*, is useful for English readers. The best brief account is by Émile Bourgeois in Petit de Julleville, *Histoire de la Langue et de la Littérature Française*, vol. v, ch. 9. Henri Sée discusses his political ideas in *Les Idées politiques en France au dix-septième Siècle*. The best history of the whole period is in Lavisse, *Histoire de France*, vols. 7–8. Sainte-Beuve's well-known essays are in *Causeries du Lundi*, XV, and *Nouveaux Lundis*, X. His essays on Dangeau are in *Causeries du Lundi*, XI.

CHAPTER IX

WILHELMINA AND FREDERICK WILLIAM I

IN the spacious field of historical memoirs France occupies the first place, England the second, Germany the third. The latter has only three contributions of outstanding importance to her credit, those of Wilhelmina of Prussia, Bismarck, and Bülow. While the political apologias appeal above all to students of diplomacy and statecraft, the recollections of the favourite sister of Frederick the Great are read by all the world. The best testimony to her literary skill is to be found in the fact that her picture of the Prussian Court during the reign of her father, Frederick William I, has coloured our outlook ever since her book appeared. Her volumes reveal one of the most fascinating personalities of the eighteenth century. A literary Hohenzollern princess, the friend and correspondent of Voltaire, the Mme de Sévigné of Germany, as she has been called, is in a class by herself. To use a modern formula, Weimar, not Potsdam, is her spiritual home. This lack of conformity to type, indeed, was the chief source of her troubles. Queen Louisa, heroine of the Napoleonic era, fulfilled herself in her short life and earned the abiding love of her people. Wilhelmina, on the contrary, is a figure of frustration, embitterment, and occasionally despair. Under happier circumstances and on a larger stage she would have played an active part in politics, like her distant cousin Caroline of Anspach, instead of being a helpless victim and tool. That she was a misfit, that her *rôle* bore no relation to her abilities, that she suffered from lifelong ill-health, must be borne in mind as we listen sympathetically to her tale of woe.

The *Memoirs*, written in such excellent French that Sainte-Beuve exclaimed, 'C'est un écrivain français de plus,' cover only the first thirty-three years of her life, 1709–42. After her death in 1758 her papers passed to her only child, the Duchess of Württemberg, and on the death of the latter in 1780 some of them were sold by auction. An incomplete German translation appeared in 1810 at Tübingen, and in 1812 the whole work in the original French was published in two volumes at Brunswick. The unsigned Preface states that many people had read the manuscript; that the author had left it to Supperville, her doctor; and that after his death a friend of the publisher had acquired it. In 1848 Pertz, the biographer of Stein, found it at the sale of a library, and to-day the folio volume, bound in calf, reposes among the treasures of the Royal Library at Berlin. Some loose sheets are bound up with it, including a diary of her Italian tour in 1755.

There are also no less than seven copies in the family archives in different hands, differing considerably from each other and from her final autograph version. She began the composition in 1734, and worked at it again in her closing years. Her manuscript contains corrections, usually unfavourable to her parents. For instance her description of the Queen as jealous, ambitious, and suspicious becomes 'Her ambition is immoderate; she is extremely jealous and of suspicious and vindictive nature.' Occasionally her chronology is confused, and incidents are differently recorded in the different versions, which suggests a shaky memory. In a few instances one of her letters provides an account much less damaging to her relatives than that enshrined in the *Memoirs*. In the words of Ranke, who undertook the first careful examination of the work, her stories cannot be wholly false but are mixed with falsehood. A later and still more detailed analysis by Droysen leads him to the crushing verdict that as a source for Prussian history they are worthless. This goes too far, but even Carlyle, who was untrained in the critical use of authorities, warned his readers to subtract twenty-five, and in extreme cases seventy-five per cent., from her testimony. Her pages swarm with errors of fact and date; her versions of letters are often incorrect; in foreign affairs she is completely out of her depth; and her credulity is suggested by her statement that Prince Leopold of Anhalt-Dessau and Grumbkow concocted a plot to murder the King.

Wilhelmina declares that she wrote to divert her mind from sad thoughts, not for publication, but such declarations need never be taken too seriously. 'Perhaps one day I shall make a sacrifice to Vulcan; perhaps I shall give it to my daughter. I repeat that I only write for my amusement, and I take pleasure in hiding nothing of my experiences, not even my most secret thoughts.' Such a finished performance was not meant to be kept for ever under lock and key. 'I am reading Sully's *Memoirs*,' she wrote to Voltaire in 1751. 'I have read all those I possess on the history of France. These secret memoirs make one far better acquainted with facts than general histories.' She was fully aware of the interest of the tale. We can imagine her seeking consolation for her disappointments in an appeal to posterity. The book was an instantaneous as well as a lasting success, and the Margravine of Bayreuth has counted for much more after her death than during her life. She was an ambitious woman, conscious of her powers and proud of her rank. Here, if nowhere else, fate has been kind.

The drama opens with the marriage of her parents in 1706, when her mother was nineteen, her father a year younger. They had fourteen children, and at their accession to the throne in 1713 the author was four years old and her brother Frederick one. Her earliest recollection was the death-bed of her kindly grandfather, King Frederick, who gave her his blessing. A brief preliminary sketch of the new Court introduces the reader to the principal actors on the Prussian stage. Her father, in her opinion, had the makings of a great man. He possessed judgment and application, and he had a good heart. The army was his idol. His fiery temperament often led him to outbursts later bitterly repented. As a rule he preferred justice to clemency. His love of money won him the reputation of a miser, which was deserved so far as himself and his family were concerned, though he was generous to those who served him well. His piety, attested by his charitable foundations and the churches that he built, degenerated into bigotry. He was suspicious, jealous, and inclined to deceit. His tutor had inspired him with contempt for the fair sex, and his low opinion of women was an affliction to his wife, of whom he was extremely jealous.

The King's two favourites, comrades from the Marlborough campaigns, are painted in the darkest colours. His cousin Prince Leopold of Anhalt-Dessau—'a very whirlwind of a man,' as Carlyle calls him—was one of the leading soldiers of the age and he had a flair for politics; but his brutal appearance inspired fear, and his face was a mirror of his character. His inordinate ambition prompted him to every crime in pursuit of his goal. He was a faithful friend, but an implacable enemy to those who had the misfortune to offend him. Though cruel and false he was a cultivated man and could talk agreeably when he chose. General Grumbkow, a Pomeranian noble, combined brains with polished manners and he was a witty conversationalist; yet his external accomplishments concealed a base, selfish, and treacherous heart. His life was loose, his whole character a tissue of vices which sickened decent folk. These men, working in partnership, were quite capable of corrupting the heart of the young ruler and ruining the state. Their ambitious projects were challenged by the King's marriage to Sophia Dorothea, daughter of the Elector of Hanover, soon to ascend the English throne as George I. The Prince of Anhalt strove to counteract her influence by encouraging her husband's jealousy. The unscrupulous and venal Grumbkow deserved the lash of Wilhelmina's whip, but the portrait of The Old Dessauer, as he was often called, is a caricature. These snapshots warn us that the author knew nothing of the larger problems which confronted her father and his colleagues, nor of the hard work which went to the governance of the little state of two millions and made it count on the chessboard of Europe.

Wilhelmina introduces her mother in the same detached and critical spirit. Though she was no beauty, her majestic demeanour inspired respect; yet her experience of society and a brilliant mind seemed to promise more solidity than she possessed. She had a good and generous heart. She liked the arts and sciences, but had given them little attention. All the pride and *hauteur* of the House of Hanover were concentrated in her. Her ambition was inordinate. She was excessively jealous, suspicious, and vindictive, and never forgave those whom she believed to have offended her. Wilhelmina never fully understood that her mother had plenty of troubles of her own. Reared in the luxurious Hanoverian Court, she was never at home in the Sparta of Frederick William I. Possessing literary and artistic tastes, and preferring to talk French, she disliked the gross and mindless Court into which she had married, and chafed against the economy enforced by her thrifty lord. She was happiest at Monbijou, now the Hohenzollern Museum, the miniature palace in the heart of Berlin on the bank of the Spree, where she showed sympathetic visitors the library which meant nothing to the King. She liked late hours, while he rose early and went early to bed. Despite the dissimilarity of temperament and taste, the marriage was fairly happy till political differences concerning the two eldest children wrecked the family peace. Olympia, as foreign diplomats called her, was a handsome woman, and she was graceful till she grew too fat. She was generally considered to be kindly, but she could be harsh enough if opposed. She was inclined to severity with her daughters, but Frederick, who never thwarted her ambitions till he came to the throne, felt a mild affection for her to the end.

On the death of her grandfather, testifies Wilhelmina, the whole face of Berlin was changed. Those who wished to retain the favour of the new monarch had to don helmet and cuirass. Everything became military, and no trace of the old Court remained. Grumbkow took the helm, and the Prince of Anhalt devoted himself to the army. The first task was to reform the finances, which had been deranged by the extravagance of the late King. Frederick William, who preferred Potsdam to Berlin, lived like a private gentleman and his table was frugal. His chief occupation was the training of a regiment of tall soldiers which he had begun to form when he was heir to the throne. All the sovereigns of Europe were on the look-out for recruits, and the regiment might be called *le canal des grâces*, for a gift of tall grenadiers secured whatever one wished. In the afternoon he hunted, and the evening was spent in the Tabagie. Wilhelmina always speaks as if her father had little to do except to amuse himself and bully his family. That he was one of the hardest workers in his kingdom, the creator of an efficient central adminis-tration, the author of conscription, the founder of the bureaucratic-military Prussian state, she never understood. Her book, to quote Carlyle, paints the outside savagery of the man and leaves the inside vacant and undiscovered. Her outlook was purely personal. We have only to glance at his correspondence with the Prince of Anhalt, and other ponderous volumes of the *Acta Borussica*, to realise that he was a conscientious ruler according to his lights, busying himself with every detail of the national machine. He kept the general control of foreign affairs in his hands, cut down the expenses of the Court, sold jewels to pay off the debts of his father, and increased the army, though he loved it too much to expose it rashly to the hazard of war. He only took up arms twice, against Sweden at the beginning of his reign, and against France in the War of the Polish Succession, and in neither case was he seriously engaged. Krauske's examination of the household accounts shows that his stinginess is greatly exaggerated.

Some memoirs inspire a growing confidence as we proceed: with Wilhelmina it is exactly the opposite. The more she piles up the horrors the less we are inclined to believe. We are conscious throughout of a tendency to lay on the colours too thick, of nerves frayed almost beyond endurance, of a leaning to caricature. All that can be said for the Spartan Frederick William has been advanced by Carlyle, to whom the ideology of the soldier king, 'a dumb poet,' 'the great drill-sergeant of the Prussian nation,' strongly appealed. The ideal of this Old Testament Christian, as he has been described, was to be the Landesvater, the thrifty landlord, the model soldier, the embodiment of discipline, the apostle of the strenuous life, dedicated to the public weal. 'Tell the Prince of Anhalt,' he wrote in one of his first letters after his accession, 'that I am the Finance Minister and the Field Marshal of the King of Prussia.' The safety of the state, he believed, was to be found in money and arms. 'Halte Dich an das reelle,' he exhorted his son: 'Keep your feet on the solid earth.' Frederick pays generous tribute to his merits in his *Memoirs of the House of Brandenburg*; but as that work was written for publication during the author's lifetime he had more reason than his sister to omit the darker details. His ideal of kingship is set forth in his striking Political Testament in 1722. Theodor von Schön, himself an active reformer, pronounced Frederick William I the greatest of Prussia's kings in the field of domestic policy. It is his misfortune that the memoirs not only of his daughter but of Fassmann and Pöllnitz, his cronies of the Tobacco Parliament, are as untrustworthy as they are picturesque. He was uncultured and unrefined, but his faults are better known than his virtues.

Wilhelmina correctly describes herself as a lively and precocious child with an exceptional memory and a taste for languages, history, and music. She had good teachers, her mother was

delighted with her progress, and her father loved her best of his
flock. The sole recreation of the busy little girl was the society of
her brother Frederick. 'Never was there such a tender relationship. He was clever but of sombre disposition; learned with
great difficulty, and was expected to have more good sense than
brains.' Unhappily he was detested by his father, who sensed
opposition to his will at an early age. One day when Wilhelmina,
at her mother's wish, was writing to Frederick about what she
calls several matters of contraband, the King entered the room;
she hastily hid the letter in a cabinet and put the inkpot in her
pocket, where she held it erect. When her father embraced her
she had to let go, with the result that the ink ran over her clothes.
She was half dead with fright, but the unwelcome visitor left
without noticing the catastrophe. Though mother and daughter
worked together in the interest of the Crown Prince, the King's
demonstrative affection for his eldest daughter aroused the
jealousy of the Queen, which was stimulated by some of her
ladies.

The *Memoirs* illustrate the baneful influence of female functionaries in the life and quarrels of eighteenth-century courts. The
author's first governess, an Italian named Letti, was a bully who
knocked her about, but her successor, Fräulein von Sonsfeld,
became a friend for life. Even if we discount the tendency to
magnify her misfortunes, it is clear that Wilhelmina's childhood
was shadowed by miserable health and domestic disputes. Neither
for the members of the royal family nor for their servants was the
Court of the peppery martinet a happy place. Long before she
herself became a victim of his ungovernable temper she learned
from his treatment of her mother and brother what she might
expect when she grew up. On one occasion, she declares, the crafty
Grumbkow persuaded his master that the Queen was unfaithful,
and the King returned to Berlin after a short absence mad with
jealousy. The fit quickly passed, for her fidelity was beyond
reproach, and the incident closed with his request for pardon and a
flood of penitent tears. Yet the barometer was never set fair.

Two royal visits are caustically described by the precocious
child. She possessed an observant eye, but her highly flavoured
descriptions must be taken with many grains of salt. When Peter
the Great arrived from Holland in 1717 his host knew only too
well what to expect, and the Queen removed the most perishable
articles from Monbijou, where he was to stay. The barbarian of
genius was coldly received. When he attempted to embrace the
Queen she repulsed him, and she took no notice of his female
entourage. There were four hundred *soi-disant* ladies, mainly
German—ladies-in-waiting, chambermaids, cooks, and laundry-
women. 'Nearly all these creatures carried richly clothed babies

in their arms, and when asked if they were theirs they replied that
the Tsar had done them that honour.' In revenge for the Queen's
neglect of 'these creatures' the Tsarina treated the princesses with
disdain. Wilhelmina, a child of eight, had not been present, and
her lively imagination embroidered the stories she heard; but on
the following day she took part in the reception at the Schloss.
The gigantic Tsar, dressed in sailor's clothes, was handsome, but
his countenance inspired fear. He took her in his arms and
scratched her face in an effort to kiss her. She struggled to free
herself, exclaiming that she disliked such familiarities. He laughed
heartily at such a notion and they proceeded to converse. Having
been well coached, she talked to him of his fleet and his conquests.
He was so delighted that he kept saying to the Tsarina that for
such a child he would gladly surrender a province. The Tsarina's
caresses were equally unwelcome, for she had only to be seen to
realise her humble origin. Small, squat, and sunburnt, she might
have been taken for a German *comédienne* by the way she dressed.
Her clothes were adorned with a dozen orders and as many
portraits of saints and relics, which collided and jangled when
she walked.

At dinner there were fresh surprises. Having been poisoned in
his youth, Peter was subject to convulsions, and he brandished his
knife so close to the Queen that she started back in alarm. In
reassuring her he took her hand with such violence that she begged
for mercy. He laughed, and remarked that her bones were more
delicate than those of his Catherine. In the King's cabinet of
medals and antiques he discovered a pagan deity in an indecent
posture which he ordered the Empress to kiss. This and other
treasures he desired to possess, and it was impossible to refuse.
When 'this barbarian Court' had departed the sorely tried Queen
hastened to her beloved little palace. 'The desolation of Jerusalem
prevailed. I never saw anything like it. Everything was so
ruined that she had to rebuild almost the whole edifice.' That the
Imperial wanderer had the habits of a pig we know from Evelyn's
account of the visit to Deptford; but the statement about the
reconstruction of Monbijou is a fresh warning that the author loves
to draw a long bow.

A more civilised though less interesting visitor was the father
of the Queen. George I was hard, cold, selfish, and at Berlin he
won no hearts. While the royal family awaited him at the Palace
of Charlottenburg in 1723, Wilhelmina's heart was beating. Her
grandfather embraced her, remarking to the Queen that her
daughter was very tall for her age. On reaching his apartments
he took a candle, for he had arrived in the evening, and looked her
up and down from head to foot without uttering a word. She
stood motionless as a statue, greatly embarrassed. His English

attendants were bidden by the Queen to talk in their own language with Wilhelmina, for they would see that she spoke very well. 'As I spoke English as well as my mother-tongue I scored and everyone seemed charmed with me. They sang my praises to the Queen, telling her that I had the English manner and was made to be their sovereign one day. That was saying a good deal, for that nation considers itself so much above ours that its inhabitants think they are paying a fine compliment when they say one has English manners.' The King hardly spoke to anyone, and his icy reserve froze the spirits of the lively girl of fourteen. 'Is she always 'so serious,' he inquired, 'and is she of a melancholy disposition?' 'Nothing of the sort,' replied the faithful Sonsfeld, 'but her respect for Your Majesty prevents her from being as bright as usual.' At table he was equally silent, and at the end of the meal he tumbled over in a faint, his wig falling one way and his hat another. For an hour he lay unconscious and passed a bad night, but he was up again next day and went through the programme of business and festivities. His departure took place in an atmosphere as frosty as that of his arrival.

There were political reasons for George I to have a good look at Wilhelmina. He had accepted in principle the double union of the royal families desired at Berlin, though he refused a written contract. His grandson, the Duke of Gloucester, later to be known as Poor Fred, was to have Wilhelmina, and the Crown Prince of Prussia was to take his granddaughter Amelia. It was an old project, and the girl grew up in the thought of its fulfilment. Everyone expected the eldest daughter of the King of Prussia to wear a crown, and this was the best match in Europe open to a Protestant princess. She corresponded with her little unknown lover and received presents in return. In theory it was excellent. In practice it inaugurated a period of domestic discord and political intrigue which for several years poisoned her health and happiness. For the scheme had its enemies no less than its friends. The House of Hapsburg disliked it from the start as calculated to make Prussia independent of Vienna.

At this point Count Seckendorff, the Austrian representative, becomes a leading figure on the stage. An old military comrade of the King from the Marlborough wars, a good soldier and a Protestant from Anspach, he had paid occasional visits to Berlin on secret missions from the Austrian and Saxon courts, but in 1726 he was appointed personal envoy to Frederick William in the belief that he could work more effectively for the Emperor without an official position. Knowing exactly how to deal with the King, he was a welcome addition to the Tabagie, and was tireless in his efforts to procure tall grenadiers. A pension to Grumbkow, the principal adviser of the King till his death in

1739, terminated his championship of the English marriage project. Gundling received a medal, high officers were flattered by banquets, and even minor Court officials were not overlooked. He even bribed the Prussian residents in London to write as he and Grumbkow desired, and he described Wilhelmina as ugly in his efforts to frustrate the English match.

Frederick William had never been so eager as his wife, who championed Wilhelmina's English prospects with passionate zeal. One reason for his lukewarm attitude was his resentment at the procrastination of George I; another, his dislike of the prospect of providing a large dowry; a third, his distaste for binding himself in regard to Frederick. The credit of Seckendorff, declares the author, waxed from day to day, and the majority of the Generals and the King's household were in his pay. Recognising the Queen as his chief enemy, he resolved to weaken her influence by sowing disunion in the royal family. He also fed the credulous monarch with inventions about his two eldest children. Frederick was depicted as an ambitious intriguer, eager for his father's death, extravagant, and no friend of the army; Wilhelmina as insufferably arrogant and imperious, the counsellor of her brother and a disrespectful critic of the King. The father's favour was now transferred to a younger daughter and never fully restored. So long as George I was alive it was impossible to break off the marriage project, for his son-in-law held him in respect; but on his death in 1727 the Courts began to drift apart, for George II and his cousin disliked one another.

Wilhelmina was now eighteen, and her father began to look round for alternative suitors. On a state visit to Dresden, she declares, he had discussed a match with the magnificent Augustus, Elector of Saxony and King of Poland, recently become a widower, the father of almost as many bastards as there are days in the year; but this project seems to have existed only in her imagination. The visit was returned and she was introduced to the most dissolute monarch in Europe, who brought not only his legitimate heir but samples of his unauthorised brood, one of them the future Marshal Saxe, another reputed to be also his mistress. Though a dignified and polished figure, his face bore the traces of his debauchery. For once the parsimonious ruler opened his purse-strings and provided the sumptuous food, drink, and entertainments to which his guest was accustomed. Among his numerous suite was a certain Duke of Weissenfeld, who paid marked attention to Wilhelmina. 'I attributed it to politeness, and I could never have imagined that he would dare to lift his eyes to me and think of marriage. He was a cadet of the Saxon house, but his was not reckoned among the illustrious families of Germany. And though my heart was free from ambition, it was also free from baseness,

which blinded me to his true intentions.' Before long she was to
hate the sound of his name.

Soon after the departure of the King of Poland, when the royal
family were in residence at Wusterhausen, the dreary hunting
lodge twenty miles south of Berlin described by Wilhelmina as
'this terrible place,' a conversation took place between her parents.
Though she and a younger sister were sent into an adjoining room,
and the door was shut, she heard a violent altercation and, to her
horror, the frequent mention of her name. After an hour and a
half her father emerged in a fury, and she found her mother in
tears. 'She embraced me and held me tight in her arms without
speaking a word.' Then came the dreadful news. 'I am in utter
despair. They want to find you a husband and the King is set
on the worst possible match. He plans to marry you to the Duke
of Weissenfeld, a wretched cadet and pensioner of the King of
Poland. I shall die of grief if you are base enough to consent.'
The girl thought she was dreaming: her father could not have
been serious, she exclaimed. 'Mon Dieu,' replied her mother, 'he
will be here in a day or two to ask for your hand. You must be
firm. I will support you with all my power, provided you stand
firm.' The girl promised to follow her mother's advice, for the
mere thought of a match with a cadet of a minor branch of the
Saxon house was an insult to her Hohenzollern pride. The mere
project, it was clear, would cause a rift in the family. Her brother,
who desired the English connection, strengthened her resolve. 'You
will ruin us all if you make this ridiculous marriage. Of course we
shall all have a bad time, but anything is better than falling into
the power of our enemies. England is our only support, and if your
marriage to the Prince of Wales is broken off, we shall all collapse.'

When the suitor arrived the Queen was ordered to receive him
as her future son-in-law, and at church on the following day he
stared at Wilhelmina throughout the service. Since her father's
will had been announced she had had no rest by night or day.
After church the King presented the Duke to the Queen, who
turned her back on him without a word. Wilhelmina could not
eat a morsel, and her face told its sorry tale. After another
terrible scene with the King the Queen called Frederick and the
Sonsfeld into council. Weissenfeld was well spoken of though not
brilliant, and it was decided that an emissary should explain the
situation to him. The Queen, he was informed, would never
consent, and the family harmony would be destroyed if the courtship was pursued. She felt sure that as a man of honour he would
not wish to make her daughter unhappy. The Duke replied that
he was greatly attracted by the charms of the Princess, and that
he would never have ventured to think of the marriage if his hopes
had not been aroused; but seeing it was contrary to their wishes

he would be the first to dissuade the King. He kept his word, only craving a preference over other non-royal suitors if the English project fell through. The King was surprised, but he finally agreed to his wife writing to Queen Caroline to beg for a definite declaration. 'If the reply is favourable, I will break off any other engagement. If ambiguous, I shall not be their dupe, and then I shall dispose of my daughter as I wish. In that case, Madam, do not imagine that your tears and cries will avail.' He added that he would never allow Frederick to marry an English princess. 'I don't want a daughter-in-law who gives herself airs and fills my Court with intrigues as you do.' He added that he detested his son and that, unless he changed his ways, he would get more than he bargained for.

The permission to try again brought little comfort. When Wilhelmina remarked that George II would reply: 'A double marriage or none,' and spoke of the gloomy prospects when such a letter arrived, her mother lost her self-control. 'She could see that I was already intimidated and was resolved to accept the fat John Adolf. She would rather see me dead than married to him. If she could imagine that I had the slightest such intention, she would strangle me with her own hands.' In addition to her official letter, which was shown to the King, she and the Crown Prince sent private letters through the English minister. The Queen could talk of nothing else, but her unflattering portrait of the Prince of Wales was calculated to diminish the girl's desire for a match which had never been more than tepid. He had a good heart, but little brains; he was ugly and a little misshapen. 'Provided you are willing to overlook his debaucheries, you will rule him entirely and be more of a King than he when he comes to the throne. Just think of the *rôle* you would play. You would decide the fate of Europe.' Such talk grated on Wilhelmina, whose idea of marriage was very different. 'Je me souhaitois un vrai ami, auquel je pusse donner toute ma confiance et mon cœur.' Neither the Prince nor the Duke fulfilled these conditions. The latter was forty-three, fat, coarse in his person, and very debauched.

It was a time of utter misery. 'We suffered the pains of purgatory.' Her father's temper was worse than ever, for he was suffering from a bad attack of gout and he crawled about on crutches. Wilhelmina was denounced as *canaille Anglaise*, her brother as *le coquin de Fritz*. If we are to believe her, the children had not enough to eat, and were forced to eat and drink what was so distasteful to them that they brought it up again in his presence. One morning when his family came to pay their respects he shouted at the Queen, 'Go away with all your accursed children, I wish to be alone.' The family was delighted at the prospect of escaping from the royal table, 'for my brother and I were becoming as thin as hacks for lack of nourishment.' Hardly were they seated when a valet rushed in: 'In God's name, madam, come quick, the King wants to strangle himself.' He was found with a cord round his neck.

The fit of fury passed, but at supper his self-control again gave way. He had heard that the young Margrave of Anspach would be coming to Berlin to marry his younger daughter. Did the news please her, he inquired of the latter, and how would she arrange when she was married? Her father's favourite audaciously rejoined that she would have a table nicely served, 'better than yours, and if I have children I will not maltreat them as you do, and force them to eat what they hate.' What was the matter with his table? cried the King in a fury; but all his wrath was directed against his two elder children. He flung plates at their heads, which they dodged, and followed up the assault with a volley of abuse. The Queen was saddled with the bad education of her children. 'You ought to curse your mother,' he exclaimed to Frederick; 'it's her fault that you are so out of hand.' On rising from table they had to pass his chair, and Wilhelmina dodged a blow from his crutch. He pursued her in his chair, but the lackeys who pulled it gave her time to escape. She reached her mother's room half dead with fright and fainted away. Fever and delirium followed, in the intervals of which she longed for death. 'I am the cause of all the troubles of the Queen and my brother,' she explained to her ladies. 'If I must die, tell the King that I have always loved and respected him, and that I hope he will give me his blessing before my death. Tell him that I implore him to be kinder to the Queen and my brother and to bury all disunion in my grave.' That she developed smallpox failed to soften her father's heart, and, fearing that his favourite daughter might catch it, he treated the patient like a prisoner of state. Her room was terribly cold, and the soup was only salt and water. When something better was proposed, he replied that it was good enough for her. Her brother visited her secretly, but the Queen did not dare to disobey the King's commands.

The royal temper improved as the gout abated, but Wilhelmina remained in disgrace. Her offence was her opposition to the Weissenfeld match, and when her sister's marriage to the Margrave of Anspach had taken place the conflict was renewed. Quarrels went on all day at Wusterhausen. 'He let my brother and me die of hunger. He carved himself and served everyone except us; and if anything was left on a plate he spat on it to prevent us eating it. We lived on *café au lait* and dried cherries which upset my stomach. To make up for it I was fed with insults and invective, for I was called all sorts of names before everybody.' Since he forbade them to show themselves except at meals, their

9

mother sent for them when the tyrant was out hunting and stationed observers to give warning of his return. One day he slipped through the cordon and his footsteps were heard approaching the Queen's room. There was no time to decamp and there was only one entrance, so Frederick darted into a closet while Wilhelmina dived under the Queen's bed. The King, exhausted by the chase, flung himself on the bed and slept for two hours, while his daughter poked her head out at intervals for air. Was there nothing to be done to improve the situation? she inquired piteously. Nothing, rejoined her mother. Only her consent to his choice of a husband would help, and that was unthinkable.

The King, determined to marry his daughter without delay, allowed his wife to knock once more at the English door; if his offer was refused, Wilhelmina must accept Weissenfeld or the Margrave of Schwedt, a descendant of the Great Elector and therefore a distant cousin. The Queen promised to write but without consenting to the alternative. Before the reply arrived the angry ruler decided against the English alliance and demanded a prompt decision between the two suitors. Well aware that the Queen, not Wilhelmina, was the obstacle, he threatened to separate from her if she resisted, to imprison the girl in a fortress, and to disinherit the Crown Prince. The Queen stoutly rejoined that she would never consent to make Wilhelmina unhappy by either of these matches. The English reply reiterated the familiar condition that there must be a double marriage or none. The reaction of the angry monarch was to threaten to shut up his daughter with Weissenfeld. Her sufferings in mind and body had reduced her to a condition in which through sheer exhaustion she was ready to accept her fate, but to obey the family tyrant was to infuriate the Queen. When the conflict of loyalties was at its height, the problem was complicated by a new factor. She loved Frederick more than all the rest of her family put together and more than he loved her, for she had a warmer heart. In childhood her chief joy was to have his company, in the years of adolescence to share his interests, his secrets, and his sorrows. Detesting debauchery she grieved to see him sowing his wild oats at an early age, but her remonstrances were in vain. His spirits declined with his health, and his formidable father was the last person to help him through the temptations of youth. 'I loved him passionately, and when I asked him what was the matter he always replied that it was the bad treatment of the King.' They passed the afternoons together, reading, writing, and composing satires on the personages of the Court. Looking back on these scenes she blames herself for lack of respect to the King, though she recalls that their literary efforts were encouraged by the Queen. They were soon to be thinking of other and graver things.

CHAPTER X

WILHELMINA AND FREDERICK THE GREAT

THE most dramatic portion of the *Memoirs* of Wilhelmina describes the attempted flight of the Crown Prince in 1730 and his father's terrible revenge. The King, she testifies, never saw him without threatening him with his cane. He would bear everything, declared the victim, except blows, and if it came to the worst he would seek safety in flight. His sister welcomed the departure on military service of the page Keith whom she regarded as an evil influence, but his next favourite seemed to her much more dangerous. The son of General Katt had been destined for the law and received an excellent education, but as the army was the only avenue to success under Frederick William I he changed his profession. His intellectual interests and polished manners attracted Frederick, but according to Wilhelmina he was ugly, ambitious, and dissolute. Soon after the formation of this friendship she was horrified to read a letter from her brother to the Queen. That morning, it ran, the King had forgotten that he was his son and had beaten him unmercifully. He had tried to defend himself, but his father had lost all self-control and continued the performance till he was tired. That was more than honour would allow him to stand, and he was resolved to put an end to it in one way or another. This phrase, correctly interpreted as a project of flight, led Wilhelmina to propose to her mother to accept the detestable Weissenfeld. She realised that it would mean misery, but as a sacrifice was needed to restore the family harmony she preferred that she, not Frederick, should pay the price. 'You wish me to die of grief,' was the angry response; 'if you are capable of such cowardice I will disown you and never see you again.' These words were pronounced with such excitement that Wilhelmina promised to do nothing to upset her mother. Henceforth the Queen appears in almost as unpleasant a light in the *Memoirs* as the King.

After further canings the exasperated Frederick resolved to act. As far back as 1728, at the age of sixteen, he had begun to think of flight, complaining bitterly that the King mistook the Crown Prince for a Prussian officer. One evening, after saying good night to him in her mother's room, Wilhelmina was getting into bed when a young man entered her room smartly dressed in the French style. She uttered a cry and sought refuge behind a screen. A moment later she recognised her brother, who was in excellent spirits. He had come to bid her good-bye, for his patience was at an end. From Dresden, whither he was to

accompany his father on a visit to the King of Poland, he would
flee to England; once there he hoped to rescue his sister and they
would meet again where they could live in peace. When her first
protests proved unavailing she threw herself at his feet, and he
promised to abandon the plan. About this time the Queen, who
was pregnant, became so ill that the King was recalled. Her
sufferings reduced him to tears, and he exclaimed that he would
not survive her if she passed away. He repeatedly begged her
forgiveness for the chagrin he had caused her—an indication, in
Wilhelmina's eyes, that his conduct had been mainly due to evil
counsellors. Seizing her opportunity the Queen implored him to
be reconciled to his two elder children before she died. Wilhelmina
was summoned and threw herself at his feet. Her voice was stifled
by her sobs, and everyone present shed tears. After embracing
her the King sent for Frederick, but the welcome was chilly
enough. He would forgive the past for his mother's sake, but the
young man would have to change his conduct and obey his
father's wishes, in which case he could count on his paternal
love.

The patched-up peace aided the Queen's recovery, but directly
she was out of danger the feud broke out again. To spare her
feelings the King controlled himself in her presence, but maltreated
his children elsewhere; the climax was reached one morning at
Potsdam when he seized the Crown Prince by the hair, threw him
on the ground, dragged him to a window, and tried to strangle him
with the cord. Frederick seized the madman's hands and cried
for help till a valet arrived. In relating this outrage to his sister
he added that only violent remedies would suffice. Katt would
follow him to the ends of the earth in case of need, and Keith
would join them. This time Wilhelmina knew that it was useless
to protest; but she sensed the danger of a plan that was certain
to fail, and only succeeded in extracting a promise to await the
English reply to the latest matrimonial soundings from Berlin.
At first sight the response, brought by Sir Charles Hotham in 1730,
seemed favourable. The double match was still pronounced
essential, but Wilhelmina and the Prince of Wales could be married
first. The British envoy, however, verbally explained that
Grumbkow must go; he was the tool of Vienna, and intercepted
letters proved his intrigues. For a brief space the Chief Minister
seemed in disgrace, but Seckendorff came to his rescue by fostering
the King's distrust of the English Court. Losing his temper the
monarch, according to Wilhelmina, tore up the letters, threw them
in Hotham's face, and raised his foot as if to kick. The envoy left
the room without a word, a message of apology was ignored, and
he returned to England. Unfortunately for her veracity Hotham
makes no reference to the kick in his report, but the interview was

stormy, for the irascible king could never bridle his tongue.   The end of the wearisome marriage negotiations seemed to have come at last, and the final obstacle to Frederick's flight was removed.

When the Queen learned that Frederick was meditating flight but was well watched, she asked Wilhelmina's advice.   Her daughter endeavoured to calm her : she did not believe that he would carry out plans born of despair.   Katt, whom she reproved for incautious talk, denied that he had encouraged his master to fly, though he believed that no harm would come to a Crown Prince. 'You are gambling for high stakes,' retorted Wilhelmina; 'I fear I am a good prophet.'   'If I lose my head,' replied Katt, 'it will be in a good cause, but the Crown Prince will not abandon me.' It was the last time they met.   A few days later the Queen gave a ball at Monbijou, and Wilhelmina, who had not danced for six years, was for once enjoying herself.   At a late hour her eye fell on the Queen in a corner of the room, pale as death, talking to two of her ladies.   Was it about the Crown Prince? she asked Countess Bülow.   'I know nothing,' she replied, shrugging her shoulders. Mother and daughter drove home in ominous silence, the girl's heart beating violently.   What was the matter? she asked the Sonsfeld when they were alone.   'The Queen has pledged me to silence,' replied the faithful friend with tears in her eyes.   Believing Frederick to be dead the girl gave way to such despair that she was told the tragic truth.   An angry letter from the King had arrived stating that he had arrested the Crown Prince who had attempted to fly.   After a sleepless night Wilhelmina was summoned at an early hour by her mother, who showed her the letter.   Wilhelmina fainted, and the condition of her mother and herself, she declares, would have melted a heart of stone.   Katt, added the Queen, had also been arrested.   The two ladies hastened to burn the compromising letters which Frederick had entrusted to her, and to fabricate others to fill the gap.

Frederick's project was doomed from the start, and the fugitive was trapped at Wesel.   When the demented parent saw his son he flew at him, tore out his hair, and would have strangled him had not a general intervened.   The Prince was deprived of his sword and cross-examined.

THE KING. Why did you wish to desert?

FREDERICK. Because you treated me not as your son, but as a miserable slave.

THE KING. So you are only a cowardly deserter, with no sense of honour?

FREDERICK. I have as much as you.   I have only done what you have told me a hundred times you would do if you were in my place.

The last thrust was too much for the monarch, who drew his sword as if to run him through. A general threw himself between them, exclaiming: 'Slay me, Sire, but spare your son.'

The King's first words to the Queen on his return to Berlin were a cruel lie: 'Your unworthy son is dead.' 'What,' she cried, 'you have been barbarous enough to kill him?' 'Yes, but I want the casket.' When she went to fetch it Wilhelmina heard her moaning: 'My God, my son!' While her husband was smashing the casket and removing the letters the anguished mother came to Wilhelmina's room. A moment later, Mme Ramen, who is always depicted as a spy of the King and the evil genius of the Queen, reported that the Crown Prince was alive. The two ladies in relief hastened to kiss the King's hand. 'When he saw me he overflowed with rage. His face darkened, his eyes flashed with fury and there was foam at his lips. "Infamous *canaille*, do you dare to enter my presence? Go and keep your rascal of a brother company." With these words he seized me with one hand and beat my face with his fist. One blow on the forehead knocked me over, and I should have broken my skull if Mme Sonsfeld had not caught me. As I lay unconscious the King, quite beside himself, wanted to trample me under his feet: the Queen, my brothers, and sisters, and the rest prevented it.' They stood round her in a circle, lifted her into a chair and fetched water and stimulants.

On regaining consciousness Wilhelmina reproached her rescuers, death being a thousand time preferable to such a life. The Queen uttered shrill cries, pacing up and down the room. The King's face, disfigured by anger, was terrible to see. The brothers and sisters, the youngest only four, fell on their knees in an attempt to soften him by their tears. The Sonsfeld held her battered and swollen head. Admitting that Frederick was alive, the King poured forth horrible threats of death for his son and of lifelong confinement for his daughter. When she was accused of being Frederick's accomplice in high treason, and of having several children by Katt, the Sonsfeld courageously exclaimed: 'It is not true, and whoever has told Your Majesty so has lied.' The fear of losing her brother impelled Wilhelmina to promise that she would marry Weissenfeld if Frederick's life was spared. There was such a noise in the room that the King did not hear, and when she tried to repeat the words the Sonsfeld put a handkerchief over her mouth. Trying to free herself Wilhelmina turned her head and saw Katt crossing the court, guarded by four gendarmes who were bringing him to the King and carrying the boxes belonging to him and his master. Katt, looking pale and broken, raised his cap in salutation when he thus saw her for the last time.

The King left the room exclaiming that now he had enough evidence against the rascal Fritz and the *canaille de Wilhelmine* to cut off their heads. The Queen's ladies followed him. 'If you wish the Crown Prince to die,' said Mme Ramen, 'spare at any rate the Queen, who is innocent of all this. Treat her gently and she will do all you wish.' The assurance, needless to say, was unauthorised, and another of the ladies struck a firmer note. He had hitherto prided himself on being a just and godfearing prince. God had punished Philip II and Peter the Great, the executioners of their sons; their countries had been a prey to foreign and civil war and their names were the horror of mankind. 'Control yourself, Sir. Your first outburst of anger may be pardoned, but it will become criminal if you do not strive to overcome it.' After looking at her for a few moments in silence he replied: 'You are very bold to talk to me like that, but I am not angry, for your intentions are good and it increases my esteem for you. Go and quiet my wife.' Wilhelmina praises both parties to this brief dialogue, but the King's fury was unabated. When Katt was brought in for examination, and threw himself at the feet of the King, the latter responded with kicks and blows which drew blood. Grumbkow persuaded him to moderate himself and to allow the interrogation to proceed.

On its conclusion the King returned to inform the Queen in an angry voice that Wilhelmina was in the plot, for Katt had confessed to bringing her letters from Frederick. She must stay in her room, and after a rigorous examination she would be moved to a place where she would do penance for her crimes. The threatened examination did not take place, but she was haunted by anxiety for her brother and had made up her mind to marry Weissenfeld if it would save his life. Meanwhile Katt had been beheaded in the fortress of Kustrin under the window of the prison of the Crown Prince, who had been compelled to watch and had fainted at the grisly spectacle. His life may have been saved by the intervention of the Emperor, to whom his mother appealed. Whether in the absence of such protests the furious parent would have proceeded to extremities we cannot be sure. The dispatches of Guy Dickens, the British Envoy, and other diplomats prove that in her account of this terrible incident at any rate she did not exaggerate. The King was considered quite capable of the crime by those who knew him best. Koser, the supreme authority on Frederick the Great, pronounces it not impossible, but Lavisse argues that a death sentence was never seriously considered.

While the Crown Prince remained a state prisoner at Kustrin Wilhelmina's matrimonial destiny was settled at last. The Queen, though still eager for the English match, realised that there was little hope of success; but she was adamant against the King's two nonentities whom she considered unworthy of her daughter's hand. After one of many altercations, in which she reiterated her unyielding opposition to Weissenfeld, he declared that he would at once arrange a marriage with the other suitor, the Margrave of Schwedt. Here, however, he was balked by the Margrave's mother, who refused her consent unless the match was approved by the Queen and the Princess herself. At this point the Queen consulted the trusted veteran, Marshal Borck, who advised her to look round for a more suitable match, and suggested the heir of the Margrave of Bayreuth, a man well spoken of and of suitable age. The Queen followed his advice, telling the King that she renounced the English project, but he must drop his two odious candidates.

THE QUEEN. Choose a suitable match and a husband with whom she can be happy, and I will be the first to give you support.

THE KING. Not a bad idea! But I cannot think of anyone better. If you can, well and good.

THE QUEEN. The Hereditary Prince of Bayreuth.

THE KING. So be it, but there is only one little difficulty, of which I must warn you. I will provide neither dowry nor trousseau, and I will not be present at the wedding, since she will have preferred your wishes. If she had fallen in with mine, I would have treated her best of my children. It is for her to choose between her parents.

THE QUEEN. You drive me to despair. I do everything possible to satisfy you and you are never content. You wish to kill me. All right, let her marry your dear Duke of Weissenfeld. I will not oppose it, but I will lay my curse on him if it happens in my lifetime.

THE KING. Well, madam, as you will. I will write to the Margrave and show you the letter. You can speak to your unworthy daughter, who can have till to-morrow to make up her mind.

The Queen hurried to her daughter and embraced her joyfully. Wilhelmina received the news without enthusiasm and begged time for consideration.

WILHELMINA. How can I marry without the King's approval and the usual formalities? I can only inform the King that I am ready to marry any of the three princes, provided that Your Majesty and he are agreed.

THE QUEEN (angrily). Then take the Grand Turk or the Great Moghul. I would never have let myself in for all this trouble if I had known you better. Obey the King's orders, and I will wash my hands of you. And please spare me the pain of your odious presence, which I cannot bear.

The Queen's promise to withdraw from the struggle was not serious, for she was full of fight. Though there could now be little hope of catching the Prince of Wales she tried to make

Wilhelmina swear to marry no one else. 'I loved the Queen to adoration, for she possessed some fine qualities, but this was asking too much.' That it was impossible to please both parents was her misfortune, not her fault.

On May 10, 1731, which Wilhelmina describes as the most memorable day of her life, Grumbkow and other officials came to inform her that the King proposed the Bayreuth prince. 'You can have no objections to this match. He becomes the mediator between the King and the Queen. She proposed it herself. He is of the House of Brandenburg and will inherit a fine country. As you do not know him, madam, you cannot dislike him. Moreover, everyone speaks very highly of him.' The King, he added, promised to liberate Frederick after the wedding and to forget the past. If, however, she refused, he had with him an order to take her to the fortress of Memel and to treat the Sonsfeld and her other ladies with the utmost rigour.

WILHELMINA. I ask only one favour, that I am allowed to obtain the Queen's consent.

GRUMBKOW. Impossible. The King desires us to bring him an unconditional reply.

WILHELMINA. All right, I consent. I sacrifice myself for my family.

Grumbkow dictated her letter to the King and the deputation withdrew. He replied in cordial terms, but the Queen's reaction was even worse than was feared. 'You pierce my heart. I placed all my hopes in you, but I did not know you. I do not recognise you any longer as my daughter and shall henceforth regard you as my cruel enemy. Count on me no more. I vow eternal hatred and will never forgive you.' This broadside was followed by similar volleys in the next few days; but her fury was partially assuaged by a hint that the Bayreuth engagement was a means of putting pressure on the English Court.

Wilhelmina liked the look of her future husband when he came to Berlin for the exchange of rings. The Queen received him with sour looks, and the news of the approaching marriage was a shock to the public. Anxious to escape from her prison-house she regarded the Prince without the aversion she had felt to the previous candidates. At this point of her narrative she anticipates and paints a portrait of the man she had come to know. He was gay, lively, good-hearted, easily angered but able to control himself, and his country adored him. He was a little inclined to frivolity, but in this he had improved. She could not know all this before her marriage, though she confesses that she began to respect him and had no complaint to make of his person and character. The behaviour of her parents, on the other hand, was a sore trial, and the old complaint of being half-starved recurs.

The Queen bullied her in public and private, and when she was ill snapped out: 'You will be the death of me.' The King told her that she was only fit to be a *femme de chambre*, and he was nettled to find his prospective son-in-law so different from himself. 'The polished and reserved manners of the Prince were not to his taste. He wished the husband of his daughter to be a person with German manners who cared only for soldiers, wine, and thrift. To discover his character and try to amend it, he made him drink, but the Prince had such a strong head that he kept sober when the others collapsed. This enraged the King, who complained to Grumbkow and Seckendorff that he was only a dull fop whose manners were an offence to him.' To placate the King the young man, acting on Grumbkow's advice, craved and received permission to command a Prussian regiment. Wilhelmina regretted the step which, she feared, would make him a slave and introduce him to undesirable company.

On the eve of his departure to take up his command the Prince met his *fiancée* in the garden of Monbijou. 'This is my first opportunity of telling Your Royal Highness of my despair at your aversion for me. I should never have aspired to your hand if the King had not proposed it. Since I do not know how long I shall be away I beg you to say whether you feel an insurmountable hatred of me. If so, it shall be an eternal farewell, though it would mean unhappiness for the rest of my life and provoke the wrath of my father and the King.' He had tears in his eyes and seemed deeply touched. When Wilhelmina blushed and remained silent, he remarked that her silence confirmed his fears. At last she found her tongue. 'My word is inviolable. I gave it at the King's command, but you may rely on it being faithfully kept.' To her relief the conversation was interrupted by the approach of the Queen. If this record is reasonably accurate, the Prince appears to have sensed his good fortune in securing the most accomplished princess of her time, a woman with shining qualities of head and heart.

On her wedding day the bride was sad and pensive. The King tried once again, with some success, to make the bridegroom drunk. The Queen was in a vile temper, for 'she only loved her children in so far as they served her ambitions.' The Margrave of Bayreuth was annoyed by the King's stingy provision for his daughter. Worst of all, Frederick, who was allowed to return to Berlin after fifteen months of banishment at Kustrin, was unexpectedly cold. Before leaving for Bayreuth she had a frank talk with her father, who confessed that he had been misinformed about her. At their parting he showed genuine emotion, while her mother was cold as ice.

The second and less interesting volume of the *Memoirs* opens

with the author's arrival in Bayreuth in January 1732, and covers
the first ten years of her married life. Her early impressions were
unfavourable, though we must remember that this fastidious and
cultivated lady was difficult to please. The Margrave had read
only two books, *Télémaque* and a history of Rome, so his conversation lacked variety. He is described as vain, ignorant, false,
suspicious, and addicted to drink, though not bad at heart. He
had divorced his first wife, and his daughters were impossible.
Since he was only forty-three it seemed likely that he would reign
for many years. The corridors of the palace were festooned with
cobwebs, Wilhelmina's rooms unwarmed, the windows broken.
The food was so bad on the first evening that she had to withdraw.
The first night was one of sadness and suffering. There was
poverty everywhere. She felt herself among rustics instead of
courtiers, a sheep among wolves. She was too poor even to buy
clothes, and there were no recreations. Court jealousies and
intrigues were as rife as at Potsdam, Wusterhausen, and Berlin.
Her faithful friend the Sonsfeld was equally depressed. The
Prince did his best to console her, and her increasing love for him
was the one ray of light in a dark sky. Discounting her tendency
to exaggerate her trials, we may accept her picture of her new
home as fairly typical of the boorish little courts of eighteenth-
century Germany.

Wilhelmina was expecting a baby, and her health was worse
than ever. She had frequent fainting fits and was haunted by
fears of a miscarriage. Her father invited her to Berlin for her
confinement, and she longed to go. She started but was too ill
to continue the journey. The King arrived, gracious and
sympathetic for once, and renewed the invitation when her troubles
were over. He talked frankly to the Margrave about the condition
of his principality, censured his idleness, advised him to associate
his son with the administration, and offered the services of an
expert to tidy up the finances. Frederick William was not a
tactful person at any time, and the Margrave's resentment was
visited on Wilhelmina. Everything seemed to go wrong. She
nearly died in childbirth, and the sex of her only child was a
disappointment to the little principality. That her husband was
now ordered to Berlin to take command of his Prussian regiment
was a bitter blow. 'I loved him passionately, and it was the
happiest union.' She dreaded not only the separation but the
temptations to debauchery and drink. She was ordered to visit
Anspach on the way to Berlin, in order to establish good relations
between the two little courts. She found her sister and brother-
in-law living a cat-and-dog life, the Margrave a contemptible
debauchee whose *maîtresse en titre* bore him three children. When
she reached Berlin her father was away, and her mother greeted

her with the cruel words 'Que venez-vous faire ici?' Both
parents displayed contemptuous pity for her poverty, and the
King remarked that the poor child had not a chemise to her back.
No wonder her husband blushed. Happily her own letters of this
period testify that she was well received and enjoyed herself.

Frederick's welcome helped Wilhelmina to bear her disappointments, but he too had his troubles. That he was ordered to
marry Elizabeth Christina of Brunswick Bevern she knew. 'I
pity the poor creature,' he had written even before he saw her;
'there will be one more unhappy princess in the world.' The
match was engineered by Seckendorff and Grumbkow in the
interest of the Hapsburgs, in the belief that a marriage with the
niece of the Empress would bring Berlin into the orbit of Vienna.
Wilhelmina was disgusted at the conversation of the royal family.
'Your brother,' observed the Queen at table, 'is in despair, as he
has a right to be. She is just an animal. She replies to everything with Yes or No, accompanied by an inane laugh which
makes one sick.' Princess Charlotte chimed in with the remark
that she exhaled an insufferable odour. Frederick changed colour,
and after supper Wilhelmina asked him about his future bride.
He did not dislike her as much as appeared, was the reply. 'I
pretend I can't bear her in order to exploit my obedience to the
King's commands.' She was nice-looking, but she lacked education and was very badly got up, but Wilhelmina would doubtless
be good enough to polish her. 'I recommend her to you, my dear
sister, and I hope you will take her under your wing.' Though
lacking personality and charm she was gentle, friendly, and un-
pretentious. She tried to please Frederick, whom she married in
1733, and earned his lasting respect. They corresponded when he
was away, and after the separation which followed his accession
she looked back with pleasure on the Rheinsberg years.

In response to an inquiry as to his relations with the King,
Frederick explained that they were subject to constant change.
One moment he was in favour, the next in disgrace. 'You know,
my dear son,' he had written after the Kustrin period, 'that if my
children are obedient I love them very much.' They understood
their totalitarian parent only too well and were happiest when
they were away. Frederick liked the life with his regiment;
reading and music were his principal occupations. The Queen,
he added, with her miserable intrigues, was the sole cause of their
troubles. When Wilhelmina had left for Bayreuth she had tried
to marry Princess Amelia to the Prince of Wales. The King was
furious, and Seckendorff advised him to end these intrigues by
marrying Frederick to the Brunswick princess. Though she had
urged him to stand firm, and promised him her support, he had
refused to have another row with his father.

Acting on Frederick's advice Wilhelmina told Seckendorff of her trials at Bayreuth, at which he was not surprised. 'I know the Margrave intimately; he is false and suspicious.' She must be patient, for there was nothing to be done till he drank himself to death. With her miserly father, he added, there was equally little hope. He had intervals of generosity, but they soon passed and he regretted his promises. At Bayreuth she had sighed for her old home, but life at Berlin proved as disagreeable as ever. The King drank with his cronies till they could not stand, and he continued to abuse his abstemious son-in-law. The young couple were forced to go to the dull German comedies in which he found delight, and at the royal table there was not enough to eat. Her husband lost weight and his perpetual cough filled her with alarm. After dinner the King snored in an armchair, and his family had to look on. Wilhelmina had to read to her mother in the afternoon, an occupation she hated, and the conversation at dinner was as dull as an ordinary sermon. 'I was ill-treated on every side. I had not a sou and I was in continual pain. My only comfort was the thought that my death was at hand. For two whole years I lived on dry bread and water, as even soup was too much for my stomach.' Such patent exaggerations diminish the effect of these bitter complaints. The Queen bullied her, criticising her dress and her coiffure, treating her as if she were still a child, and pretending to believe that her ill-health was a sham. The King was sometimes kind, but she knew his inconstancy. 'I loved him tenderly, and but for the Queen I could have regained his heart.' She remained long enough in Berlin to witness the arrival of Frederick's *fiancée*, whom he introduced to 'the sister whom I adore.' Wilhelmina embraced her, but the frightened girl stood silent and motionless as a statue.

Cheering news arrived at last from Bayreuth; the Margrave's health was failing and he had fallen downstairs drunk. Frederick William wished to keep Wilhelmina and her husband in Berlin, where the latter would be better employed than in planting cabbages at home. At last, in August 1732, they were allowed to leave. The King was cold at the parting. 'It was the last time I saw this dear father, whose memory I shall always revere.' For once the Queen shed tears. Wilhelmina hardly recognised her infant daughter—'the prettiest child you could see.' The Margrave was thin and weak, and the doctor warned him that unless he renounced his liquor he was doomed. 'But he was so used to it that he could not pass the day without getting drunk twice.' Yet there seemed always to be some unexpected element of bitterness in her cup. The King desired her husband to take part in a campaign on the Rhine, and the latter wished it too. She feared he would expose himself to danger—'the dearest of my

possessions. We were one heart and one soul. We had no
secrets from one another, and I believe that no hearts were ever
so united as ours.' She persuaded the Margrave to veto the
project, but her father's imperious will prevailed. Frederick,
who visited her on his way to the campaign, assured her
that there would be no fighting and therefore no danger;
but her anxiety remained. 'Only those who love as I do
can imagine my sufferings, for I believed I should never see
him again.'

The Prince made himself beloved in the army and returned
safely, but reported that Frederick was a changed man. It was
only too true, as Wilhelmina discovered to her distress when he
passed through Bayreuth shortly afterwards. His sarcasms about
'the little prince' and 'the little court' were a shock. He seemed
to have lost his affection for her and to think of nothing but his
own plans. Their father, he declared, would not outlive the
month. 'I know I have made you great promises, but I shall not
be in a position to keep them. I will leave you half the sum he
lent you, and I think you will be quite satisfied with that.' Her
affection, rejoined Wilhelmina, had never been mercenary; she
asked nothing more than the continuance of his friendship, and
she did not wish for a sou if it caused him the slightest incon-
venience. 'No, no,' he replied, 'you will have the hundred
thousand crowns. People will be surprised to see me acting quite
differently from what they expected. They thought that I should
squander my treasures, and that money would become as common
in Berlin as stones. On the contrary I shall increase the army
and leave everything on the present footing. I shall treat my
mother with the greatest consideration and load her with honours,
but not let her interfere in my affairs. If she does it will be the
worse for her.'

Wilhelmina listened with distress and wondered if she was
dreaming. After inquiring about the affairs of the little state her
visitor proceeded to wound both her heart and her pride. 'When
your silly father-in-law is gone, I advise you to dismiss the whole
Court, and to live like ordinary gentlefolk in order to pay your
debts. You do not need so many people, and you must reduce
the salary of those you retain. You shall come to Berlin from
time to time; that will save you expense.' Her heart, already
full, overflowed at these indignities. 'Why do you cry? I will
banish this gloomy mood by the music of my flute.' She seated
herself at the harpsichord in an adjoining room, wetting it with
her tears, and one of her ladies stood in front of her to hide her
trouble. On the fourth day of his visit an urgent message from
the Queen begged him to return, since the King was in extremity.
Wilhelmina's loving heart always tried to find excuses for

Frederick, but she felt that he was no longer an understanding friend.

Frederick William recovered from the dropsy in 1735, and it was the Margrave of Bayreuth who went first. His last days were a trial, which Wilhelmina bore patiently, knowing that deliverance was at hand. Her husband had never murmured against his father except on the day he tried to cane him. Yet, just as the young couple, after four years of happy marriage, were about to take command, a new trouble arose. Believing that she would try to secure a share of political power, the Prince became less open with her. She promised not to interfere, but for the first time he was chilly and silent. His increasing coldness after his father's death moved her to tears, and her protest only evoked harsh words. Usually, she declares, she could control herself. 'Mais je suis femme et j'ai mes faiblesses comme les autres. Je me brouillai à toute outrance avec mon époux. J'étois dans un tel désespoir que je tombai en faiblesse.' It was the first rift within the lute, and it was quickly repaired. Fearing for her life, the Margrave's affection returned. He admitted that wrong ideas had been put into his head, and both parties begged forgiveness. She repeated her promise not to meddle in his business, asking in return that he should not listen to evil tongues. To prove her good-will she borrowed money to pay for two special embassies. His heart was so good, she declares, that he could not refuse the smallest request. He retained all the officials at Court, declaring that he had forgotten the past and wished everyone in his state to be happy. He gave her the Hermitage, a miniature Sans Souci, as a birthday present. It was there that she spent her happiest hours, with her garden, her music, her books, and the composition of her memoirs. For the first time in her adult life it seemed as if there was not a cloud in the sky. They danced for hours at a stretch, and the exercise did her good. 'Nous étions tous de la meilleure humeur du monde. Le Margrave aimait la joie et la bonne compagnie. Ses manières polies et obligéantes le faisoient adorer et nous vivons tous dans l'union la plus parfaite.' The Court became a brighter place, drinking was frowned on, a new palace and a fine opera-house were built, an orchestra was formed, and a university was founded at Erlangen. The only thing lacking to Frederick the Well-beloved and his wife was a male heir.

It was too good to last. Ill-health returned, and in 1739 the life of the Margravine was despaired of. She wrote tenderly to her father, craving forgiveness for all the worries she had involuntarily caused him, asking his blessing, and begging him to send her his French doctor Supperville, an able and cultivated man who became her valued friend. When the latter expressed his desire to transfer his allegiance from Berlin to Bayreuth she remarked that Frederick would object. Supperville replied that he was in high favour with the Crown Prince, but he knew him only too well. 'Ce prince a un grand génie, mais un mauvais cœur et un mauvais caractère. Il est dissimulé, soupçonneux, infatué d'amour-propre, ingrat, vicieux; ou je me trompe fort, ou il déviendra plus avare que le roi son père ne l'est à présent. Il n'a aucune religion et se fait une morale à sa guise; toute son étude ne tend qu'à éblouir le public; mais malgré sa dissimulation bien des gens ont démélé son caractère.' The Prince was trying to increase his knowledge, for the study of the sciences was one of his chief passions; but when he had learned all he needed himself, his teachers, like others, would be cast aside. Wilhelmina challenged this cruel analysis, but the Margrave, who entered the room during the argument, confirmed it. That Frederick had changed she already knew, and for the next few years his affection for her seemed almost dead. She consulted him about visiting her dying father, but received a snub. 'Que diable voulez-vous venir faire ici dans cette galère? Vous serez reçue comme un chien, et l'on vous saura peu de grè de vos beaux sentiments. Jouissez du repos et de plaisirs que vous goûtez à Bayreuth, et ne songez point à venir dans un enfer, où l'on ne fait que soupirer et souffrir, et où tout le monde est maltraité. La reine désapprouve comme moi votre beau projet.'

When her father passed away in May 1740 Wilhelmina wrote several times to the new King, and wrote from her heart. For six weeks, she complains, there was silence and then came a cold reply not in his own hand. Unfortunately for her veracity we possess several of his letters during this period seemingly as affectionate as ever. Several weeks later she was secretly informed that he was about to visit her incognito at the Hermitage. She nearly died of joy and welcomed him with open arms. His caresses, on the other hand, were strained, his face betrayed embarrassment, his talk was of indifferent things. He was equally distant when in the autumn she visited Berlin for the second time since her marriage. Mother and daughter opened their hearts to one another after the long estrangement: this time it was Sophia Dorothea who needed sympathy, for her day was over. That the new King was unpopular his sister learned from many sources, and she was not surprised. The old intimacy was gone. 'Je remarquai qu'il ne se souçioit plus de moi.' Even at Rheinsberg, where she was invited, she saw little of him. An attack of fever kept him indoors, but he was hard at work all the time. The brief intervals of relaxation were passed with the Huguenot Jordan, the Venetian Algarotti, and other literary friends; in the evening he played the flute or read poetry. She enjoyed her first meeting with Voltaire, but it was not a time of unalloyed happiness. Craving the loving confidence of her brother, she fretted when it was withheld. His conversation, she complains, was marked by embarrassment and seasoned with sarcasms on the state of the Margrave's finances. Only when the visit was over did she learn that the author of *Anti-Machiavel* had been immersed in the final preparations for the rape of Silesia.

The *Memoirs* break off in 1742, and the later portions were written in 1744 when the sky was dark with clouds. She could not know that the estrangement from her favourite brother was soon to end, and that their renewed friendship was to be her chief delight for the rest of her days. Even harder to bear was the wreck of a marriage which had turned out so much better than she had ever dared to hope. In dark hours she had found consolation in the loving companionship of the Sonsfeld and her niece Albertine, the daughter of General von Marwitz. 'Pour la Marwitz, je l'aimois de passion; nous n'avions rien de caché l'une pour l'autre. Je n'ai jamais vu un rapport de caractère pareil au nôtre; elle ne pouvoit rien sans moi ni moi sans elle; elle ne faisoit pas un pas sans me consulter, et elle étoit approuvée de tout le monde.' That the girl would steal her husband's heart she could not conceive. During convalescence after a dangerous illness the Margrave displayed extreme coldness to his wife and unconcealed satisfaction in the company of the attractive girl. A terrible jealousy possessed her heart. 'I could not forgive the Margrave for his altered attitude towards me. I had been blind for a year, and had not noticed a thousand little things which now stared me in the face.' The Marwitz, she believed, was still attached and virtuous, and would leave the Court if she noticed her distress. The faithful Sonsfeld spoke plainly to the Margrave, who made his excuses to his wife, attributed his behaviour to the fever, and resumed his tender ways. Wilhelmina redoubled her kindness to the Marwitz, and for a time it seemed as if the storm might pass. When the General, wounded in the Silesian campaign, invited his daughter for a long visit, she came to her mistress in tears. 'I must leave you, for charges against me are believed and my father wants to marry me.' Trusting in her loyalty, Wilhelmina persuaded her to remain in her service. They were almost always together, and when the Margravine saw her with the Margrave her behaviour was discreet. 'I slept tranquilly while they plotted my ruin. Can the reader believe she betrayed me?' It became more credible when the girl returned from the visit to her father a changed being. Treated coolly by her mistress on account of her new-found arrogance, she complained to the Margrave, who in turn became cool to his wife once more.

1741, we are told, was the last tranquil year, and in 1742 a new phase of her life opened, more difficult than any through which she had passed. She confesses to having committed political but not moral mistakes. At last she discovered that the evil was too deeply rooted to be cured. The curtain falls on a poignant cry of distress. 'This girl had unbounded ambition. To satisfy this passion it was necessary to lead the Margrave into dissipations to which he was only too much disposed in order to divert him from his official duties. It was also necessary to throw dust in my eyes by informing me of the principal things and to lull my suspicions by the confidence which the Margrave showed me. The Marwitz reserved to herself the distribution of appointments and favours and above all the finances. She was consumed by the desire to shine. Realising his weakness for her she used it to secure power. She believed that in maintaining my confidence, and in avoiding all occasion of arousing my suspicion, she would blind me while becoming so formidable that, if I saw through her game, I should be powerless to thwart her. Indeed her conduct and that of the Margrave was so discreet that I noticed nothing of their secret understanding.'

The unfolding of the drama of deceit and infidelity was doubtless considered too distressing a theme both for the *Memoirs* and her letters, and the last sixteen years of Wilhelmina's life must be constructed from her correspondence with her brother and Voltaire. Here she appears in a more attractive light than in the *Memoirs*, written or revised when she was ill and depressed; for her letters deal less with politics and persons than with the arts. Her daughter's marriage to Karl Eugèn, the Duke of Württemberg, later the enemy of Schiller, was a failure, but she does not appear to have broken her heart about it. Her supreme consolation was the knowledge that she had recovered the affectionate confidence of her brother, was initiated into his plans, shared his anxieties, his triumphs, and his fame. Had she continued the *Memoirs* her story might have been of greater value to the political historian. No one knew her character and thoughts so well as he, and no one admired her so much. Her last letter was to him. They were two bodies, he declared, and one soul. 'It is to her that I owe in great measure what little good there is in me,' he remarked to de Catt. 'The most affectionate, the most faithful friendship united the King and his noble sister,' he wrote in a glowing tribute in his *Memoirs*. She was a princess of rare worth, he added, with a fine intellect, a special talent for the arts, and a generous heart. The Margravine had her failings, but her brother's carefully chosen words are true. So long as the world retains its interest in the meteoric rise of Prussia and the formidable personality of Frederick the Great the vivid *Memoirs* of Wilhelmina will continue to be read.

Bibliographical Note.—A critical edition is badly needed. The best biographies are by Edith Cuttell, *Wilhelmina, Margravine of Bayreuth*, 2 vols., and Fester, *Die Bayreuther Schwester Friedrichs des Grossen*. There is a sympathetic study in Arvède Barine, *Princesses et Grandes Dames*. Sainte-Beuve's essays are in *Causeries du Lundi*, XII. Her correspondence with Frederick the Great is edited by Volz in 2 vols., her correspondence with Voltaire by Horn. The historical value of the *Memoirs* was investigated for the first time in Ranke's address to the Prussian Academy, *Ueber die Glaubwürdigkeit der Memoiren der Markgräfin von Bayreuth*, in *Abhandlungen und Versuche, Erste Sammlung*, 57–70. A more detailed and even more devastating analysis is in Droysen, *Geschichte der Preussischen Politik*, vol. iv, 33–96. The best accounts of the early life of Frederick the Great are by Koser, *Friedrich der Grosse als Kronprinz*, and Lavisse, *La Jeunesse du Grand Frédéric*, and *Frédéric le Grand avant l'Avenement*. Carlyle, *Frederick the Great*, vols. 1–3, is a literary rather than an historical masterpiece. For foreign affairs Droysen, *Friedrich Wilhelm I*, 2 vols., is indispensable. Berney, *Friedrich der Grosse*, vol. 1, is the best recent survey. The administrative reforms of Frederick William I are admirably summarised in Hintze, *Die Hohenzollern*. The best account of the Old Dessauer is in Krauske's massive Introduction to *Briefwechsel Friedrich Wilhelms I mit Leopold von Anhalt-Dessau*; of Grumbkow in Koser's Introduction to *Briefwechsel Friedrich des Grossen mit Grumbkow*. Ranke's *Zwölf Bücher Preussischer Geschichte* should be read in the annotated edition published by the Prussian Academy. The reigns of Frederick William I and Frederick the Great are described in vols. 2 and 3. Reddaway, *Frederick the Great*, is still the best English biography. Pierre Gaxotte, *Frederick the Great*, contains a useful bibliography.

CHAPTER XI

LORD HERVEY AND GEORGE II

LORD HERVEY'S *Memoirs* are unique in English literature, for nowhere else do we find such a photographic picture of Court life over a term of years. Known to his age merely as a clever intriguer, he sprang into fame a century after his death, just as Pepys, after a similar interval, was promoted from an Admiralty official to the greatest diarist in the world. The Vice-Chamberlain to George II and Queen Caroline, judging by contemporary references, was not a pleasant person. 'I think he has fewer amiabilities and more disagreeables in him than most people,' wrote Hanbury Williams. 'He has certainly parts and wits,' declared old Sarah Duchess of Marlborough in 1737, 'but is the most wretched profligate that ever was born, besides ridiculous; a painted face and not a tooth in his head.' Lady Mary Wortley Montagu, a not unfriendly witness, coined the well-known aphorism that the human family consisted of men, women, and Herveys. Pope pierced him with his rapier in some of the bitterest satires in the language:

> this bug with gilded wings,
> This painted child of dirt that stinks and sings,
> Fop at the toilet, flatterer at the board,
> Now trips a lady, and now struts a lord.

Nero had a minion named Sporus, and it is as Sporus that Hervey survived before the publication of his *Memoirs* gave him a better title to immortality:

> that thing of silk
> Sporus, that mere white curd of asses' milk,
> Who, at the ear of Eve, familiar toad,
> Half froth, half venom, spits himself abroad.

Sir George Young, the biographer and champion of Poor Fred, dismisses him as a blackguard, and good haters like Hervey cannot complain if they are hated in return. His character affects the value of his judgments but not the brilliance or interest of his narrative. Standing at the heart of events with his notebook in his hand, a keen observer and a master of caustic phraseology, he brings his actors back to life by a thousand deft touches of his brush. He is as intimate as Pepys, as pungent as Saint-Simon, as skilful a recorder of conversation as Boswell. Without Hervey and Horace Walpole our knowledge of the personal side of English politics during the eighteenth century would be meagre indeed.

John, Lord Hervey, the eldest of the first Earl of Bristol's seventeen children by his second marriage, was born in 1696.

Neither of his parents meant anything to him. From his mother he inherited the persistent ill-health—gall-stones, epilepsy, and other troubles—which embittered his life, and gave him a reputation of effeminacy among his full-blooded contemporaries. She taught him to be an expert card-player, an accomplishment which enabled him to increase his income without much effort in a gaming age. The usual Continental tour, following the years at Westminster and Cambridge, led him to Paris and to Herrenhausen, where budding politicians were anxious to peg out claims. When the Hanoverians arrived in England he became Gentleman of the Bedchamber to the Prince of Wales, afterwards George II. In 1720 he married the beautiful but rather mindless Molly Lepel, a Maid of Honour to Caroline, Princess of Wales, who bore him eight children. The bridegroom was equally good-looking. Gay described him as 'Hervey fair of face,' Pulteney and Chesterfield in a joint ballad as 'Hervey the handsome.' It was, however, a feminine rather than a masculine type of beauty, and he was conscious of the feminine elements in his character. If a stranger were to read his letters to Stephen Fox (the future first Lord Ilchester), he confessed, he would certainly conclude that they came rather from a mistress than a friend. On another occasion he describes how he blushed at a dinner-party. To Pope he was Lord Fanny, an amphibious thing.

The death of his half-brother in 1723 brought him the courtesy title of Lord Hervey, the reversion of the earldom, and a family seat in Parliament. He was elected for Bury St Edmunds in 1725 but took his duties very lightly, for his main concern in these early years was his miserable health. His hope that the accession of George II would bring him some office was disappointed, but he was allotted a pension of a thousand a year till a vacancy occurred. His condition improved so greatly as the result of adopting a milk diet and a year in Italy in 1728–29 that he was at last ready to begin his political career. He was appointed Vice-Chamberlain (the Chamberlain being the Duke of Grafton, a grandson of Charles II) and a member of the Privy Council. It was not a high post, but it opened the way to the enduring friendship with the Queen which brought him his chance and gave us the *Memoirs*. Lord Rosebery describes him as the tame cat of the family circle.

The working up of his journals into the finished article seems to have begun in 1733. The story begins with a brief statement of the author's credentials. Having lodged all the year round at Court, he must have been deaf and blind not to have seen and heard much that more distant observers could never know. He was immune to the temptations of flattery, since his narrative would not be published till after his death. He wrote to inform rather than to please, excluding what was generally known. To diminish the impression of egotism he would refer to himself in the third person. 'I leave those ecclesiastical heroes of their own romances, Retz and Burnet, to aim at that useless imaginary glory of being thought to influence every considerable event they relate, and I very freely declare my part in this drama was only that of the Chorus in the ancient tragedies, who, by being constantly on the stage, saw everything that was done and made their own comments upon the scene without mixing in the action or making any considerable figure in the performance.' His sole object was to describe what he had seen: that it was not always a pretty story was not his fault. 'I am determined to report everything just as it is, or at least as it appears to me; and those who have a curiosity to see courts and courtiers dissected must bear with the dirt they find in laying open such minds with as little nicety and as much patience as in a dissection of their bodies; if they wanted to see that operation they must submit to the stench.'

The drama opens with vivid sketches of the principal performers on the Parliamentary stage. Pulteney, the ablest member of the Opposition, is painted in dark colours, and we must bear in mind that a bitter quarrel had taken place. 'He was a man of most inflexible pride, immeasurable ambition, and so impatient of any superiority that he grudged the power of doing good even to his benefactor, and envied the favour of the Court to one who called him in to share it. He had as much lively ready wit as ever man was master of, and was, before politics soured his temper and engrossed his thoughts, the most agreeable and coveted companion of his time. He was changeable in his wishes, vehement in the pursuit of them, and dissatisfied in the possession. He had strong passions, was seldom sincere but when they ruled him, cool and unsteady in his friendships, warm and immovable in his hate.' The author had lived in friendship and intimacy with him for many years till the deterioration of his character led to a breach. 'Those who thought that Mr Pulteney was never good-humoured, pleasing, honourable, friendly and benevolent, knew him not for long; for no two men ever differed more from one another in temper, conduct and character, than he from himself in the compass of a few years.' This rapid and complete change sounds unconvincing; yet the final verdict is that, with all his imperfections, he was a great man.

Of Bolingbroke Hervey speaks with less authority, for they had never been friends. That he had served the Pretender ruined him with the Whigs, and he was hated by the Jacobites, who believed that he had betrayed his Stuart master. His character was so mixed that he possessed qualities which the greatest might envy and others of which the worst would be ashamed. 'He had fine talents, a natural eloquence, great quickness, a happy memory, and very extensive knowledge; but he was vain much beyond the general run of mankind, timid, false, injudicious and ungrateful, elated and insolent in power, dejected and servile in disgrace. Few people ever believed him without being deceived or trusted him without being betrayed. He was one to whom prosperity was no advantage and adversity no instruction. Those who were most partial to him could not but allow that he was ambitious without fortitude and enterprising without resolution; that he was fawning without insinuation and insincere without art; that he had admirers without friendship and followers without attachment; parts without probity, knowledge without conduct, and experience without judgment.' Eighteenth-century writers loved these metallic antitheses, but in the case of Macaulay's 'brilliant knave' the strong lights and shadows require no great subtlety of delineation.

The portrait of Walpole is the most convincing of the introductory series, for Hervey saw him at close quarters for many years and the stage is dominated by his ample figure. 'No man ever was blessed with a clearer head, a truer or quicker judgment, or a deeper insight into mankind; he knew the strength and weakness of everybody he had to deal with, and how to make his advantage of both. He had more warmth of affection and friendship for some particular people than one could have believed it possible for any one who had been so long raking in the dirt of mankind to be capable of feeling for so worthless a species of animals. Whether his negligence of his enemies, and never stretching his power to gratify his resentment of the sharpest injury, was policy or constitution, I shall not determine; but I do not believe anybody who knows these times will deny that no minister ever was more outraged or less apparently revengeful. In all occurrences and at all times and in all difficulties he was constantly present and cheerful. There never was any minister to whom access was so easy and so frequent, nor whose answers were more explicit. He knew how to oblige when he bestowed, and not to shock when he denied; to govern without oppressing, and conquer without triumph. He pursued his ambition without curbing his pleasures, and his pleasures without neglecting his business; he did the latter with ease, and indulged himself in the other without giving scandal or offence. In private life, and to all who had any dependence upon him, he was kind and indulgent; he was generous without ostentation and an economist without penuriousness; not insolent in success nor irresolute in distress; faithful to his friends, and not inveterate to his foes.' That is not quite the whole Sir Robert, for we miss a reference to his cynical debasement of the moral currency of public life.

The narrative opens with the accession of George II, when

Walpole was momentarily replaced by Sir Spencer Compton, Speaker of the House of Commons and Treasurer to the new ruler, but personally a cipher. Hervey paints the usual repulsive picture of the courtiers turning shamelessly away from the fallen minister and worshipping the rising sun. 'There were none among the many his power had obliged (excepting General Churchill and Lord Hervey) who did not in public as notoriously decline and fear his notice as they used industriously to seek and covet it.' The author sent Walpole an unsigned letter, introducing himself as 'one of the many you have obliged, and one of the few who will never forget it.' A scheme was afoot, he continued, to use the ex-Premier to secure a lavish Civil List for the new ruler and then to cast him aside. Walpole showed the letter to the new Queen, who assured him of her interest and support. Her intervention proved decisive, for Mrs Howard, the *maîtresse en titre*, of whom her lover had begun to tire, was kept in the background and the keen-witted Caroline advanced to the centre of the stage. The *Memoirs* are a drama without a hero, for neither the monarch, the Prime Minister nor the author himself can qualify for that *rôle*. But there is a heroine—a woman of solid character, unflinching courage and considerable intelligence, utterly unromantic, devoid of illusions, content to enjoy the reality of power without the form. Caroline of Anspach is Hervey's masterpiece, and no more convincing portrait is to be found in historical literature. Seldom, declares Carlyle, had foolish husband so wise a wife.

'When the King was Prince there were so few occasions for the Queen to show her credit with him that some were apt to imagine this latent dormant power was much less than it proved itself when the time came that made it worth her while to try, show and exert it. But as soon as ever the Prince became King the whole world began to find out that her will was the sole spring on which every movement in the Court turned; and though His Majesty lost no opportunity to declare that the Queen never meddled with his business, yet nobody was simple enough to believe it. Her power was unrivalled and unbounded. She managed this deified image as the heathen priests used to do the oracles of old, when, kneeling and prostrate before the altars of a pageant god, they received with the greatest devotion and reverence those directions in public which they had before instilled and regulated in private.' Everyone knew who stood at the helm, and the satirists were quickly at work.

You may strut, dapper George, but 'twill all be in vain;
We know 'tis Queen Caroline, not you, that reign.

That her tact was equal to her ambition was shown by her encouraging her unfaithful husband to retain his deaf and middle-aged mistress, Mrs Howard, afterwards Lady Suffolk, for fear of making room for a successor whom he might really love. In Hervey's words, Mrs Howard's apartment, if she were banished, would not be empty for long.

It was not till more than a year after his accession that George II summoned his elder son from Hanover, where he had been left when his parents came to England in 1714. His ministers told him that if the Prince's coming were longer delayed an address from Parliament and the voice of the nation would oblige him to act. 'These persuasions prevailed, and the King, as children take physic, forced himself to swallow this bitter draught for fear of having it poured down his throat in case he did not take it quietly and voluntarily.' He was friendly enough at first, but he and his son knew nothing of each other. The affections of the parents were centred on their second son William, Duke of Cumberland, who, they hoped, would follow them on the English throne, leaving Hanover to Frederick. 'The Prince's character at his first coming over, though little more respectable, seemed much more amiable than it was upon opening himself and being better known. For though there appeared nothing in him to be admired, yet there seemed nothing in him to be hated—nothing great nor nothing vicious. He was as false as his capacity would allow him to be, and was more capable in that walk than in any other, never having the least hesitation in telling any lie that served his future purpose. He had a much weaker understanding, and, if possible, a more obstinate temper, than his father; that is, more tenacious of opinions he had once formed, though less capable of ever having right ones. Had he had one grain of merit at the bottom of his heart, one should have had compassion for him in the situation to which his miserable poor head soon reduced him, for his case in short was this: he had a father that abhorred him, a sister that betrayed him, a brother set up to pique, and a set of servants that neither were of use to him nor were capable of being of use to him nor desirous of being so.' The King kept him at arm's length, allowed him only half the income he had himself enjoyed as Prince of Wales, and made the Queen, instead of the Prince, Regent during his absence from England. If he had been such a futile mediocrity as Hervey suggests he would have had an easier life, for his parents and Walpole would have had no ground for dreading him as a potential leader of the Opposition.

What was the cause of the hatred and contempt expressed in Hervey's *Memoirs* which have long coloured the judgment of historians? The explanation is not to be found in the two mutilated manuscripts which survive, but we learn enough from other sources to reconstruct his part in the story. As Vice-Chamberlain he saw a good deal of the Prince after his arrival in

England, and for two years they got on well together. Frederick
was godfather to Hervey's third son, and when the epileptic
courtier had a fit he sat by his bedside all day. Having literary
leanings, Hervey helped him with his verses and they collaborated
in an unsuccessful play. Stephen Fox seems to have been a little
jealous of their intimacy, for in 1731 Hervey wrote denying that
he ever wished to love the new friend as much as the old. By the
end of the same year, however, an icy wind swept over the land-
scape. 'That fool plagues my heart out,' wrote Hervey to Fox;
'he is as false as he is silly.' In March 1732 it was noted that the
Prince had transferred his political patronage to Bubb Dodington.

It was the old story of *cherchez la femme!* A certain Miss Vane,
better known as Vanella, daughter of Lord Barnard, had been a
Maid of Honour to Queen Caroline, and had recently switched over
from Hervey to the Prince. The latter claimed the paternity of a
son born in June 1732 and christened him Fitzfrederick, though
Hervey and Lord Harrington were asserted by wagging tongues to
have quite as good a right. On discovering that the Prince's
friendship had rapidly cooled, Hervey wrote an angry letter to
Vanella, blaming her for treachery in undermining his influence
and threatening to expose her unless she recovered the lost ground.
The Prince was incensed by his threat to his new mistress and the
last remnants of friendship disappeared. The King, Queen, and
Walpole, all enemies of the Prince, blamed Hervey's conduct, and
for a time he lost favour at Court. Even without their quarrels
about a worthless woman the partnership would doubtless have
come into an open scandal. Hervey had been glad to have a foot
in both camps. But if compelled to choose, he naturally sided
with the reigning sovereigns, not the heir, for without the favour
of the Queen he would have been little more than a cipher.

After sketching the chief actors on the stage the writer proceeds
to describe a painful crisis in his career. In 1729, on returning
from his long sojourn in Italy, he was tempted by the Leader of
the Opposition. 'He loved Mr Pulteney and had obligations to
Sir Robert Walpole. He lived in long intimacy and personal
friendship with the former, and in his public and political conduct
he always attached himself to the latter. But as the dissensions
of these two men were now grown to such a height that it was
impossible to live well with both, Lord Hervey at his return found
he should be brought to the long-feared disagreeable necessity of
quitting the one or the other.' His wife, we are assured, loved
Pulteney and hated Walpole, who had unsuccessfully made love
to her. During her husband's residence abroad she and Pulteney
had concocted a plan by which Lord Bristol should be induced to
indemnify his son for resigning his Court pension of £1000 a year.
The father, himself a member of the Opposition, was prepared to

settle £600 a year on his heir if he would oppose the Government in the House of Commons. At this point the author admits that he played his cards badly and should have rejected the project out of hand. Fearing to anger Pulteney, he had replied that his father would never consent.

Pulteney concluded that the only obstacle to the success of his scheme lay in the uncertainty as to Lord Bristol's pecuniary response, and accordingly he pressed the latter to play his part. Six hundred was not a thousand, but Pulteney had other arrows in his quiver. The Government, he argued, could not possibly last six months longer. Walpole had shattered the Whig party into fragments; the King was hated, the Queen despised, the Prince of Wales both hated and despised. When Hervey inquired what sort of Ministry the Opposition proposed, the clumsy tempter replied that some had hopes of a popular Government, others perhaps of a new King under new restrictions. 'But who is that King to be?' interjected Hervey. 'Not the Pretender, I hope?' 'Why the little Duke (of Cumberland) or anybody but this puppy, this huffing military jackanapes of a King, or the timid, poor, mean, weak wretch, the Prince of Wales.' The pretext for such a revolutionary step would be found in the continuation of the Hessian troops in English pay for the defence of Hanover. Pulteney added that Walpole would never allow anyone to share his power, and that, if he himself took office, there was nothing Hervey could not ask. The author was now forced to say 'with the air of a mean shuffle and double dealing, which he might have done with openness and reputation, which was throwing up his pension and yet acting on with those who had procured it for him.' Pulteney's invitation to join the Opposition and Lord Bristol's conditional offer of an allowance were declined. The Court pension was resigned, and the Prime Minister was asked to procure him a position which he would not be ashamed to own. The friendship with Pulteney quickly cooled and ended in a duel when the Opposition chief printed an abusive reply to a pamphlet which he wrongly attributed to Hervey. Walpole was assured of his follower's unchanging fidelity. There had never been and there never was to be any love lost between the two, but Hervey sincerely believed the Prime Minister the best man for the highest post.

When the narrative resumes after the violent hiatus of 1730–32 the author has become a prominent figure at Court. He used to describe the debates in Parliament to the Queen, who in turn told him of noteworthy conversations in which she had taken part. The King was an equally interested listener to his reports during the passionate debates on the Excise Bill in 1733. 'During the whole progress of this Bill, which lasted about three weeks, the

King was under the greatest anxiety for the event of it. Lord
Hervey and Mr Pelham were with him and the Queen almost
every day to give them accounts, not only how people voted and
talked in the House, but how they looked, how they spoke, how
they caballed in the town. Every division showing a decrease in
the majority, the King grew more and more uneasy.' One day,
too impatient to wait till the evening, he had made Hervey write
from the House at five o'clock. When the author came to St
James's Palace after the sitting the King took him into the Queen's
bedchamber and kept him there without dinner till nearly three in
the morning, asking him ten thousand questions. The Bill proved
so unpopular, partly owing to its attempt to control the drink
traffic, that Walpole reluctantly dropped it and offered to resign.
'This dance,' he declared to a meeting of his supporters, 'it will
no further go'; and for once there were tears in his eyes. It was
a statesmanlike scheme and would have yielded a substantial sum
to the revenue, but the country was too excited to consider it on
its merits. 'The Queen chid him extremely for having so ill an
opinion of her as to think it possible for her to be so mean, so
cowardly, and so ungrateful, as to accept of such an offer, and
assured him that as long as she lived she would not abandon him.
When Sir Robert Walpole made the same offer to the King, His
Majesty (as the Queen told me) made the most kingly, the most
sensible, and the most resolute answer that it was possible for a
wise, a just, and a great prince to make to the most able and
most meritorious servant; but whether she dictated the words
before he spoke them, or embellished them afterwards, I know
not.' On learning that the Bill was lost, the tears ran down the
Queen's cheeks and for some time she could not speak. The King
asked for the names of the deserters and loaded each of them with
abuse. The author had energetically supported the Bill and was
rewarded by a peerage.

Hervey's services were by no means confined to his support of
the ill-fated Excise Bill, for he was the Queen's permanent partner
in the unceasing effort to keep Walpole at the helm. George II,
he declares, possessed physical but not moral courage, and the
anger aroused by misrepresentation of the Bill might have induced
him to bow to the storm had not domestic influences been at work.
On his accession he had held Walpole at arm's length, avoiding
every opportunity of speaking to him in public, so anxious was he
to show that he was his own master. All this had gradually
changed. 'He very apparently now took all occasions to declare
him his first, or rather his sole minister; singled him out always
in the drawing-room, and received no application (military affairs
excepted) but from him; and most certainly, if he loved anybody
in the world except the Queen, he had not only an opinion of the

statesman but an affection for the man. When Lord Hervey gave
him accounts of attacks in the House and the things Sir Robert
had said in defence of himself and in retaliation on his adversaries,
the King would often cry out, with colour flushing his cheeks and
tears sometimes in his eyes, and with a vehement oath: He is a
brave fellow; he has more spirit than any man I ever knew. The
Queen, if she was by, always joined in chorus on such occasions;
and Lord Hervey in these partial moments never failed to make
the most he could of his friend and patron's cause.'

Hervey points out that the Queen had changed the King's plan
of government. He had intended that all his ministers should be
clerks, not to give advice, but to receive orders. After five years
on the throne, however, she had convinced him that he should
have one outstanding minister and that Walpole's incomparable
abilities made him the only possible choice. 'But this work,
which she now saw completed, had been the work of long time,
much trouble, and great contrivance. For though, by a superiority
of understanding, thorough knowledge of his temper, and much
patience in her own, she could work him by degrees to any point
where she had a mind to drive him, yet she was forced to do it by
slow degrees and with great caution. For, as he was infinitely
jealous of being governed, he was never to be led but by invisible
reins, neither was it ever possible for her to make him adopt her
opinion but by instilling her sentiments in such a manner as made
him think they rose originally from himself. She always at first
gave in to all his actions, though never so extravagant, and made
him imagine any change she wrought in them to be an afterthought
of his own. To contradict his will directly was always the way
to strengthen it, and to labour to convince was to confirm him.
Besides all this he was exceedingly passionate, and his temper
upon these occasions was a sort of iron reversed, for the hotter it
was the harder it was to bend, and if ever it was susceptible of any
impression or capable of being turned, it was only when it was
quite cool.'

CHAPTER XII

LORD HERVEY AND QUEEN CAROLINE

QUEEN CAROLINE could never have too much of Lord Hervey's company. Their pathological hatred for the Prince of Wales was a bond of union, but there were better reasons for their friendship. She was a woman of intellectual tastes with a *penchant* for philosophy, while the Court of George II was the dullest place on earth and the King the greatest of its bores. Hervey could feed her with first-hand information about Parliament and the latest gossip about society. 'Wednesdays and Saturdays, the King's days for hunting, he had her to himself for four or five hours, Her Majesty always hunting in a chaise; and as she neither saw nor cared to see much of the chase, she had undertaken to mount Lord Hervey the whole summer (who loved hunting as little as she did) so that he might ride constantly by the side of her chaise, and entertain her whilst other people were entertaining themselves with hearing dogs bark and seeing crowds gallop. Sunday and Monday Lord Hervey lay constantly in London; every other morning he used to walk with the Queen and her daughters at Hampton Court. His real business in London was pleasure; but as he always told the King it was to pick up news, to hear what people said, to see how they looked, and to inform Their Majesties what was thought by all parties of the present posture of affairs, he by these means made his pleasure in town and his interest at Court reciprocally conducive to each other. These excursions put it also in his power to say things as from other people's mouths which he did not dare to venture from his own.' The accomplished and not over-scrupulous courtier mixed his counsels with adroit eulogies of the monarch's courage and wisdom. 'The King's vanity had such an ostrich digestion for flattery that, let the dose be ever so potent, there was no danger of making it too strong for his appetite.'

One of the most justly celebrated passages in Lord Hervey's *Memoirs* is the full-length portrait of the Queen, which ranks with the masterpieces of Clarendon and Burnet. 'Her predominant passion was pride, and the darling pleasure of her soul was power; but she was forced to gratify the one and gain the other, as some people do health, by a strict and painful régime which few besides herself could have had patience to support or resolution to adhere to. She was at least seven or eight hours *tête-à-tête* with the King every day, during which she was generally saying what she did not think, assenting to what she did not believe, and praising what she did not approve; for they were seldom of the same opinion, and he too fond of his own ever at first to dare to contra-

dict it. She used to give him her opinion as jugglers do a card,
by changing it imperceptibly, and making him believe he held the
same with that he first pitched upon. But that which made
these *tête à têtes* seem heaviest was that, as he neither liked reading
or being read to (unless it was to sleep), she was forced, like a
spider, to spin out of her own bowels all the conversation with
which the fly was taken. However, to all this she submitted for
the sake of power and for the reputation of having it; for she was
with regard to this as some men are with regard to their amours,
the vanity of being thought to possess what she desired was
equal to the pleasure of the possession itself. Her every thought,
word and act therefore tended and was calculated to preserve her
influence there; to him she sacrificed her time, for him she morti-
fied every inclination; she looked, spake and breathed but for
him, was a weathercock to every capricious blast of his uncertain
temper, and governed him (if influence so gained can bear the
name of government) by being as great a slave to him thus ruled
as any other wife could be to a man who ruled her. For all the
tedious hours she spent then in watching him while he slept, or
the heavier task of entertaining him while he was awake, her
single consolation was in reflecting she had power, and that people
in coffee-houses and *ruelles* (private circles) were saying she
governed the country without knowing how dear the government
of it cost her.'

Caroline liked reading and the conversation of men of wit and
learning. 'But she did not dare to indulge herself as much as she
wished to do in this pleasure for fear of the King, who often
rebuked her for dabbling in all that lettered nonsense (as he termed
it), called her a pedant, and said she loved to spend her time more
like a schoolmistress than a Queen. The King used often to brag
of the contempt he had for books and letters; to say how much
he hated all that stuff from his infancy; and that he remembered
when he was a child he did not hate reading and learning merely
as other children do upon account of the confinement, but because
he despised it and felt as if he was doing something mean and
below him.' It is not a pretty picture, but happy royal marriages
had never been the order of the day. George II admired his wife,
but fundamentally he loved no one but himself.

The author's relations with Caroline were not only those of the
courtier but the friend, and he could stand up to her when he
thought she was wrong. 'Lord Hervey was this summer (1734)
in greater favour with the Queen, and consequently with the King,
than ever; they told him everything and talked of everything
before him. The Queen sent for him every morning as soon as
the King went from her, and kept him while she breakfasted till
the King returned, which was generally an hour and half at least.

By her interest, too, she got the King to add a thousand pounds a year to his salary, which was a new subject of complaint to the Prince. She gave him a hunter, and on hunting days he never stirred from her side. She always called him her child, her pupil, and her charge; used to tell him perpetually that his being so impertinent and daring to contradict her so continually was owing to his knowing she could not live without him, and often said: It is well I am so old, or I should be talked of for this creature. Lord Hervey made prodigious court to her and really loved and admired her.' The King trusted his wife, and there was no reason for jealousy.

Caroline and the Vice-Chamberlain agreed about most political questions, but the harmony was threatened when she supported her husband's desire to intervene in the War of the Polish Succession. George II, loving armies, despising civil affairs, and fancying himself as a commander, longed to strike a blow at the French. 'He could not bear,' he said, 'the thought of growing old in peace and rusting in the Cabinet whilst other princes were busied in war and shining in the field.' Caroline had no love of war, but she could never forget the land of her birth. 'Wherever the interest of Germany and the honour of the Empire were concerned, her thoughts and reasonings were often as German and Imperial as if England had been out of the question.' Walpole, the most pacific of our prime ministers, fought hard for neutrality and told her: 'Madam, there are fifty thousand men slain this year (1734) in Europe and not one Englishman.' Hervey backed up his arguments so vigorously that for once he received very rough replies. He returned to the charge the same evening in a long and able Memorandum, and had the satisfaction, not of converting her, but of being received next day rather with added than diminished favour. Walpole had his way and kept England out of war, though only for another five years.

The Prime Minister realised Hervey's value as an ally, and they often discussed political tactics. He visited his beloved Norfolk home twice a year, for ten days in the summer and twenty in November. On the evening before starting for his autumn holiday in 1734 he went from Hervey's lodgings to bid the Queen good-bye. He found her coughing incessantly, her head aching and heavy, her eyes half-shut, her cheeks flushed, her pulse quick, her flesh hot, her spirits low, her breathing oppressed. The anxious minister implored her to take care of herself. 'Madam, your life is of such consequence to your husband, to your children, to this country, and indeed to many other countries, that any neglect of your health is really the greatest immorality you can be guilty of. When one says these sort of things to princes, I know, madam, they must sound like flattery; but consider particular circumstances, and Your Majesty will quickly find what I say to be strictly true. Your Majesty knows that this country is entirely in your hands, that the fondness the King has for you, the opinion he has of your affection, and the regard he has for your judgment, are the only reins by which it is possible to restrain the natural violences of his temper or to guide him through any part where he is wanted to go. Should any accident happen to Your Majesty, who can tell into what hands he would fall; who can tell what would become of him, of his children, and of us all? Some woman, Your Majesty knows, would govern him, for the company of men he cannot bear.' The Queen, with tears in her eyes, challenged his estimate of her importance and returned the compliment. 'He has now such a love for you, and so just a value for your services, as well as such an opinion of your abilities, that, were I removed, everything would go on just as it does.' Walpole interjected that he could do nothing without her; he could merely suggest, while she must execute. 'You, madam, are the sole mover of this court; whenever your hand stops, everything must stand still.' His proposal to postpone his journey was disallowed, and he returned to Hervey's room to report the conversation.

The more Hervey saw of his master the more he despised him. George II had little heart, less head, and no manners, and the chief sufferers were the members of his family. He was particularly disagreeable after his periodical visits to his old home. In the lifetime of his father everyone had imagined that he loved England and hated Germany. This was only part of the game of opposition which Hanoverian heirs were always playing, and on his accession he threw off the mask. His vanity was flattered by the title of King of England, but the charm of Hanover was that there he could do as he liked. On returning to London in 1735 he showed in his usual boorish way the call of the blood. 'After this last visit Hanover had so completed the conquest of his affections that there was nothing English ever commended in his presence that he did not always show or pretend to show was surpassed by something of the same kind in Germany. No English or even French cook could dress a dinner; no English confectioner set out a dessert; no English player could act; no English coachman could drive, or English jockey ride, nor were any English horses fit to be drove or ridden; no Englishman knew how to come into a room, nor any English woman how to dress herself; nor were there any diversions in England, public or private, nor any man or woman in England whose conversation was to be borne—the one, as he said, talking of nothing but their dull politics, and the others of nothing but their ugly clothes. Whereas at Hanover all these things were in the utmost perfection.

'The men, declared the King, were patterns of politeness,

11

bravery and gallantry; the women, of beauty, wit and entertainment; his troops there were the bravest in the world, his counsellors the wisest, his manufacturers the most ingenious, his subjects the wisest, and at Hanover, in short, plenty reigned, magnificence resided, arts flourished, diversions abounded, riches flowed, and everything was in the utmost perfection that contributes to make a prince great or a people blessed. In truth he hated the English, looked upon them all as king-killers and republicans, grudged them their riches as well as their liberty, thought them all overpaid, and said to Lady Sundon one day as she was waiting at dinner, just after he returned from Germany, that he was forced to distribute his favours here very differently from the manner in which he bestowed them at Hanover; that there he rewarded people for doing their duty and serving him well, but that here he was obliged to enrich people for being rascals and buy them not to cut his throat.' We must take this brilliant passage with a grain of salt; but it is true enough that the ill-tempered monarch took a malicious delight in hurting the feelings of his entourage, and that, in Hervey's words, everybody who came near him had some share of his bilious temper at this time. The deeper reason for his lack of self-control was that he had found a new mistress in Mme Walmoden, whom he had bought from her husband and longed to rejoin. With such a foolish little peacock on the throne there could be no more of the Stuart nonsense about the divinity that doth hedge a king. Several of our rulers have been worse men, but none has commanded less affection or respect.

Queen Caroline remained a German princess, though she controlled her tongue more successfully than her foolish and irascible partner. At times she would speak indignantly about the limitation of the power of a king—'the humble servant of the Parliament, the pensioner of his people and a puppet sovereignty that was forced to go to them for every shilling he wanted, that was obliged to court those who were always abusing him, and could do nothing of himself. A good deal of that liberty that made them so insolent, if she could do it, should be much abridged.' When she was on her guard she would praise our free institutions, declaring that no sensible prince would try to take them away; but this lip-service never impressed the Vice-Chamberlain. 'At the very moment Her Majesty was uttering these truths, the love of rule, the thirst of dominion, and the jealousy of prerogative were so strongly implanted in her, the German and the Queen so rooted in her mind, that the King himself had not more at heart all the trappings and pageantry of sovereignty than she the essential parts of it; nor could she more easily brook any checks to the authority of the Crown than he any contradiction to his opinion.' She loved the sight of troops as much as the King, though she did not talk of them so often; and when Hervey enlarged on the public demand for a reduction of the army he found a bolted door.

The marriage of the Prince of Wales was the chief event of 1736. Princess Augusta of Saxe-Gotha, a girl of seventeen, knew no one in England and could speak no English and little French. 'The Princess was rather tall and had health and youth enough in her face, joined to a very modest and good-natured look to make her countenance not disagreeable; but her person, from being very ill-made, a good deal awry, her arms long and her motions awkward, had in spite of all the finery of jewels and brocade an ordinary air, which no trappings could cover or exalt.' She seemed at first a complete nonentity and excited more pity than interest. Everyone believed that Princess Prudence, as Horace Walpole called her, obeyed the orders of her husband. 'Poor creature,' exclaimed the Queen to Hervey. 'If she were to spit in my face, I should only pity her for being under such a fool's direction and wipe it off.' Caroline detested her son, but she was kind enough to his wife, declaring that there was no sort of harm in her, that she never meant to offend, and was very modest and respectful; that she was dull company was not her fault. When Hervey visited the Queen after the young couple had dined with her she used to greet him with yawns. The silly gaiety of her son, she explained, joined to the silent stupidity of her daughter-in-law, had left her ready to cry with the fatigue of their company; she felt more tired than if she had carried them round the garden on her back.

If the company of her daughter-in-law was a fresh trial, the absence of the King at Hanover during the summer of 1736 was a blessed relief. Hervey had never known her in better health and spirits. That her husband hurried away to his new mistress, who had recently given birth to a son, was a further blow to her pride; but she never broke her heart about such trifles. The clouds soon dispersed, for 'the being freed from his ill-humour seemed to be a full compensation for all his good-humour being bestowed elsewhere.' When, however, his stay was prolonged beyond expectation, she rationed both the length and the warmth of her letters. Fearing that she might thereby lose her influence, Hervey reported the situation to Walpole and begged him to intervene. The Prime Minister replied that nothing could ever quite destroy her power, since the King respected both her understanding and her loyalty; but he agreed that her resentment might be pushed too far. He proceeded to remind her that, being no longer young, it was useless to threaten the inconstant monarch with the loss of her affection. Only soothing, complying, softening, bending, and submitting could avail. If, as he advised,

she pressed the King to bring the woman to England, he guaranteed
that she would get the better of her.   Tears came into Caroline's
eyes, but she decided to swallow the bitter pill.   A day or two
later she showed the Prime Minister the submissive letter in which
she begged her husband to bring Mme Walmoden to England and
promised her every consideration.   'Vous voyez mes passions, ma
chère Caroline,' replied the grateful King.   'Vous connaissez mes
foiblesses, il n'y a rien de caché dans mon cœur pour vous,'   Mme
Walmoden, he added, would do whatever he wished and she relied
on the Queen's goodness.   He proceeded to describe the lady as
agreeable in countenance though not a beauty.   Her mind, he
added, was not remarkable, 'mais à l'égard du cœur elle est
sûrement la meilleure créature du monde.'   In conclusion the
Queen was asked to prepare the lodgings recently vacated by Lady
Suffolk.   Walpole believed that, despite this letter, she would not
come.   The King's prolonged absence naturally diminished the
popularity of the throne.   If he must have a mistress, it was
asked, could not England supply the need?   The satirists were
again at work, and the contemporaries of Hogarth did not mince
their words.   Never had the silly little monarch been so despised.
Not till the middle of January 1737 did he return—without Mme
Walmoden.   For once he was in a good temper, full of praise for
Walpole and the Queen.   On the day after his return the Prime
Minister whispered, *Optime, optime, omnia rident,* to which Hervey
replied with an appropriate quotation from Horace.

The two most celebrated scenes in the third volume of the
Memoirs are those of the first confinement of the Princess of Wales
and the death of the Queen, both of which occurred in 1737.
Court and society circles were aware that his parents detested
their eldest son and that he had as little love for them, and the
circumstances of the birth of his first child emphasised the ferocity
of the feud.   One evening at Hampton Court 'the King played at
commerce below stairs, the Queen above at Quadrille, the Princess
Emily at her commerce-table, and the Princess Caroline and Lord
Hervey at cribbage, just as usual.'   They separated at ten and
went to bed at eleven, without hearing that the Princess was ill
or even of her not being in the house.   At 1.30 A.M. a courier
arrived with the news that she was in labour.   The King and
Queen were awakened, and Caroline exclaimed: 'My God, my
nightgown!   I'll go to her this moment.'   'Your nightgown,
madam,' replied the Woman of the Bedchamber, 'and your
coaches too, the Princess is at St James's.'   'Are you mad,'
interrupted the Queen, 'or are you asleep, my good Tichbourne?
You dream!'   The King flew into a violent passion and scolded
his wife in German.   'You see now, with all your wisdom, how
they have outwitted you.   This is all your fault.   There is a false

child will be put upon you!' The Queen said little, dressed as fast as possible, ordered her coaches, and sent for the Duke of Grafton (the Chamberlain), Hervey, and the two princesses. They were off at 2.30 A.M. and reached St James's Palace at 4 A.M., to learn that a daughter had been born before their arrival. The Queen wished the mother joy and kissed the child, exclaiming: 'Le bon Dieu vous bénisse, pauvre petite créature! Vous voilà arrivée dans un désagréable monde!' To the mother the Queen remarked: 'My good Princess, is there anything you want or anything you would have me do? Here I am; you have but to speak and ask; and whatever is in my power, I promise you I will do it.' The Princess thanked her and said that she had nothing to ask.

What had happened to cause all this commotion? The Prince himself supplied some information to his irate mother. Her pains in the coach, he confessed, were so strong that he thought he should have been obliged to carry her into some house on the road. He added that, by holding her and her pillows in the coach, he had got such pains in his back that he could hardly stir. The Queen, desiring not to cause a scene, did not ask the reasons for this strange behaviour, merely remarking that it was a miracle the mother and child had not been killed. When he announced his intention of coming the same day to Hampton Court, Caroline replied: 'I fancy you had better not come to-day; to be sure the King is not well pleased with all this bustle you have made.' He was, in fact, commanded to leave St James's Palace as soon as the Princess was well enough to move.

After this interview the Queen dispatched a short letter to the King, and then went to Hervey's room to drink chocolate. Her fears of foul play, she remarked, had been removed. 'Well, upon my honour, I have no more doubt of this poor little bit of a thing is the Princess' child than I doubt of either of these two being mine, though I own to you I had my doubts upon the road that there would be some juggle; and if, instead of this poor, little, ugly she-mouse, there had been a brave, large, fat, jolly boy, I should not have been cured of my suspicion, nay, I believe they would have been so much increased, or rather that I should have been so confirmed in that opinion that I should have gone about this house like a madwoman, played the devil, and insisted on knowing what chairman's brat he had bought.' There was, of course, not the slightest reason to fear a trick. No one judged the Prince with such brutal severity as his mother. 'You do not know my filthy beast of a son so well as I do," she remarked to Walpole. His conduct on this occasion, in Hervey's view, was due to the advice of some of his counsellors to show that he was his own master and accountable to nobody in the affairs of his family. A simpler and more probable explanation is that neither the

Prince nor the Princess desired the birth of their child to take place in such an unsympathetic atmosphere as that of Hampton Court. Though the Prince detested both his parents, his fiercest hatred was reserved for his mother, whom he justly suspected of hardening his father's heart. Princess Caroline, who grudged him every hour he continued to live, sent a message that all of them, except the Princess of Wales, deserved to be hanged. The Prince spat into the fire and exclaimed: 'Ah! vous savez la manière de Caroline; elle est toujours comme ça.' The degree of their hatred, testifies Hervey, could not be conceived by people who did not hear the names his family called him, the character they gave him, the curses they lavished on him, and the fervour with which they prayed every day for his death. Even now this ferocious detestation is difficult to explain. Sir George Young is quite right to remind us that till recently we have known the Prince almost entirely through his enemies, above all Hervey and Horace Walpole, and that a very different human being emerges from the diary of his reputable friend, the Earl of Egmont. That Frederick was far more popular than his father is beyond doubt, for he was a much more likeable person. When, however, his biographer suggests that the pupil of Bolingbroke would have proved the true patriot King if he had come to the throne, and that the man generally regarded as a failure might have changed the course of history, some readers may find it difficult to agree.

The friendship of the Queen had its disadvantages for Hervey, who was the recipient of so many secrets that he had to be on his guard not only with the King but with the Prime Minister. During a violent attack of gout, which confined her to bed for several days, Caroline broke through Court etiquette by admitting the Vice-Chamberlain to her room for hours at a time. Her character was beyond reproach, but such familiarities produced the usual crop of jealousies. Even Walpole was affected, not because he regarded the Queen's favourite as a rival to his power, but 'from a weakness in this great man's composition which made him grudge this show of favour even where, I believe, he had not the least suspicion, or where I am sure at least he had no reason given him to justify suspicion that this would ever be employed for his disservice. For Lord Hervey always looked upon Sir Robert as his benefactor, who had placed him in that station; as an able master, from whom he had learned all he knew in the beginning of the secrets of the Court and most of what he knew of the policy requisite for his conduct there; and was sensible it was to his favour, protection and commendations that he owed originally his having any credit there. But that credit was now higher than Sir Robert wished it.'

The Queen's last months were darkened by the feud with her

son. 'I hope in God I shall never see the monster's face again,'
she exclaimed, and her wish was gratified. 'You once thought—
you fool to be so imposed upon—that he loved me. You thought,
too, that he loved you, poor my Lord Hervey. He laughed at you
all the time for believing him. I told you he never loved anybody;
he cannot love anybody. Yet once I would have given up all my
children for him. I was fond of that monster; I looked upon him
as one that was to make the happiness of my life, and now I wish
he had never been born.' 'Poor Mama,' interrupted Princess
Caroline, 'do not throw away your wishes for what cannot happen,
but wish that he may *crever*, and that we may all go about with
smiling faces, glad hearts, and crape and bands for him.' At this
moment the King entered and joined in the chorus of abuse.
'I am weary of the puppy's name. I wish I was never to hear it
again, but at least I shall not be plagued any more with seeing his
nasty face.' He could forgive his injuries to himself, he continued,
but not to his mother. 'I must say you have been an excellent
mother to all your children, and if any of them behave ill to you
they deserve to be hanged. Bad subjects are very provoking;
bad servants are still more provoking; and bad children are the
most provoking of all.' The Prince, it was believed at Court,
retaliated by threats what he would do to all his family except his
brother if he came to the throne. 'For me,' said the Queen, 'I am
to be fleeced and flayed, and minced; for Emily, she is to be shut
up between four walls; and for Caroline, she is to be sent to
starve.' In an elaborate parallel between the Prince and Nero,
filling twenty pages, Hervey discharges his venom with equal
gusto and exaggeration. Except that both of them hated their
mothers, no one ever less resembled Nero than Poor Fred.

The last fifty pages of the third volume describe the illness and
death of the Queen. On November 9, 1737, she complained of
colic, took to her bed, vomited incessantly, was blooded, and
developed fever. She told Caroline that it mattered nothing what
they did to her, for she should certainly die. Hervey was never
out of her room more than four or five hours at a time, sometimes
not two out of the twenty-four, and he never left the King without
being exhorted to return as soon as possible. Walpole was
summoned from his autumn holiday at Houghton, but the request
of the Prince of Wales to pay his respects was angrily declined.
'He wants to come and insult his poor dying mother,' cried the
King to Hervey who brought the message, 'but she shall not see
him. You have heard her, and all my daughters have heard her
very often this year at Hampton Court, desire me, if she should be
ill and out of her senses, that I would never let him come near her.
No, no! He shall not come and act any of his silly plays here,
false, lying, cowardly, nauseous puppy.' When the Queen

expressed her fear that he might try to see her, the King told her
of the message and his reply. He added, however, that if she had
a mind to see him, he had of course no objection. 'I am so far
from desiring to see him,' said the Queen, 'that nothing but your
absolute command should ever make me consent to it. For what
should I see him? For him to tell me a hundred lies? If anything
I could say to him would alter his behaviour, I would see him with
all my heart; but I know that is impossible.' Sometimes when
she talked of dying she would say: 'At least I shall have one
comfort in having my eyes eternally closed—I shall never see that
monster again.' The Prince, comments Hervey, fully deserved
her blame; for while he was pretending to desire to see her, he
was railing at her to his favourites and counting the days till she
was gone. 'Well, sure, we must have some good news soon. It's
impossible she can hold out long. I think I am a very good son,
I wish her out of her pain.' These utterances, declares Hervey,
were reported to him by the Duke of Marlborough.

The Queen had suffered from an umbilical rupture for many
years, though she had concealed it from everybody except the
King. She knew she was doomed, but she had not the slightest
fear of death. When the rest of the family were in tears she
displayed no grief. William, Duke of Cumberland, the younger
son, was exhorted to be a support to his father in order to make
up for the disappointment and vexation caused by his profligate
and worthless brother. When the King was advised to marry
again he sobbed out the famous response: 'Non, j'aurai des
maîtresses.' 'Ah, mon Dieu, cela n'empêche pas,' retorted the
sorely tried wife. She received Walpole, who had hurried back to
London, and recommended her husband, her children, and the
kingdom to his care. The end came on November 20, after
eleven days of agony bravely borne. The King had shown a
tenderness which surprised his entourage but made little impression
on Hervey. He would cry for her for a fortnight, he remarked to
the Prime Minister, and forget her in a month. That the King
could not live without women was recognised on all hands, and
it was not long before Mme Walmoden was brought over, made
Lady Yarmouth, and installed as *maîtresse en titre*.

Hervey proved an equally good prophet in a matter of far
greater importance. 'Oh! my Lord,' exclaimed Walpole when
the end was near, 'if this woman should die, what a scene of
confusion will there be! Who can tell into what hands the King
will fall or who will have the management of him? I defy the
ablest person to foresee what will be the consequence of this great
event.' Hervey found no difficulty in answering these rhetorical
questions. 'You will have all the credit, more power than you
ever had, and govern him more absolutely than ever you did.'

The Minister reiterated his conviction that the death of the Queen would make a great difference. 'Though he will hear nobody but me, you do not know how often he refuses to hear me when it is on a subject he does not like; but by the Queen I can with time fetch him round to those subjects again; she can make him do the same thing in another shape, and when I give her her lesson can make him propose the very thing as his own opinion which a week before he had rejected as mine.' The Prime Minister had never had an easy task, but his difficulties were not materially increased by the loss of the Queen. When he fell five years later it was not the King but the serried ranks of the Opposition who brought him down.

Ten days after Caroline's death Hervey dispatched the long and querulous letter to Walpole with which the work concludes. Now she was gone the post of Vice-Chamberlain was hardly worth having. He began by reiterating his conviction that the Prime Minister's position would be stronger than ever, since 'as I have often said of you, though never before to you, what I really think true, that your great talents and abilities are so much superior to anybody I ever knew or I believe ever shall know.' He then came to the point. 'I have long made it my sole business to please the Queen and you. How well or ill I have succeeded is immaterial.' The refusal of some honorary trifles and other more essential favours showed that the Minister was either afraid or unwilling to promote him, and judged him fit for nothing but to carry candles and set chairs all his life. 'I once had it in my power to serve you (or my vanity gave me pleasure in thinking so). That time is over. I know I am now as insignificant as any other of the dignified ciphers about you. All I mean to say is that I will be refused or disappointed no more, for I will ask and expect no more; that my enemies shall not conquer, for I will not struggle; that I could have made my peace with my greatest enemy (Pulteney) if I would have done it at your expense; that I scorned it, and do not repent the part I have acted; that I submit to be a nothing, and wish whoever you honour with your confidence, or benefit with your favour, may always serve you with as honest a mind, as warm a heart, and as unshakable an attachment.' To this shrill cry of distress Walpole gave a verbal reply next day. With what Hervey coldly describes as a very well-acted concern, the old statesman declared that of all his transactions this letter had surprised and affected him most, and that after his own children there was nobody he loved so well. 'I mean to serve you, I wish to please you; for God's sake, go on with me as you used to do. Commit your future interest to my care.' Hervey promised not to alter his conduct nor complain to anybody unless he thought he had any fresh reason to be displeased; but, as he confides to his readers, he was beginning to know his leader too well to trust the most lavish professions of kindness and esteem.

The Vice-Chamberlain had to wait for the fulfilment of Walpole's promise, and it was not till the close of 1739 that he was appointed Lord Privy Seal with a seat in the Cabinet. The Prime Minister was aware of his unpopularity, but in 1739, when he was forced into the Spanish War, he felt the need of Hervey's support. The Duke of Newcastle particularly resented the appointment, knowing how the sharp-tongued courtier despised him; and Hardwicke, the Lord Chancellor, also disliked him. Walpole was now losing control over his Cabinet colleagues as well as over the House of Commons, and his fall in 1742 was promptly followed by the eviction of his *protégé*. By this time, however, Hervey was a dying man. Reporting his death in 1742 to Horace Mann in Florence, Horace Walpole added that he had outlived his last inch of character. We should do him little injustice in describing him as one of the least attractive and least respected figures of an age when the standards of public and private conduct were lamentably low. Yet the man who won and kept the friendship of Queen Caroline cannot have been wholly vile.

Bibliographical Note.—An expurgated edition of the *Memoirs* was published in three volumes in 1848 by Croker, the famous editor of the *Quarterly Review*, who complained of the omissions which he was compelled by the first Marquis of Bristol to make. A complete edition, based on a collation of the original manuscript with an early copy preserved at Windsor, appeared in 1931 with an admirable Introduction by Romney Sedgwick. The new matter amounts to about a hundred pages. Even now we do not possess the whole, for there is a gap of more than two years (1730–32) both in the original and the copy. The missing material doubtless related to the bitter quarrel with Frederick, Prince of Wales, which Lord Bristol may have thought too compromising to preserve. The case for the Prince of Wales is ably presented in *Poor Fred, the People's Prince*, by Sir George Young. Wilkins, *Caroline of Anspach*, 2 vols., is a popular biography. John Morley, *Walpole*, explains the constitutional significance of our first Prime Minister. F. S. Oliver, *The Endless Adventure*, 3 vols., is a discursive commentary on Walpole's long Ministry by a brilliant amateur. The best brief survey of the period is by Basil Williams, *The Whig Supremacy, 1714–1760*. Sichel, *Life of Bolingbroke*, offers a spirited defence of the author of *A Patriot King*. Vaucher, *Robert Walpole et la Politique de Fleury*, is indispensable for foreign affairs. Vaucher, *La Crise du Ministère de Walpole*, discusses the struggle over the Excise Bill. The best sketch of Queen Caroline is in Alice Greenwood, *Lives of the Hanoverian Queens*, vol. 1. Michael, *Englische Geschischte im achtzehnten Jahrhundert*, vols. 2–4, contains the most authoritative account of the whole Walpole period.

CHAPTER XIII

HORACE WALPOLE AND GEORGE II

HORACE WALPOLE lives as the most famous letter-writer in our language, but his voluminous *Memoirs* cannot be ignored. Though they lack the kindliness of Burnet, the pungency of Hervey, and the delicate charm of Fanny Burney, he knew so much that generations of historians have quarried in his mine. Entering Parliament in 1741, a few weeks before the fall of his father, he made his maiden speech resisting a motion for a Committee of Inquiry into the conduct of the Prime Minister. He sat for twenty-seven years without a break, and though he seldom intervened in debate he listened and made copious notes. Macaulay's description of Chesterfield as a man of the world among men of letters, and a man of letters among men of the world, is equally suited to the host of Strawberry Hill. Had he not been a son of the chief statesman of the time he would probably have devoted himself exclusively to literature and the arts, for he lacked ambition and the gift of speech. He was impelled to play his part on the public stage by two powerful impulses—devotion to his father and the urge to know everything that was going on. The first shaped his course as a moderate Whig; the second made him an eager spectator of the political game.

We must begin by emancipating ourselves from the spell of Macaulay, whose scintillating essay has moulded opinion for over a century. Whatever was little seemed to him great, we are told, and whatever was great seemed to him little. Serious business was a trifle to him, and trifles were his serious business. Politics were an amusement, and he cared nothing for them. Though he called himself a Whig, he was essentially a courtier, a gentleman-usher at heart. His books swarmed with foolish observations and contradictory judgments. He sneered at everybody and put the worst construction on every deed. He lacked the power of discerning the finer shades of character. What a difference between his daubs and the masterly portraits of Clarendon! Having no sense of values, he lived in easy idleness, focusing his attention on trifles and curiosities. His letters were better than his books because in the former his bitter, scoffing, depreciating disposition reveals itself less nakedly. 'What then is the irresistible charm of his writings? It consists in the art of amusing without exciting. He never convinces the reason or fills the imagination or touches the heart; but he keeps the mind of the reader constantly attentive and constantly entertained. No man who has written so much is so seldom tiresome. His writings are a literary *pâté de foie gras*,

ranking high among the delicacies of the intellectual epicure, but
the reflection of an unhealthy and disorganised mind.'

Macaulay's indictment is as unconvincing as his even more
celebrated denunciation of Boswell. Horace Walpole was not a
great man and he knew it, but he was more than the elegant trifler,
the drawing-room performer, the *petit-maître*. That he supplies
varied entertainment is true enough, but he also gives us solid food.
Living to the age of eighty he spans the era between the reign of
his father and the wars of the French Revolution. His main
theme in the *Memoirs* is Parliament, as Hervey's theme was the
Court. There is no need for us to accept all his verdicts or to
share his many animosities, and no one would call his record a
work of art like his incomparable letters. But we may be grateful
for the mass of first-hand information enshrined in the three
volumes on the last decade of George II, the four volumes on the
first decade of George III, the two volumes of *Journals* on the
years 1771–83, and the brief *Reminiscences* relating to the courts
of George I and George II written in 1788 for the amusement of
the Miss Berrys. Like other writers of memoirs he was often
unfair, but he was not a mere cynic and he hated cruelty and
intolerance. He was stirred to the depths by the execution of
Admiral Byng, 'most unjustly and wickedly put to death.'

The *Memoirs of the Reign of King George II* open with the
year 1751. He left no instructions as to publication, but the
care he devoted to the work leaves no doubt that he wished it to
appear. The first sketch and the corrected copy are in his own
hand, while the third version, written by his secretary, contains
autograph corrections and notes. The first edition was prepared
for the press by the third Lord Holland, who furnished a critical
Introduction and explanatory notes. 'He was too much under
the influence of personal feelings and resentments,' declares the
distinguished editor, 'and too apt to sacrifice his friendships to
his aversions; and as the latter were often excited by trivial and
accidental causes, his political conduct, though unexceptionable
on the score of interest or ambition, was fluctuating and uncertain,
and his judgment of men variable and capricious. Where his
resentments did not cloud his judgment, his indifference to the
common objects of ambition rendered him an impartial spectator.'
His summaries of debates are particularly valuable because the
Parliamentary reports from the fall of his father to the American
war are most unsatisfactory. He took down striking phrases and
arguments, and his descriptions of the impression made by
speakers are of genuine interest. Many anecdotes based on
personal knowledge are woven into the narrative. His portraits
in general incline to severity, though a few of his friends are overpraised. They were often dictated by the latest events rather

than by a comprehensive view of their career, and subsequent
references sometimes contradict first impressions and soften the
blame.

'The Author's Postscript,' as Walpole entitles his brief Preface,
claims to have painted the actors as they were. 'Many, from
private connections of party and family, will dislike meeting
such unflattered portraits of their heroes or their relations. Yet
this, I fear, must always be the case in any history written impartially by an eye-witness. I never assert anything positively
unless from very good authority. Where I am not certain I
always say, it was said, it was believed, it was supposed. The
speeches, every one of them, I can affirm to be still more
authentic, as I took notes at the time. It will perhaps be thought
that some of the characters are drawn in too unfavourable light.
I have endeavoured to illustrate my assertions by facts. Here are
no assassins, no poisoners, no Neros, Borgias, Catilines, Richards of
York! Here are the foibles of an age, no very bad one; treacherous
Ministers, mock Patriots, complaisant Parliaments, fallible Princes.
Another objection I foresee is that I may have prejudices on my
father's account. I can answer this honestly in a word: all who
know me know that I had no such prejudice to him as blinded me
to his failings which I have faithfully mentioned in my character
of him. If more is necessary, let me add his friends are spared no
more than his enemies, and all the good I know of the latter I
have faithfully told. Have I concealed my father's own failings?
Some of my nearest friends are often mentioned in these Memoirs,
and their failings I think as little concealed as those of other
persons. Some whom I have little reason to love are the fairest
characters in the book. Indeed if I can call myself to account
for heightening characters, it is on the favourable side. With
more reason I can avow myself guilty of having inserted too many
trifling circumstances; but they are trifles relating to considerable
people, and such all curious persons have ever loved to read.' His
claim to impartiality has been challenged by friend and foe.
Croker, the diehard Tory, described the book as a party pamphlet
in two quarto volumes, written under all the excitements of party
feeling, offended vanity, and personal disgust; and the author is
compared to a tiger-cat, now sportive, now cruel. This is the
verdict of a partisan; yet even Miss Stuart, in her monograph
in the *English Men of Letters*, complains of the pervading atmosphere of malice, self-seeking, and chicane almost justifying
Macaulay's strictures at times. To such critics Walpole would
doubtless have replied that he had known the actors in the flesh.
On re-reading his survey of the year 1751 he comments: 'I find
the truth rigidly told. Avaunt, flattery! Tell the truth, my
pen!'

The narrative opens with Oxenstiern's celebrated question: *An nescis, mi fili, quantilla prudentia regitur orbis?* The author proposed the motion for the Address, but throughout the ten volumes of the *Memoirs* and *Journals* there is relatively little about himself. The Whigs had been so long in power that they had broken up into warring groups, and since Walpole's fall no one had dominated the scene. The King was old and in these pages he plays a secondary part. Since the defeat of the Young Pretender in 1745 no great issue was at stake. 'At this time all was faction and splitting into little factions. The Pelhams were ill with one another, and ill with the Bedfords. The latter Duke would have set up Fox against Mr Pelham, and the former Duke was countenancing Mr Pitt against all. Mr Pelham supported Pitt and his clan against the Duke of Cumberland, who was united with the Bedfords. The Prince's Court, composed of the refuse of every party, was divided into twenty small ones.' This satirical passage may serve as a prologue to the arid drama of ambition and intrigue. As a young M.P. he had witnessed the closing scenes of his father's gallant fight against a host of enemies. He could never forgive the men who had acted with him, had in some cases owed their careers to him, and had ultimately joined his foes. False friends, in his eyes, were infinitely worse than open enemies.

'I am no historian,' writes Walpole in opening his survey of 1754. 'I write casual Memoirs; I draw characters; I preserve anecdotes.' The main interest to modern readers lies in his portraits. The full-length picture of the Duke of Newcastle, the chief performer between Walpole and the great days of Chatham, has passed into history, though we must bear in mind the writer's undying resentment at his part in the overthrow of his father. 'He succeeded young to an estate of about thirty thousand a year and to great influence and interest in several counties. This account contains his whole character as a Minister, for to the weight of his fortune he solely owed his every-other-way most unwarrantable elevation. His person was not naturally despicable; his incapacity, his mean soul, and the general low opinion of him, grew to make it appear ridiculous. A constant hurry in his walk, a restlessness of place, a borrowed importance, a real insignificance, gave him a perpetual air of a solicitor, though he was perpetually solicited; for he never conferred a favour till it was wrested from him, but often omitted doing what he most wished done. He had no pride but infinite self-love: jealousy was the great source of all his faults. There was no expense to which he was not addicted but generosity. His speeches in Council and Parliament were flowing and copious of words, but empty and unmeaning. He aimed at everything, endeavoured nothing. He was a Secretary of State without intelligence, a Duke without money, a man of infinite intrigue, without secrecy or policy, a Minister despised and hated by his master, by all parties and ministers, without being turned out by any.' This picture of a fussy mediocrity, severe though it be, yields in severity to the crushing verdict of the author's father, 'His name is Perfidy.' The portrait of the Duke's brother and colleague, Henry Pelham, is only a little less contemptuous. 'It may appear extraordinary that Mr Pelham, who had not so much levity in his character, should consent to be an accomplice in his brother's treacheries, especially as upon every interval of rivalry the Duke grew jealous of him. The truth was that Mr Pelham, who had as much envy in his temper and still more fondness for power, was willing to take advantage of his brother's fickleness and reaped all emolument without incurring the odium of it. Sir Robert Walpole was a man of genius, but the younger man had done what his master had failed to achieve—he had exercised power without unpopularity. Sir Robert Walpole was bold, open, steady, never dejected. Mr Pelham was timorous, reserved, fickle, apt to despair. Presumption made Sir Robert Walpole many enemies; want of confidence in himself kept from Mr Pelham many friends. Sir Robert Walpole loved power so much that he would not endure a rival; Mr Pelham loved it so much that he would endure anything. Sir Robert Walpole never professed honesty, but followed it; Mr Pelham always professed it, and kept his word when nothing happened to make him break it. Sir Robert Walpole, with the greatest confidence in himself, had no pride; Mr Pelham had the most, with the least self-sufficience. Both were loved in private life. Sir Robert Walpole was forgiving to a fault, if forgiveness can be faulty; Mr Pelham never forgave but when he durst not resent. All men thought Mr Pelham honest till he was in power; the other never was thought so till he was out.' Such, if we are to believe Horace Walpole, were the Pelhams, in whose reign the Parliamentary opposition which had lasted from the days of Elizabeth ceased to exist. 'All were now sunk into a dull mercenary subjection to two brothers.' On recording the death of the younger in 1754 the chronicler makes partial amends by admitting that he lived without abusing his power and died poor.

Pulteney, a much more brilliant but less effective figure, is dismissed in a few lines of concentrated venom. 'Lord Bath is so known a character that it is almost needless to draw him. Who does not know that Mr Pulteney was the great rival of Sir Robert Walpole, whose power he so long opposed, at last over-turned, and was undone with it? Who does not know that his virtue failed the moment his inveteracy was gratified? Who does not know that all the patriot's private vices, which his party

would not see while he led them, were exposed and if possible
magnified the instant he deserted them? Who does not know
that he had not judgment or resolution enough to engross the
power which he had forfeited his credit and character to obtain?
And who does not know that his ambition, treachery, irresolution,
timidity, and want of judgment were baffled and made advantage
of by a man who had all those vices and deficiencies in a stronger
proportion—for who does not know the Duke of Newcastle?'

Carteret, another brilliant enemy of Sir Robert, a Secretary of
State and Lord Lieutenant of Ireland, the only minister who could
converse with the King in German, is treated a little better. 'His
person was handsome, open, engaging; his eloquence at once
rapid and pompous. He was an extensive scholar, master of
classic criticism and of all modern politics. It is difficult to say
whether he was oftener intoxicated by wine or ambition; in fits
of the former he showed contempt for everybody; in rants of the
latter for truth. His genius was magnificent and lofty; his heart
without gall or friendship, for he never tried to be revenged on
his enemies or to serve his friends.' In refusing to recommend
to the King a certain promotion he replied: 'What is it to me
who is a Judge or a Bishop? It is my business to make Kings
and Emperors, and to maintain the balance of Europe.' Lord
Hardwicke, the Lord Chancellor, whose rise is attributed to Sir
Robert Walpole, repeatedly feels the cut of the lash. He had
good parts, we are assured, but no character. The best thing
about him was his fidelity to his patrons, 'for, let the Duke of
Newcastle betray whom he would, the Chancellor stuck to him
in his perfidy, and was only not false to the falsest of mankind.
In the House of Lords he was laughed at, in the Cabinet despised.'
Here is one of the worst injustices in the *Memoirs*, for the great
lawyer's influence was deservedly immense.

The rivals Henry Fox and the elder Pitt are introduced in the
first volume and studied in more detail in the later parts of the
work. Writing in 1751 Walpole found most to praise in the
former, who was his favourite statesman till he joined the detested
Newcastle in 1755. A comparison of the two men as speakers
tells us exactly what we desire to know. 'Pitt was undoubtedly
one of the greatest masters of ornamental eloquence. His language
was amazingly fine and flowing; his voice admirable; his action
most expressive; his figure genteel and commanding. Bitter
satire was his forte; when he attempted ridicule, which was very
seldom, he succeeded happily; when he attempted to reason,
poorly. But where he chiefly shone was in exposing his own
conduct. Having waded through the most notorious apostasy in
politics, he treated it with an impudent confidence that made all
reflections upon him poor and spiritless when worded by any

other man. Out of the House of Commons he was far from being
this shining character. His conversation was affected and un-
natural, his manner not engaging, nor his talents adapted to a
country where ministers must court if they would be courted.
Fox, with a great hesitation in his elocution, a barrenness of
expression, had conquered these impediments and the prejudices
they had raised against his speaking by a vehemence of reasoning
and closeness of argument that beat all the other orators of the
time. His spirit, his steadiness and humanity procured him
strong attachments, which, the more jealous he grew of Pitt, the
more he cultivated. Fox always spoke to the question, Pitt to
the passions; Fox to carry the question, Pitt to raise himself;
Fox pointed out, Pitt lashed the errors of his antagonists; Pitt's
talents were likely to make him soonest, Fox's to keep him First
Minister longest.' On one occasion when Pitt was speaking Fox
said to his neighbour, 'He is a better speaker than I am, but,
thank God, I have more judgment.' Pitt's pre-eminence only
became manifest to Walpole when he was captain of the ship in
stormy weather.

The portraits of the royal family are much less intimate than
of the politicians. He boasts that he never went to Court and
always leaned towards the Opposition, but he had learned a great
deal from his father and his friends. Of George II he thought as
meanly as the rest of his subjects, though he is described as never
despotic except in his insistence on paying visits to Hanover.
'He had fewer sensations of revenge, or at least knew how to
hoard them better, than any man who ever sat upon a throne.
In general his disposition was merciful if the offence was not
murder. His avarice was much less equivocal than his courage.
His understanding was not near so deficient as it was imagined.
His passions were Germany, the army, and women. There were
few arts by which he was not governed at some time or other of
his life. The Queen governed him by dissimulation, by affected
tenderness and deference; Sir Robert Walpole by abilities and
influence in the House of Commons; Lord Granville by flattering
him on his German politics; the Duke of Newcastle by teasing
and betraying him; Mr Pelham by bullying him. Who indeed
had not sometimes weight with the King, except his children and
his mistresses? With them he maintained all the reserve and
majesty of his rank. He had the haughtiness of Henry VIII,
without his spirit; the avarice of Henry VII, without his
exactions; the indignities of Charles I, without his bigotry for
his prorogative; the vexations of King William, with as little
skill in management of parties. He might perhaps have been
honest if he had never hated his father or had ever loved his
son.' The Stuarts are contemptuously dismissed as a worthless

12

and exploded race. In his refusal to be overawed by royalty, and
in his preference for what he calls 'most limited monarchy,'
Horace Walpole was a true Whig.

Though the King had so few merits the death of the Prince of
Wales in 1751 caused no tears to flow. An anonymous Jacobite
Royalist gave him a parting kick in an elegy which was sold in the
streets and has found its way into all the history books:

> Here lies Fred,
> Who was alive, and is dead.
> Had it been his father,
> I had much rather.
> Had it been his brother,
> Still better than another.
> Had it been his sister,
> No one would have missed her.
> Had it been the whole generation,
> Still better for the nation.
> But since 'tis only Fred,
> Who was alive and is dead,
> There's no more to be said.

Walpole declares that the breach with his parents was not
entirely his own fault. The King had refused to pay his debts at
Hanover, and it was a tradition in the family to hate the eldest
son. The Queen is accused of a narrow prying into his conduct,
and his favourite sister Emily betrayed to their mother any of
his secrets that might do him prejudice. Whoever was unwelcome
at Court was sure of a welcome from the Prince of Wales, but his
attachment to his followers was no stronger than theirs to him.
'His chief passion was women, but, like the rest of his race, beauty
was not a necessary ingredient. Gaming was another of his
passions. He was really childish, affectedly a protector of arts
and sciences, fond of displaying what he knew. His best quality
was generosity; his worst insincerity and indifference to truth.'

The strong man of the royal family was the Duke of Cumberland, commonly known as the Duke. When Fox was asked by
George II whom he wished to be Regent if the new Prince of Wales,
a boy of thirteen at the death of his father, ascended the throne
during his minority, he replied that the Duke of Cumberland had
the first claim. He had spoken in this sense on the Regency Bill.
'I thank you for that,' rejoined the King. 'My affection is with
my son. I assure you, Mr Fox, I like you better for wishing well
to him. The English nation is so changeable. I don't know
why they dislike him. It is brought about by the Scotch, the
Jacobites and the English that don't love discipline, and by all
this not being enough discouraged by the Government.' The
chief reason for his unpopularity, as his father was well aware,
was his savage repression of the rebels after the battle of Culloden.

Walpole depicts a hard soldier who never sought the applause of the crowd. 'He loved indiscriminate submission. Flattery did not come up to his ideas of obedience, and consequently he over-looked it, but the least opposition he never forgave. With the most heroic bravery he had all the severity that levels valour to cowardice, and seemed to love war for itself without feeling the passions that it gratifies. It is certain that his martial genius did not proceed from love of glory nor much from ambition. Glory he despised, and he had taken every step to make himself un-popular both with the people and the army, and thought it so much beneath his rank to have any share in the Ministry that he would not be of the Cabinet Council. His strongest principle was the dignity of the Blood Royal, and his maxim to bear anything from his brother if he had lived to be king rather than set an example of disobedience to the royal authority. These prejudices and this pride were the swellings of his heart and temper, not the errors of his head, for his understanding was strong, judicious and penetrating, though incapable of resisting partialities and piques. He despised money, fame and politics; loved gaming, women and his own favourites, and yet had not one sociable virtue.'

The death of Henry Pelham in 1754 left his brother, the Duke of Newcastle, in Walpole's phrase, absolute. 'He had all the advice from wise heads that could make him get the better of rivals, and all the childishness in himself that could make them ashamed of his having got the better. If his fickleness had been tied down to any stability, his power had been endless.' Acquies-cence in all Hanoverian measures was the only homage he paid to the King. The decade preceding the Seven Years War was a dreary time, but our interest never flags when Pitt is on the stage. Walpole heard all his great speeches, among them the celebrated comparison of the union of Fox and Newcastle to the junction of the Rhône and the Saône which he had been taken to see at Lyons in his youth. He had to be seen as well as heard, for his action, we are assured, would have added reputation to Garrick. There were plenty of good speakers in Parliament, but Pitt alone studied eloquence as an art, and he was aided by his commanding figure. Yet Walpole was by no means an unreserved admirer. His greatest failure was in argument; he spoke too often and too long, and he was better in attack than in defence. 'Illustrious as he was in the House of Commons, he would have shone still more in an assembly of inferior capacity; his talents for dazzling were exposed to whoever did not fear his sword and abuse, or could detect the weakness of his arguments.' In other words, if his antagonists stood up to him he was much less formidable than he seemed. He had no party, and the King had no desire to see him in power. 'I am sure Pitt will not do my business,' he remarked, remembering his hostility to purely Hanoverian interests. When Newcastle resigned in 1756 Pitt became Secretary of State, and took control of foreign policy. 'What a strange country is this!' remarked the King to Fox. 'I have never known more than two or three men in it who understood foreign affairs. You do not study them—and yet here comes one man and says he had not as much as read Wicquefort, has all to learn, and demands to be Secretary of State.' Pitt's worst failing was not his ignorance of foreign affairs but his difficult temperament, aggravated as it was by bad health. 'Pitt used to call me madman,' complained Lord Granville (Carteret) after a meeting, 'but I never was half so mad as he is.'

Walpole interrupts his narrative in 1756 to assure his readers that, despite his criticisms, England was not so badly off. 'Considering how seldom the world is blessed with a government really good, and that the best are generally but negatively good, I am inclined to pronounce the times of which I have been writing happy. Every art and system that brings advantage to the country was permitted; commerce was in no way checked; liberty, not being wanton, nay, being complaisant, was not restrained. The Church was moderate, and when the Ministry required it, yielding. If the Chancellor (Hardwicke) was ravenous and arbitrary and ambitious, he moved too deliberately and too gravely to bring on any eminent mischief. If the Duke of Newcastle was fond of power, and capricious, and fickle, and false, they were the whims of a child. If the King was too partial to Hanover, and was unnecessarily profuse of subsidies to Germany, perhaps it was the only onerous grievance; and the King, who did no more harm, and the Ministers, who by yielding to this passion purchased the power of doing no more harm, certainly constituted no very bad Government.'

The third volume describes the triumphs of the Seven Years War, the prowess of our ally Frederick the Great, and the genius of Pitt, who directed foreign affairs while Newcastle, the nominal Premier, controlled the machinery at home. Pitt, in Walpole's words, lacked simplicity, and the *Memoirs* abound in pictures of the most accomplished actor on the Parliamentary stage. Here is a vivid snapshot taken on the eve of the most glorious chapter in his life: 'Pitt, it was expected, would take advantage of illness and not appear. But he refined on that old *finesse*; and pretending to leave the care of a broken constitution when his country demanded his service, and as a pledge of his sincerity in the scrutiny, he came to the discussion in all the studied apparatus of a theatre valetudinarian. The weather was unseasonably warm (April); yet he was dressed in an old coat and waistcoat of beaver laced with gold; over that a red surtout, the right arm

lined with fur, and appendent with many black ribands, to
indicate his inability of drawing it over his right arm, which
hung in a crape sling, but which, in the warmth of speaking, he
drew out with unlucky activity and brandished as usual. On
his legs were riding stockings. In short, no aspiring Cardinal
ever coughed for the Tiara with more specious debility.'

Yet the accomplished *poseur* was also a great man of action.
'I am sure I can save this country and nobody else can,' he
exclaimed to the Duke of Devonshire. 'It were ingratitude to
say that he did not give such a reverberation to our stagnating
councils as exceedingly altered the appearance of our fortune.
He warded off the evil hour that seemed approaching; he infused
vigour into our arms; he taught the nation to speak again as
England used to speak to foreign Powers; and so far from dreading
invasions from France, he affected to turn us into invaders.' On
the other hand he was vain, rash, and extravagant; and he did
not possess all the talents he supposed in himself or seemed to
possess owing to the lack of great men around him. Walpole
had only seen five—his father, the Duke of Cumberland, Granville
(Carteret), Mansfield, and Pitt. Granville, in his opinion, had
most genius. Sir Robert intended the happiness, not the grandeur,
of mankind. 'Pitt's was an unfinished greatness: considering
how much of it depended on his words, one may almost call his
an artificial greatness; but his passion for fame and the grandeur
of his ideas compensated for his defeats. He aspired to redeem
the honour of his country and to place it in a point of giving law
to nations.'

The book closes with the death of George II 'full of years and
glory.' Though there is no warmth in the final verdict, the
contempt of the earlier years is gone. His greatest merit was the
calmness with which he bore both calamities and triumphs, and
he left his family firmly established on a long-disputed throne.
His faults were more the blemishes of a private man than of a
king. He used his power with moderation, and his resentments
were mild. He was more patient with his ministers than with his
mistresses. 'Content to bargain for the gratification of his two
prominent passions, Hanover and money, he was almost indifferent
to the rest of his royal authority provided exterior observance
was not wanting; for he comforted himself if he did not perceive
the diminution of Majesty, though it was notorious to all the rest
of the world. Yet he was not so totally careless of the affection
and interests of this country as his father had been. George I
possessed a sounder understanding and a better temper; yet
George II gained more by being compared with his eldest son
than he lost if paralleled with his father. His treatment of his
second son, to whose valour he was indebted for the preservation

of his crown, and to the silence and tenderness of whose duty he owed the preservation of his honour, was punished by the ingratitude of the Princess of Wales.' No one could make a hero of George II, but in Walpole's eyes he was a far better ruler than George III.

At the end of 1759 the author, aged forty-two, painted an elaborate portrait of himself in the third person. He was without the least tincture of ambition, but the persecution of his father made him a politician. In middle life he withdrew to the amiable activities of a tranquil life—arts, books, painting, architecture, antiquities—not only because he had always loved them, but because none of the leading actors—Newcastle, Fox, Pitt—commanded his allegiance. 'Walpole had a warm conception, vehement attachments, strong aversions; with an apparent contradiction in his temper, for he had numerous caprices and invincible perseverance. His principles tended to republicanism, but without any of its austerity; his love of faction was unmixed with any aspiring. He had a great measure of pride, especially apt to resent neglect, and scorning to stoop to any meanness or flattery. A boundless friend; a bitter but a placable enemy. His humour was satiric though accomplished with a most compassionate heart. One virtue he possessed in a singular degree— disinterestedness and contempt of money—if one may call that a virtue which really was a passion. In short, such was his promptness to dislike superiors, such his humanity to inferiors, that, considering how few men are of so firm a texture as not to be influenced by their situation, he thinks, if he may be allowed to judge of himself, that had either extreme of fortune been his lot, he should have made a good prince but not a very honest slave.' To complete the portrait we may add the celebrated aphorism which suggests that he was something more than a dilettante: 'This world of ours is a comedy to those who think, a tragedy to those who feel.'

CHAPTER XIV

HORACE WALPOLE AND GEORGE III

HORACE WALPOLE'S *Memoirs of the Reign of King George III* were begun in 1776 and ended with the death of the Princess Dowager of Wales, the widow of Poor Fred, in 1772. The first-hand reports of debates cease when he retired from Parliament in 1768, but he continued to pick up a good deal from his friends, some of whom lent him their notes. Vanity, he declares, played no part in his narrative, for his *rôle* was not brilliant. 'My counsels might have been more serviceable to my country if they had been more followed.' He repeats that he is writing memoirs, not history, and when he altered his opinion of men he left his first judgments on record. That the picture was not altogether pleasant he was well aware. 'Reader, I offer you no more than the memoirs of men who had many faults, written by a man who had many himself.' If he really entertained this modest opinion of himself there is little sign of it in his censorious pages.

The drama opens with the death of George II, 'crowned with years and honours and respected from success,' and the accession of his grandson at the age of twenty-two under the fairest auspices. No monarch, in the author's opinion, had ascended the throne with so many advantages. The first Hanoverian born in England was in the flower of youth, possessed a handsome, open, and honest countenance, and was free from vice. Pitt, 'the most successful genius that ever presided over our councils,' was at the height of his powers, and conquest had crowned our arms. Unfortunately there was another side to the balance-sheet. 'A passionate, domineering woman, and a Favourite without talents, soon drew a cloud over this shining prospect.' Walpole detested them both and pursues them with angry contempt to the end. That Bute was a champion of the royal prerogative was bad enough, but there were other reasons for his unpopularity. 'The Favourite was unknown, ungracious and a Scot, and his connection with the Princess an object of scandal.' The Tories at last came to Court, but they retained their principles, and Prerogative became a fashionable word. Placards were placed at the Royal Exchange and in Westminster Hall with the words: 'No Petticoat Government! No Scotch Favourite!' The King was naturally humane and benevolent, but he resigned himself obsequiously to the government of his mother and Bute. He bowed to the veto on his marriage to Lady Sarah Lenox, with whom he had fallen in love, and accepted the plain Mecklenburg princess chosen for him by his mother. It took time to discover that he was the most obstinate man in the kingdom.

In the struggle between Pitt and the Favourite which began with the new reign the statesman was bound to fail, for England was not yet a democracy. Finding his foreign policy vetoed, he resigned. 'It is difficult to say which exulted most on this occasion, France, Spain, or Lord Bute, for Mr Pitt was the common enemy of all three.' At this moment, unfortunately, he made a tactical mistake. 'The King was advised to heap rewards on his late Minister. The Princess pressed it eagerly. A peerage, a vast pension, the government of Canada (as a mark that it was not to be restored at the peace) were offered to him. He had the frailty to accept a peerage for his wife, and a pension of three thousand a year for their lives.' His great days were over, and Walpole's frequent references to the lost leader, 'a chief without a party,' became increasingly critical.

When the Duke of Newcastle followed Pitt into retirement, Bute, to the disgust of the nation, became First Lord of the Treasury. 'The facility which the Favourite found of mastering so great and victorious a kingdom, and of removing the man who had carried the glory of the country so high, was not the only evidence that, however enlightened an age may be, knavery and folly need never despair.' They are bitter words, but not too severe for the régime of the only Favourite in English history since Buckingham was murdered. Power, we are told, sucked the weak bladder of his mind to the highest pitch. His behaviour was haughty and distant, that of his creatures insolent. To Walpole's horror his old friend Henry Fox helped the Prime Minister by buying votes for the Treaty of Paris, which is described as a shameful and scandalous peace. When it was approved the Princess exclaimed: 'Now my son is King of England.'

The glove thrown down to constitutional tradition was picked up by Wilkes, who occupies a large space in the *Memoirs* and is treated with a mixture of gratitude and disdain. He was a bad speaker and his countenance was horrid. He had ill-used his wife, debauched a girl by an informal promise of marriage, committed frauds and other breaches of trust. He was more of a cynic than a martyr, and there was nothing in his principles that led him to care under what government he lived. 'To laugh and riot and scatter firebrands with him was liberty. Despotism will for ever reproach Freedom with the profligacy of such a saint.' Yet there were many things in *The North Briton* which Walpole approved, especially the famous Number 45 which denounced the Treaty of Peace. The adventurer's career suggests the reflection that nations are usually saved by their worst men, since the virtuous are too scrupulous to go to the lengths needed to rouse the people against their tyrants. 'Wilkes and Liberty' made a good cry, but the antics of the libertine demagogue proved too much for

the fastidious Whig. His triumph, we are told, deprived him of
the little discretion he possessed, and he seemed to put himself
into the situation of a king.

When England, in Walpole's phrase, seemed submissively
prostrate at the Favourite's feet, it was announced that he would
resign for reasons of health. He had occasionally declared that
he would go when he had made the peace, but few believed it,
and even his Cabinet colleagues were amazed. What was the
cause? Fear, replies the author without hesitation. 'The best
comment on his behaviour at that moment was his subsequent
conduct. The fondness he retained for power, his intrigues to
preserve it, the confusion he helped to throw into almost every
succeeding system, and his impotent and dark attempts to hang
on the wheels of the Government, which he only clogged and to
which he dreaded even being suspected of recommending drivers,
all proved that neither virtue nor philosophy had the honour of
dictating his retreat, but that fear and fear alone was the immediate inconsiderate and precipitate cause of his resignation.'
His pusillanimity, however, was a blessing. 'Had he been firm
to himself, there was an end of the Constitution. A happy panic
blew up the system of absolute power when it had lasted but five
months.' Whether our liberties were in such a desperate plight
as Walpole suggests may be doubted, but the nation was glad
enough to see his back. Yet even now he did not leave the stage:
he merely went behind the wings. Whatever the ministers might
think, he declared, they should find that he himself was minister
still. Poor Fred, the founder of his fortunes, had tired of him
before his death and said to him: 'Bute, you would make an
excellent ambassador to some proud little court where there is
nothing to do.'

The successor of the Favourite was scarcely more to Walpole's
taste. George Grenville had few admirers. The King declared
that he would rather see the devil enter his closet than his new
Prime Minister, and the author does not spare the patron of the
American Stamp Act. 'Mr Grenville had hitherto been known
but as a fatiguing orator and indefatigable drudge, more likely to
disgust than to offend. Beneath this awful unpromising outside
lay lurking great abilities: courage so confounded with obstinacy
that there was no drawing the line betwixt them; good intentions
to the public, without one great view; much economy for that
public, which in truth was the whole amount of his good intentions;
excessive rapaciousness and parsimony in himself; infinite self-
conceit, producing impossibility of instructing, convincing, or
setting him right; implacability in his temper and a total want
of principles in his political conduct; for, having long professed
himself uncommonly bigoted to the doctrines of liberty, he became

the staunchest champion of unwarrantable power. As all his passions were expressed in one livid smile, he never blushed at the variations in his behaviour. His ingratitude to his benefactor Lord Bute, and his reproaching Mr Pitt with the profusion of a war which he had sometimes actively supported and always tacitly approved, while holding a beneficial place, were but too often paralleled by the crimes of other men; but scarce any man ever wore in his face such outward and visible marks of the hollow, cruel and rotten heart within.'

Walpole's hatred of the Grenville Ministry turned to fury when General Conway, his first cousin and closest political ally, was dismissed from his command of a regiment of dragoons. It was the penalty for voting against General Warrants, though our author is uncertain whether the chief agent was the King, the Prime Minister, the Duke of Bedford, or Lord Bute. 'The temper and fairness of the man disgraced, his aversion to faction, the disinterestedness of his character, his general co-operation with the measures of government, his being recently recommended by Prince Ferdinand [of Brunswick] for his services in Germany, and his being brother to the ambassador at Paris [Lord Hertford], all these were considerations that made the measure amazing.' Conway bore the unmerited disgrace like a man. 'His temper, decency and submission were unalterable and unequalled. He neither complained nor tried to instil a sense of his injuries into a single friend.' That his family feared to take up the challenge increased Walpole's zeal. Never before or after was he so excited by any political incident. Though not a rich man he offered Conway six thousand pounds, which were declined; and he altered his will, leaving almost the whole of his fortune to his cousin unless his regiment should be restored to him. He shut himself up in the country for three days till he had conquered the first ebullitions of rage.

What more could be done? The plan of gingering the Opposition broke down. 'Every step I took I found discouragement and disappointment. There was no union in our party, nor could I bring about any. At first I laboured to form a little junta of the most considerable of our friends in the House of Commons, who should plan our future measures and conduct them. But of those I could not prevail on any three to assemble and enter into concert.' Newcastle, still the titular head of the Whig party, he had always despised. 'He was still the same; at once busy and inactive, fond of plotting, but impossible to be put in motion.' Pitt was equally unhelpful, refusing to see Conway, and Conway was too proud to make advances to Pitt. Walpole had planned many other strategems for annoying the Government, but they were 'damped or annihilated by the supineness of my confederates.'

In championing the cause of his cousin, Walpole was flying at higher game. Like every Whig worthy of the name he desired to limit the power of the Crown. 'The higher we could raise the flame of opposition, the sounder benefit we conferred on our country. Prerogative was the object of the Court, and corruption so flagrant in both Houses of Parliament that, if the people were not animated enough to hold both in check, no resource would be left but a civil war. Early opposition was the only preservative against the latter. My nature shuddered at the thoughts of blood, and I felt, what every good man will feel in civil commotions, that there is nothing so difficult as to make the people go far enough and prevent their going too far.' He wished to make the ministers both odious and ridiculous, but they were so profligate that they were the first to laugh and the last to fall. It was all in vain, and he relieved his feelings in a pamphlet. Once again he found that a country will never be saved by its best men. The whole Conway incident showed how little men are, 'though riding at what is called the Top of the World.' Filled with disgust, he resolved to quit Parliament, 'that splendid theatre of pitiful passions.' It was an additional mortification that the injured Conway displayed little gratitude or affection.

When the detested Grenville fell in 1765, Walpole wished Pitt to succeed and endeavoured to rally his friends. 'Nobody knew his faults better, but nobody admired his genius more; no man had felt greater pride than I had from the glorious position in which he had placed my country.' It was not to be, and the new Prime Minister was Lord Rockingham, the patron and hero of Burke. Though a great improvement on Grenville and Bute, he found little favour in Walpole's critical eyes. 'More childish in his deportment than in his age, he was totally void of all information. Ambitious, with excessive indolence; fond of talking of business, but dilatory in the execution, his single talent lay in attracting dependants; yet, though proud and self-sufficient, he had almost as many governors as dependants. To this unpromising disposition he had so weak a frame of person and nerves that no exigence could surmount his timidity of speaking in public; and having been only known to the public by his passion for horse-races, men could not be cured of their surprise at seeing him First Minister. His personal character was blameless—unfortunately the times required something more than negative qualities.' The best feature of the new Ministry in Walpole's view was the appointment of Conway as one of the two Secretaries of State. Rockingham had wished to make him Chancellor of the Exchequer; but he knew nothing of finance, and 'the disgusting coldness of his manner, which would revolt those he ought to court,' was a further disability.

The formation of a Whig Ministry with his cousin in one of the chief posts might have been expected to earn the writer's approval, but no blessings came from that quarter. With such a colourless chief it could hardly be expected to last long, but there was also a personal reason for this unfriendly attitude. The injustice inflicted on Conway had inspired Walpole with the fixed resolve to overthrow the Grenville Ministry, but in this programme there was no thought of personal interest. When he declares that he lacked political ambitions there is no need to disbelieve him. He was too thin-skinned to elbow his way through the Parliamentary throng; yet, though he had no desire for office, it was a shock to find himself overlooked. 'I flattered myself that if ever our party were successful, I should have the payments of my place settled on some foundation that should not expose me to the caprice or wanton tyranny of every succeeding Minister; for court I was resolved to make to none, whether friend or foe;—a haughtiness I maintained throughout my life, never once condescending to go to the levee of any First Minister.'

Walpole had mentioned this wish to Conway when they were in opposition, but it was received in silence and the hint was not renewed. 'As disinterestedness was my ruling passion, I did hope that on the change some considerable employment would be offered to me, which my vanity would have been gratified by refusing. It was mortifying enough to me, when Mr Conway reported the proposed arrangement of places, to find that my name had not been so much as mentioned.' It was Conway's fault, for if he took no action who else could be expected to move? 'For him I had sacrificed everything; for him I had been injured, oppressed, calumniated. The foundation of his own fortune, and almost every step of his fortune, he owed solely to me. Whatever was due to me, much or little, he totally forgot it; and so far from endeavouring to secure my independence, in his whole life after he never once mentioned it. Such failure of friendship, or, to call it by its truer name, such insensibility, could not but shock a heart at once so tender and so proud as mine. I had enough command of myself not to drop a word of reproach on a friendship so frozen.' Whether the services to his cousin had been so transcendent we have no means of knowing. Conway seems to have been unaware of his friend's gnawing resentment, for he continued to consult him and trusted him with secrets hidden from his brother and his wife.

The Rockingham Ministry lasted only a year, but it did not live in vain, for it repealed Grenville's American Stamp Act. The death of the Duke of Cumberland, a supporter of the Ministry and an enemy of Bute, was a damaging blow. 'The Butcher of Culloden' is painted in brighter colours than in the *Memoirs of*

George II. 'He would have made a great King, but probably too great a King for so corrupt a country.' Though he loved war, he was always beaten in his foreign campaigns; and he was excluded from political influence by his father and later by his sister-in-law. It was a frustrated life, for he had too much dignity and too great a respect for the Crown to be a *frondeur.* The chief weakness of the Rockingham Ministry was the hostility of the King, without whose support no Ministry in the eighteenth century could hope to survive. Moreover Pitt was anxious to resume office.

Walpole welcomed the return of the Great Commoner, who, despite failing health, towered above all other actors on the stage; but his acceptance of a peerage as the Earl of Chatham seemed to him a deplorable mistake. 'That fatal title blasted all the affection which the country had borne to him, and which he had deserved so well. The people, though he had done no act to occasion reproach, thought he had sold them for a title, and, as words fascinate or enrage them, their idol Mr Pitt was forgotten in their detestation of the Lord Chatham. The blow was more ruinous to his country than to himself. While he held the love of the people, nothing was so formidable in Europe as his name. The talons of the lion were drawn when he was no longer awful in his own forests.' Walpole exaggerates the evil effect of the peerage, but his verdict that peace was not his element is true enough. Finding the author at Bath the new Prime Minister visited him and had a frank talk of two hours, praising Conway whom he had taken over from the Rockingham team. But 'his presumptuous impracticability' made him a difficult chief, and he treated Conway with such lack of consideration that Walpole had to implore his cousin not to resign.

'Like oracles and groves, whose sanctity depended on the fears of the devout, and whose mysterious and holy gloom vanished as soon as men dared to think and walk through them, Lord Chatham's authority ceased with his popularity and his godhead when he had affronted his priests. Lord Chatham had been the arbiter of Europe; he affected to be the master of the English nobility; he failed, and remained with a train of domestics whom he could not pay. Yet British posterity will ever remember that, as Lord Chatham's first Administration obtained and secured the most real and substantial benefits of his country, the puerilities of his second could not efface their lustre. Even the shameful Peace of Paris, concluded in defiance of him, could not rob the nation of all he had acquired, nor could George III resign so much as Pitt had gained for George II. Half the empire of Hindostan, conquered under his Administration by the spirit he had infused, still pours its treasures into the Thames. Canada was subdued by his councils, and Spain and France, that yet dread his name, attest the reality of his services. The memory of his eloquence, which effected all these wonders, will remain when the neglect of his contemporaries and my criticisms will be forgotten.' It is one of Walpole's most finished portraits, and the twentieth-century historian finds little to add.

When the Duke of Grafton, a great-grandson of Charles II, succeeded Chatham in 1768, Walpole carried out his project of withdrawing from Parliament. Henceforth, he declares, he was detached from all parties and in the secrets of none; and though he learned a good deal from Conway, who was in the Grafton Cabinet, the value and interest of the *Memoirs* wane. Increased leisure enabled him to pay long visits to Paris during the closing years of the reign of Louis XV. In 1765 he saw much of Choiseul, still at the height of his power, the dissolute old Marshal Richelieu, and other prominent actors. But 'the great source of my intelligence was the celebrated old blind Marquise du Deffand, who had a strong and lasting friendship for me.' How ardent and indeed embarrassing her attachment became we learn not from his *Memoirs* but from her celebrated letters. Walpole is one of our many witnesses to the degradation of the Court under the sway of Mme du Barry. 'The doting Monarch was enchanted with her indelicacy, vulgarism, and indecencies, the novelty of which seemed to him simplicity. Her mirth was childish romping; her sallies, buffoonish insults; her conversation, solecisms and ignorance. She pulled off the Chancellor's wig, spat in the Duc de Laval's face at her levee—he deserved it, for he let her repeat it; and the King, who deserved it still more, she called "fool" and bade him hold his tongue.'

The fall of the Grafton Government in 1770, in Walpole's view, was due to the faults of its chief. 'His haughtiness, indolence, reserve and improvidence had conjured up the storm; but his obstinacy and fickleness were the radical causes of all the numerous absurdities that discoloured his conduct and exposed him to deserved reproaches; nor had he a depth of understanding to counterbalance the defects of his temper. He was the fourth Prime Minister in seven years who fell by his own fault. Lord Bute was seized with a panic and ran away from his own victory. Grenville was undone by his indolence. Lord Rockingham's incapacity overturned him; and now the Duke of Grafton, by a complication of passions and defect of system, destroyed a power that had depended on himself to make as permanent as he could desire.' Thus the way was cleared for a new system under the nominal leadership of Lord North.

The elaborate portrait, drawn from the life, of the man who held the office of Premier for twelve years is the last and one of the best in Walpole's crowded gallery. He admires his pluck in undertaking the post at a moment's notice, possessing neither connections with the nobility nor popularity with the country. The first contentious division was awaited with anxiety. 'If the Court should be beaten, the King would be at the mercy of the Opposition or driven to have recourse to the Lords—possibly to the sword.' When the Government won by a majority of forty the King wrote to his Minister that a little spirit would soon restore a degree of order in his service. The spirit was in the ruler, not in the Minister, for George III now became his own Premier and governed England till he lost the American colonies. The easy-going North was as much the servant of the King as the younger Pitt was his master.

'Frederic, Lord North, eldest son of the Earl of Guildford, was now in the thirty-eighth year of his age. Nothing could be more coarse or clumsy or ungracious than his outside. Two large prominent eyes that rolled about to no purpose (for he was utterly short-sighted), a wide mouth, thick lips, and inflated visage, gave him the air of a blind trumpeter. A deep untunable voice, which, instead of modulating, he enforced with unnecessary pomp, a total neglect of his person, and ignorance of every civil attention, disgusted all who judge by appearance. But within that rude casket were enclosed many useful talents. He had much wit, good-humour, strong natural sense, assurance and promptness, both of conception and elocution. His ambition had seemed to aspire to the height, yet he was not very ambitious. He was thought interested, yet he was not avaricious. What he did, he did without a mask, and was not delicate in choosing his means. He had knowledge, and, though fond of his amusement, seemed to have all necessary activity till he reached the summit. Yet that industry ceased when it became most requisite. He had neither system, nor principles, nor shame; sought neither the favour of the Crown nor of the people, but enjoyed the good luck of fortune with a gluttonous epicurism that was equally careless of glory and disgrace. His indolence prevented his forming any plan. His indifference made him leap from one extreme to another, and his insensibility to reproach reconciled him to any contradiction. He proved as indolent as the Duke of Grafton, but his temper being as good as the Duke's was bad, he was less hurt at capital disgraces than the Duke had been at trifling difficulties.'

North's conduct in the American war, the outstanding event of his ill-fated Ministry, illustrates the qualities noted by Walpole. 'He engaged in it against his opinion, and yet without reluctance. He managed it without foresight or address, and was neither ashamed when it miscarried, nor dispirited when the Crown itself became endangered by the additional war with France.

His good-humour could not be good-nature, for at the beginning of the war he stuck at no cruelty, but laughed at barbarities with which all Europe rung. It could not be good sense, for in the progress he blushed at none of the mischiefs he had occasioned, at none of the reproaches he had incurred. If he had ambition, it was of very mean complexion, for he stooped to be but a nominal Prime Minister, and suffered the King's private junto to enjoy the whole credit of favour, while, between submission and laziness, Lord North himself was seldom the author of the measures in which he bore the principal part. This passive and inglorious tractability, and his being connected with no faction, made him welcome to the King: his having no predominant fault or vice recommended him to the nation, and his good-humour and wit to everybody but the few whom his want of good breeding and attention offended. He was a man whom few hated, fewer could esteem. If he was free from vices, he was as void of virtues. Yet he was the least odious of the Ministers with whom he acted; and though servile to a Prince who meant so ill, there was reason to think that Lord North neither stimulated, nor was more than the passive instrument of, the black designs of the Court.' In other words, the Prime Minister was a cipher and George III the villain of the piece.

Critics and biographers of Horace Walpole who depict him as merely a gifted dilettante loitering through life do less than justice to the strength and sincerity of his political convictions. The horror of the French Revolution threw him off his balance, as it rattled much greater men; but he remained to the end a champion of the sound Whig theory that the royal power should be limited. The Hanoverian rulers, he believed, were constitutionalists by necessity, not by choice, and the maxims of the Stuarts were still secretly revered. The attempt to revive the influence of the Crown is traced back to the later years of George II, when the conduct of his ministers inspired the Princess of Wales and her husband Prince Frederick (Walpole places them in this order) with the desire of emancipating themselves. 'I am persuaded that she, her husband, and her son (if the latter at first had any plan) meditated humbling the aristocracy rather than invading liberty. Yet every increase of prerogative is so fatal, and so sure are the people of being trampled upon in such contest whether the Crown or the nobility get the better, that it was true patriotism to resist the attack, and the people were in the right not to consider the motives to the attempt, since in general questions the privileges of all the subjects are equally concerned.'

Walpole rings down the curtain on the death in 1772 of the woman whom he holds responsible for many of the disasters of the reign. She had given her family a wretched education. Her intimacy with Bute was spoken of by all her children with disgust, and they could have heard nothing but passionate lamentations on the impotence of English sovereigns. 'This unfortunate mother's fate is a speaking lesson to princes. Had the credit and happiness of her children been her object, her own life, except in those she lost, would have been prosperous and renowned. Her own ambition, and the desire of making her son more powerful than the laws allowed, led her and him into disgraces, mortifications, humiliations. Reviled, traduced, hated, she scarce dared to appear out of her own palace; her Favourite she saw driven from his country, and his life frequently endangered. Her younger children disgraced her; and the eldest, as well as herself, missed the despotism she sought for both, and obtained only that preeminence of Turkish sultans, being shut up with mutes in their own seraglio.'

Walpole's *Last Journals*, as he called them, continued his *Memoirs* to 1783. 'This Journal,' he wrote in 1772, 'is rather calculated for my own amusement than for posterity. I like to keep up the thread of my observations: if they prove useful to anybody else I shall be glad; but I am not to answer for their imperfections, as I intend this Journal for no regular work.' Though he attached less importance to the later enterprise, and though there are many entries of no special significance, it possesses considerable interest. The notes were worked up into a narrative, and additions were made as fresh information came to hand. He kept in close touch with his cousin Conway, the Duke of Richmond, and other political friends, and on rare occasions he attended debates in the House of Commons.

Walpole never approved of George III, either as a ruler or a man, and the King's heartless conduct in regard to the marriage of his brother excited his angry disgust. The Duke of Gloucester had secretly married Walpole's beautiful niece, the widow of Lord Waldegrave, and when the coming of a child rendered further concealment impossible, the King pretended to doubt whether the marriage had actually taken place. His other brother, the Duke of Cumberland, had also married a commoner, and it was this union, which had not been concealed, that led to the Royal Marriage Act of 1772. Though Cumberland was a rake and Gloucester an affectionate husband, the ruler's wrath was concentrated on the latter. Walpole had disapproved the match for fear of complications, but when the storm broke he stood loyally by his beloved niece. No one can read the letters reproduced in the *Journal* and the repeated references to this painful theme without feeling that he had a tender heart. The King was finally convinced of the validity of the marriage, but he yielded with a singularly bad

13

grace and never admitted the Duchess to Court. 'Thus ended this memorable transaction, with the complete triumph of the Duke, and to the signal credit of his sense and character. The King through the whole showed so much pride, ill-nature, duplicity and pusillanimity that one may almost conclude the whole had been concerted and conducted by himself, the Queen, her woman, and a man as silly as her woman, Lord Rochford. Satisfactory as the Archbishop's letter was at last [the King's recognition of the validity was communicated to the Duke by the Archbishop], I soon learned that the avowal had been wrung most reluctantly from a mind that had harboured disingenuity to the last moment, and which, as deceit pursued to its inmost retreat never pardons, His Majesty resolved not to forgive.' While Gloucester, having done nothing of which he was ashamed, made no effort to regain favour, Cumberland expressed contrition for arousing the royal wrath. 'The King, whose joy and talent lay in fomenting division in all connections, was charmed with these overtures, and affected to favour his contemptible brother, whom he always hated, in order to mortify and affront his favourite brother, for folly and demerit never wanted His Majesty's countenance if they were but abject enough. Sense and virtue might awe him, but were sure of his aversion.'

Walpole detested the American war, the dominating theme of the *Last Journals*, and wished the Opposition to display more spirit. It was an additional reason for disliking the King, whose desire to increase the power of the Crown he, who described himself as almost a Republican, could never forgive. He speaks contemptuously of the gay indolence, the jocose levity, of Lord North, a pliant tool without system or principle; of the knaves who surrounded him, of the ecclesiastics who favoured the revival of Stuart views. But his sharpest arrows were reserved for the villain of the piece, to whom he allows obstinacy but not courage; and he sought comfort in the prospect that the war was bound to reduce the royal power. 'If America gets the better,' he wrote at the outset, 'it will be independent, or will not return to us without effectuating by stipulation a total change of administration and a blow to despotism. If Britain prevails, it cannot be but by ruining the towns and trade of America, and by wasting the King's fleet, armies and treasure, his best means of despotism. If a middle way, an ignominious treaty, ensues, what disgrace to the Crown, and what a damp to its further innovations! No case can happen in which, if the King prevails, he will not be a far less potent monarch than before the war. These kingdoms are more likely to grow shocked at so ignominious a reign, compared with its glorious commencement, and few princes that grow despised augment their power. If a civil war will not dispel our delusion, a French or Spanish war, or both, will tear the bandage from the eyes that wink most obstinately. Then will our absolute Monarch know the difference between the constitutional glory of such a King as his grandfather, and that of a despotic sovereign who has revolted and laid waste his colonies, and impoverished and exhausted his subjects at home.' This slashing indictment is not the language of a man who cared for little beyond the leisured ease of Strawberry Hill with his library, his printing press, and his antiques. He had always hated cruelty, and he denounces 'our barbarities and folly' in America which 'shocked everybody but the English and the Scotch.'

The loss of the American colonies ended the disastrous partnership of George III and Lord North. 'The Administration had given the most fatal stab to the glory and interests of England, by (I believe) planning (certainly by taking no step to prevent), pushing on, and persisting in the American war, and had, by the countenance of the Crown, and by the arts of the Scotch and the intoxication of the nation, maintained themselves under the greatest disgraces and losses that ever this country had sustained.' An additional satisfaction, both on personal and national grounds, was the appointment of Conway as Commander-in-Chief by the short-lived Second Rockingham Ministry. 'This was the centre of my wishes. I had long dreaded lest success or despair should infuse resolution enough into the King to endeavour to establish absolute power by the army. Had the conquest of America been achieved, I have not the smallest doubt but a triumphant army, returned from subduing the King's enemies and stigmatised by the Americans as Tories, would have been unbounded, being ready to make war on all called Whigs and all the King should call his enemies.'

The closing chapters of the *Journals* describe the confusion on the home front after the fall of North: 'The King greatly unhappy. He said that every morning he wished himself eighty or ninety, or dead.' To Lord North he remarked: 'You have often seen me keep my temper, but now I often cannot command it.' Exasperated by defeat and by the loss of his spineless Premier, he was sometimes barely civil to his new advisers. On the death of the feeble but blameless Rockingham the most distrusted figure on the political stage took his place. The *Journals* lack the elaborate portraits which are a feature of the *Memoirs*, but in his characterisation of Lord Shelburne Walpole is blinded by hatred and lets himself go. 'His falsehood was so constant and notorious that it was rather his profession than his instrument. He was so well known that he could only deceive by speaking truth. His plausibility was less an artifice than a habit, and his smiles were so excited that, like the rattle of the snake, they warned before he had time to bite. Both his heart and his face were brave; he feared neither danger nor detection. He was so fond of insincerity as if he had been the inventor, and preached it with as little caution as if he thought nobody else had discovered the secret. He not only had no principles, but was ready for any crimes that suited his plans, which seemed drawn from histories of the worst ages. Thus a Catiline or a Borgia were his models in an age when half their wickedness would have suited his purpose better. He determined to be Prime Minister by any means, but forgot that character is a necessary ingredient towards acquiring or preserving power. The King hated him.' How unfairly Walpole treated this distinguished but unpopular statesman was shown a century later in the monumental biography of his ancestor by Lord Edmund Fitzmaurice.

The portrait of Charles James Fox is less studied but far more true to life in its recognition both of merits and defects. He knew him much less intimately than his father, but, like almost everyone except the King, he yielded to the charm of the man whom Burke described as made to be loved. 'Fox lodged in St James's Street, and as soon as he rose, which was very late, had a levee of his followers and of the members of the Gaming Club at Brookes's, all his disciples. His bristly black person, and shaggy breast quite open, and rarely purified by any ablutions, was wrapped in a foul linen night-gown, and his bushy hair dishevelled. In these cynic weeds, and with epicurean good humour, did he dictate his politics, and in this school did the heir to the Crown attend his lessons and imbibe them. When not in office he thinks of nothing but his pleasures, nor of business except when he is doing it in the House of Commons. Void of art or design, if nature had not made him the most powerful reasoner of the age, he would never have distinguished himself. He never stooped to any of the manœuvres of a politician. Had not Pitt so early aspired to be his rival, Fox would have cherished him as his friend and disciple.' Pitt's abilities were rated by Walpole as infinitely inferior to those of Fox, 'but his attention to character, and future experience, is more likely to set him at the head of this country than any man.' This prophecy, written in May 1783, when Pitt was only twenty-four, was about to be fulfilled in a Premiership of seventeen memorable years. With the opening of the new era the *Journals* end. For Walpole's verdict on his performances we must turn to the letters which he continued to write till his death in 1797 in his eightieth year. He had never been happy without a pen in his hand.

Bibliographical Note.—The volumes on the reign of George II, edited by the third Lord Holland, appeared in 1822, and a new edition in 1847. The volumes on the first decade of the reign of George III were published by Sir Denis le Marchant in 1845, and a new edition by G. F. Russell Barker appeared in 1894. The *Later Journals, 1771–1783,* were edited by A. F. Stewart. The fragmentary *Reminiscences of the Court of George II* were first published in full by Paget Toynbee in 1924. The best short survey of the life and writings is by Dorothy M. Stuart in the *English Men of Letters.* The best portrait of the man is by Stephen Gwynn. Austin Dobson's monograph is good on the art collector but weak on the political side, which is best studied in the massive French biography by Paul Yvon. Leslie Stephen's essay is in *Hours in a Library,* vol. 1. In addition to the older histories by Stanhope and Lecky, Basil Williams, *The Whig Supremacy, 1714–60, Carteret and Newcastle, The Life of Chatham*; Ilchester, *Henry Fox*; Fitzmaurice, *The Life of Shelburne*; Keith Feiling, *The Tory Party, 1714–1832*; Turberville, *The House of Lords in the Eighteenth Century*; Namier, *The Structure of Politics at the Accession of George III* and *England in the Age of the American Revolution* are useful. The descriptions and verdicts in the *Memoirs* and *Journals* should be compared with those in the *Letters,* edited by Mrs Paget Toynbee. A sumptuous American editions of the correspondence by W. S. Lewis is in course of publication.

CHAPTER XV

FANNY BURNEY AND QUEEN CHARLOTTE

THE publication by her niece of Mme d'Arblay's *Diary and Letters* in 1842 revealed the author of *Evelina* and *Cecilia* not only as a gifted and lovable woman but as one of the most accomplished recorders in English literature. Dr Johnson's 'little character-monger,' it was discovered, was no less skilled in the delineation of living people and historic events than in clothing the creations of her fancy with flesh and blood. Jeffrey, the veteran editor, declared that many of her portraits of celebrities were as good as anything in Boswell; and when Croker attacked her in the *Quarterly*, Macaulay did her full justice in the *Edinburgh Review*. The book became and has remained a popular favourite, ranking with Pepys and Evelyn. The publication in 1889 of her *Early Diaries*, extending from her sixteenth to her twenty-sixth year, was a further indication that the public had taken her to its heart, for they had been held back by her niece as of too little general interest. In a journal composed for her family and a few intimate friends there is naturally a good deal of trivial detail, but there are many chapters from which both literary and political historians cut and come again. No such intimate picture of the Court of George III and Queen Charlotte has ever been painted; the narrative of the King's illness in 1788 and the snapshots of the Warren Hastings trial are testimony of the first importance; while her marriage to General d'Arblay opened the door to French society in the time of the Revolution and brought her to Paris and Brussels during the Hundred Days. Croker challenged the accuracy of her full-length conversation pieces, and it is obvious that such exchanges are always a little touched up. But we have her father's testimony to her 'bird-lime memory,' and the book is based on entries written up from day to day.

In a work on Courts and Cabinets there is no need to linger over the pre-*Evelina* period of the *Early Diaries*, and we may begin when the young novelist took London by storm. Her adored father, Dr Burney, an accomplished musician, a friend of Handel, and an erudite historian of music, attracted celebrities to his musical parties, many of whom extended their friendship to his precocious child. Garrick called her 'the old lady' at the age of ten. There is the freshness of a spring morning in the story of the literary and social *début* of the shy girl who at the age of twenty-six published the best English novel of manners before Jane Austen, and was welcomed, not as a nine days' wonder but as a valued friend, by several of the first men of the age. 'My

little Burney,' as Dr Johnson called her in paternal affection, gives
us both the tenderness and the fun of the oracle of Fleet Street
in richer measure than Boswell himself. Mrs Thrale introduced
her to her famous literary salon at Streatham and took her to her
heart. Burke and Reynolds displayed an enduring interest in her
welfare. Goldsmith, Windham, Garrick, Nollekens the sculptor,
Sheridan, Arthur Young the agriculturist, Mrs Montagu the Queen
of the Bluestockings, Horace Walpole, Gibbon, and a host of other
celebrities cross the stage. Like every healthy human being she
delighted in her success, but neither sales nor compliments turned
her head. The Fannikin of Daddy Crisp, her 'second father,'
remained an unspoiled and affectionate woman, devotedly attached
to her family and her many friends.

In 1783, at the age of thirty-one, shortly after the publication
of her second novel, *Cecilia*, Fanny met Mrs Delany, widow of one
of the few intimate friends of Swift, and loved her at first sight.
The old lady of eighty-three was a valued friend of the King and
Queen, who lent her a small house at Windsor and provided an
allowance of £300 a year. One day at the end of 1785, when
Fanny was staying with her, the King walked in and began to
talk about *Evelina*.

THE KING. How came you? How happened it?

F. B. I only wrote, Sir, for my own amusement, only in some
odd, idle hours.

THE KING. But your publishing, your printing, how was that?

F. B. I thought, Sir, it would look very well in print. (I do
really flatter myself this is the silliest speech I ever made. He
laughed very heartily himself.)

THE KING. But your father—how came you not to show him
what you wrote?

F. B. I was too much ashamed of it, Sir, seriously.

THE KING. But you have not kept your pen unemployed all
this time?

F. B. Indeed, I have, Sir.

THE KING. But why?

F. B. I believe I have exhausted myself, Sir.

THE KING. I believe there is no constraint to be put on real
genius; nothing but inclination can set it to work. Miss Burney,
however, knows best.

At this moment the Queen arrived, and joined in the appeal to
use her pen. 'I would not say it, only that I think from what has
been done there is a power to do so much good—and good to
young people—which is so very good a thing that I cannot help
wishing it could be.' Fanny was delighted with her first glimpse
of the royal pair. 'The Queen is a most charming woman. She
appears to me full of sense and graciousness, mingled with delicacy

of mind and liveliness of temper. She speaks English almost perfectly well, with great choice and copiousness of language, though now and then with a foreign idiom and frequently with a foreign accent. Her manners have an easy dignity with a most engaging simplicity, and she has all that fine high breeding which the mind, not the station, gives, of carefully avoiding to distress those who converse with her, or studiously removing the embarrassment she cannot prevent. The King, however he may have power in the Cabinet to command himself, has in private the appearance of a character the most open and sincere. He speaks his opinions without reserve, and seems to trust them intuitively to his hearers, from a belief they will make no ill use of them. All I saw of both was the most perfect good humour, good spirits, ease and pleasantness. Their behaviour to each other speaks the most cordial confidence and happiness. In their different ways, and allowing for the difference of their characters, they left me equally charmed both with their behaviour to each other and to myself.' The Queen was equally pleased with the meeting, and sent a kind message through Mrs Delany.

A day or two later the King came to tea and talked about literature and the stage. When Rousseau was condemned for savage pride and insolent ingratitude, Fanny told how her father had visited him in Paris and found the King's portrait over the mantelpiece—a sign of gratitude for the pension he had bestowed. Mrs Siddons was preferred to Garrick, the want of good modern comedies was deplored, and the immorality of most of the old ones denounced. At last he came to Shakespeare.

THE KING. Was there ever such stuff as great part of Shakespeare? Only one must not say so. But what think you? What? Is there not sad stuff? What? What?

F. B. Yes, indeed, I think so, Sir, though mixed with such excellence that——

THE KING (*laughing good-humouredly*). I know it is not to be said, but it's true. Only it's Shakespeare, and nobody dare abuse him.

He stayed two hours, for this time Fanny found her tongue. 'He is a pattern of modest but manly superiority to rank,' she reported. Next day, December 20, 1785, accompanied by Mrs Delany, she was summoned to a 'very delightful' private conversation.

THE QUEEN. Miss Burney, have you heard that Boswell is going to publish a life of your friend, Dr Johnson?

F. B. No, ma'am.

THE QUEEN. I don't know for the truth of it, and I can't tell what he will do. He is so extraordinary a man that perhaps he will devise something extraordinary. Is Mme de Genlis about any new work?

F. B. Yes, ma'am; one which she intends 'pour le peuple.'

THE QUEEN. Ah, that will be a good work. Do you like the *Sorrows of Werther*?

F. B. I have not read it, ma'am, only in part.

THE QUEEN. I don't know how it is translated, but it is very finely writ in German, and I can't bear it.

F. B. I am very happy to hear that, for what I did look over made me determine never to read it. It seemed only writ as a deliberate defence of suicide.

THE QUEEN. Yes, and what is worse, it is done by a bad man for revenge.

The conversation then passed to Klopstock's *Messiah*, which the Queen complained was badly translated, to Milton, Wycliffe, Cranmer and the practices of the Roman Church.

Fanny returned to London for Christmas, blissfully unaware of the significance of her contacts with the royal family. Five months later, in May 1786, she paid another visit to Mrs Delany at a time when the Second Keeper of the Robes, who had accompanied the Mecklenburg Princess to England on her marriage, returned to Germany. The post was promptly offered to her with time for consideration. 'I was led to think of Miss Burney,' explained the Queen to Mrs Delany, 'first by her books, then by seeing her, then by always hearing that she was loved by her friends, but chiefly by your friendship for her.' The offer, which carried a salary of £200 a year, was received with consternation, and Fanny explained to the bearer of the royal message that 'no situation of that sort was suited to my taste or promising to my happiness.' Her greatest terror, she wrote to a friend, was lest the Queen should make her promise herself a length of years. 'Anything that has a period is endurable; but what can I object that will not sound ungrateful to the honour she is doing me and meaning me? She is one of the sweetest characters in the world, but I have always had a horror of a life of attendance and dependence.' She was persuaded to accept by her father and Mrs Delany, the two people whose judgment had the most weight, and all her friends approved. Burke left a card at Dr Burney's house with congratulations 'upon the honour done by the Queen to Miss Burney and to herself.' 'I was in the very joy of my heart,' wrote Hannah More, 'on seeing the other day in the papers that our charming Miss Burney has got an establishment so near the Queen. How I love the Queen for having so wisely chosen!'

Everybody was delighted except Fanny herself. 'Everything is settled,' she wrote to her father on June 19, after an interview with the Queen, 'and to-morrow morning I go to the Queen's Lodge to see the apartments and to receive my instructions. I must confess myself extremely frightened and full of alarms at a change of situation so great, so unexpected, so unthought of. Whether I shall suit it or not, Heaven only knows, but I have a thousand doubts. Yet nothing could be sweeter than the Queen, more encouraging, more gentle, or more delicate. She did not ask me one question concerning my qualifications for the charge. She only said, with the most condescending softness, "I am sure, Miss Burney, we shall suit one another very well." The pre-possession the Queen has taken in my favour is truly extra-ordinary, for it seems as if her real view was to attach me to her person.' The Court, added Fanny, would hear of the appointment with the utmost astonishment. 'Everybody has settled some successor to Mrs Haggerdorn; and I have never, I am very sure, been suggested by a single person.' She was told that the place had been solicited distantly by thousands of women of fashion and rank. 'Everybody so violently congratulates me that it seems as if all was gain. However I am glad they are all so pleased. My dear father is in raptures, that is my first comfort.' She felt as if she had been married against her will. 'The knot is tied. What then now remains but to make the best wife in my power? I am bound to it in duty, and I will strain every nerve to succeed.' There could be no gladness in her heart as she thought of unwritten books and unvisited friends.

Fanny's period of service began on July 17, 1786, and she quickly settled into the wearisome routine. Closer acquaintance with the royal couple confirmed the impressions formed in the chance meetings under Mrs Delany's roof. 'A noble sovereign this is,' she wrote in her journal, 'and when justice is done him he will as such be acknowledged.' During her five years at Court she received nothing but kindness from him, and in no contem-porary work does he appear in such an attractive light. She had been bred a Tory, and her instinctive loyalty ripened into affec-tionate reverence. Knowing nothing of politics and parties, she was unaware of the less amiable features of his régime. She saw merely the devoted husband, the tender father, who lived frugally, gave himself no airs, cared nothing for pomp, stopped gambling at Court, worked hard, and had a kindly word for everyone. He often dropped in when Mrs Delany visited her friend. Hating loose living as she did, she was grateful to the King for setting the example of a happy family life. That she was unhappy at Windsor was certainly not his fault.

The portrait of her mistress is naturally far more elaborate, and the two volumes on Fanny's life at Court are our best authority on Queen Charlotte, who lived for her family and took no part in politics. Such a retiring person needed a good deal of knowing, and it was only by degrees that the Second Dresser realised how much there was in her. 'The Queen was unremittingly sweet and gracious,' she wrote after a few weeks of service. 'For the excellency of her mind I was fully prepared, but the depth and soundness of her understanding surprised me. Good sense I expected: to that alone she could owe the even tenor of her conduct, universally approved, though examined and judged by the watchful eye of multitudes. But I had not imagined that, shut up in the confined limits of a Court, she could have acquired any but the most superficial knowledge of the world and the most partial insight into character. But I find now I have only done justice to her disposition, not to her parts, which are truly of that superior order that makes sagacity intuitively supply the place of experience. In the course of this month I spent much time quite alone with her, and never once quitted her presence without fresh admiration of her talents.' She cared nothing for the trappings of royalty, though she was always ready to play her part with fitting dignity on ceremonial occasions. 'She told me with the sweetest grace imaginable how well she had liked at first her jewels and ornaments as Queen. "But how soon," cried she, "was that over! Believe me, Miss Burney, it is a pleasure of a week—a fortnight at most—and to return no more." She told me she had never in her most juvenile years loved dress and show, nor received the smallest pleasure from anything in her external appearance beyond neatness and comfort. Yet she did not disavow that the first week or fortnight of being a Queen, when only in her seventeenth year, she thought splendour sufficiently becoming her station to believe she should henceforth choose constantly to support it. But her eyes alone were dazzled, not her mind, and therefore the delusion speedily vanished.' No Queen was ever less of a mischief-maker, and she lived out her long life without making an enemy.

Fanny liked the six princesses, and Amelia, the youngest, was the darling of the Court. They often came to her room, and they are depicted as healthy and unaffected though not particularly intelligent girls. That they admired her novels was a good start. Of the princes we hear little, most of them having grown up and left the nest. The second son, Frederick Duke of York, described as gay, modest, yet unembarrassed, was the favourite of his parents, and his return from Germany after an absence of seven years was a happy day at Windsor. The King's joy and pride went to her heart. The Prince of Wales is hardly even a shadow on the screen.

While the royal family surpassed her expectations, Fanny was shocked by her chief, Mrs Schwellenberg. The Senior Keeper of Robes had accompanied her mistress from Mecklenburg, and her fidelity to the royal couple was beyond dispute. But that was her only virtue, for the old hag from Germany, as Macaulay describes her, had a vile temper and no manners. She was utterly selfish, could only talk broken English, and was almost illiterate. Some of the unpublished entries in the diaries are even more critical, and according to Mrs Papendiek, who also detested her, the King would have sent her back to Germany but for the opposition of his wife. Next to the Queen she is the most finished portrait in the Windsor gallery. Perhaps because she was short-sighted, Fanny describes people by their talk, not by their looks, and Cerbera or La Présidente lives again in these dialogues and monologues. The Second Dresser had to spend about six hours of utter boredom daily with her chief, to listen to her garrulous talk, to bear with her rude outbursts, and to take unwilling part in the card games which she loved. Her happiest times were when the Schwellenberg was away or laid up with the gout.

Fanny quickly realised that she had made a fatal mistake. The life, she confessed, was dead and tame. 'Can you blame the plan that I have gradually been forming,' she wrote to her sister after a month's experience, 'namely to wean myself from myself, to lessen all my affections, to curb all my wishes, to deaden all my sensations? This design I formed so long ago as the first day my dear father accepted my offered appointment. I thought that what demanded a complete new system of life required, if attainable, a complete new set of feelings for all enjoyment of new prospects and for lessening regrets at what were quitted or lost. Such being my primitive idea, merely from my grief of separation, imagine how it was strengthened and confirmed when the interior of my position became known to me, when I saw myself expected by Mrs Schwellenberg not to be her colleague but her dependent deputy; not to be her visitor at my own option but her companion, her humble companion, at her own command. This has given so new a character to the place I had accepted under such different auspices that nothing but my horror of disappoint-ing, perhaps displeasing my dearest father, has deterred me, from the moment that I made this mortifying discovery, from soliciting his leave to resign. Kind, good, indulgent as he is to me, I have not the heart so cruelly to thwart his hopes, his views, his happiness in the honours he conceived awaiting my so unsolicited appointment. The Queen, too, is all sweetness, encouragement and gracious goodness to me, and I cannot endure to complain to her of her old servant. You see then my situation: here I must remain. The die is cast, and that struggle is no more. Little does the Queen know the slavery I must either resist or endure.' Macaulay defines her duties as mixing snuff and sticking pins.

Except for Mrs Schwellenberg the members of the household, male and female, were pleasant enough, and Colonel Digby, always mentioned as Mr Fairly, the Queen's Vice-Chamberlain, an elderly widower, became a devoted friend. But the Court was a dull place, the duties were exacting, and everybody wearied of the monotonous routine. 'After all one's labours, riding, and walking, and standing, and bowing,' exclaimed Colonel Golds-worthy, one of the equerries, 'what a life it is! Well, it's honour! That's one comfort. It's all honour! royal honour! One has the honour to stand till one has not a foot left; and to ride till one's stiff, and to walk till one's ready to drop,—and then one makes one's lowest bow, and blesses one's self with joy for the honour. All the comfort of my life in this house is one half-hour in a day spent in this room. How do you like it, ma'am? Though it's hardly fair to ask you yet, because you know almost nothing of the joys of this sort of life. But wait till November and December, and then you'll get a pretty taste of them! You'll get knocked up in three days, take my word for that!' There was an element of humorous exaggeration in this outburst, and Fanny points out that as a man of means he could have resigned had he wished; but the prophecy of ill-health was correct. The early rising, late hours, long standing, the absence of leisure and holidays, the isolation from family and friends, added to the strain of adapting herself to a position for which she felt herself radically unsuited.

Despite physical weariness, boredom, and a numbing sense of intellectual frustration, Fanny resolved to make the best of a bad job. On January 16, 1787, the day appointed to move to town for the winter, the King came in, asked kindly how she was and whether she had sufficiently recovered from a short illness to undertake the journey. The four days in bed, she tells us, had been a time of useful meditation. 'I reflected upon all my mental sufferings in the last year; their cause seemed inadequate to their poignancy. In the hour of sickness and confinement the world, in losing its attractions, forfeits its regrets. A steady plan, calm yet no longer sad, deliberately formed itself in my mind: my affection was already subsided; I now banished also discontent. I found myself as well off, upon reflection, as I could possibly merit, and better, by comparison, than most of those around me. The beloved friends of my own heart had joined me unalterably, inviolably to theirs; who, in number, who, in kindness, has more? Now, therefore, I took shame to myself and *resolved to be happy*. And my success has shown me how far less chimerical than it appears is such a resolution. To relinquish without repining frequent intercourse with those I love; to settle myself in my monastery without one idea of ever quitting it; to study for the approbation of my lady abbess, and make it a principal source of content as well as spring of action; to associate more cheerily with my surrounding nuns and monks: these were the articles which were to support my resolution. I thank God I can tell my dearest friends I have observed them all. And now, I thank God, the task is at an end. What I began from principle and pursued from resolution is now a mere natural conduct. My destiny is fixed, and my mind is at ease; nay I even think, upon the whole, that my lot is altogether the best that can betide me, except for one flaw in its very vitals, which subjects me at times to a tyranny wholly subversive of all power of tranquillity.' The flaw was Mrs Schwellenberg, whose yoke became ever heavier with the advancing years.

In November 1787 Fanny and her mistress were upset by a newspaper announcement that she had resigned her place about the Queen and had been promoted to attend the princesses—'an office far more suited to her character and abilities which will now be called forth as they merit.' The news was brought by Dr Burney, and Fanny hoped that it would not be known at Court. Next day she was told that everyone knew about it, and the princesses, though they never read newspapers, had been told by the Duke of York. The Queen was particularly gracious that day, softer and gentler than ever. 'Looking at me very steadfastly, she said, Miss Burney, do you ever read newspapers?'

F. B. Sometimes, but not often: however I believe I know what Your Majesty means.

THE QUEEN. Do you?

F. B. Yes, ma'am, and I have been very much hurt by it: that is, if Your Majesty means anything relative to myself.

THE QUEEN (*looking at her earnestly*). I do.

F. B. My father, ma'am, told me of it last night, with a good deal of indignation.

THE QUEEN. I did not see it myself. You know how little I read the newspapers.

F. B. Indeed, as it was in a paper not taken in here, I hoped it would quite have escaped Your Majesty.

THE QUEEN. When the Duke of York came yesterday for dinner he said, 'Pray, ma'am, what has Miss Burney left you for?' 'Left me?' 'Yes, they say she's gone. Is she not gone?' 'Not that I know of.'

The Queen had been staggered, for she apparently thought that there was something behind the paragraph, and Fanny seized the first occasion to clear the matter up. 'They little know me, ma'am, who think I should regard any other place as a promotion that removed me from Your Majesty.' 'I did not take it ill,' replied the Queen gently. 'Indeed, ma'am, I am far from having a wish for any such *promotion*—far from it. Your Majesty does not bestow a smile upon me that does not secure and confirm my attachment.' 'You are very good,' replied the Queen in a gentle voice.   Thus the incident ended happily, for the Queen had shown beyond all doubt her desire to retain her services.   'I can hardly tell you,' she reported, 'how sweet was her whole manner nor how marked her condescension.   Oh, were there no Mrs Schwellenberg!' She now renewed her resolve 'that, in total disregard of all that belongs to myself, I must cherish no thought of retreat, unless *called* hence by willing kindness to the paternal home, or *driven* hence by weakness and illness from the fatigues of my office.' At the opening of 1788 we read that the Queen's graciousness had grown into the most perfect, the most flattering kindness.   The beloved Mrs Delany seized the opportunity to assure her of Fanny's gratitude for her goodness.

MRS DELANY. Fanny Burney has only one fault.

THE QUEEN. What?

MRS DELANY. She wants so much drawing out.

THE QUEEN. Yes, but she's very well worth it.

1787 had been an uneventful year, but 1788 was memorable for two events in which Fanny took the keenest interest and on which her testimony has passed straight into the history books.   Apart from her attachment to the royal family she had little interest in affairs.   We hardly hear of the American War of Independence, and there is very little about the French Revolution till her marriage took her into a wider world; but the trial of Warren Hastings stirred her to the depths.   Macaulay's belief that she borrowed her opinions from the sovereigns, warm champions of the great proconsul, is too simple an explanation.   Burke, the moving spirit in the impeachment, had been for many years the honoured friend of her father and herself, and no one felt greater reverence for his character and genius.   But she had also met Hastings, and, though it had only been a fleeting contact, she had formed so favourable an impression that all Burke's eloquence was in vain.   Moreover, one of her sisters had recently married his private secretary, who confidently foretold that 'the prosecution would turn out to Mr Hastings' glory.'   Gratefully accepting the offer of one of the Queen's tickets, she was present in Westminster Hall on February 13, 1788, at the opening of the most famous state trial since that of Charles I.   Fascinated by the pageant and passionately interested in the fate of the defendant, she came again and again, reporting her experience in detail to her royal mistress when the latter could not attend.

'I shuddered and drew involuntarily back when, as the doors were flung open, I saw Mr Burke, as Head of the Committee, make his solemn entry.   He held a scroll in his hand and walked alone, his brow knit with corroding care and deep labouring thought, a brow how different to that which had proved so alluring to my warmest admiration when first I met him: so highly as he had

been my favourite, so captivating as I had found his manners
and conversation in our first acquaintance, and so much as I had
owed to his zeal and kindness to me and my affairs in its progress.
How did I grieve to behold him now the cruel Prosecutor (such to
me he appeared) of an injured and innocent man!' A wave of
emotion surged over her when Hastings was summoned to the bar.
After a few words from the Lord Chancellor he bowed to the Court
and answered: 'My Lords, impressed, deeply impressed, I come
before Your Lordships, equally confident in my own integrity and
in the justice of the Court before which I am to clear it.' This
brief speech confirmed her favourable anticipations, 'and all my
best wishes for his clearance and redress rose warmer than ever
in my heart.' While the lengthy indictment was being read he
surveyed the scene. 'Pale looked his face—pale, ill and altered.
Had I looked at him without restraint, it could not have been
without tears. I felt shocked, too, shocked and ashamed to be
seen in that place. His eyes were not those I wished to meet in
Westminster Hall.' She was terrified lest he should see her, and
it was a relief when Reynolds bowed, smiled and nodded to her
with his usual good humour and intimacy. Hastings was now
quite at his ease. 'He seemed composed after the first half-hour,
and calm; but he looked with a species of indignant contempt
towards his accusers that could not, I think, have been worn had
his defence been doubtful. Many there are who fear for him;
for me, I own myself wholly confident in his acquittal.'

As a holder of the Queen's ticket Fanny occupied a conspicuous
place in Westminster Hall. She was visited by various acquaintances, among them the brother and son of Edmund Burke; but
with one alone did she enter into earnest conversation. Her
brother, who sat behind her, leaned down and told her that a
gentleman desired to be presented. 'Who?' 'Mr Windham.'
'What could I do? There was no refusing; yet a planned meeting
with another of the Committee, and one deep in the prosecution,
and from whom one of the hardest charges has come—could
anything be less pleasant as I was then situated?' She had only
seen him twice, and anywhere else would have been much gratified
by his desire for a meeting, as he was one of the most agreeable,
spirited, well-bred, and brilliant talkers she had ever met. 'I was
sorry to see him make one of a set that appeared so inveterate
against a man I believe so injuriously treated; and my concern
was founded upon the good thoughts I had conceived of him, not
merely from his social talents, which are yet very uncommon,
but from a reason dearer to my remembrance. He loved Dr
Johnson, and Dr Johnson returned his affection.'

After a few remarks on the brilliant scene Windham fixed his
gaze on Hastings and exclaimed: 'What a sight is that! To see

that man, that small portion of human clay, that poor feeble machine of earth, enclosed now in that little space, brought to that Bar, a prisoner in a spot six foot square—and to reflect on his late power! Nations at his command! Princes prostrate at his feet! What a change! How must he feel it!' Fanny was relieved to hear these words, hoping they indicated a softening of enmity, but a moment later she received a shock. Suddenly arousing himself he passionately exclaimed: 'Oh, could those— the thousands, the millions, who have groaned and languished under the iron rod of his oppressions—could they but be permitted one dawn of light to look into this Hall and see him *there*! *There*—where he now stands—it might prove, perhaps, some recompense for their sufferings. In the history of human nature how memorable will be the records of this day—a day that brings to the great tribunal of the nation a man whose power, so short a time since, was of equal magnitude with his crimes!' Good heaven! thought Fanny, did he really believe all this? She heard him with a shudder and felt that the time had come to explain her own view of the prisoner. Might she speak frankly? He looked surprised, laughed at the question, and eagerly cried, 'Oh, yes, yes, pray speak out, I beg it.' After she had avowed both her prepossessions and her ignorance of the case, Windham urged her to come again and hear Burke—hear truth, reason, justice, eloquence. 'You will then see in other colours that man. There is more cruelty, more oppression, more tyranny, in that little machine, with an arrogance, a self-confidence, unexampled, unheard of.' That did not appear to those who knew him, replied Fanny: she had met him directly after his return from India, and had felt a strong interest in his favour.

F. B. I found him so mild, so gentle, so extremely pleasing in his manners.

W. Gentle?

F. B. Yes, indeed, gentle, even to humility.

W. Humility? Mr Hastings and Humility!

F. B. Indeed it is true. He is perfectly diffident in the whole of his manner, when engaged in conversation; and so much struck was I at that very time by seeing him so simple, so unassuming, when just returned from a government that had accustomed him to a power superior to our monarchs here, that it produced an effect on my mind in his favour which nothing can erase.

W. (*with great energy*). Oh, yes, yes, you will give it up. It will be plucked away, rooted wholly out of your mind.

F. B. (*steadily*). Indeed, sir, I believe not.

W. (*with added animation*). You believe not? Then there will be the more glory in making you a convert.

To Fanny's surprise Windham paid her another visit in the

afternoon. It was a welcome sign that her frankness had caused
no offence; but she declined his friendly offer to fetch some
refreshment, confiding to her journal that, well though she liked
him, she could not break bread with him. He now played his
trump card, for he knew her admiration for his own adored leader.
'Come and hear Burke,' he cried. "'Tis an eloquence irresistible,
a torrent that sweeps all before it with the force of a whirlwind.
It will cure you of your prepossession, but it will give you truth
and right in its place; what discoveries has he not made! what
gulfs has he not dived into! Come and hear him, and your
conflict will end.' Yet there seemed to be a conflict in his own
heart as he gazed fixedly at the prisoner. On rising to leave he
exclaimed: 'I must shake all this off, dismiss it, forget he is
there.'

F. B. (*earnestly*). Oh! no, do not forget it.

W. Yes, yes, I must.

F. B. No, remember it. I could almost (putting up my hands
as if praying) do this; and then, like poor Mr Hastings just
now to the House, drop down on my knees to you, to call out
Remember it.

W. Yes, yes, how else shall I go on? I must forget that *he*
is there and that *you* are here.

The Queen had witnessed the whole scene, and when Fanny
described the conversation she was moved to tears. It was a
comfort to know that 'the finest gentleman of the age,' as Macaulay
calls him, 'the ingenious, the chivalrous, the high-souled Windham,'
was free from personal malignity in the case which stirred and
divided opinion only less than the fate of Dreyfus a century later.

Fanny listened to Burke on the second day of his long introductory speech, and Windham came for her impressions. 'I told
him that his opening had struck me with the highest admiration
of his powers, from the eloquence, the imagination, the fire, the
diversity of expression, and the ready flow of language with which
he seemed gifted in a most superior manner for any and every
purpose to which rhetoric could lead. And when he came to his
two narratives, when he related the particulars of those dreadful
murders, he interested, he engaged, he at last overpowered me;
I felt my cause lost, but I could hardly keep on my seat. My
eyes dreaded a single glance towards a man so accused as Mr
Hastings; I wanted to sink on the floor that they might be saved
so painful a sight. I had no hope that he could clear himself;
not another wish in his favour remained. But when from this
narration Mr Burke proceeded to his own comments and declama-
tion—when the charges of rapacity, cruelty, tyranny were general,
and made with all the violence of personal detestation, and continued and aggravated without any further fact or illustration;

then there appeared more of study than of truth, more of invective than of justice; and, in short, so little of proof to so much of passion, that in a very short time I began to lift up my head, my seat was no longer uneasy, my eyes were indifferent which way they looked or what object caught them; and before I was myself aware of the declension of Mr Burke's powers over my feelings, I found myself a mere spectator in a public place, and looking all round it, with my opera-glass in my hand.' Windham listened patiently to this spirited attack on his idol, shrugged his shoulders, and merely remarked: 'I comprehend you perfectly.'

The great orator was unaware of the sentiments of his former admirer, to whom he bowed with the utmost civility when he came to a lady seated in front of her. It was a painful moment. 'My courtesy was the most ungrateful, distant and cold. I could not do otherwise; so hurt I felt to see him the head of such a cause, so impossible I found it to utter one word of admiration for a performance whose nobleness was so disgraced by its tenor, and so conscious was I the whole time that at such a moment to say nothing was almost an affront; that I hardly knew which way to look or what to do with myself. How happy and proud would any distinction from such a man have made me had he been engaged in a pursuit of which I could have thought as highly as I think of the abilities with which he conducted it.'

Still blissfully unconscious of her frowns Burke came to her on her fourth visit to Westminster Hall. She trembled as he approached, dreading that he would extract a disapprobation which she could not disguise and which he might well resent. 'Near-sighted as I am,' he began, 'I knew you immediately. I knew you from our box the moment I looked up; yet how long it is, except for an instant here, since I have seen you!' 'Yes,' answered Fanny hesitatingly, 'I live in a monastery now.' Windham joined them, and after a few exchanges on neutral subjects Burke returned to the Manager's Box. 'However I might be obliged to him, which sincerely I felt, I was yet glad to have him go. My total ill-will to all he was about made his conversation merely a pain to me.' He came twice again the same day, but she bridled her tongue. 'So brief was my speech and so long my silences that of course he was soon wearied into a retreat.' His place was taken by Sheridan, who was tarred with the same brush. 'Cold therefore was my reception of his salutations, though as civil as I could make it.'

Fox's speech of five hours had not impressed her, and his face struck her as hard and callous. His violence, she complained, had the monotony that seemed to result from its being factitious, whereas Burke's extravagances were at least unaffected. 'Mr Fox appeared to have no such excuse. He looked all good humour and negligent ease the instant before he began a speech of uninterrupted passion and vehemence, and he wore the same careless and disengaged air the very instant he had finished. A display of talents in which the inward man took so little share could have no power of persuasion to those who saw them in that light.' Windham briefly defended his gifted friends, adding that she would like Pitt better than any of his competitors. 'Then he made his panegyric in very strong terms, allowing him to be equal, ready, splendid, wonderful. He was in constant astonishment at his powers and success; his youth and inexperience never seemed against him. Though mounted to his present height after and in opposition to such a vortex of splendid abilities, yet, alone and unsupported, he coped with them all. Take the testimony of an enemy—a very confirmed enemy of Mr Pitt.'

Windham evidently enjoyed these conversations, for he came again and again. Finally she explained the reason for her frankness with him and him alone. 'Dr Johnson! What I have heard from him of Mr Windham has been the cause of all this openness.' ''Twas a noble cause,' he replied, 'and noble has been its effect. I loved him sincerely. He has left a chasm in my heart, a chasm in the world.' They proceeded to sing the praises of their friend and parted in peace. Nowhere do we come so near to Windham as in these conversations so vividly described. And nowhere does the *Diary* supply better proof that Fanny Burney was a good deal more than a charming little blue-stocking.

CHAPTER XVI

FANNY BURNEY AND GEORGE III

IN the summer of 1788, after two gruelling years in the Queen's service, Fanny Burney pronounced judgment on Courts and Court life in a conversation with her good friend Colonel Digby. 'I frankly said I like them not, and that, if I had the direction of any young person's destination, I would never risk them into such a mode of living. For though vices might be as well avoided there as anywhere, and in this Court particularly, there were mischiefs of a smaller kind, extremely pernicious to all nobleness of character, to which this Court, with all its really bright examples, was as liable as any other—the mischiefs of jealousy, narrowness and selfishness.' The home-coming after a sojourn in Cheltenham, where the King had been advised to drink the waters, filled her with gloomy thoughts. 'Melancholy—most melancholy—was the return to Windsor; destitute of all that could solace, compose, or delight; replete with whatever could fatigue, harass, and depress. Ease, leisure, elegant society, and interesting communication were now to give place to arrogant manners, contentious disputation, and arbitrary ignorance.' Yet an event was now to occur which banished all thought of self, and united high and low in a common sentiment of anxiety and grief. Though Fanny was like a fish out of water, her affection for the royal family was deep and never changed.

The long agony of the King's derangement, signs of which had appeared in 1762, 1763, and 1765, is described in realistic detail. The trouble began in October 1788. Here are a few extracts from the *Diary*:

October 17. The King is not well. He has not been quite well some time, yet nothing I hope alarming, though there is an uncertainty as to his complaint not very satisfactory.

October 18. The King was this morning better.

October 19. The King is but very indifferent. Heaven preserve him! There is something unspeakably alarming in his smallest indisposition. I am very much with the Queen, who, I see, is very uneasy, but she talks not of it.

October 20. The King was taken very ill in the night, and we have all been cruelly frightened, but it went off.

October 25. I had a sort of conference with His Majesty, or rather I was the object to whom he spoke, with a manner so uncommon that a high fever alone could account for it: a rapidity, a hoarseness of voice, a volubility, an earnestness, a vehemence rather, it startled me inexpressibly; yet with a graciousness exceeding even all I ever met with before—it was almost kindness.

October 26 (Sunday). The King was prevailed upon not to go to Chapel this morning. I met him in the passage from the Queen's room; he stopped me, and conversed upon his health near half an hour, still with that extreme quickness of speech and manner that belongs to fear. He hardly sleeps, he tells me, one minute all night; indeed if he recovers not his rest, a most delirious fever seems to threaten him. He is all agitation, all emotion, yet all benevolence and goodness, even to a degree that makes it touching to hear him speak. He assures everybody of his health; he seems only fearful to give uneasiness to others.

November 1. The King is very sensible of the great change there is in himself. 'My dear Effy (Lady Effingham), you see me all at once an old man.' He then produced a walking-stick which he had just ordered. He could not, he said, get on without it; his strength seemed diminishing hourly. He took the bark, and said 'but the Queen is my physician, and no man need have a better.' How the Queen commanded herself I cannot conceive; but there was something so touching in this speech, from his hoarse voice and altered countenance, that it overset me very much. He then applied to me, saying he was really very well, except in that one particular, that he could not sleep. The kindness and benevolence of his manner all this time was most penetrating: he seemed to have no anxiety but to set the Queen at rest, and no wish but to quiet and give pleasure to all around him. To me he never yet spoke with such excess of benignity.

November 3. The King is better and worse so frequently, that everything is to be apprehended if his nerves are not some way quieted. I dreadfully fear he is on the eve of some severe fever. The Queen is almost overpowered with some secret terror. I am affected beyond all expression in her presence to see what struggles she makes to support serenity. To-day she gave up the conflict when I was alone with her, and burst into a violent fit of tears. It was very, very terrible to see.

November 5. Oh, dreadful day! The King at dinner had broken forth into positive delirium, which long had been menacing all who saw him most closely; and the Queen was so overpowered as to fall into violent hysterics. All the princesses were in misery, and the Prince of Wales had burst into tears. I do not suppose an eye was closed in the house all night.

When Fanny entered the Queen's bedroom next morning she hastened to her, but in trying to speak burst into a flood of tears. 'She looked like death, the tears gushed from her eyes and a perfect agony of weeping ensued which, once begun, she could not stop; she did not indeed try; for when it subsided, and she wiped her eyes, she said, I thank you, Miss Burney, you have made

me cry, it is a great relief to me.   I had not been able to cry before
all this night long.'   After this outburst of delirium no concealment of the gravity of the situation was possible.   'General hope
seemed universally to abate, and the Prince of Wales now took
the Government of the house into his own hands.   Nothing was
done but by his orders, and he was applied to in every difficulty.
The Queen interfered not in anything; she lived entirely in her
two new rooms, and spent the whole day in patient sorrow and
retirement with her daughters.'   On November 29 there is the
first mention of a Regency, 'a word which I have not yet been
able to articulate.'   When Colonel Digby asked if she had recently
heard anything of Windham, an old friend of his, Fanny replied
severely that she had done with the whole set at present, owing to
their behaviour in regard to the King and the Regency.

The most exciting episode during the anxious winter occurred
on February 2, 1789, when Fanny was chased by the King in the
gardens of Kew Palace.   'What an adventure had I this morning,
one that occasioned me the severest personal terror I ever experienced in my life.'   Since everybody had been ordered to keep out
of sight, she ran away directly she saw him.   'But what was my
terror to hear myself pursued! to hear the voice of the King
himself loudly and hoarsely calling after me Miss Burney! Miss
Burney!   I protest I was ready to die.   On I ran, too terrified to
stop.   The steps still pursued me, and still the poor and altered
voice rang in my ears.   More and more footsteps resounded fright-
fully behind me, the attendants all running to catch their eager
master, and the voices of the two Dr Willises loudly exhorting him
not to heat himself so unmercifully.   Heaven, how I ran!   Soon
after I heard other voices, shriller though less nervous, call out
Stop! Stop! Stop! Dr Willis begs you to stop.   It hurts the
King to run.   Then I stopped.   When they were within a few
yards of me the King called out: Why did you run away?   I
looked up and met all his wonted benignity of countenance,
though something still of wildness in his eyes.   Think of my
surprise to feel him put both his hands round my two shoulders,
and then kiss my cheek!'

His obvious pleasure at the meeting banished her fears, and the
two walked quietly side by side, out of hearing of the doctors.
'He assured me he was quite well, as well as he had ever been in
his life; and then inquired how I did, and whether I was more
comfortable.   He asked after the coadjutor (Mme Schwellenberg)
laughing, and saying, Never mind her!   Don't be oppressed!   I
am your friend.   I know you have a hard time of it, but don't
mind her.   I will protect you—I promise you that—and therefore
depend upon me!'   The talk passed to Dr Burney and his *History
of Music*, which brought him to Handel.   'He tried to sing some

of the airs and choruses, but so dreadfully hoarse that the effect was terrible. When the doctors begged him to return home, he cried No! No! I want to ask her a few questions. I have lived so long out of the world, I know nothing.' After further inquiries about various persons the conversation ended. Agitating though the experience had been, Fanny was inexpressibly relieved to learn that his sanity was almost restored. She hurried to the Queen with the good news, discreetly omitting all reference to Mme Schwellenberg. Next day she was assured by the doctors that the invalid had suffered no harm. The worst was now over, and on February 18 she watched the King and Queen arm in arm in Richmond Gardens, accompanied by a doctor—'the highest gratification, the purest feeling of delight I have been regaled with for many months.' A few days later he remarked to her, 'I am quite well now—I was nearly so when I saw you before, but I could overtake you better now.' The journey of the Court to Weymouth was a resounding triumph. He had won the love of his subjects by an unspotted life, declares Fanny. *God save the King!* was sung and played incessantly, even when he was bathing.

The warm-hearted Fanny had felt the long strain as much as anyone outside the family circle, and her drawn face told its own tale. 'She does not look well,' remarked the King to the Queen on March 1; 'she looks a little yellow, I think.' The Queen, though equally kind, was far less observant. 'Illness here—till of late—has been so unknown that it is commonly supposed it must be wilful, and therefore it meets little notice till accompanied by danger or incapacity of duty. This is by no means from hardness of heart, far otherwise; there is no hardness of heart in any one of them; but it is prejudice and want of personal experience.' She never omitted her daily three attendances, but they were often a sore physical trial. Her health steadily deteriorated, and in the autumn of 1790 she drafted a petition to resign which received her father's full approval. By this time everyone except the Queen and Mme Schwellenberg realised that it could not go on. 'Were your talents given you to be buried in obscurity?' wrote Horace Walpole at this moment. 'You have retired from the world to a closet at Court.' No one was more ardent in the cause of emancipation than Windham, whom Fanny had again met in Westminster Hall, and who argued that it was Dr Burney's task to cut the knot. 'It is resolution, not inclination, he wants. I will set the Literary Club about him. Miss Burney has some very true admirers there, and I am sure they will all eagerly assist. We will present him a petition, an address.' Boswell added his voice to the swelling chorus. Meeting her at Windsor he exclaimed: 'I am happy to meet you, madam, for I was told you were lost,

closed in the unscalable walls of a royal convent. It won't do.
You must come forth. Besides I want your Johnson letters for
my book.'

Fanny's memorial to the Queen, drawn up in October 1790, was
not presented till two months later. Bark had done her good, but
the effect had soon worn off. 'I have long felt creeping upon me
a langour, a feebleness, that makes at times the most common
attendance a degree of capital pain to me. At length, as my
constitution itself seems slowly yet surely giving way, my father
became alarmed.' That was the gist of the letter, which concluded with warm expressions of affection and gratitude. At
their next meeting the Queen was 'kind and sweet and gentle,'
but it was not till July 1791 that the drooping invalid at last
escaped, for it took time to find a suitable successor. The Queen
gave her a pension of £100 a year. Mrs Schwellenberg, who had
at first made stormy scenes, softened when the moment of parting
arrived. 'She would take no leave of me, but wished me better
hastily, and, saying we should soon meet, she hurried suddenly
out of the room. Poor woman! If her temper were not so
irascible, I really believe her heart would be by no means wanting
in kindness.' She even offered Fanny the succession to her own
place when it was vacated by retirement or death, though it was
not hers to give.

In her last talk with the Queen Fanny begged still in some
measure to be considered her servant, either as reader, or to assist
occasionally if her successor should be ill. 'When your health
is restored,' was the reply, 'perhaps sometimes.' When the King
came to say good-bye she was speechless and turned her head
away. 'He stood still and silent for some minutes, waiting to see
if I should turn about; but I could not recover myself sufficiently
to face him, and perceiving me quite overcome he walked away and
I saw him no more. His kindness, his goodness, his benignity,
never shall I forget—never think of but with fresh gratitude and
reverential affection.' She had spent exactly five years at Court
and left it with mixed feelings. 'My heart was a little sad in
spite of its contentment. My joy in quitting my place extended
not to quitting the King and Queen.' On her rare subsequent
visits she was received with unfailing kindness.

With her liberation from a deadening routine Fanny's health
and spirits quickly revived, and she again enjoyed the best conversation that London could provide. Burke's *Reflections on the
French Revolution* atoned for his heresies in the Hastings trial,
and renewal of social intercourse with 'the very first man of true
genius now living in this country' was a delight. 'You look
quite renewed, revived, disengaged,' he began; 'you seemed, when
I conversed with you last at the trial, quite altered; I never saw

such a change for the better as quitting a Court has brought about.' As he talked to her at a dinner-party given by Mrs Crewe she felt her first enthusiasm return. With Burke at this time all roads led to Paris, and he was soon denouncing the principles and practices of the Revolution: 'This it is that has made me an abettor and supporter of Kings. Kings are necessary, and if we would preserve peace and prosperity, we must preserve them. We must all put our shoulders to the work.' Fanny wished that her sisters could meet this wonderful man 'when he is easy, happy, and with people he cordially likes. But politics, even on his own side, must always be excluded; his irritability is so terrible on that theme that it gives immediately to his face the expression of a man who is going to defend himself from murderers.' He expressed the opinion that Fox did not really like the Revolution: he was entangled, but he had too much taste really to approve. When Richard Burke spoke of the censures on his illustrious brother for being the friend of despots and the abettor of slavery, the old statesman good-humouredly poured out a glass of wine, and, turning to Fanny, said, 'Come then—here's slavery for ever.' 'That would do for him completely if it got into the newspapers,' cried the hostess amidst laughter. So the fun continued till Richard Burke gave a new toast, 'Here's confusion to confusion!'

For the next twenty years the main interest of Fanny Burney's life was France. While staying with friends at Norbury Park, near Mickleham, she made acquaintance with the remarkable group of *émigrés* who had found temporary refuge at Juniper Hall, a pleasant house on the road to Dorking. Among them were Talleyrand, Narbonne, and Mme de Staël. The latter addressed her as 'la première femme d'Angleterre,' and she is described by Fanny as one of the cleverest women she had ever met. The budding friendship wilted when Fanny, a strict moralist, learned that she and Narbonne were lovers; but General d'Arblay, a less brilliant but more dependable member of the little colony, now advances towards the centre of the stage. 'He is tall and a good figure, with an open and manly countenance,' reported Fanny to her sister; 'about forty, I imagine.' An artillery officer, he had been Adjutant-General to Lafayette when the latter was taken prisoner by the Prussians, and he was a bosom friend of Narbonne. They exchanged lessons in French and English, and a few months later were married in Mickleham Church. She was forty-one, and in 1794 their only son was born. It was a union of unclouded happiness, for d'Arblay was a man of sterling character and literary tastes. Their political views were the same, for the Revolution was anathema to both. The execution of Louis XVI was the greater shock since she had thought it inconceivable.

'M. de Narbonne and M. d'Arblay have been almost annihilated.
They are for ever repining that they are French, and break our
hearts with the humiliation they feel for their guiltless birth in
that guilty country. "Est-ce vrai," cries M. de Narbonne, "que
vous conservez encore quelque amitié pour ceux qui ont la honte
et le malheur d'être nés Français?" Poor man, he has all the
symptoms upon him of the jaundice. And M. d'Arblay, from a
very fine figure and good face, was changed as if by magic by the
receipt of this inexpiable news.'

Fanny's marriage brought poverty as well as love in its train,
for her husband had lost everything and for a year or two their
chief resource was her little pension. The publication of her third
novel, *Camilla*, in 1796, eased the situation; for its financial yield
exceeded that of its predecessors as much as its merits fell short
of them. It was dedicated to the Queen, who responded hand-
somely with a hundred guineas; and when the author took
presentation copies to Windsor she was warmly received by the
whole royal family. A year later a more intimate conversation
with the Queen occurred. 'I raised my eyes and saw in hers a
look of sensibility so expressive of regard, and so examining, so
penetrating into mine, as to seem to convey, involuntarily, a
regret I had quitted her. This, at least, was the idea that struck
me, from the species of look which met me; and it touched me
to the heart, and brought instantly, in defiance of all struggle, a
flood of tears into my eyes. I was some minutes recovering; and
when I entreated her forgiveness, the voice with which she spoke,
in hoping I was well, told me she had caught a little of my sensation, for it was by no means steady. I longed to kneel and beseech
her pardon for the displeasure I had felt in her long resistance of
my resignation; for I think now it was from a real and truly
honourable wish to attach me to her ever.' The Queen looked ill,
pale, and harassed, but showed a lively interest in Fanny's new
life. The King looked in for a few minutes, and she left the
sovereigns more attached to them than ever.

The Peace of Amiens in 1802 interrupted the long conflict with
France for a year, and the d'Arblays were among the throng of
visitors to Paris. Fanny was glad to meet the relatives and
friends of her husband, and she saw the First Consul at a reception
at the Tuileries. 'I had a view so near, though so brief, of his
face as to be very much struck by it. It is of a deeply impressive
cast, pale even to sallowness, while not only in the eye but in
every feature care, thought, melancholy, and meditation are
strongly marked with so much of character, nay genius, and so
penetrating a seriousness, or rather sadness, as powerfully to sink
into an observer's mind. He has by no means the look to be
expected from Bonaparte, but rather that of a profoundly studious

and contemplative man.' She saw a good deal of the newly married Louis Bonaparte, 'a young man of the most serious demeanour, a grave yet pleasing countenance, and the most reserved yet gentlest manners. He was very kind to my little Alex whom he never saw without embracing, and he treated M. d'Arblay with a marked distinction extremely gratifying to me.' Mme de Staël once more attempted to rebuild the bridges, but in vain.

The renewal of the war caught the family in Paris, and for the next nine years the journal and correspondence become a trickle. 'My grief, I who feel myself now of two countries, is far greater than I can wish to express. The General suffered almost as much, refusing to fight against England, declining several high military appointments, and accepting only a minor post in the civil service in order to earn a living.' Fanny made friends everywhere, but she longed to revisit her aged father, and to remove her son before he was forced into the French army. Women were occasionally granted passports for a brief period, and the General had influential contacts. 'Whenever Bonaparte left Paris there was always an immediate abatement of severity in the police; and Fouché, though he had borne a character dreadful beyond description in the earlier and most horrible times of the Revolution, was at this period, when Ministre de la Police, a man of the mildest manners, the most conciliatory conduct, and the easiest access in Paris. He had least of the glare of the new imperial court of any one of its administration; he affected, indeed, all the simplicity of a plain Republican; I have often seen him strolling in the shady and unfrequented parts of the Elysian Fields, giving le bras to his wife without suite or servant, merely taking the air. On these occasions, though he was universally known, nobody approached him. Yet such was the impression made upon me by the dreadful reports that were spread of his cruelty and ferocity at Lyons that I never saw him but I thrilled with horror.' That no personal application was necessary was due to the intervention of Narbonne, her old acquaintance in the Juniper Hall days.

It was a joy to be back in England, but her father was near his end. Though the Queen and the princesses were as cordial as ever, dark shadows had fallen on the Court in 1810. Princess Amelia had died and George III had lost his reason. 'The beloved King is in the best state possible for his present melancholy situation; that is, wholly free from real bodily suffering or imaginary mental misery, for he is persuaded that he is always conversing with angels.' She was presented to Louis XVIII on the eve of his return to France. 'I am very happy to see you,' he said in excellent English, 'for I have read you and been charmed with your books, charmed and entertained. I have read them often, I know them very well indeed, and I have long wanted to know *you*.' The Duc de Duras, Master of the Ceremonies, filled the cup of her joy by remarking, 'Et M. d'Arblay, Sire, bon et brave, est un des plus dévoués et fidèles serviteurs de votre Majesté.' 'Je le crois,' replied the King, and took her hand for the third time, saying, 'Bonjour, Mme la Comtesse.' For a countess she was by marriage, though they never used the title for lack of means. She was invited to the Palace to see the Tsar, the King of Prussia and his sons, and the other princes who flocked to London after the overthrow of Napoleon. Alexander, as usual, won all hearts. 'How was I charmed with his pleasing, gentle and so perfectly unassuming air, manner and demeanour! The King of Prussia made friends of all who most nearly approached him. Blücher is still the general idol, and he seems to enjoy as well as merit so being.'

Fanny hurried back to rejoin her husband in Paris, where, on the recommendation of Queen Charlotte, she was received in audience by the Duchess of Angoulême, the only surviving child of Louis XVI and Marie Antoinette. Hearing that the Duchess was reading her latest work in a French translation, Fanny dispatched a copy of the original, and in February 1815 found herself once again in the Tuileries. The conversation ranged over the ten years which she had spent in Paris. Her story of her husband's refusal to serve in the Napoleonic army evoked the comment, 'Il a agi bien noblement.' The conversation turned to the British royal family, of whom the Prince Regent was evidently her favourite. The noble style in which he had treated her and all her family at his Carlton House fête in the midst of their misfortune did so much honour to his heart, and proved so solacing to their woes and humiliations, that she could never revert to that public testimony of his esteem and good-will without the most glowing gratitude. 'Il a été parfait.' The conversation, which lasted three-quarters of an hour, revealed powers of pleasing which were little known, though her courage and piety were universally recognised.

Fanny was in Paris when Napoleon escaped from Elba, and her husband was Officier Supérieur in the King's Body-Guard at the Tuileries. The full account of the Hundred Days is one of the most dramatic and valuable portions of the *Diary*. Like most other people, the d'Arblays concluded that the ex-Emperor would be prevented from landing or be taken prisoner. The apprehensions aroused by his arrival at Lyons were partially removed by Ney's bombastic promise that he would bring him to Paris in an iron cage, and the King announced that he would never quit his capital. Both promises were broken, and the frail foundations of the restored monarchy were speedily revealed. 'The dread necessity which had reduced the King to be placed on his throne by foreigners would have annihilated all enthusiasm of loyalty if any had been left by the long underminings of revolutionary principles.' Her husband, despite broken health, expected and desired to take the field as the only chance of saving the throne, but he had no illusions. 'Rien ne tient,' he wrote, 'ou plutôt tout nous trahit.' Himself the soul of loyalty, his military honour was wounded by the inertia which seemed to paralyse all effort to save the King and his cause. When the Emperor was at the gates of the capital and the King was forced to flee, d'Arblay scribbled a line to his wife: 'Tout est perdu. Partez! Le plutôt sera le mieux.'

Fanny fled to Brussels, where the atmosphere was in striking contrast. 'All was quiet and tame. The Belgians had lost their original antipathy to Bonaparte without having yet had time to acquire any warmth of interest for the Bourbons. Naïvely phlegmatic, they demand great causes or strong incitement to rouse them from that sort of passiveness that is the offspring of philosophy and timidity—philosophy that teaches them to prize the blessings of safety, and timidity that points out the dangers of enterprise. In all I had to do with them I found them universally worthy, rational and kind-hearted, but slow, sleepy and uninteresting. Surely our colloquial use of the word phlegm must be derived from the character of the Flemings.' She found it impossible to discover whether they were at heart Bourbonists or Bonapartists, though nearly everyone believed the Emperor to be invincible, all the more since Louis XVIII had fled to Ghent. On June 17 she heard the roar of cannon in battle for the first time and watched from her windows the return of the wounded. 'We want blood, madam! What we want is blood!' exclaimed Colonel Jones, to whom Wellington had entrusted the military command of Brussels in his absence. When Fanny applied for a passport, he was unwilling to sanction an evacuation which he deemed premature. It was not for the English, he said, to spread alarm. He had not sent away his own wife or children, and he had no doubt that victory would repay his confidence. 'I was silenced but not convinced, the event was yet uncertain, and my stake was, with respect to earthly happiness, my existence.' As a compromise he signed her old passport, she promising to remain till the last extremity. 'The motive of Colonel Jones was that all should yield to the glory of the British arms and the Duke of Wellington.'

At six o'clock on June 18, the morning of Waterloo, Fanny was awakened by two English friends rapping at her door. 'Open! There is not a moment to lose.' She must join them by eight, proceed to the wharf, and set sail for Antwerp, whence they

would journey to England if Brussels were captured. As she
walked to the rendezvous, no fiacre being available, she heard the
thunder of the guns. It was too late to escape, for on reaching
the wharf the party were ordered to return. It was said that all
was lost; that the Emperor was advancing on Brussels; that
Wellington had ordered the seizure of every barge and boat for
the use of the army and the wounded. As they trudged back to
their lodgings the roar of the guns became louder and louder.
'We could only gaze and tremble, listen and shudder. Yet
strange to relate, on re-entering the city, all seemed quiet and
tranquil as usual, and though it was in this imminent danger of
being invested and perhaps pillaged, I saw no outward mark of
distress or disturbance, or even of hurry or curiosity.' Search
for a carriage or cart proving fruitless, she and her friends had no
alternative but to await the decision of arms. In the absence of
authentic news rumours followed one another in rapid succession.
Her host and hostess came to announce 'Bonaparte est pris!
le voilà! le voilà!' She flew to the window and saw a French
general on horseback. A quarter of an hour later she heard a
howl, violent, loud, affrighting, and issuing from many voices.
'I ran to the window, and saw the Marché aux Bois suddenly
filling with a populace, pouring in from all its avenues and hurrying
on rapidly, and yet as if unconscious in what direction; while
women with children in their arms, or clinging to their clothes,
ran screaming out of doors; and cries, though not a word was
ejaculated, filled the air and from every house I saw windows
closing and shutters fastening. All this, though long in writing,
was presented in a single moment, and was followed in another
by a burst into my apartment to announce that the French were
come. Without waiting to speak to the people of the house I
crammed my papers and money into a basket and throwing on a
shawl and bonnet I flew downstairs and out of doors.' It was a
false report, and late in the evening unofficial news of victory
arrived. Not till June 20 did she learn the full significance of the
stricken field of Waterloo.

Fanny joined her husband at Treves, where he was recovering
from an operation, and they set out by easy stages for Paris.
'Notwithstanding this complete victory over Bonaparte, the
whole of the peasantry and common people, converse with them
when or where or how I might during our route, with one accord
avowed themselves utterly incredulous of his defeat. They all
believed he had only given way in order that he might come
forward with new forces to extirpate all opposers and exalt himself
on their ashes to permanent dominion.' The object of the visit
was to bid farewell to their friends, for the General, now an
elderly man and in broken health, had yielded to his son's eager

desire that they should all live in the land of his birth. Among
Fanny's old acquaintances was the most brilliant member of the
Juniper Hall circle whom she had last seen in her cottage at
Bookham, and who, since those distant days, had filled Europe
with his fame. 'In passing the chair of M. de Talleyrand, who
gravely and silently but politely rose and bowed, I said, "M. de
Talleyrand m'a oublié, mais on n'oublie pas M. de Talleyrand."
I left the room with quickness, but saw a movement of surprise
by no means unpleasant break over the habitual placidity, the
nearly imperturbable composure of his made-up countenance.'

Returning to England in the autumn of 1815, at the age of
sixty-three, Fanny Burney fades quietly out of history. She
lived for her ailing husband and her promising son, both of whom
she adored. Both predeceased her, and her pen had lost its
cunning. Jane Austen had passed her in the race, and the *Diaries*
were still in manuscript. Her three-volume biography of her
father was written in a style so pompous and unreadable that,
despite its wealth of material, it came stillborn from the press.
She died in 1840 in her eighty-eighth year, forgotten by the
younger generation though visited by Scott, Rogers, and a few
other celebrities. It was a peaceful close to a life of exciting
experiences such as have never fallen to the lot of an English
woman writer before or since. She is not a star of the first
magnitude, yet our literary heritage would be poorer without
Evelina and the *Diary*. No fitter epitaph for this loving and
loyal soul is to be found than in the brief eulogy by her old mistress
—'as true as gold.'

Bibliographical Note.—The *Diaries and Correspondence* should be read in
the six-volume edition by Austin Dobson. *The Early Diaries*, in 2 vols.,
cover the less interesting period before the publication of *Evelina* made her
a celebrity. The three-volume biography, *Memoirs of Dr Burney*, is disfigured by the mannerisms of her later style, but contains useful material.
Macaulay's essay is sympathetic. The best biography is by Austin Dobson
in the *English Men of Letters*. Tourtellot, *Be Loved No More*, is rather cool
in tone. Unpublished material from her papers is utilised by Constance Hill
in her trilogy, *The House in St Martin's Street, Fanny Burney at the Court of
Queen Charlotte*, and *Juniper Hall*. Some interesting portions of journals
during her residence in Paris, omitted in the published edition, are printed
in R. Brimley Johnson, *Fanny Burney and the Burneys*. *The Daughters of
George III*, by Dorothy M. Stuart, contains new material. An American
psychiatrist, Dr Guttmacher, investigates the King's mental trouble in
America's Last King. An Interpretation of the Madness of George III (Scribner,
1941). The *Memoirs of the Court of Queen Charlotte*, by Mrs Papendiek, whose
father came over with her, are full of errors. The best sketch of the Queen
is in Alice Greenwood, *Lives of Hanoverian Queens*, vol. 2.

CHAPTER XVII

MME CAMPAN AND MARIE ANTOINETTE

WHILE most of the famous writers of memoirs require space to tell their tale, Mme Campan has compressed her thrilling testimony into a single volume. Marie Antoinette, she declares, intended to write her own memoirs and preserved many documents for the purpose, but after the first invasion of the Tuileries she committed most of them to the flames. Mme Campan's home was also pillaged and many of her papers were destroyed, but the tragedies she had witnessed were too deeply engraved in her memory to be blurred by the lapse of time. Writing in the closing years of her life, when the Bourbons were back on the throne, she read parts of her story to friends, and was busy with revision when she died, in 1822. The manuscript was printed in the same year with omissions by the editor in order to spare august susceptibilities. Flammermont, the severest of her critics, pointed out various small inaccuracies, but he exaggerated their importance. She knew little of what was going on in the political world, but her veracity in her limited field is generally recognised.

Henriette Genet, sister of the notorious republican diplomatist, was born in 1752. Her father was Premier Commis or Director of the Foreign Office, a travelled, thoughtful, and highly cultivated man. Scholars and writers, among them Marmontel, Quesnay, and the elder Mirabeau, frequented the house. Twenty years before the Revolution, she tells us, she heard talk of the decadence of the monarchy, which her father compared to a statue on a shaky pedestal, of the misery of the people, the growing influence of the *Philosophes*, and the probability of a crisis at the end of the century. She received an excellent education, learning to speak English and Italian and studying music. She read aloud so well that at the age of fifteen she was appointed *lectrice* to Mesdames de France, the four unmarried daughters of Louis XV. Great changes had recently taken place at Court, for the Queen, the Dauphin, the Dauphine, and Mme de Pompadour had died about the same time. Choiseul was at the helm and for the moment there was no *maîtresse en titre*.

The *Memoirs* open with a description of the dreary life of Versailles before the arrival of Marie Antoinette. Louis XV thought of nothing but hunting, and when he stayed at home the courtiers used to say: 'Le Roi ne fait rien aujourd'hui.' The etiquette established under Louis XIV was preserved, but there was neither dignity nor piety, neither gaiety nor wit. He was more interested in public affairs than Mme Campan was aware,

15

for the story of his subterranean diplomatic activities had to wait till the Duc de Broglie published *Le Secret du Roi*, nearly a century after his death. Every morning he visited Mme Adelaide, the eldest daughter, often bringing his coffee, and the other three, Victoire, Sophie, and Louise, were summoned. The youngest, small and misshapen, hobbled along from her distant apartments so slowly that sometimes she had only just time to greet her father before he hurried away to the chase. At six in the evening Mesdames returned the call, received a ceremonial kiss, and were soon back in their rooms. They were all lacking in charm. Adelaide had most brains, but she was autocratic and had political ambitions which she was unable to fulfil. Victoire had good looks and was adored by her staff. Sophie, a nonentity, was the ugly duckling of the family. They were nothing to their father and he was nothing to them.

It was a dull life for these middle-aged women who had no public duties, and the youngest of them found it intolerable. Louise loved history, and the little *lectrice* often read to her till her throat was sore. One day the princess disappeared. She had always lived a very retired life and secretly yearned to take the veil, but it was long before the King's consent could be obtained. One evening, when Mlle Genet was reading aloud, a letter arrived and was eagerly perused. It was the anxiously awaited permission, and next day Louise entered the convent of the Carmelites at Saint-Denis. Adelaide was furious, and Victoire cried quietly. On two or three occasions the *lectrice* visited her late mistress, who apologised for driving her so hard. 'I overworked your young lungs; but I knew I should only be able to read books of edification here, so I wanted to finish the historians who interested me.' The moralists, she added, were right when they said that happiness was not to be sought in palaces.

Soon after the appointment of Mlle Genet in 1767 the disreputable Mme du Barry, a *protégée* of Choiseul's enemies, was officially installed. Never had such a low-born adventuress occupied the coveted and lucrative post of *maîtresse en titre* at the French Court, but the King was a lonely old widower who had long ceased to care about appearances. Despite the frowns of his children and grandchildren, the new Favourite was firmly entrenched when Marie Antoinette arrived in 1770, at the age of fourteen and a half. She had received little education, could neither speak nor write French correctly, had read nothing and was mentally indolent, though she had learnt Italian and liked music. The Abbé de Vermond, dispatched by Choiseul to Vienna to coach her, was a much better man than Mme Campan admits, but he had too little personality to exert real influence. Maria Theresa herself, cumbered with an enormous family and affairs of state, had little time to prepare her daughter for the perils and duties of a throne.

Louis XV, like his people, was delighted by the freshness and warm-hearted friendliness of the little Dauphine, the living symbol of the Austrian alliance which he and Choiseul had made. 'Vive et un peu enfant,' he remarked, 'mais c'est bien de son âge.' The first official visit of the young couple to Paris was a triumph, and on their frequent visits to the opera and the theatre they always received an ovation. Paris, reported Mercy, the Austrian Ambassador, was enchanted. Yet there were clouds in the sky. On the evening of her arrival the princess supped with the royal family and the Favourite. She concealed her disapproval in public, but she avoided all intimacy, describing the du Barry as 'la plus sotte et impertinente créature qui soit imaginable.' The mistress was well aware of her aversion and was an enemy from the first. Politics also played a part; for Choiseul's enemies, who had engineered her triumph, hated the Austrian alliance and secured his fall soon after the arrival of the Austrian princess. Maria Theresa, declaring that the rupture of the compact would be her death, pressed her daughter into the service and recommended a certain minimum of consideration for the Favourite, though without any sacrifice of dignity and honour. A second trial was Mme de Noailles, the *dame d'honneur*, a good woman of limited intelligence, who would not allow the slightest departure from the traditional forms which meant nothing to a child brought up in the simplicity of the Austrian Court. It was natural that she chafed at the admonitions of 'Mme l'Etiquette,' whose sway only lasted till the Dauphine blossomed into the Queen.

A third difficulty was the character of the Dauphin, a blameless mediocrity, shy, *gauche*, almost boorish, only a year older than herself. She assured her mother that she preferred him to his brothers, but he was rather a trial. 'Mais m'aimez-vous bien?' he inquired after three years of matrimony. 'Oui, et vous ne pouvez pas en douter. Je vous aime sincèrement, et je vous estime encore davantage.' There was, indeed, at this stage more respect than love, as Maria Theresa complained to Mercy. 'La froideur du dauphin, jeune époux de vingt ans, vis-à-vis d'une jolie femme m'est inconcevable.' She never cared about the Comte de Provence, afterwards Louis XVIII, a calculating intellectual who looked down on his elder brother. The Comte d'Artois, afterwards Charles X, was an elegant *charmeur*, living for amusement. With their unattractive Italian wives she never became intimate. Mme Elizabeth, on the other hand, the unmarried sister and the saint of the family, was later to become a real friend, to share the trials of the young couple, and to wear the crown of thorns. The aunts were no help, and Mme Adelaide coined the sinister phrase *l'Autrichienne*. The pitfalls which surrounded Marie Antoinette during her first ten years at Versailles are minutely described in the touching correspondence with her mother and in the voluminous secret reports of Comte de Mercy d'Argenteau, published by Arneth from the Vienna archives in three stout volumes. Maria Theresa was a devoted but formidable parent, and her letters, which sometimes contained sharp censure, were opened with apprehension. Her information came from two men who possessed her entire confidence, the Abbé de Vermond, no longer tutor but *lecteur*, and the admirable Ambassador, who worked with him in unbroken harmony. Mercy felt the same fatherly affection for the Austrian princess as Melbourne entertained for the young Victoria. That the girl had a very difficult part to play was fully recognised by all three, for the Court was full of cliques, ambitions, and intrigues, and their frequent criticisms never extended to the graver aspects of her life. Failings she had, but no vices, and nature had given her a loving heart.

Mlle Genet became one of the Dauphine's *femmes de chambre*, talked Italian with her, and accompanied her on the harp. The two young women, with only three years between them, took to each other from the first, and liking gradually ripened into affection. The Dauphine had enemies among the du Barry clique, while her high spirits, indiscretions, and innocent games were censured in some quarters as levity. The *Memoirs* depict a healthy, unspoiled, warm-hearted girl, hating flattery and craving for happiness and love. Mercy complained to her mother of her extreme repugnance to serious occupations, particularly reading; but we must remember that when this was written she was not yet fifteen. When, in 1774, Mlle Genet married Campan, Maître de la Garderobe to the Comtesse d'Artois and son of the Queen's secretary and librarian, she received a dowry of 15,000 francs a year from the new King. The marriage was not a success and was later dissolved.

The death of the dissolute old monarch in 1774 was hailed with delight by all but the members of the du Barry clique. When the end was near the Favourite left Versailles, never to return. The Dauphin had decided to quit the palace directly his grandfather ceased to breathe, and everything was ready for the departure of the Court to Croisy. The signal was given by the extinction of a candle placed at the window of the dying man, but the new King and Queen learned the news in another way. A terrible noise, just like thunder, was heard. It was the crowd of courtiers who left the antechamber of the dead sovereign to come and salute Louis XVI. Hearing this strange sound, Marie Antoinette and her husband realised that they had begun to reign, and, by an instinctive movement which touched all present, they fell on their knees in tears, exclaiming, 'Mon Dieu, guidez-nous, protégez-nous,

nous régnons trop jeunes.' The Comtesse de Noailles, after
saluting the Queen, begged the new rulers to emerge from their
private apartments and to receive the princes and high officials
who desired to pay homage. Leaning on her husband, holding a
handkerchief to her eyes, and in a most touching attitude, Marie
Antoinette greeted her first visitors. Then the whole Court drove
away from the germ-infested palace. The passage reads like a
faint echo of Saint-Simon, but its brevity and simplicity have an
art of their own. Mme Campan's salary was raised, and the vast
number of candles in the Queen's apartments, which were changed
daily whether lighted or not, were the perquisite of her ladies.
As the chief of them was often absent, she took her place and
finally succeeded to her post. The rise of a bourgeoise to wealth
and influence excited jealousy in certain circles, but the new
rulers knew her worth. She is never mentioned by name in the
voluminous Mercy correspondence, but the Ambassador assured
the Empress that they could count on the honour and fidelity of
the two principal *femmes de chambre*.

Marie Antoinette's wish for the return of Choiseul was disappointed, for the aged Maurepas became the Chief Minister.
Vergennes, an experienced diplomatist, was called to the Foreign
Office, and Turgot became Controller-General. Mme du Barry,
'the creature,' as Marie Antoinette called her, disappeared from
sight. The Queen's popularity was now at its height, though it
did not last long. The charge of extravagance is too lightly
dismissed by Mme Campan as a libel, for the next few years were
the least admirable period in the life of a noble woman, and Mercy
expressed his disappointment in tactful terms. With the exception of the King, as Mme Campan admits, all the young members
of the royal circle, above all the Comte d'Artois, were occupied in
pleasure. Marie Antoinette loved balls, theatres, riding, expensive
jewels, and yielded to the fascination of play for high stakes.
Her mother rejoiced in her popularity, but she knew the trials of
rulers, and expressed the opinion that her daughter's happiest days
were over. 'Je crains seulement votre paresse et dissipation, le
seul ennemi que vous avez à craindre.' The young Queen meekly
confessed her shortcomings. 'Je dois avouer ma dissipation et
paresse pour les choses sérieuses. Je désire et espère me corriger
peu à peu.' The mood of contrition, however, quickly passed and
the temptations resumed their hold. The correspondence of Mercy
and the Empress becomes more sombre in 1776, and the latter's
letters are filled with forebodings no less than rebukes. Rulers
live in glass houses and the Queen's popularity rapidly waned.
The young King disliked her frivolous entourage and in particular
hated gambling, but he trusted her absolutely, let her go her own
way, and paid her debts. How gravely she damaged not only her

own reputation but compromised the monarchy Mme Campan, like her mistress, was too unpolitical to comprehend. The best of Marie Antoinette's many biographers, La Rocheterie, speaks of her period of dissipation and attributes it in the main to the frustration of a married woman's hopes. She would be beyond reproach, reported Mercy to the Empress, if she were left to herself.

The fairest judgment of the Queen in the opening years of her reign was pronounced by her austere and rather self-righteous brother Joseph after his long visit in 1777. He found much to criticise and disliked his sister's extravagance, but on the deeper issues of conduct he reported that there was no cause for alarm. 'Sa vertu est intacte,' he wrote to his brother Leopold. 'Elle est même austère, par caractère plus que par raisonnement. C'est une aimable et honnête femme, un peu jeune, peu réfléchie, mais qui a un fonds d'honnêteté et de vertu dans sa situation vraiment respectable.' If she were not his sister, he gallantly declared, he would like her to be his wife. Except for the few occasions on which his rebukes were too roughly presented, she enjoyed his company. 'Mon frère a eu une conduite si parfaite avec tout le monde,' she wrote to her mother, 'qu'il emporte les regrets et l'admiration de tous les états.'

Mercy pronounced the visit a complete success, and found the Queen resolved to follow his advice; but subsequent letters regretfully reported that the gambling habit had proved too strong to be broken and that the situation at Court was as unsatisfactory as ever. Maria Theresa replied that perhaps nothing but misfortune would change her, and the change might come too late. 'Votre avenir me fait trembler,' wrote the anxious mother; 'il faut s'arracher tout d'un coup de cette passion.' The Queen's friendship with the Princesse de Lamballe, a young widow of Italian birth whom she made Surintendante de la Maison, and with Countess Jules de Polignac brought new happiness into her life. Unfortunately the ladies were rivals and both had their critics, Mercy among them. Moreover, every successive favourite involved new expense, new jealousies, and new claims. Now that her husband was at last beginning to be in love with her, her only sorrow was her childlessness. When the Comtesse d'Artois gave birth to a son, all members of the royal family, according to custom, were present. 'Mon Dieu, que je suis heureuse!' exclaimed the proud mother. The Queen controlled her feelings till she returned to her apartments, where she shut herself up with Mme Campan to weep that she herself was denied a similar joy. How often did her mother inquire, and how often did she sadly reply that there was nothing to report!

Mme Campan's portraits of the leading figures at Court, with the exception of the Queen, are not works of art, but we welcome the testimony of a spectator who stood so close to events. Though she respected the King's virtues, she stresses the absence of the qualities required in a ruler. His gait was clumsy, his person neglected, his hair untidy, his voice unmelodious, his hands often dirty from working at his keys and locks. He was not without intellectual tastes, for he liked history and the drama, knew English well, and translated passages of Milton. Modest, timid and tongue-tied, simple and pious, he was a kind master, a good husband, a tender parent. He hated all forms of extravagance. This instinct led him to welcome reforms, but he lacked self-confidence and resolve. 'His principles, his prejudices, his fears, and the clamour of the privileged intimidated him and made him abandon the plans which his love for his people had led him to adopt.' His brother, Monsieur, had more dignity, loved literature, and wrote verse. Artois was the most expansive and frivolous of the three.

In 1778, after eight years of marriage, Marie Antoinette gave birth to her first child and the period of dissipation came to an end. According to the barbarous custom of the time her bedroom was open to spectators, and when the doctor called out 'La reine va accoucher,' there was such a rush that the screens round the bed were almost swept away. The room was so full that it was impossible to move, and two men climbed on to the furniture to get a better view. It was a daughter, but for a moment it looked as if the mother might die. The blood rushed to her head, her mouth was contorted, and the accoucheur cried: 'De l'air, de l'eau chaude, il faut une saignée au pied!' The windows, which had been plastered up, were forced open by the King. The Queen was lanced, and when the blood spouted she opened her eyes. So critical had it been that the Princesse de Lamballe fainted and was carried out. When the danger was over, the valets drove away the crowd of sightseers, and henceforth the right of establishing the legitimacy of the royal offspring was confined to members of the royal family and the ministers. Men and women alike shed tears of relief. In later years Mme Campan often regretted that her beloved mistress had been snatched from the jaws of death to undergo indescribable sufferings and to perish by the guillotine. Three years later a Dauphin was born.

For some years the Queen had lived for herself; henceforth she lived for her children. Childish things were put away and her interest in affairs of state increased, though she exerted little influence till the revolutionary storm broke over her head. In home affairs she was ready—at any rate in theory—for moderate reforms, but she knew nothing of the needs of France. She had helped to secure the fall of Turgot after two short years of office, though she denied all responsibility in a letter to her mother; and she began by admiring Necker, but later joined his critics. The growing *malaise* of the country filled her with a vague alarm, and she began to realise that her popularity was gone. When Mme Campan was ordered to read the *Mariage de Figaro* to the King and Queen in manuscript the King resented the criticisms of the government and declared that it could not be produced. The public was angered by the veto, and the masterpiece of Beaumarchais was soon being played to crowded audiences. Belief in the Queen's extravagance seemed to find confirmation when the King bought Saint-Cloud from the Duke of Orleans for her and as a place where the Court could live during structural alterations at Versailles.

The most dramatic pages in Mme Campan's pre-Revolution chapters describe the celebrated scandal of the Diamond Necklace in 1785, on which her testimony is of the first importance. The Queen was the innocent victim of a contemptible intrigue, but her love of jewels prepared the soil for poisonous growths. Boehmer, the Crown jeweller who had sold her expensive diamond ear-rings in the early part of the reign and from whom the King had bought other valuable gems, had gradually collected large diamonds for a necklace which he hoped to sell to Mme du Barry and, after her fall, to the Queen. When it was ready he asked Mme Campan to take it to her mistress, but met with a refusal. It was shown to the King who, despite his dislike of extravagance, wished to present it to his wife. The price was 1,600,000 francs, and Marie Antoinette, sobered by the responsibilities of motherhood and happy at last in possessing the love of her husband, did not wish such expense to be incurred. She had diamonds enough, she replied, and a warship would be a much more suitable object for investment. Boehmer tried to sell it at different courts but the price was too high, and a year later he again offered it to the King for payment by instalments and shares. Mme Campan was present when Louis XVI consulted his wife, who remarked that if it was a good bargain it might be bought and kept for the marriages of the children: she herself would not wear it. When the King rejected this plan, the importunate jeweller obtained an audience, threw himself on his knees, burst into tears, and threatened suicide. 'Madame, je suis ruiné, déshonoré, si vous n'achetez pas mon collier. Je ne veux pas survivre à tant de malheurs. D'ici, Madame, je pars pour aller me précipiter dans la rivière.' The Queen rebuked him as sharply as he deserved. 'Levez-vous, Boehmer; les gens honnêtes n'ont pas besoin de supplier à genoux.' She would regret his death but would be in no way responsible. Not only had she not ordered the necklace, but she had told him again and again that she had enough diamonds. 'Je vous a refusé votre collier; le roi a voulu me le donner; je l'ai refusé de même; ne m'en parlez donc jamais. Tâchez de le diviser et de le vendre, et ne vous noyez pas. Sortez.'

The jeweller withdrew, and soon afterwards he told Mme Campan that he had sold the necklace at Constantinople. The Queen's satisfaction at the news was premature, for the statement was untrue. On the occasion of the baptism of the Duc d'Angoulême, son of Artois, the King gave his wife some diamonds and ordered Boehmer to bring them. The jeweller accompanied them with a letter declaring his happiness to know her in possession of the most beautiful diamonds in Europe, and begging her not to forget him. She thought the man was mad, and burned the letter in a candle with the words: 'Cela ne vaut pas la peine d'être gardé.' Mme Campan was charged to tell him, when next they met, that she would never buy any more diamonds, and that if she had money to spend, she would enlarge her property at Saint-Cloud. Surprised at receiving no reply to his letter, he visited the author of the *Memoirs* in her country home and learned that it had been burned, as the Queen did not understand its meaning.

BOEHMER. Ah! Madame, cela n'est pas possible; la reine sait qu'elle a de l'argent à me donner.

MME CAMPAN. De l'argent, M. Boehmer? Il y a longtemps que nous avons soldés vos dernier comptes pour la reine.

BOEHMER. Madame, vous n'êtes pas dans la confidence? On n'a pas soldé un homme que l'on ruine en ne le payant pas, lorsqu'on lui doit plus de quinze cent mille francs.

MME CAMPAN. Avez-vous perdu l'esprit? Pour quel objet la reine peut-elle vous devoir une somme si exorbitante?

BOEHMER. Pour mon collier, madame.

MME CAMPAN. Quoi! encore ce collier pour lequel vous avez inutilement tourmenté la reine, que vous l'aviez vendu pour Constantinople?

BOEHMER. C'est la reine qui m'avait fair ordonner de faire cette réponse à tous ceux qui m'on parleraient.

The jeweller proceeded to explain that she wanted the necklace and had bought it through Cardinal de Rohan, the former Ambassador, Archbishop of Strasbourg and Grand Almoner of France.

MME CAMPAN. Vous êtes trompé. La reine n'a pas adressé la parole une seule fois au Cardinal depuis son retour de Vienne; il n'y a pas d'homme plus en défaveur à sa cour.

BOEHMER. Vous êtes trompée vous-même, madame. Elle le voit si bien en particulier que c'est à son Eminence qu'elle a remis trente mille francs qui m'ont été donnés pour premier à-compte, et elle les a pris, en sa présence, dans le petit secrétaire de porcelaine de Sèvres qui est auprès de la cheminée de son boudoir.

MME CAMPAN. Et c'est le Cardinal qui vous a dit cela?
BOEHMER. Oui, madame, lui-même.
MME CAMPAN. Ah! quelle odieuse intrigue!
BOEHMER. Mais à la vérité, madame, je commence à être bien effrayé, car son Eminence m'avait assuré que la reine porterait son collier le jour de la Pentecôte, et je ne le lui ai pas vu; c'est ce qui m'a décidé à écrire à Sa Majesté.

Madame Campan rebuked him for acting without the orders of the King, the Queen, or the head of the King's household. The incautious jeweller replied that he possessed documents signed by the Queen, and had been compelled to show them to several bankers in order to obtain an extension of time for his payments.

When Boehmer presented himself at Trianon, saying that Mme Campan had advised him to do so, the Queen exclaimed: 'Il est fou, je n'ai rien à lui dire, et je ne veux pas le voir.' She had not yet heard Mme Campan's report, which not only shocked but mystified her. The key was supplied when Cardinal Rohan was summoned to the palace.

THE KING. You bought diamonds from Boehmer?
ROHAN. Yes, sir.
THE KING. What have you done with them?
ROHAN. I thought they had been sent to the Queen.
THE KING. Who charged you with this commission?
ROHAN. A lady called Countess de Lamotte-Valois, who showed me a letter from the Queen, and I thought to please Her Majesty.
THE QUEEN. How, sir, could you believe—you to whom I have not spoken for eight years—that I should choose you to conduct this negotiation and through the instrumentality of such a woman?
ROHAN. I realise that I have been cruelly deceived. I will pay for the necklace. My desire to please Your Majesty blinded me. I did not suspect crooked dealings, and I am sorry.

When Rohan produced the Queen's pretended letter to Mme Lamotte, a disreputable adventuress descended from a bastard of Henri II, the King pointed out that it was not in her writing. And how could a prince of the House of Rohan, a Grand Almoner of France, believe that she would sign herself Marie Antoinette de France? Pressed to explain his dealings with Boehmer, the Cardinal turned pale and supported himself against a table. 'Sire, je suis trop troublé pour répondre à Votre Majesté d'une manière. . . .' The King bade him write his reply, and a quarter of an hour later he reappeared with a document. The King read it and curtly remarked: 'Retirez-vous, monsieur.' He was arrested and taken to the Bastille, but not before sending a message to a friend to burn the compromising correspondence with Mme Lamotte. For once Louis was firm, for the incident had stirred him to the depths. When pressed to overlook the Cardinal's offence, he replied that neither as King nor as husband could he consent. He explained his decision in a letter to Vergennes, who wished to hush the matter up. 'Il faut en finir avec l'intrigue d'un besogneux qui a compromis si scandaleusement la Reine et qui, pour se laver, n'a rien de mieux à faire que d'alléguer sa liaison avec une aventurière de la dernière espèce. Il déshonore son caractère ecclésiastique. Pour être devenu Cardinal, il n'en est pas moins sujet de ma couronne.' Marie Antoinette shared his wish. 'Je désire,' she wrote to her brother Joseph, 'that this horror and all its details should be cleared up in the eyes of the world.'

The King allowed the Cardinal to choose between a confession of guilt and a trial by the Parlement of Paris. His choice of the latter was deplored by the French clergy and the Vatican for submitting to a civil court, and the higher nobility complained of the outrage to one of its members. The trial was a first-class sensation and lasted nine months. 'I was completely blinded by my intense desire to regain the good opinion of the Queen,' declared Rohan. Mme Lamotte, who had arranged for the forging of letters from Marie Antoinette and had employed a woman to impersonate the Queen in a secret rendezvous with the Cardinal, denied everything. Rohan was acquitted by a majority of votes, while Mme Lamotte was sentenced to be whipped, branded and imprisoned. When the verdict was announced the Cardinal became a popular hero, and Mme Campan found her mistress in tears. 'Venez plaindre votre reine outragée et victime des cabales et de l'injustice.' At this moment the King entered, remarking that she had good reason to be distressed. Rohan, he continued, wanted money, and he had been tricked. He was now deprived of all his offices and was exiled from Paris. Though the innocence of the Queen had been established beyond challenge, the revelation of her unpopularity was a bitter grief. It was particularly hard to bear, for she no longer gave the slightest cause of offence. 'Mme Déficit' became the target of innumerable verses, pamphlets, and caricatures, many of them obscene, and her enemies took care that she should see them. The long-expected revolution was in sight.

CHAPTER XVIII

Mme Campan and the French Revolution

Marie Antoinette, declares Mme Campan, took no part in politics till the eve of the Revolution, when Maurepas and Vergennes were dead and the hated Calonne had resigned. She herself deplored the change, all the more since she had never been initiated into affairs of state. 'Il n'y a plus de bonheur pour moi depuis qu'ils m'ont fait intrigante,' she remarked with a sigh. Mme Campan protested. It was the right word, replied her mistress. 'A woman who interferes in matters outside her knowledge and her duty is an *intrigante*.' One day, she added, on her way to a committee in the King's room, she overheard the remark of a Court musician: 'Une reine qui fait son devoir reste dans ses appartements à faire du filet.' 'Malheureux, tu as raison,' she thought to herself, 'mais tu ne connais pas ma position; je cêde à la nécessité et à une mauvaise destinée.' Mme Campan realised the danger, for the more active *l'Autrichienne* became the more enemies she was certain to make. Carried away by the glib tongue of Archbishop Loménie de Brienne, she helped to secure his appointment to the Treasury, and on the fall of the unpopular Minister she sent him her portrait with expressions of confidence. She was always a poor judge of statesmen and had no flair for politics. Neither she nor Mme Campan ever seriously attempted to understand why she had lost the affection of the people or why a revolution occurred. Courage she possessed in plenty, and Mirabeau described her as the only man in the King's entourage, but in such critical times a brave heart was not enough. Her moral stature grew with misfortune, but political wisdom she never learned.

When it became necessary to convoke the States-General, the question arose whether they should meet at Versailles or far away. Marie Antoinette, dreading the pressure of Paris on the deputies, argued for the latter, but Necker's advocacy of Versailles prevailed. A second difference of opinion arose on the double representation of the Tiers État. The opposition of Artois to the King's decision cooled her friendship for her flighty brother-in-law, and Mme de Polignac's adoption of the same view was a blow. At the opening of the States-General on May 4 she appeared in full state for the last time, but there was no warmth in the atmosphere and no happiness in her heart. While the King was still trusted and popular, the campaign of calumny against her had done its work, and she was widely believed to be the chief obstacle to reform. Some women in the crowd cried 'Vive le Duc d'Orléans!' with such concentrated venom that she nearly fainted. She lost her sleep, and one evening at the end of May a curious incident occurred. Four candles were placed on the table. The first went out, and was relit by Mme Campan; then the second and the third. The Queen seized her hand, saying, 'Misfortune can make one superstitious. If the fourth goes out I must regard it as an evil omen.' The fourth followed suit, and the suggestion that there was something wrong with the wicks failed to convince. Private sorrow was added to public anxieties when the sickly Dauphin died, a year after the death of his sister. Two of her four children were gone.

The insurrections in Paris, culminating in the murders which accompanied the fall of the Bastille, caused bitter tears to flow, and the thought that the King had lost the confidence of his subjects broke her heart. He was urged to come to Paris, and she favoured the suggestion. On July 16, two days after the destruction of the Bastille, she asked Mme Campan to put her diamond ornaments in a little box which she could take in her carriage, and the two women burned a quantity of papers, fearing that an armed mob might any day storm the palace. The King was ready for the move, but the majority of the ministers were against it. At this moment Artois, Condé and the first batch of *émigrés* fled abroad. The parting from the Duchesse de Polignac was a grief to the Queen, for their old affection had revived under the discipline of sorrow.

The long-dreaded raid took place on October 5, when the angry women of Paris marched on Versailles. Mme Campan was not on duty, but her sister, also a *femme de chambre*, supplied the information enshrined in the *Memoirs*. The Queen only went to bed at two in the morning, and at half-past four shots and cries were heard outside her room. Opening the door the sister saw a *garde-du-corps* assailed by the mob, his face covered with blood. 'Madame, sauvez la reine,' he cried, 'on vient pour l'assassiner.' Marie Antoinette jumped out of bed and made for the King's room. He had already left it, but her children joined her there and in response to demands all three appeared on the balcony. When someone shouted 'Pas d'enfants!' she sent the children indoors and faced the surging crowd alone. At midday the sovereigns, obeying the imperious cry 'À Paris!' left the palace, never to return. Mme Campan found her in tears and hardly able to speak, looking as if all the blood in her body had rushed to the head. 'Come to Paris,' were her first words after an embrace. 'I will lodge you at the Tuileries. Come and do not leave me. We are lost and perhaps doomed to die.'

Next morning the women who had convoyed the royal family from Versailles gathered under the Queen's windows at the

Tuileries and asked to see her. When she showed herself, one of them bade her dismiss the courtiers and to love the citizens of her good city. She had loved them at Versailles, was the reply, and would also love them at Paris. 'Yes, yes,' cried another, 'but on July 14 you wanted to besiege and bombard the city, and on October 6 you wanted to cross the frontier.' That was the misfortune both of kings and the people, she rejoined quietly; they were told such stories and believed them. When a third spoke to her in German she replied that she had become so French that she had forgotten her native tongue. They asked for the ribbons and flowers from her hat, and cried '*Vive Marie Antoinette! Vive notre bonne reine!*' as she tossed them to the crowd.

The King missed his hunting, felt ill and depressed, and could never express himself, but the children were a consolation and the new Dauphin was a bright and thoughtful lad. One day he asked his father why his loving people had turned against him so suddenly. The King took him on his knees, and tried to explain. 'My child, I wished to increase their happiness. I needed money for the wars. The Magistrates said that only the people could give consent. So I assembled the leading men of every town—what we call the States-General. But they made demands I could not accept, and there were some evil persons who stirred them up.' The Queen encouraged her son to be friendly to everybody, and the boy would occasionally whisper to his mother: 'Est-ce bien comme cela?' Too worried to read, she busied herself with tapestry, and the Revolution was the sole topic of conversation. In trying to discover why she had lost the people's love, she found a partial clue in the enmity of the Duke of Orleans. That her life was in danger she was well aware. One day she discovered Mme Campan changing the powdered sugar she used for her *eau sucrée*, smiled sadly, and begged her not to trouble. 'They will not use poison. They will kill me by calumny, which is much more effective.'

If anyone could save the monarchy it was Mirabeau, and one day, after preliminary negotiations with the Court, Marie Antoinette, who had spoken of him as *le monstre*, consented to receive him at a quiet spot in the gardens of Saint-Cloud. The interview was friendly, and on leaving he exclaimed grandiloquently, 'Madame, la monarchie est sauvée,' and received permission to kiss her hand. 'Elle est bien grande, bien noble et bien malheureuse,' he exclaimed to his nephew, 'mais je la sauverai. Rien ne m'arrêtera, je périrai plutôt que de manquer à mes promesses.' The Queen was less impressed, and neither she nor the King trusted him sufficiently to follow his advice. Mme Campan had no confidence in the ugly nobleman who, as she says, believed himself to be the political Atlas of the world. It was true enough that he could not deliver the goods, but his belief in consti-

tutional monarchy was sincere.   The Queen regretted his early
death, unaware that he had already lost all influence and that his
acceptance of money from the Court could not remain a secret.
She judged Lafayette much more severely, regarding him as a
false friend and exclaiming that she would rather perish than owe
her safety to him.

Despairing of salvation at home, her eyes turned increasingly
to the frontier.   The walls of palaces have ears, and in the spring
of 1791, when the King entered his carriage to start for Saint-
Cloud, the guard shut the gates of the Tuileries.   Here was a fresh
reason for trying to escape.   At last even Louis was converted,
and the plan was worked out by Fersen, the faithful Swede.
Mme Campan, who was on duty during March, carried out most
of the secret orders of her mistress.   When she argued that large
purchases would excite suspicion, the incautious Queen replied
that she wished to arrive at Brussels with a complete trousseau for
herself and her children.   Accordingly Mme Campan and her
sister, partially disguised, ordered the garments in different shops
and packed them in a trunk addressed to one of her ladies who was
on leave at Arras, ready to start for Brussels or some other place
at the word of command.

The Queen only proposed to take her first *femme de service*, but
hoped that Mme Campan would join her at a later stage.   When
she asked her to forward the luggage on the pretext that it was a
present to the Austrian Archduchess Christina, the Governor of
the Low Countries, the faithful servant pointed out that the story
might not be believed.   All she could obtain was that the Austrian
Chargé should come and request a list of articles for the Governor
of the Low Countries precisely similar to those which were waiting
to be sent.   Thereupon the Queen, in the presence of her ladies,
ordered Mme Campan to make the necessary purchases.   This
elaborate farce was useless, for an unnamed *femme de garde-robe*
who had been with Marie Antoinette since her marriage, but whom
Mme Campan had long suspected, was disloyal.   After the return
from Varennes the Mayor of Paris forwarded to the Queen a statement by this woman, dated May 21, that preparations for a journey
were being made and that the dispatch of articles as a present to
the Archduchess at Brussels was only a pretext.

In the middle of May, Marie Antoinette inquired if the articles
she had ordered would soon be ready.   On hearing that a further
six weeks were needed, she declared that she could not wait, as
she would have to leave in June.   Since Mme Campan's turn of
service did not synchronise with the royal plans, her mistress
pressed her to accept 500 louis for holiday expenses till she could
rejoin her, but the offer was gratefully declined.   The King, it
was explained, would only go to the frontier in order to treat with

the Assembly, and would only cross it if his proposals failed. Many members, she added, were by this time cured of their first exaltation. The flight was made in the night of June 20, and the news that the royal family had been arrested at Varennes was quickly followed by an unsigned letter to Mme Campan dictated by the Queen and posted in Paris. ' Je vous fais écrire de mon bain où je viens de me mettre pour soulager au moins mes forces physiques. Je ne puis rien dire sur l'état de mon âme; nous existons, voilà tout. Ne revenez ici que sur une lettre de moi, cela est bien important.' Returning to her post in August, Mme Campan was horrified at the change in her mistress, whose hair had turned white. Another witness attributes it to the night of October 5, 1789.

The acceptance of the new Constitution by Louis XVI brought a momentary lull, but the prestige of the monarchy was gone and the Tuileries had become a prison. 'Ces gens ne veulent point de souverains,' remarked the Queen sadly. 'Nous succomberons à leur tactique perfide, mais très bien suivie; ils démolissent la monarchie pierre par pierre.' The Legislative Assembly was much more radical than the Constituent, but there seemed just one ray of hope. Barnave, a refined and cultivated lawyer, who with Pétion had shared the later stages of the sorrowful return from Varennes, strove to restore harmony, but there were so many enemies in the Tuileries that meetings were difficult to arrange. The advice of the Constitutional trio, Barnave, Lameth, and Duport, to the sovereigns to identify themselves with the Constitution and to ignore the *émigrés* was sound enough in theory, but it came too late. The Queen had learned to distrust the Princes, and she regarded Calonne as the evil genius of Artois; but she corresponded with the *émigrés* and Vienna in cipher, and it was part of Mme Campan's duty to arrange for the couriers. When her brother, the diplomatist Genet, came out as a champion of the Revolution she proposed to resign her post, but the suggestion was rejected by her grateful mistress. A few minutes after this conversation a letter from the Queen was brought to her room. ' Je veux vous dire par écrit que je crois à votre honneur et à votre fidélité, autant qu'à vos autres bonnes qualités et que je compte toujours sur le zèle et l'intelligence que vous employez à me servir.' Scarcely had she read the letter when there was a knock at her door. She was surprised to see the King. After sympathising with her anxieties, he added: 'Si nous avons le bonheur de voir tout ceci terminé, je dirai chez la reine, en présence de mes frères, tous les services que vous nous avez rendus et je vous en récompenserai, vous et votre fils.' She knelt and kissed his hand. 'Allons, allons, ne vous chagrinez pas; la reine qui vous aime croit à vos sentiments aussi bien que moi.'

In the early summer of 1792 it was clear that a fresh storm was about to break. The National Guard controlled the entrance to the Tuileries, the Queen's visitors were insulted, and ribald jokes were heard under her windows. The King seemed paralysed and for ten days he never uttered a word, but he remained unafraid. He vetoed decrees ordering the deportation of priests and the formation of a camp of 20,000 men under the walls of Paris. A few days later, on June 20, the anniversary of the oath of the Jeu de Paume and the flight to Varennes, the mob stormed the palace with the cry, 'Vive la Nation! A bas le veto!' Marie Antoinette, with the Dauphin, Mme Elizabeth, and her ladies took refuge behind a large table while the invaders filed past. They had brought some horrible symbols, among them a gallows from which a doll was hanging, with the legend 'Marie Antoinette à la lanterne.' When a woman hurled furious imprecations against her, the Queen asked if she had done her any harm. 'No, but you have harmed the nation.' 'So you have been told,' was the reply, 'but you are mistaken. Wife of a King of France and mother of the Dauphin, I am French. I shall never revisit my country, and I can only be happy or unhappy in France. I was happy when you loved me.' The woman began to cry, asked forgiveness, and added: 'C'est que je ne vous connaissais pas; je vois que vous êtes bien bonne.'

The royal couple had shown superb courage during these terrible hours, but having narrowly escaped death the Queen redoubled her appeals to the Princes and her Austrian relatives. 'J'existe encore,' she wrote to Fersen, 'mais c'est un miracle.' Louis read up the story of Charles I, and the Queen exclaimed: 'I am beginning to fear they will try the King. As for me, I am a foreigner and they will assassinate me. What will become of our poor children?' She burst into tears, and when Mme Campan offered a sedative she rejoined that in her cruel position such alleviations were useless. She refused to wear a padded corset which Mme Campan had ordered for her, adding, 'If they assassinate me it will be a blessing, for that will end my troubles.' A few days later the King, meeting Mme Campan on a staircase, took her hand and kissed her on both cheeks without uttering a word.

The story closes with the storming of the Tuileries, the most blood-curdling event of the writer's life. The invasion of the palace on June 20 had revealed the dire peril of the royal family, and the Queen ceased to sleep on the ground floor. She had not quite given up hope, and one night she confided to Mme Campan that in a month she and the King would be free. The itinerary of the Princes and the King of Prussia was in her possession, but she was aware of the difficulties, among them the temperament of the King. He had plenty of passive courage, but he suffered from an incurable inferiority complex. A few bracing words to the Parisians would make all the difference, but he could not utter them. 'I could act and mount a horse in case of need, but that would play into the hands of his enemies, who would raise the cry of *l'Autrichienne*. A Queen who is not the Regent must keep in the background and prepare to die.' The crowd in the Tuileries Gardens was a perpetual reminder of danger, and it was no longer possible for the family to take the air. At the beginning of August offers of money came from loyal friends, but they were declined. The tension had become so unbearable that the Queen longed for an end of the crisis, whatever it might be. On the last Sunday of his reign, as the monarch walked through the gallery to the chapel, half the soldiers of the National Guard cried, 'Vive le roi!' which provoked the counter-cry, 'Non, pas de roi! A bas le veto!'

On the evening of August 9, Pêtion, the Mayor of Paris, informed the Assembly that a large-scale insurrection was planned for the following day, that the tocsin would sound at midnight, and that he lacked the means to resist. The Assembly took no action, for the crazy Brunswick Manifesto had sounded the death-knell of the monarchy, but the faithful Swiss Guard was at its post. The tocsin duly sounded at midnight and before long the first shot rang out in the court of the Tuileries. At four the Queen emerged from the King's room to say that she had no more hope. The official who was entrusted with the safety of the palace, and who had been summoned to the Hôtel de Ville for further orders, had been murdered, and his head was carried through the streets. At daybreak the royal family and Mme Elizabeth came downstairs and walked past the National Guard. There were some cries of 'Vive le roi!' but there were also shameful insults. Louis was as pale as death. On their return the Queen remarked to Mme Campan, who had watched the sorrowful procession from a window, that all was lost, that the King had displayed no energy, and that this little review had done more harm than good.

The defenders inside the Tuileries were so badly armed that effective resistance was impossible. The Carrousel and the adjacent streets were filled with armed bands, the fiery Marseilles contingent at their head, and the guns were trained on the palace. A message to the Assembly conveyed by the Minister of Justice, asking for a delegation to safeguard the Executive Power, was ignored. At eight the King was informed that the royal family and their attendants were doomed to perish unless they at once repaired to the National Assembly. He consented, saying: 'Allons, Messieurs, il n'y a plus rien à faire ici.' Marie Antoinette was accompanied by Princess de Lamballe and another of her ladies. Mme Campan watched them depart through the crowd, which pressed so closely on them that the Queen's watch and purse were stolen. When they had gone the Swiss Guards were overpowered and massacred, and the mob streamed into the palace, shooting and stabbing as they went. Mme Campan had been seized by a burly Marseillais when someone called out, 'On ne tue pas les femmes,' and the man released his grip with the words 'Lève-toi, coquine, la nation te fait grâce.' Her own home having been pillaged she fled to her sister's house amid scenes of carnage.

It was too dangerous to stay under her sister's roof, for a crowd gathered, crying that the Queen's confidante was there and that they must have her head. She hurried in disguise to the house of a friend, and next day a member of the Assembly brought a summons from her mistress. Still disguised and accompanied by her sister, Mme Campan reached the Feuillants and was conducted to a little room where they found the King. They tried to kiss his hand, and he embraced them in silence. The Queen was lying down in the next room. 'Venez, malheureuses femmes, venez en voir une encore plus malheureuse que vous, puisque c'est elle qui fait votre malheur à toutes. Nous sommes perdus, nous succomberons dans cette horrible révolution; bien d'autres périront après nous. Tout le monde a sa part dans nos malheurs.' It was their last meeting, for the request for the company of her faithful friend was refused and further visits were forbidden. At this point Mme de Tourzel, Gouvernante des Enfants de France, becomes our guide. Soon afterwards the royal family were transferred to the Temple. On the day after the King's execution Mme Campan received his verbal message of thanks: 'Elle est du nombre des gens que je regrette de ne pouvoir récompenser de leur fidélité à ma personne et de leurs bons services.'

The fall of the monarchy forced Mme Campan at the age of forty to start a fresh career, for she was now almost penniless. She had obtained a judicial separation from her husband, and was debarred by her Royalist sympathies from public employment. She therefore undertook the education of the orphaned daughters of her sister, who had jumped from the window at the moment of arrest in order to preserve her fortune for her family, of which they would have been deprived had she been condemned by the Revolutionary Tribunal. Two years later, when the Terror ended with the death of Robespierre, she opened a *pensionnat* at Saint-Germain. Within twelve months there were sixty pupils, and the number soon rose to a hundred. Since the religious houses were closed, there was a demand for educational facilities among the circles who had suffered from the Revolution. She had found her vocation and her reputation spread rapidly.

The fortune of the school was made when Hortense Beauharnais and the sisters of Napoleon became boarders. The First Consul often visited Saint-Germain and admired her gifts of organisation.

'If ever I were to create a Woman's Republic,' he declared, 'I would make you First Consul!' In 1807 the Emperor appointed her head of a school for daughters of officers at Écouen, the first of what were officially described as Maisons de la Légion d'Honneur. The Tsar visited the establishment in 1814, but on the fall of the Empire the château was restored to the Condé family. The execution of Marshal Ney was a heavy blow, for he had married one of her nieces. She retired to Mantes, where an old pupil was married to a kindly doctor. The Royalists blamed her for her contacts with the Empire, but the grateful Hortense continued a small pension. She died of cancer in 1822 at the age of seventy, having lost her only son. Her wish that her *Memoirs* should be published directly after her death was fulfilled. 'The proofs of my conduct, which had been so unjustly attacked, are there.' 'Je dois à la vérité ce témoignage,' writes Mme de Tourzel in her poignant *Memoirs*, 'que Mme Campan, malgré les calomnies qu'on n'a cessé de répandre sur son compte, n'a jamais abusé de la confiance que la Reine lui a témoignée en divers circonstances.' Her readers will agree with those who knew her best that she had no reason to be ashamed of the part which she had played in helping her beloved mistress to bear the long martyrdom of her reign.

Bibliographical Note.—The best edition is by Funck-Brentano. The *Correspondance de Mercy d'Argenteau*, published by Arneth from the Vienna Archives in three stout volumes, contains not only the reports of the Austrian Ambassador but the letters exchanged between the Empress Maria Theresa and her daughter from the arrival of the latter in France in 1770 till the death of the former in 1780. The best biography of Marie Antoinette is by La Rocheterie, 2 vols. The best brief survey of the years 1770–89 is in Lavisse, *Histoire de France*, vol. 8. The brilliant volumes on Turgot and Necker, entitled *Au Couchant de la Monarchie*, by the Marquis de Ségur should be consulted. The best summaries of the French Revolution are by Madelin and J. M. Thompson.

CHAPTER XIX

MME DE RÉMUSAT AND THE FIRST CONSUL

THE publication of the *Memoirs* of Mme de Rémusat in 1880 was an event in the history of Napoleonic studies. Sainte-Beuve had been allowed to see them for his essay in the *Revue de deux Mondes* in 1842, republished in his *Portraits de Femmes*, but he gave no indication of their merit. Here in three volumes was the testimony of a refined and intelligent woman, who lived for a good part of seven years under the same roof as the dictator and witnessed the process of moral deterioration as his power and temptations increased. Since her husband was also a Court official, her record and reflections embody his experiences and impressions as well as her own. Nowhere else do we find a more convincing picture of the atmospheric change which occurred between the radiant dawn of the Consulate and the stormy close of the Empire. She confesses that they had hoped too much, but adds that the whole country made the same mistake. The greatest of historic men, as Acton described him, dug his own grave. To shrewd observers at home and abroad the attack on Russia was the beginning of the end. France was as delighted to see him go as she had been to see him come. After the horrors of the Revolution and the squalid anarchy of the Directory the nation cried aloud for order, liberty, and peace. Order he had given; but the conception of liberty was beyond him, and the most gifted soldier in history loved war as the drunkard craves for drink.

Though readers of first-class memoirs owe an immeasurable debt to their authors, we must inquire in every case when and for what reason they were composed. Mme de Rémusat, herself a novelist and author of the once popular *L'Éducation des Femmes*, enjoyed writing, and her position at Court inspired her to keep a journal in the form of letters to a fictitious friend. Of this not a page remains, for on the escape of Napoleon from Elba she threw the whole bundle into the fire. Since she and her husband had now openly joined the royalists, she feared the effect of discovery on the family fortunes. The loss of her record is irreparable, for the sparkling *Memoirs* are no adequate compensation to the historian hungry for strictly contemporary records of scenes, conversations, and moods. But for an incident in literary history we might have had nothing at all, and her name would be forgotten. Mme de Staël's *Considérations sur la Révolution Française*, published in 1818, with its sharp attack on the Emperor, made a deep impression on France, and inspired Mme de Rémusat to follow her into the witness-box. Throwing aside a novel on which she was engaged, and encouraged by her adored son Charles, who was later to win fame as a statesman and a scholar, she began to describe the central years of her life. 'Me voilà mordue du besoin de parler de Bonaparte,' she wrote. She started off with the tragedy of the Duc d'Enghien, and after a few lines found herself transported back to that terrible week at Malmaison. 'Les faits et les paroles me reviennent comme d'eux-mêmes; j'ai écrit vingt pages entre hier et aujourd'hui, cela m'a assez forte-ment remuée.'

Her pen raced along, and four months later she reported that she had written five hundred pages. 'Quel homme! Quel homme, mon fils! Il m'épouvante à retracer; c'est un malheur pour moi que d'avoir été jeune quand je vivais auprès de lui. Je ne pensais assez sur ce que je voyais, et aujourd'hui que nous avons marchés, mon temps et moi, mes souvenirs me remuent davantage que ne faisaient les événements. J'éprouve quelque chose de pénible et de mes illusions passées, et de mes sentiments présents.' Henceforth her *Memoirs* filled her thoughts and days. When she died three years later in 1821, at the age of forty-one, she had covered the years 1802–8. In reading her unfinished masterpiece we must bear in mind that it is a drama of disillusion, composed when the glittering soap-bubble had burst.

Mme de Rémusat was the daughter of a state official and a great-niece of Vergennes, the Foreign Minister of Louis XVI. Her father and grandfather were guillotined together only three days before the fall of Robespierre ended the butchery. In 1796, at the age of sixteen, she married Rémusat, a solid, kindly lawyer, twice her age. How happy they were may be seen in the two volumes of her letters published by her grandson in 1881. Her clever and attractive mother, Mme de Vergennes, was an acquaint-ance of Josephine Beauharnais, and on the establishment of the Consulate she begged her aid in securing a post for her son-in-law. Josephine's best quality was her readiness to help, and in 1802 even more was given than had been asked. Rémusat became *Préfet du Palais* to the First Consul and his wife a *dame du palais*. It was an excellent double appointment. The one was a tactful, competent, and conscientious official, the other a young woman of exceptional charm. Their opinions fitted into the new régime without difficulty, for they were neither ardent royalists nor republican doctrinaires. Rémusat, like other civil servants, was ready to do his duty under any tolerable régime. He would have preferred a purely administrative post in the service of the state, for there was nothing of the courtier about him, but for the time he and his wife were content. Josephine was kind and gracious to everybody, and the First Consul was still at his best.

Mme de Rémusat prefaces her story with a series of portraits.

The elaborate study of the personal appearance and habits, conversation and character of Napoleon is a pearl of great price. His legs, we are told, were too short for his body, his complexion colourless, his regular features like a classical medallion, his mouth agreeable when he smiled, his chin rather short, his jaw heavy and square, his hands and feet delicate. His expression in repose was melancholy and meditative, but in anger his glance became fierce and menacing. He dressed simply and wore no decorations. He would break or tear in pieces anything which caused him the slightest *malaise*. His smile was attractive but rare, for his nature was serious, not from nobility of spirit but from the profundity of his meditations. In youth he was something of a dreamer; later he was often depressed, and later still almost continually in a bad temper. Lacking social training, he seemed destined to live in a tent where nothing mattered, or on a throne where everything was permitted. He did not know how to enter or leave a room, how to sit down or get up, how to greet visitors. His speech was forced and he never seemed quite at home either in Italian or French; yet it was often a delight to listen to the rapid flow of his talk.

Passing to more important matters she leaves hardly a rag to cover his nakedness. 'Rien de si rabaisse que son âme. Nulle générosité, point de vraie grandeur. Je ne l'ai jamais vu admirer, je ne l'ai jamais vu comprendre une belle action. Il redoutait les liens d'affection, il s'efforçait d'isoler chacun, il n'a vendu ses faveurs qu'en éveillant l'inquiétude, pensant que la vraie manière de s'attacher les individus est de les compromettre, et souvent même de les flétrir dans l'opinion. Il ne pardonnait à la vertu que lorsqu'il avait pu l'atteindre par le ridicule.' When he came into the world his heart seemed to have been forgotten, or perhaps he had stifled it. 'Il ignore à peu près les liens du sang, les droits de la nature; je ne sais même si la paternité n'eut pas échoué devant lui.' Despising women he was never quite at home in their company and did not understand how to talk to them. He felt some affection for Josephine, whom at first he looked up to as his social superior, but never allowed it to interfere with his liaisons. 'Vous devez vous soumettre à toutes mes fantaisies, et trouver tout simple que je me donne de pareilles distractions. J'ai le droit de répondre à toutes vos plaintes par un éternel *moi*. Je suis à part de tout le monde, je n'accepte les conditions de personne.' His occasional tears were the result of nerves rather than genuine emotion.

Madame Mère is described as thoroughly mediocre in mind and caring chiefly for money. Joseph was never up to the lofty positions he occupied. Lucien had brains, but he was loose and self-willed. Louis was cleverer than Joseph, but he had no heart,

plained he would gradually abandon himself to the most disgraceful passions. Had he not seduced his own sisters, one after the other? Would not his family, trading on his weaknesses, persuade him to abandon her? Did not the coming of a new mistress always make him hard and sharp to his wife? Did he not say 'Je ne suis pas un homme comme un autre, et les lois de morale ou de convenance ne peuvent êtres faites pour moi?' It was in vain that Mme de Rémusat counselled patience and resignation.

On one occasion Josephine kept her talking late in the Tuileries, and an hour after midnight resolved to catch her faithless husband in the act. 'Je n'y peux plus tenir; Mlle Georges est sûrement là-haut, je veux les surprendre. Suivez-mois, nous monterons ensemble.' Protests at being dragged into such perilous espionage were unavailing, but the adventure ended undramatically, for a slight noise alarmed the injured wife. 'Perhaps it is Rustan, Bonaparte's mameluke, on the watch, and he might cut our throats.' Mme de Rémusat shuddered at the thought and fled back with the candle, leaving her mistress alone in the dark. Josephine followed a few minutes later, and the sight of such a terrified countenance made her laugh. The project was abandoned, and as they parted Mme de Rémusat remarked that her fright had served a useful purpose.

It was a novel experience to witness Napoleon's tactics during an official journey to the cities of north-eastern France and Belgium in 1803. The grace and charm of Josephine won all hearts, and the dictator knew how to stimulate enthusiasm where it was not spontaneously displayed. Finding the citizens of Ghent a little chilly, he remarked to his wife: 'These people are under the influence of their priests. To-morrow we must go to church, gain the clergy by a caress, and thus win back the ground.' He was present at High Mass, conversed with and conquered the bishop, and gradually secured the acclamations of the crowd. When he restored the family property to some acquaintances of Mme de Rémusat she told him of their gratitude. 'Gratitude,' he replied, 'is a purely poetical expression, devoid of meaning in times of revolution. What I have just done would not prevent your two friends from rejoicing if some royalist agent were to murder me. You are young, you do not understand political hatreds. People see everything through their party spectacles: nothing is intrinsically good or bad. This suits us quite well, for we too have our glasses through which we watch over our interests.' For whom, then, she asked, was he spending himself in great tasks, often in dangerous efforts? 'Oh, c'est qu'il faut être l'homme de sa destinée. Qui se sent appelé par elle ne peut guère lui résister. Et puis l'orgueil humain se crée le public qu'il souhaite dans ce monde idéal qu'il appelle la posterité.' 'But how can you risk your life for the sake of glory if you inwardly despise the people of your own time?' 'I do not despise them, madame, and in particular I esteem the French.' On another occasion he referred to his wife's complaints of his infidelity. 'She worries much more than she need, fearing that I shall fall seriously in love. She does not know that love is not for me. What is love? It means forgetting the whole universe and seeing only the beloved object. I am not made like that. What does it matter to her if I find distractions in which my affections are not engaged?' The dictator disliked blue-stockings, but he spent so much time in conversations with Josephine's vivacious *dame du palais* that tongues began to wag, though the character of the devoted wife and mother was beyond reproach.

Two years after her appointment an event occurred which opened her eyes to the utter ruthlessness of the master of France. The chapter on the execution of the Duc d'Enghien, which should be compared with the account by Queen Hortense, is the most dramatic in the book. The air was thick with rumours of assassination plots, and the *Émigrés*, announced the *Moniteur*, were summoned to gather on the Rhine, where a prince of the House of Condé was stationed. Josephine's four ladies took weekly turns in attendance, and Mme de Rémusat's week opened on Passion Sunday, March 18, 1804. After they had heard Mass at the Tuileries her mistress remarked that they were going to spend the week at Malmaison. She was very glad, she added, for just then she was afraid of Paris. She was silent and depressed, but when her companion made sympathetic inquiry she replied after a little hesitation: 'I will tell you a great secret. Bonaparte said this morning that he had sent M. de Caulaincourt to the frontier to seize the Duc d'Enghien and bring him here.' 'Ah! mon Dieu, madame,' exclaimed Mme de Rémusat, 'et qu'en veut-on faire?' 'Mais il me parait qu'il le fera juger.' When her companion seemed about to faint with horror, she opened the window of the carriage, and continued: 'I have done my best but I greatly fear he has made up his mind.' 'Quoi donc! vous pensez qu'il le fera mourir?' 'Je le crains.' Mme de Rémusat burst into tears, and Josephine promised to try again.

On reaching Malmaison both women were utterly worn out. The younger fled to her room where she wept bitterly. 'Toute mon âme était ébranlée. J'aimais et admirais Bonaparte, je le croyais appelé par une puissance invincible aux plus hautes destinées, je laissais ma jeune imagination s'exalter sur lui. Tout à coup le voile qui couvrait mes yeux venait à se déchirer, et par ce que j'éprouvais en ce moment je ne comprenais que trop l'impression que cet événement allait produire.' When she appeared in the salon she found the First Consul playing chess, outwardly calm and serene. On parting for the night Josephine promised to renew her appeal, but next morning she reported her failure. Women, he had told her, should not meddle in such affairs. His policy demanded a *coup*, after which he could afford to be clement. It was either this decisive act or a long series of conspiracies involving punishment from day to day. Impunity would encourage his enemies. The Duc d'Enghien had already been mixed up in a conspiracy, and his military reputation might some day cause trouble in the army. When he was dead the soldiers would have broken with the Bourbons. In politics a death which would ensure peace was not a crime. The orders had been given and there could be no drawing back. Josephine, as shallow as she was kind, reconciled herself to the inevitable, but Mme de Rémusat passed that day and the next in torment.

The dictator displayed a forced gaiety, playing with his little nephew, the child of Louis, and apparently enjoying his usual game of chess. Josephine had told him the views of her *dame du palais*, and, noticing her pallor, he asked her why she was not rouged. 'I forgot.' 'Comment? Une femme qui oublie son rouge! Cela ne l'arriverait jamais à toi, Josephine! Les femmes ont deux choses qui leur vont fort bien: le rouge et les larmes.' On the morning of the third day Mme de Rémusat came down early to the salon, where she found Savary alone, pale and haggard. His lips trembled, and there was no need to ask what had occurred. A moment later Josephine appeared. 'Eh bien, c'est donc fait?' 'Oui, madame, il est mort ce matin, et je suis forcé d'en convenir avec un beau courage.' He had come straight from the fortress of Vincennes and proceeded to describe the last hours of the victim.

It was a consolation for Mme de Rémusat when her husband arrived with news of the reaction in Paris. The Jacobins naturally rejoiced, exclaiming: 'Le voilà des nôtres.' For once the modest official stepped outside his usual sphere and gave Josephine some sound advice. There was not a moment to lose in steadying public opinion. The First Consul must prove that the event did not indicate a character turning to cruelty, and it should make him very cautious. Josephine approved, and reported the message to her husband, who remarked: 'C'est juste.' Among the many visitors to Malmaison in the course of the day was Caulaincourt, who had carried out the arrest without knowing its purpose. When he saw Mme de Rémusat shrink from him he exclaimed in tears: 'You too are going to desert me, but I am only an unfortunate. He rewards my devotion by dishonouring me. I have been basely deceived and I am ruined.' He spoke in the same way to the dictator, whose efforts to make it up he icily repelled. Napoleon asked Josephine what her *dame du palais* thought, and on hearing of her horror he remarked: 'C'est tout simple, elle fait son métier de femme. Vous autres, vous n'entendez rien à mes affaires. Mais tout se calmera, et l'on verra que je n'ai point fait une gaucherie.' At dinner he sat silent, but in rising from table he exclaimed in a harsh voice: 'Au moins, ils verront ce dont nous sommes capables, et dorénavant, je l'espère, on nous laissera tranquille.' Conscious of a chill in the salon after dinner he ordered extracts from the documents to be read aloud. 'There are the irrefragable proofs. These people wished to sow disorder in France and kill the Revolution in my person. I had to defend and avenge it. The Duc d'Enghien was a conspirator like the rest and had to be treated as such. I have shed blood, I had to do it. Perhaps I shall do it again, but without anger, for blood-letting is an item of political medicine. I stand for the state, I am the French Revolution, and I will maintain it.' After this defiant harangue the silent company was dismissed.

The First Consul made himself particularly agreeable to Mme de Rémusat, but with limited success. She began to feel ashamed of her chains, and on returning to Paris the dictator realised the atmospheric change. It was now, she believes, that he determined to assume the crown, on the principle that one strong impression was most easily removed by another. Josephine took her place as Empress with her customary tact, but the distribution of titles led to painful scenes with the greedy Bonapartes. At the first family dinner after the change of title Caroline wept whenever the Emperor addressed Hortense as Princess Louis. Elisa controlled herself but was equally hurt. On the following day there was a violent scene in the salon of the Empress, the noise being audible in the next room. Caroline's passionate complaints that she remained plain Mme Murat had no effect on the Emperor, who replied with cutting irony that he was the master and could distribute titles at his will. 'En vérité, mesdames, on croirait que nous tenons la couronne des mains du feu roi notre père.' There was certainly little in his family circle to counteract the dictator's growing contempt for mankind.

CHAPTER XX

MME DE RÉMUSAT AND THE EMPIRE

THE Court of the newly proclaimed Empire, despite its glittering surface, was not a happy place. Though many new posts and titles were created there were not enough to go round. The etiquette imposed by the master reflected the severity of military discipline, and the faces of courtiers and officials revealed their *malaise*. Rémusat was now described as First Chamberlain, and on ceremonial occasions he came immediately after Talleyrand, the Grand Chamberlain. His wife, on the other hand, was henceforth only one of several *dames du palais* to Josephine whose feminine vanity was flattered by her new position, but whose graceful tact and kindness of heart excluded all suggestion of arrogance. 'Mon excellente Impératrice' continued to pour her troubles into the ear of one of her few disinterested friends. The picture of greedy ambition, lying, and intrigue painted in these scintillating pages is repulsive in the extreme. Almost everyone was afraid of the dictator, whose moods altered from day to day and sometimes from hour to hour. Little had changed since Saint-Simon, except that Le Roi Soleil had the manners of a gentleman, whereas Napoleon, in Taine's cruel phrase, was a condottiere of the fifteenth century.

The proclamation of the Empire was accelerated by the scare of the royalist conspiracies, and the Duc d'Enghien was only the most illustrious of the victims. Among the nobles condemned to death was the Duc de Polignac. The sentences were being discussed by Mme de Rémusat, her husband, and her mother when the Duchess de Polignac and her aunt were announced. Both were in tears and the former was expecting a child. She desired to plead with the dictator for her husband's life, and believed that the *dame du palais* could open the door. After bidding her visitors return on the following day Mme de Rémusat sought the aid of her kindly mistress, who promised to receive the Duchess. While they were talking Napoleon entered the room, and the two women, undaunted by his frowns, begged him to grant an audience. He refused, explaining that the royalist party was full of young hotheads who could only be tamed by a sharp lesson. Why was Mme de Rémusat so interested in these people? It would only be excusable if they were relatives. She had never seen Mme de Polignac till yesterday, was the reply. 'Eh bien, vous plaidez ainsi la cause des gens qui venaient pour m'assassiner.' 'Non, sire, mais je plaide celle d'une malheureuse femme au désespoir et, je dirai plus, la vôtre même.' The Emperor left the

room in a bad temper, with the injunction not to worry him again.
A few minutes later the Duchess arrived and was received by
Josephine, who twice entered the study and was twice repulsed.
When she tried a third time Talleyrand, who had arrived,
supported the plea. Finally the Duchess was brought in and fell
fainting at the Emperor's feet, while Josephine was in tears and
even Talleyrand was moved. The death sentence was commuted
to imprisonment, but other conspirators paid the extreme penalty.

The Coronation fêtes brought Josephine the double satisfaction
of being crowned and of at last securing a religious solemnisation
of their marriage. Her position, however, was weakened rather
than strengthened by her elevation, for the creation of the Empire
revived the question of an heir in an acute form, and the
Bonapartes continually pressed for a divorce. Their arguments
were reinforced when she reacted violently against the latest
liaison. Rejecting the advice not to play into the hands of her
enemies she exclaimed excitedly one morning at Saint-Cloud that
she was going to see for herself. Half an hour later she returned
with the words: 'Tout est perdu!' The door of a room recently
furnished at the Emperor's orders was locked, and she heard his
voice and that of the Favourite within. She knocked loudly,
saying who she was, and when the door was tardily opened no
doubt remained. The lady wept and the Emperor began to
storm. 'I know I ought to have controlled myself,' confessed the
Empress on her return, 'but it was impossible to stifle my
reproaches. I am still all of a tremble and he is sure to come
and make a terrible scene.' 'I will withdraw,' replied her friend.
'He would never forgive you for telling me. Try to soften him
and to repair your great imprudence.' A few minutes later she
heard loud noises, and after the agitating interview she found her
mistress in tears. The Emperor in his fury smashed some of the
furniture, told her to leave Saint-Cloud, and declared his intention
to marry a woman who would bear him children. Eugène was
fetched to make arrangements for his mother's departure, and
Mme de Rémusat was commissioned to tell Hortense. The
dictator's wrath evaporated as usual in a few days, and the mistress,
not the wife, left the palace; but the vacancy was soon filled.
The position of the *dame du palais* between the dissolute husband
and the injured wife was almost intolerable, for both sides demanded
her support and accused her of being lukewarm in their cause.
She felt the ground rocking under her feet, and Court life became
ever more distasteful to her husband and herself. A partial
consolation was found in the increased contact with Talleyrand,
who took an equally detached view of their difficult master.

Mme de Rémusat continued to like her mistress, but her
superficiality was a trial, and the tone of the *Memoirs* becomes

increasingly critical.   The Empress was allowed 600,000 francs a
year for personal expenses, but it was not nearly enough.   She
also received 120,000 francs for her charities, which included her
poor relations.   She was very generous, but, as she always bought
her presents, they enormously increased her debts.   Her rooms
were filled with salesmen and artists.   She loved to be painted,
giving portraits to relations, friends, housemaids, and anyone who
wished to have them.   Diamonds, jewels, shawls, and other
fineries were brought to her in a never-ending stream.   She took
everything without asking the price, and usually forgot what she
had bought.   She told her ladies that her toilette was not their
affair.   Everything was settled with her housemaids, of whom she
had six or eight.   She rose at nine and lingered long over her
dressing, after which her hair was done.   She changed all her linen
thrice a day, and wore only new stockings.   When she had been
rouged, great baskets of robes, hats, and shawls were brought in
and she made her choice.   She possessed between three and four
hundred shawls, buying all that were brought, whatever the price,
though some cost many thousands of francs.   Despite his protests
the dictator always had to pay.   Josephine, we are assured, never
opened a book, wrote a letter, or did any work.   She loved to
embellish Malmaison, on which she spent large sums.   Her extravagance survived the divorce, and even when there were no visitors
she made herself smart.

The victories of Austerlitz, Jena, and Friedland made Napoleon
master of the Continent, but neither Mme de Rémusat nor her
husband was happy.   'We had been poor when we entered the
service of the First Consul,' she writes in describing the events of
1807, 'and his gifts had surrounded us with the luxury which he
prescribed.   Young as I was I could satisfy the tastes of my age
and enjoy the pleasures of a brilliant position.   I lived in a fine
house, I was adorned with diamonds, I could wear a different dress
every day and invite celebrities to my table.   I was invited to
every fête in Paris.   Yet from this time on a sort of dark cloud
weighed on my imagination.   Often, on returning from a glittering
circle at the Tuileries, still wearing the livery of luxury—perhaps
I may add of servitude—my husband and I used to have serious
talks.   A secret disquiet about the future, an ever-increasing
distrust of our master, oppressed us.   Without precisely knowing
what we feared, we began to confess our apprehensions.   I am not
made for this rôle and restricted court life, said my husband.   I
cannot admire what costs so much blood and tears, I replied.   We
were tired of military glory.   To these painful sentiments was
added the fear of no longer feeling able to like the master we had
to serve.   That was one of my secret troubles.   With the vivacity
of my youth and imagination I clung to the admiration for the

Emperor which I wished to preserve; I honestly strove to deceive myself about him; I sought occasions when he fulfilled my hopes. It was a painful and unequal conflict, and yet, when it ceased, I suffered still more. When in 1814 several people were surprised at my zeal for the fall of the maker of my fortunes and charged us with ingratitude they could not know all we had lived through. The return of the King ruined us, but it was balm to our feelings and ideas.'

The dictator realised that the Rémusats were drifting away. On returning home after the Treaty of Tilsit he rebuked the *Préfet du Palais* for not sending him reports on Paris, particularly on the Faubourg Saint-Germain: 'You are in a position to find out what people are saying in the salons, and it is your duty to let me know.' Rémusat replied that he heard little; people were naturally on their guard when he was present. He added that he would not care to attach such importance to unconsidered talk, often without really hostile intent. The Emperor shrugged his shoulders, and turned his back, remarking to Duroc: 'J'en suis bien fâché, mais Rémusat n'avancera guère, car il n'est point à moi comme je l'entends.' The Emperor loved praise from any quarter, and admiration, even if clumsily expressed, always paid.

The chapter in the third volume on the lengthy sojourn of the Court at Fontainebleau in 1807 has been compared to Saint-Simon, for Mme de Rémusat's descriptive powers are far above the average. The actors are alive and she could reproduce the atmosphere as skilfully as she recorded events. There is a sketch of the parvenu dictator at the height of his power. If a visitor, ignorant of history, had suddenly arrived at Fontainebleau, the splendour of the scene, the ruler's air of authority, and the obsequious reverence of the courtiers would have suggested a sovereign occupying the greatest throne in the world by the combination of power and dynastic right. Forgetting the past and having no fear of the future, he marched forward with unfaltering steps, confident that he could easily remove all obstacles in his path. It seemed to him, and to the rest of us, that he could only fall in consequence of some unpredictable event involving universal catastrophe. Master or friend of all the kings on the Continent, allied to several of them by treaties or marriages, assured of Europe by his new frontiers and his widely distributed garrisons, sole disposer of France's resources, immensely rich, in the prime of life, admired, feared, and above all scrupulously obeyed, he seemed to have triumphed all along the line. Yet there was a maggot in the fruit. England was a barrier which his armies could not pass. 'A few leagues of sea protected the civilisation of the world.' Perhaps Mahan had this sentence in mind when he wrote the most celebrated passage in his *Life of Nelson*.

At Fontainebleau as at Versailles a century earlier all details were regulated by the master's will, the officials and guests being informed of their parts. One evening in the week the Emperor held a reception, with music and card games. On two evenings there was a play or an opera. The Empress received once a week, finally Caroline and Pauline gave balls, and the princes and ministers had to give dinners in turn. Special days were set aside for sport, and all the ladies were supplied with smart hunting costumes. The Emperor liked hunting mainly for the exercise, for he was the hardest worker of them all, rising at seven and working almost uninterruptedly till five or six. Meanwhile the Empress, hating to be alone, passed the day in conversation and receiving visitors till four, when she began to dress for dinner at six. In the evening the Emperor mixed in the throng, but his conversation was usually a monologue, for people were afraid to reply. He had no wish to put them at their ease, for he resented the slightest appearance of familiarity. Everyone, including himself, was bored. He often complained of the chilly silence resulting from the constraint which he imposed. It was a queer thing, he remarked. He had collected plenty of people, wished them to enjoy themselves, and made arrangements for their pleasure; yet he saw long faces and everyone seemed tired and depressed. Pleasure, replied Talleyrand, could not be mobilised to the sound of drums. 'Here, as in the army, you always seem to be saying to us: Come along, ladies and gentlemen, forward, march!' At this time the Grand Chamberlain could say anything to his master in private, though in public he was as silent as the rest. The reigning mistress was a pretty Italian, but there was not much romance in what Mme de Rémusat described as 'cette froide liaison.'

The organisation of festivities was the task of the First Chamberlain. 'I pity you,' observed Talleyrand; 'il vous faut amuser l'inamusable.' Sometimes the piece would be changed almost at the last moment by the dictator, who replied to protests: 'Bah! avec un peu de peine vous en viendrez à bout. Je le veux, c'est à vous de trouver le moyen de le faire.' Actors and singers had to change their parts at the eleventh hour, and couriers rode away to fulfil the latest commands. One must have lived at Court, testifies Mme de Rémusat, to understand how trifles become important and how disagreeable the master's frowns. Since the dictator never praised the performance and indeed sometimes went to sleep, and since no one dared to applaud, it was a chilly affair. Yet he recognised Rémusat's ability and now added to his duties the control of the Paris theatres. It was interesting work, but by this time he and his wife were sick of the worries and pettiness of Court life. The low opinion of their master which they had come to hold was confirmed by Talleyrand, now a valued friend, who often came to their rooms for a frank talk and has left us a charming sketch of the happy couple. One day, when he had held forth on what he called the *fourberie* of the Emperor, tears came into the eyes of the hostess. 'What is the matter?' 'You hurt me,' was the reply. 'You politicians do not need to love your masters, but I, poor woman, how shall I bear the disgust your anecdotes arouse, and what is to become of me since I have to stay here without retaining any illusions?' 'You are a child,' was the reply, 'always putting your heart into what you do. Do not waste your affections on this man, but remember that with all his faults he is still necessary to France.' He was soon to change the latter opinion, for the dictator was about to plunge into the Spanish adventure which, as Talleyrand warned him, led towards the abyss.

The last chapter of importance is devoted to the coming divorce. The threatened Empress continued to confide her fears to Mme de Rémusat, who expressed her determination to leave the Court if the project were carried through. Josephine's emotions were not as a rule very profound, and she had never been ambitious; but the idea of a public repudiation stirred her to the depths. That she had ceased to worry her husband about his amours seemed for a time to strengthen her position, and the dictator often shed tears; but she had little hope of averting a catastrophe. She even pretended to believe, though without the slightest justification, that her life might be in danger. A long letter from Fouché, suggesting that she should sacrifice herself to the interests of France, which demanded an heir to the throne, seemed to settle her fate. Though it was close on midnight she sent for Mme de Rémusat, who had gone to bed. Rémusat, however, was still up, and found her in extreme agitation crying out that she was lost. Could the Minister of Police have taken a step of such importance on his own initiative? The First Chamberlain felt that it was impossible, and Josephine evidently had her doubts. 'What shall I do to avert the storm?' she exclaimed. 'Go to the Emperor this moment,' was the reply; 'show him the letter and say that you will only obey a direct order from himself.' Pretending to be angry, Napoleon declared that he knew nothing of the matter, that Fouché's zeal had outrun his discretion, and that he should be punished. These explanations were reinforced by caresses, but the trembling Empress reported that her husband seemed embarrassed. Fouché, needless to say, retained his post and his influence. Once again the storm blew over, but speculation was already rife on where the future Empress would be sought.

Every reader of these fascinating *Memoirs* will regret that they were interrupted by death when they had reached the opening of

1808. A partial substitute for the missing story of the divorce is to be found in the author's letters to her husband. The correspondence, which covers the years 1804-13, is singularly free from politics, no doubt owing to the fact that there was no guarantee of secrecy in the post; but there are some vivid snapshots of Josephine in the letters from Malmaison at the time of her fall. 'Elle pleure sans cesse et fait réellement mal à voir,' she wrote in December 1809. 'Ses enfants son pleins de courage; le vice-roi est gai, il la soutient de son mieux; ils lui sont d'un grand secours.' The Empress, said Hortense, was greatly touched by Mme de Rémusat's decision to share her fate; but ought she to make such a sacrifice? Her husband remained at the Court, and should she not transfer her services to the new Empress? The *dame du palais* had made up her mind, and Hortense, gratefully embracing her, confessed that it was also her mother's wish. Josephine certainly needed all the comfort she could find, for she was continually in tears. Every visitor seemed to revive her grief, and Napoleon's letters, protesting his affection and describing his sorrow, drove her almost mad. 'Je la soigne de mon mieux; elle me fait un mal affreux, elle est douce, souffrante, affecteuse, enfin tout se qu'il faut pour déchirer le cœur. En l'attendrissant, l'Empereur augmente cet état. Au milieu de tout cela, il ne lui échappe pas un mot de trop, pas une plainte aigre; elle est réellement douce comme un ange.'

That Josephine gradually recovered her spirits was due in part to the affectionate loyalty of her faithful friend, with whom she shared a wealth of memories. 'Elle est vraiment bonne dans la joie qu'elle a de me voir auprès d'elle,' wrote Mme de Rémusat in January 1811, 'et quand je la retrouve si affectueuse et si caressante, je m'applaudis toujours des légers sacrifices de vanité que j'ai faits à la reconnaissance que je crois lui devoir. Nous causons souvent, entre nous, de l'Empereur; elle aime à parler de lui, à se persuader qu'elle lui tient encore, et tout cela avec un tact et une modération qu'on ne saurait trop admirer.' Life became less interesting but far happier to the gifted woman who had tired of Court ceremonies and was perfectly content with her husband and children. The dictator was glad that Josephine should have such a sensible counsellor at her side. Rémusat retained his posts of First Chamberlain and Superintendent of the Theatres, while giving up that of *Grand-maître de la Garderobe*. He was free from the violent hatreds of his contemporaries, but none of the Emperor's functionaries was more delighted to witness his fall. His wife shared his satisfaction and was rebuked by Hortense for her rapid conversion to the cause of legitimacy. There was no romance about the fat and gouty old King, whose policy could hardly satisfy thoughtful Liberals, but at any rate Louis XVIII brought peace. Rémusat, as he had always wished, became a Prefect, and after the death of Josephine in 1814 his wife had time to write not only her forgotten novels but the work which keeps her name alive.

The book swelled the anti-Napoleonic tide which flowed between the collapse of the Second Empire and the appearance of Marbot's *Memoirs*, and supplied Taine with some of his most effective missiles. The famous critic and thinker was an amateur in history, as Aulard demonstrated in *Taine historien de la Révolution Française* and Prince Napoleon in *Napoléon et ses Détracteurs*. Taine, complained the latter, selected only the witnesses and the passages required to prove his thesis without assessing the value of the evidence. In his impassioned defence of his uncle the Prince puts Metternich, Bourrienne, Mme de Rémusat, Abbe de Pradt, and Miot de Melito under the miscroscope. Does Mme de Rémusat, he asks, deserve serious refutation? Is she indeed a historian at all? Certainly not, he replies. Since, however, Taine had pillaged her pages, it was necessary to deal with 'ce recueil de cancans, où éclatent toutes les petites passions, amour-propre froissé, calculs de la femme négligée et déçue.' She is condemned out of her own mouth, he adds, for her enthusiastic letters written during her period of service flatly contradict the *Memoirs* which were begun in 1818. That her narrative was coloured by the royalist reaction is true enough, but the Prince discovers much more than a change of perspective. Napoleon's attentions to such a young woman, he declares, turned her head. 'She formed dreams of grandeur and ambition which were never realised. It was these dreams which left the bitterness exhaled in her *Memoirs*. The wound was inflamed when she saw many persons, whom she regarded as of inferior merit, passing her and her husband in the race for influence and honours.' He adds that she took part in royalist intrigues and allied herself with Talleyrand, the arch *frondeur*. The real secret of her hostility, we are asked to believe, was her disappointed ambition, the failure of her plan to become the dictator's Egeria. The Emperor, adds Prince Napoleon, was immune to the influence of women, and this indifference inevitably produced hostility and misunderstanding. That there is a distinct change of attitude between the letters and the *Memoirs* is clear enough. But modern readers are as capable of explaining that difference as the nephew of the dictator, and are able to compare her published testimony with a wider range of evidence than was available two generations ago. Without claiming for Mme de Rémusat the authority of an impartial judge, we may say without hesitation that her picture of the dictator is more convincing than the apologia of his angry nephew.

Bibliographical Note.—The *Memoirs* are enriched by a valuable introduction by her grandson, Paul de Rémusat. A refutation of her charges against the

Emperor is attempted by his nephew, Prince Napoleon, in *Napoléon et ses Détracteurs*, based mainly on her *Correspondance*, published by her grandson in two volumes in 1881, which reveals her as an admirer of the ruler.   Sainte-Beuve's essay in *Portraits de Femmes* was written in 1842.   The most authoritative biography of Josephine is by Frédéric Masson, 3 vols.   There is an appreciative study of her distinguished son Charles by Jules Simon in *Thiers, Guizot, Rémusat*.

CHAPTER XXI

QUEEN HORTENSE AND NAPOLEON

THE most attractive of the ladies on the Napoleonic stage is surely Queen Hortense. The Emperor's sisters were no less unsatisfactory than his brothers, as no one knew better than himself. Pauline's good looks could not make up for her lack of mind and soul. The selfish and frivolous Josephine arouses sympathy rather than affection. Marie Louise was a doll. Madame Mère, a dignified old lady, shunned the limelight and saved half her allowance as a nest-egg for the time when, as she always foretold, the glittering bubble should burst. The Empire was a gigantic gamble, depending on the genius, the luck, and the health of a single man. All the world hastened to make hay while the sun shone, chasing madly after thrones, titles, offices, power, wealth.

The long-awaited *Memoirs* of Queen Hortense, published in 1927, surpassed anticipations. She had read extracts to friends during her lifetime, her son made comments, and champions of the great Emperor, such as Houssaye and Masson, were allowed to quote; yet no one could guess what a feast awaited them till large portions of the three volumes began to appear in the *Revue des deux Mondes*. Though she was never a highbrow she knew how to write, and the note of intimacy holds us enthralled. Here is Napoleon, from the campaign in Italy to the morrow of Waterloo, more human and therefore more real than in almost any of the countless memoirs of the period. Here is his stepdaughter, a little afraid of him, no doubt, but cherishing a genuine admiration and a measure of affection which survived his fall, a graceful, sensitive creature, full of feminine charm. Here is Louis Bonaparte, sick in mind and body, unfit for marriage and for the normal contacts of life. Here is Flahaut, the accomplished tempter to whom an impossible husband gave his chance. How Hortense drank the cup of sorrow to the dregs, how she longed for domestic happiness, how it eluded her grasp, is the most poignant revelation of the book. 'Mon cœur m'a toujours guidé dans les moindres démarches.' Her motto of resignation, 'Moins connue, moins troublée,' was turned by some friends into 'Mieux connue, mieux aimée.' This was the wish of her heart when, in the chill years of exile, she told her tale between 1816 and 1820. That she does not tell us the whole story is true enough, but that is the way of mankind. Readers who may be tempted to take her entirely at her own valuation may consult her latest biographer Pierre de Lacretelle, who presents her as a frivolous, selfish, and intriguing flirt, though few readers are likely to accept his verdict.

Hortense's father, Vicomte François de Beauharnais, a General and for a brief space President of the Constituent Assembly, was guillotined shortly before the *coup* of Thermidor brought Robespierre to the scaffold and the Terror to an end. A lucky accident saved the life of his wife, for Josephine shared his imprisonment. When they came for her she fainted and the official hastened away with the words: 'On viendra la prendre plus tard.' What Hortense describes as her first grief was the sight of her parents at a window a day or two before the end. Eugène hastened to Tallien, a friend of Josephine, but that cunning enemy of Robespierre was not quite ready with his plans. The children had been allowed to send presents to their parents, but nothing more. 'Je ne t'abandonnerai pas, sois tranquille,' said Eugène, a brave lad of thirteen, to Hortense, two years younger; 'je me ferai soldat.' He kept his word, and the unchanging devotion of brother and sister is a little patch of blue sky in the dark horizon of her life. They always agreed, she tells us, and it was a grief to her that he was so seldom at home. Her only other vivid memory of the Revolution was the *Fête de l'Etre Suprême*, when she saw Robespierre in all his glory with his powdered hair.

Hortense describes her schooldays as the only happy time of her life. This was an exaggeration, for the brief period at Malmaison before her marriage was happy enough; but she was certainly fortunate in coming under the influence of Mme Campan, who lavished on her 'la bonté, la tendresse éclairée d'une mère.' Marie Antoinette's lady-in-waiting earned her living after the Revolution by starting a boarding-school for girls of good family at Saint-Germain, where she carried on the better traditions of the *ancien régime*. Hortense was the model pupil, and, if we may believe the *Memoirs*, a general favourite, for the girls came to her with their troubles and disputes. 'Jamais je n'exerçai une plus véritable royauté que celle que mes compagnes s'étaient plu à m'accorder. Rien alors ne faisait prévoir l'élévation de ma famille. Je le devais à ce désir d'être aimée dont mon cœur était plein et qui pénétrait toutes mes actions.' It sounds a little priggish, yet it was substantially true. Throughout life she loved to please and possessed a talent for pleasing. That she enjoyed her popularity is natural enough. Mme Campan called her *petite bonne* and always remained her motherly friend. Some of her fellow-pupils also formed lifelong attachments. She was not a beauty, but she possessed a delicate charm which attracted almost everyone except the pathological specimen selected as her mate.

Josephine often invited her children to Paris, and in January 1796 she told them she was going to dine with Barras and would take them with her. Hortense, then in her fourteenth year, remonstrated. 'Comment, ma mère, tu vois ces gens-là? Tu

oublies donc les malheurs de notre famille?' Josephine gently
replied that since their father's death she had been striving to save
the remains of his property. Should she not feel grateful to
those who helped and protected her? She did not explain that
she was or had been his mistress, and Josephine's moral lapses
are discreetly omitted in the *Memoirs*. It was a big dinner-party
at the Luxembourg, the seat of the Directory, and Hortense knew
no one except Tallien and his wife. She was placed between her
mother and a man who wearied her by his vivacity. 'Sa figure
était belle, fort expressive, mais d'une pâleur remarquable. Il
parlait avec feu et paraissait uniquement occupé de ma mère.
C'était le Général Bonaparte.' The friendship had apparently
begun with an incident described in the memoirs both of Hortense
and Eugène. When an order was issued in October 1795 that no
private citizen should possess arms, Eugène went to Bonaparte,
then second in command of the Army of the Interior, and begged
to retain his father's sword. The lad pleaded so earnestly that
the General granted his wish and expressed the desire to know
the woman who had inspired him with such noble sentiments.

The children dreaded the remarriage of their mother, and their
chilly reception of the visitor told its own tale. His efforts to
break the ice by teasing Hortense only made matters worse. 'Je
concevais de lui une mauvaise opinion.' Every time she visited
Paris she noticed that Bonaparte's attentions to Josephine were
more marked. She confided her fears to her mother, who put up
a feeble defence. With tears in her eyes she begged her not to
marry again, above all a man whose position would separate her
from her children; 'but the General already had more influence
than I.' When he was appointed to command the army of Italy
Josephine accepted him. She loved him, writes Hortense; but
her love was much less than his. Mme Campan was deputed to
break the news to the children, since Josephine shirked the painful
task. 'I was profoundly afflicted. Mme Campan tried to calm
me, pointing out the advantages for my brother, who would be
happy to serve his country and could do so under no better auspices
than those of a general, his own stepfather. Moreover, he had
had nothing to do with the horrors of the Revolution. His family
was old and honourable. From every point of view it was a
suitable partnership.' The girl made the best of it, and when the
young officer returned from Italy with laurels on his brow she saw
him in a new light. All Paris resounded with his name, and
Josephine's little house, where he stayed, was crowded with people
who came to see the conqueror of Italy. Hortense, however, was
won by his kindness, not by his fame. 'Il m'accueillait avec toute
la tendresse d'un père.'

At the age of seventeen the marriage of Hortense became a

topic of eager speculation, and it was generally believed that some promising officer would be found. Mme Junot describes her in her *Memoirs* as 'fraîche comme une fleur, gaie, douce, parfaitement bonne.' Though not precisely a beauty, she was full of delicate charm. She hardly expected to be allowed to make her own choice: 'ma main semblait appartenir à tout le monde.' The First Consul had thought of Desaix, and his death at Marengo was a double blow. 'Quel homme distingué! quelle perte pour la Patrie! Je lui destinai Hortense. Elle eût été heureuse avec lui. Je le regrette vivement.' Tears came into his eyes as he spoke. 'On ne connaît pas Napoléon,' commented Josephine when he left the room. 'Il est vif mais il est bon. On le jugerait mieux s'il ne résistait pas autant à ces mouvements du cœur qu'il regarde comme des faiblesses.' The next name on the list was Duroc, whom Hortense liked, and to whom the First Consul had no objection. Josephine, however, thought it would be a *mésalliance*, adding that she could not get used to hearing her daughter called Mme Duroc.

At this stage the dictator took a hand in the game. Josephine's marriage had introduced the girl into the Bonaparte circle, and Louis often used to visit her home. 'Son attention paraissait se fixer sur moi, et je ne sais pourquoi je le redoutais.' That is the first reference to her future husband, and she was never to overcome her fears. Napoleon announced his decision to Josephine with his usual brevity. Louis, he declared, was the only suitable husband for Hortense. 'Nous n'aurons peut-être pas d'enfants. J'ai élévé Louis, je le regarde comme mon fils. Ta fille est ce que tu chéris le plus au monde. Leurs enfants seront les nôtres. Nous les adopterons, et cette adoption nous consolera de n'en pas avoir. Mais il faut que les jeunes gens se trouvent heureux de notre plan.' When Bourrienne, his secretary, was deputed to announce the wishes of the parents, Hortense promised her reply in a week. Eugène was away, but his presence would have made no difference. 'Il s'agissait de sacrifier mes idées romanesques au bonheur de ma mère.' Josephine was delighted, for it was the match on which she had set her heart. Perhaps her daughter might learn to love the man. Mme Campan encouraged her with the assurance that he was generally esteemed, and she believed he would make her happy. 'Louis me paraît bon, humain,' replied Hortense, 'mais je n'aime pas ce mépris qu'il affecte pour les femmes. Celle qu'il épouserait n'en souffrira-t-elle pas?' A virtuous wife, was the consoling reply, would alter his views.

Louis was summoned to Paris and informed of his fate. Entering the room where the brothers were closeted, Hortense heard the First Consul say: 'C'est une jeune personne douce et vertueuse.' Louis accepted the decision without protest but without enthusiasm, for he had been attracted by another girl. He proceeded to send his *fiancée* a letter of twenty pages on his life and tastes. He saw everyone at her feet, and he could not conceive that 'un intérieur simple' could suit her. She replied that he knew her tastes, and that she did not look for happiness to high place. 'Si vos succès et le grand monde ne vous ont pas gâtée,' rejoined Louis, 'vous devez être un ange, car il n'y a pas de milieu: vous êtes ou toute bonne ou toute mauvaise.' There was no warmth in these exchanges, for he was an incurable misogynist. 'Un pion (pawn) fantasque et déséquilibré,' declares Frédéric Masson, 'qui souffre autant qu'il la fait souffrir.' Moreover, he suffered from a slight curvature of the spine, partial atrophy of his right hand, and acute skin trouble which repeated visits to spas failed to cure. No more unattractive partner could have been found than this neurotic invalid whom Napoleon believed to have contracted syphilis in Italy. No woman could have made him happy or found happiness with him, and most men would have thought themselves lucky to have such a wife.

On the proclamation of the Empire in 1804, two years after her marriage, Mme Louis Bonaparte became Princess Louis and in 1806 Queen of Holland. Her husband welcomed his promotion, for he was a man of fair ability and he sincerely desired the welfare of his future subjects. The chief attraction, however, was the prospect of greater independence. His wife, on the contrary, dreaded the separation from her mother, her friends, and the Emperor to whom she could appeal in case of need. 'J'aime Hortense,' he remarked to Roederer, 'oui, je l'aime. Elle et son frère prennent toujours mon parti, même contre leur mère. Si pendant que je suis au Conseil Hortense demandait à me voir, je sortirais pour la recevoir. Si Mme Murat me demandait je ne sortirais pas.' To the end of his life he regarded her with affection and respect. When Louis told her that he was to be King of Holland she exclaimed: 'I hope you will decline.' For a moment she thought of throwing herself at the feet of the Emperor, telling him of the torments inflicted by her husband, and begging permission to remain in France. This, however, would have involved parting with her children, and she bowed to her fate.

Hortense felt no interest in Holland and the change merely aggravated her troubles. The dislike of husband and wife for each other was unconcealed. 'Plus je mettais de douceur de faire ses volontés plus il devenait exigeant.' His most repulsive characteristic was his pathological suspicion of his wife and of every young man who came near her. One day she found a valet reading one of her letters, and the man confessed that the King had promised him a hundred louis if he could find something against her. She often heard his footsteps at night as he came to

listen at her door. The Emperor's reproaches continued to irritate
the Man of Property whose idea of matrimony was possession, not
partnership. 'J'apprends la manière dont vous traitez votre
femme. Je vous ai donné une femme vertueuse et vous ne savez
pas l'apprécier.' Louis showed Hortense the letter and accused
her of writing to complain. 'You see everything I write to the
Emperor,' she meekly replied. 'Then it is the French Ambassador,'
rejoined the King. He ordered her to go nowhere without him,
not even to her adored mother, from whom he tried to separate
her by telling tales of Josephine's stormy past. Continually complaining that she did not love him, he had long killed any lingering
affection and turned it into fear and hate. The sudden death of
her eldest son, whom the Emperor adored and intended to make
his heir, prostrated Hortense with grief. Her sour husband made
more than one clumsy attempt at a rapprochement, but, as she
told him, she had suffered too much. After the birth of their
third son in 1808, the future Napoleon III, whom the neurotic
father regarded as illegitimate, the marriage came to an end in
everything but name. Resenting the tutelage of the Emperor and
in particular the strangling of Holland by the Continental System,
he was forced to resign his throne. 'Je veux manger la Hollande,'
wrote the Emperor, who proceeded to incorporate it in France.
Louis went into voluntary exile in Austria and Italy, carrying with
him an implacable hatred both of his brother and his wife.

For the first time in her life Hortense had a house of her own
and was her own mistress, but a new sorrow quickly came upon
her. The Emperor needed an heir if his work was to endure.
There was no acceptable candidate in the Imperial circle, and for
years the spectre of divorce had brooded over the scene. He
retained a mild affection for his wife, but he was not a man to let
sentiment stand in his way. The birth of a son to the *lectrice* of
his sister Caroline in December 1806 convinced him that the
childlessness of his marriage was not his fault. On returning to
France Hortense was grieved to notice the change in his behaviour.
'Plus de tendresse, plus d'égards pour ma mère. Il devenait
injuste, tourmentant.' When Josephine told her that her fate
had been definitely decided, the daughter welcomed the news as
the end of a public humiliation. 'Tant mieux. Nous partirons
tous et tu seras plus tranquille.' They knew that it was useless
to oppose the Emperor, for resistance merely stimulated his
desires. The whole of France, he explained, desired the divorce,
and he could not resist the wishes of the country; neither tears
nor prayers would change his course. 'She will submit,' rejoined
Hortense quietly, 'and we will all go away, taking with us the
memory of your kindness.' At these words his expression suddenly
changed, and tears ran down his cheeks. 'Quoi! Vous me quit-

terez tous, vous m'abandonnerez! Vous ne m'aimerez donc plus?
Si ce n'était que mon bonheur, je vous le sacrifierais, mais c'est
celui de la France. Plaignez moi plutôt d'être forcé de le faire
en renonçant à mes plus chères affections.' Hortense was touched,
but she continued to urge a complete withdrawal, and Eugène,
who was recalled to Paris, agreed. The Emperor pleaded and at
last his stepchildren gave way. Their mother, they believed,
would prefer to remain near him. For a brief space after the
divorce Napoleon visited or wrote to Josephine every day, and
sometimes there were tears in his eyes.

Hortense paints a vivid picture of the Court after the arrival of
Marie Louise. The Emperor did not expect good looks. 'Je vois
que ma femme est laide, car tous les diables de jeunes gens n'ont
pu me prononcer qu'elle est jolie. Enfin, qu'elle soit bonne et me
fasse de gros garçons, je l'aimerai comme la plus belle.' He asked
Hortense to teach him to dance, but he was clumsy and soon gave
it up. Before leaving Vienna the bride was coached by Metternich,
who had recently spent three years in the Austrian Embassy at
Paris. Pauline, he declared, was the peerless beauty, Caroline,
Queen of Naples, the wittiest, but the Queen of Holland was the
only member of the Emperor's circle of whom she could make a
friend. Hortense and Marie Louise got on excellently, though
they never became intimate friends. The Emperor insisted on
strict propriety at Court, and doubtful characters were removed.
He was gentler with his second wife, and he did not show his usual
annoyance when she kept him waiting. When he was in good
humour, we are assured, he was enchanting. 'Jamais on ne serait
douté, à le voir ainsi, que c'était le même homme qui faisait trembler
l'Europe et celui dont la grandeur naturelle nous imposait tant à
nous-mêmes ainsi qu'à toute sa Cour.' The shrieks of the Empress
during her confinement quite unmanned him. Hortense found him
pale and breathless. 'C'est fini, elle est sauvée. Son air était si
malheureux que je lui demanda avec crainte: Est-ce un garçon?
Oui, me dit-il, tout oppressé. A ce mot je l'embrassai, mais il
était tellement oppressé qu'il me repoussa. Ah! je ne puis sentir
tout ce bonheur-là; la pauvre femme a tant souffert.'

France, declares Hortense, was happy and satisfied: surfeited
with glory, the people desired the blessings of peace. The Emperor,
though aware of these feelings, was incorrigible, and plunged into
the Russian adventure. Marie Louise used to visit Hortense at
Saint-Leu, her country home on the Seine, bringing news from the
front. When bad tidings came pouring in, anxiety turned into
anguish. 'Our disasters were equalled by our grief. Everyone
was in mourning. France, long accustomed to obey a single will,
began to wish to share in the control of her destinies.' The
country pulled itself together on the return of its master, who

reached the capital almost as soon as the tidings of defeat.
Hortense hurried to the Tuileries, where she found the Emperor
tired and preoccupied but not depressed. Never was he more
master of himself, she declares, than in difficult moments. Had
the disasters of the army, she asked, been as cruel as he had
announced in the celebrated Bulletin 29 of December 3, 1812?
'I have told the whole truth,' was his reply. Had not the enemy
also sustained grave losses? 'Of course, but that is no consolation.'
He was thinking more of England than of Russia. When a fall
from his horse compelled him to stay in bed, he remarked: 'Well,
Hortense, my death would have been great news for the English.'
She believed that he would at last renounce his ambitious plans,
though perhaps a single victory would be needed to prove to the
enemies of France that the disasters in Russia had not destroyed
her strength.

One evening, when Hortense was alone with her ladies, Prince
Schwarzenberg, the Austrian Ambassador, was announced. 'You,
madame,' he whispered, 'who know the Emperor's character so
well, do you frankly believe we can expect peace? We desire it.
Europe is tired. But if he gains a success, would he not wish to
regain all his advantages?' One victory, she replied, would be
needed to restore confidence, but then he would surely obey the
desire of France for peace. 'Could you not convince him of its
necessity?' inquired her visitor. She rejoined that, in view of her
age and her position as an obedient daughter, she had never dared
to express her views. The Ambassador suggested Eugène, and
Hortense promised to write to her brother, adding that the
Emperor was too clear-sighted to need advice. She was wrong,
for even after the battle of Leipzig he believed in his star. She
went to dinner at the Tuileries on the evening that news arrived
that the Allies had crossed the Rhine. He was alone with the
Empress, holding her in his arms, apparently teasing her. 'Eh
bien! Hortense, on a donc peur à Paris? On y voit déjà les
cosaques. Ah! ils n'y sont pas encore et nous n'avons pas oublié
notre métier.' Turning to the Empress, he added: 'Sois tranquille,
nous irons encore à Vienne battre papa François.' When his son
came in for dessert he kept saying to him: 'Allons battre papa
François.' The child repeated the phrase so well that the Emperor
laughed loudly. After dinner he called Berthier and for an hour
dictated the organisation of the army in the plains of Châlons.
Other officers were summoned and questioned about their troops.
The ladies were present throughout, and at the end he remarked
cheerfully: 'Eh bien! Mesdames, êtes vous contentes? Croyez-
vous qu'on nous prenne si facilement?' But the time for such
bombast was past. The Allies marched into Paris and the
Emperor was packed off to Elba.

The victorious sovereigns drew a sharp distinction between the Beauharnais and the Bonapartes. On April 16, 1814, on arriving at Malmaison, Hortense found her mother walking in the garden arm-in-arm with the Tsar. 'Voilà ma fille et mes petit-fils,' remarked Josephine; 'je vous les recommande.' Alexander then gave his arm to Hortense and caressed her children. 'Que voulez-vous que je fasse pour eux? Permettez-moi d'être leur chargé d'affaires.' She replied that she desired nothing. When the illustrious visitor had left she was reproved by her mother for her chilly behaviour, and retorted that she could not show enthusiasm for the man who had declared himself the Emperor's personal enemy. Since Alexander, however, was a *charmeur*, the ice was soon broken and she came to look on him as the protector of her family. The King of Prussia and his sons, Wellington, the German Princes, Bernadotte, heir to the Swedish throne, the young Grand Dukes, ambassadors and other celebrities flocked to Malmaison. The Tsar came again and again, taking the children on his knees and winning the friendship and confidence of Hortense. Nowhere else, he declared, did he feel so entirely at home, and he added that he had met no one who did not speak well of her. He could hardly believe that he had known her such a short time. 'Je n'ai jamais vu une femme aussi intéressante,' he confided to her friend and secretary, Mlle Cochelet. 'Elle mérite d'être heureuse. Elle serait ma sœur.' His susceptibility to female charms was notorious, and his marked attentions to the Beauharnais family were hotly resented both in Bonapartist and royalist circles. Hortense sought and obtained an audience with Louis XVIII in order to thank him for allowing her at the instance of the Tsar to assume the title of Duchess of Saint-Leu. She was agreeably impressed by his simplicity and kindliness. At the close of the interview he kissed her hand, adding that he would be happy to see her whenever she wished. When she replied that she regarded herself as an old woman withdrawn from the world, he laughed. When she had gone he remarked that he had never met a woman with more agreeable and distinguished manners. While, however, the political sky seemed to be clearing, two misfortunes fell upon her. Her mother died and her husband procured a judicial order for the handing over of her elder son within three months.

The news that Hortense had remained in Paris and had played the hostess to his enemies reached Napoleon at Elba, and he received her coldly when she visited him on the evening of his return to the Tuileries. She had been thoughtless and imprudent, declares Masson, but she had never conspired against him. Next day she brought her children and entered his study with a beating heart. It was true enough that she had accepted the Restoration, though for a brief space she had dreamed that her brother might take the lead in France. Again she was coldly received, and after a moment of silence he let himself go.

NAPOLEON. I should never have thought you would abandon my cause.

HORTENSE. Abandon your cause, Sire! Had I the wish or even the power to do so?

NAPOLEON. You had no right to decide about my nephews without my permission. Your husband had reason to be offended.

HORTENSE. Sire, you do not know the circumstances which made me remain in France. My mother desired it, and she had nobody but me. My husband offered me no support. Where could I go?

NAPOLEON. With your brother.

HORTENSE. But he had no post, and he had gone to Vienna to see about it.

NAPOLEON. You could have gone there too.

HORTENSE. The Emperor of Russia has been a generous enemy. He wished to assure the future of my children. Could I refuse him?

NAPOLEON. You ought not to have remained in France. A piece of black bread would have been preferable. Besides, do not imagine your children would have profited by these pretended advantages. They would have been cancelled. You have behaved like a child. When one has shared in the rise of a family one should also share in its misfortunes.

HORTENSE (*bursting into tears*). Ah! Sire, I have miscalculated. I thought I was fulfilling a duty in saving your nephews from exile. I could not write to you. I tried. Where are the friends to whom I could have entrusted them?

NAPOLEON (*in softer tones*). You have no sound reason to offer me, but you know I am a good father. I forgive you!

Now that a full reconciliation had taken place Hortense was constantly at the Élysée, whither the Emperor had moved on account of its private garden. When she sang the praises of the Tsar, emphasising his desire for peace and his repugnance to the return of the Bourbons, he remarked: 'Did he say so? Then he is very false.' Hortense was oppressed by the thought that a new and hopeless struggle was at hand. She worried more than he, for he had been encouraged by his rapturous reception. He liked to see people, granted audiences without difficulty, and talked about literature and art. At the family dinner on June 11, on the eve of his departure for the front, he was quite gay, though Hortense felt that he was putting it on. In saying good-bye to Mme Bertrand he remarked: 'Pourvu que nous ne regrettons pas l'île d'Elbe!'

The greatest gambler in history was back in Paris on June 21, only a few hours after the news of Waterloo had arrived. Hortense hurried to the Élysée, where she found him alone in the garden, and was greeted with the words: 'What have you been told?' 'That you have been unfortunate, Sire.' He made no reply and they went to his study. He seemed overwhelmed by fatigue and by his thoughts, opening letters without reading them. He begged her to stay while he had his dinner, but uttered hardly a word. She went to him every day, obsessed by fears for his safety, to which he seemed to give no thought. Encouraged by Madame Mère, she urged him to leave without a moment's delay. 'The Emperor of Austria might perhaps remember that you are his son-in-law. The English would shut you up in the Tower. The Emperor of Russia is the only man in whom you can trust. He was your friend; he is loyal and generous. Write to him.' Napoleon listened almost apathetically and then remarked: 'And you, what are your plans? Will you go to your place near Geneva?' 'I am not thinking of myself but solely of you,' she replied; 'the worst of my proposals is preferable to this inaction.' On the following day, when Caulaincourt gave similar advice, the fallen dictator replied: 'Pour l'Autriche, jamais. Ils m'ont touché au cœur en gardant ma femme et mon fils. Pour la Russie, c'est se donner à un homme. Pour l'Angleterre, au moins, ce serait se donner à une nation.'

Though his mother and brothers were with him, Hortense was now his chief comfort, and he expressed a desire to spend the last days at Malmaison. Friends warned her that to identify herself so openly with him would estrange the Allied sovereigns. She replied that the time of his misfortune was the moment to show her gratitude, and that she wanted nothing from the sovereigns except passports for her retreat. During the following days Malmaison was crowded, while some officers and soldiers formed a miniature garrison of defence. The weather was superb, and the Titan was in his gentlest mood as he walked in the garden with Hortense. On the last evening he exclaimed: 'Que c'est beau, la Malmaison! N'est-ce pas, Hortense, qu'il serait heureux d'y pouvoir rester?' It was a relief to her when he drove away on June 29, after a last embrace, eleven days after Waterloo. The close of her public career had come. Accepting the baseless rumour that she had helped to arrange the return from Elba, the Tsar refused to see her, remarking to Mme Walewska: 'I protected her in 1814, and now she is the cause of all the misfortunes of France.' Hortense returned his letters and the mild flirtation was at an end. There was no longer a place for the woman who had been proud to solace the last hours in Paris of the fallen Emperor, and at the age of thirty-two she became a wandering exile.

CHAPTER XXII

QUEEN HORTENSE'S LOVE STORY

WHEN the *Memoirs* of Queen Hortense were published in 1927 we all wondered whether they would reveal the secret which was at once her torment and her joy. That she was attracted to Flahaut almost from the first, that she told him of her love while still under the authority of her husband, and that she was aware of his amorous escapades, she frankly admits. Starving for affection she strove in vain to resist, and in October 1811, after the final parting from Louis, she became the mother of the Duc de Morny. Her surrender is not mentioned in the *Memoirs*, though they make it clear enough that she was over head and ears in love. We must turn to the exquisite work of Henri Bordeaux, *Le Cœur de la Reine Hortense*, for the information which she fails to supply. While almost everything in her life is sad, its most poignant experience was that she compromised herself for a man unworthy of such devotion.

Charles de Flahaut's nominal father, like the father of Hortense, perished by the guillotine, but it is understood that he was an illegitimate son of Talleyrand. Born in 1785, and therefore two years younger than Hortense, he entered the army as a volunteer at the age of fifteen, was rapidly promoted, and became successively aide-de-camp to Murat, Berthier, and the Emperor himself, accompanying the latter in the Russian campaign and to the stricken field of Waterloo. His military rank, added to his personal charm, opened all doors at Paris, and it was at a dance that he first saw Hortense soon after the proclamation of the Empire. She loved dancing, and she tells us that at balls people sometimes stood on chairs to watch her. On one occasion the young officer, in a moment of enthusiasm, applauded. Annoyed at this exhibition she complained to his mother, a friend of Josephine, now Mme de Souza, wife of the Portuguese Ambassador. Princess Louis, she explained, danced for her own pleasure, not for applause.

Next day mother and son called to ask forgiveness. Henceforth Flahaut was a frequent visitor, for he was in the regiment of Prince Louis Bonaparte. At first Hortense was not impressed. Despite his talents and good looks, she writes, his levity made her regard him as an agreeable young man, but not in the least dangerous. He often came to her husband and gave her a look on his way out. Since she liked to reserve the morning for herself she sometimes declined to see him, except when she was having a singing lesson, when they sang duets, as they had the same teacher. Once when he was announced she replied with a little irritation, 'Say I am

not at home.' The visitor, however, was so close behind the valet
that he overheard the words, and walked in. She was confused,
but her effort to excuse herself failed to remove his expression of
gloom. He ceased to come, and she attributed his absence to this
incident. She sought to remove the painful impression, and,
meeting him at the house of Caroline Murat, reproached him for
dropping his visits. He had come, was the reply, but had not
been admitted. She asked the porter for the list of callers, and
there was his name, not once but often. Her husband, she learned,
had imposed a veto. 'Cette jalousie me parut encore plus bizarre
que les autres: un jeune homme si peu fait pour me plaire, puisqu'il
ne me paraît que léger, auquel j'ai fait même des impolitesses!'
What would he think of a woman who invited his visits and
apparently refused to receive him? She worried about it till they
met again at a ball, when he complained of being sent away while
others were admitted. 'It is not my fault,' she replied, 'but please
do not come again.' She at once felt her imprudence, for he
expressed his happiness that the veto was not hers. 'Vous ne me
verrez plus,' he added with emotion, 'car l'idée que je pourrais
être la cause d'une peine pour vous me serait insupportable.'

Hortense had revealed in a phrase both the jealousy of her
husband and her own good-will. 'Un étourdi, qui ne devait être
rien pour moi, m'avait montré un véritable intérêt: me fuir,
respecter mon repos, c'était m'aimer comme je l'entendais. Malgré
moi, j'y pensais souvent.' Soon afterwards they met at a large
lunch-party given by her brother Eugène. This time, however, it
was not Hortense, but another lady, a Pole, in whom Flahaut was
interested. She was to leave Paris next day, and seemed in
despair. He also had tears in his eyes, and Hortense began to see
him in a new light. 'Il est susceptible d'aimer,' she reflected;
'il souffre, il m'intéresse. Je m'était trompée de le juger léger;
il m'a montré de l'amitié; il aura la mienne; il la mérite, et je
puis m'y livrer puisque, amoureux d'une autre, il est sans danger
pour moi.' She had not yet discovered that he was as unstable
as water and could pay attentions to two charming women at the
same time. In the words of Countess Potocka, another of his
Polish flames, he was a very seductive person.

Louis Bonaparte was away from Paris when Hortense was
expecting her second child, combining a sojourn at Plombières for
the waters with a duty visit to Italy. The young wife, always
thankful to be alone, would have had a peaceful time but for the
thought of Flahaut. How serious it was she hardly realised,
though by her own account the symptoms were ominous. 'Si
quelqu'un causait avec moi, j'amenais la conversation sur les
impressions de ceux qui aiment; j'avais peur de sentir ce que je
redoutais tant et, lorsque l'on me peignait l'amour avec sa passion

et ses extravagances, je respirais et je me disais: Quel bonheur! Ce n'est pas de l'amour que j'éprouve.' Flahaut, however, was busy laying siege to the fortress. Knowing that Hortense went daily to the Bois de Boulogne with her eldest son and a lady-in-waiting, he took his ride at the same time and occasionally dismounted for a walk. 'Je ne le recevais plus chez moi, mais il se trouvait toujours où j'étais et ne manquait jamais l'occasion de me parler de ses sentiments.' In fact he rather overdid it; remembering his grief when the Polish lady went away, and believing that one can love only once, she realised that he was 'l'homme léger qui ne voulait que plaire et que séduire.' Yet she was unable to shake him off, and her heart beat when she saw his grey horse in the distance. They also met at the house of Caroline Murat, for the flirtatious hostess was numbered among his admirers. One day in the presence of the servants she rallied him on his attentions to her sister-in-law. It occurred to him that such talk was damaging to the reputation of his friend, and that thought, he told Hortense, filled him with despair—a mark of affection by which she was duly impressed. Caroline now strove to regain her influence over his wayward heart. Hortense, she argued, was good and gentle, but too cold for tenderness, and she was rendered so miserable by her husband's jealousy that it would be a crime to add to her torments.

Caroline's medicine seemed to work, for Flahaut was no more to be seen. Hortense passed so quickly from surprise to grief that for the first time she looked into her heart and took fright at what she found. 'L'ascendant impérieux que me révélait ma souffrance même me dominait trop pour ne pas être répréhensible. Il fallait le vaincre; c'est la seule chose qui m'occupa.' She confided her trouble to a devoted school friend, but it was in vain. On the pretext of sending a new novel, Flahaut wrote her a letter full of tenderness. 'Je souffrais. Mon cœur était oppressé; je priais Dieu avec ferveur; j'étais atteinte et pourtant j'espérais encore.' When she next saw him arm in arm with Caroline the blood rushed to her heart. The more he tried to talk to her, the more she strove to avoid him, but the effort told its own tale. 'J'aimais. Cette conviction achevait mon malheur.' She was to struggle against her passion for years, but with such an accomplished seducer it could only have one end. Her first resolve on reaching home was to tell her husband after his return from Italy, but the plan was upset by a curious coincidence. Believing him to be in Turin, it was a shock to a woman far gone in pregnancy when he suddenly walked into her bedroom in the middle of the night. Everyone except Hortense was asleep. 'What a fright you gave me!' she exclaimed. This revelation of his mistrust put an end to all thought of seeking his help. She merely begged him to take her into the country. On hearing of her departure, Flahaut wrote that he needed only a word to consecrate his life to her, but she sent no reply.

Balls and Court ceremonies still brought them together. Believing herself to have regained self-control she invited him to dance, when to her horror he accused her of coquetry, the failing she most despised. 'Moi coquette!' 'Yes,' he replied, 'you have shown your friendliness. That is all I ask, and it made me happy, and now it seems that you hate me.' Poor Hortense, forgetting that people were watching her, felt her eyes fill with tears, and Flahaut at last learned the depth of her affection. 'Why did you not tell me you were interested in me? It would have spared me much pain, and now, when I love you alone, I am committed to another.' 'No, no,' cried Hortense, 'I do not love you. If I dreaded it for a moment, that is over.' 'Then give me your friendship,' he replied; 'that will console me for what I have lost.' She promised, and they parted. She was no longer afraid of a man who confessed to a liaison. Everyone noticed the change in her, but only she and Flahaut knew the cause.

NAPOLEON. Hortense has lost her colour. Her husband does not make her happy, and we may have a terrible time with her. If ever she loves, it will be intensely, and love causes great follies.

JOSEPHINE. You know how sensible she is.

NAPOLEON. Yes, but the passions are very strong.

JOSEPHINE. She is so gentle and calm, with never a moment of vivacity.

NAPOLEON. Don't be so sure; watch her gait, listen to her talk. Everything in her breathes sensibility, otherwise she would not be your daughter.

Hortense listened to her mother's repetition of this dialogue with downcast eyes and responded with a smile. Her stepfather read her heart better than Josephine.

Now that the relationship had been verbally defined as friendship, not love, Hortense wrote her first letter to Flahaut in reply to his condolences on the departure of Eugène to become Viceroy of Italy. Unfortunately the friendship formula was merely a phrase. When she read that he had been wounded in the wars she was luckily alone, for, as she confesses, no one would have believed that her distress was merely that of a friend. On the day she was to start for Holland, to take up her new duties as Queen in 1806, a man was announced by the only attendant left in the house as desiring to see her alone, 'presque déguisé,' she writes, though the words in the manuscript were afterwards crossed out. For the first time since she had loved him they were alone. Fear and emotion paralysed her for a moment, and then she uttered a cry. 'Remember that someone may come and that you would be compromised,' said her visitor. 'Let them think evil of me as much as they like, so long as I keep straight,' was her response. 'Alors, avec la plus grande simplicité je lui avouai que je l'aimais, mais que la vertu m'était encore plus chère que lui.' Once again she promised her friendship and they parted in tears.

In 1808, on the eve of her departure to assume the crown of Naples, Caroline Murat poured out her heart to her sister-in-law. 'Tu ignores le sentiment qui me lie à M. de Flahaut. Que de fois j'ai craint qu'il n'éprouvât un trop tendre pour toi! Tu es la seule femme au monde que j'eusse redoutée. Il paraissait te distinguer, mais j'ai été promptement reassurée. Quoique jeune, quoique léger, il ne pourra jamais aimer que moi. On ne ressent pas deux fois un attachement comme celui que je lui ai inspiré et, sans mes devoirs et mon amour pour Murat, je ne sais si j'aurais la force de lui résister. J'appréhende la douleur qui lui causera mon départ. Il cherchera peut-être à se consoler près de toi, mais promets-moi de ne pas l'écouter. Il doit me rester fidèle puisque son amour était si vif. Je ne pourrais penser sans chagrin qu'une autre pût lui plaire.' Hortense replied with an effort: 'Qu'as tu à craindre de moi? Je ne puis intéresser personne.' Here was a new shock for her bleeding heart. Had she been deceived by the man who had sworn to be true? Yes, he had deceived her, she said to herself, but perhaps he was unhappy to lose Caroline. 'S'il souffre, je lui pardonne. Peut-être avais-je besoin d'être trompée. Cependant il m'en resta un sentiment de méfiance qui ôta toute sécurité à mon âme.' Flahaut went off to the wars and was again wounded. He returned the same plausible creature as ever, with his tears and protestations of eternal devotion on his lips. The moth was fluttering round the lamp, and his triumph was at hand.

In July 1810, after the brief episode of the Kingdom of Holland was over, Louis Bonaparte broke with the Emperor and went abroad in the sulks. He pretended to believe that his third child, the future Napoleon III, was illegitimate, and the marriage was at an end in everything but name. 'Ce que je trouve consolant,' he wrote, 'c'est de vivre loin de vous, de n'avoir rien a démêler, rien à faire avec vous, rien à en attendre. Adieu donc et pour toujours.' If she replied, he added, her letter would be returned unopened. Sick in mind and body, Hortense joined her mother at Aix. As she drove from Geneva she saw two riders galloping towards her. One of them, we are not surprised to learn, was Flahaut, who had just ended his liaison with Countess Potocka and had been granted a month's leave. Never before had they seen so much of one another and for so long a period. Only a

page is devoted to this meeting, when, in the belief of Henri
Bordeaux, she surrendered at last.   Her words reveal her feverish
state.   'Je voulais tout combattre, tout surmonter, et je ne savais
que me retirer précipitamment chez moi, pleurer, blâmer ma
faiblesse et rougir d'apercevoir dans mon âme, au lieu du calme
de l'amitié, tous les tourments de l'amour.   Mes yeux étaient sans
cesse mouillés de larmes, malgré la tendre solicitude de ma mère
et les soins empressés de tout le monde.'   It was the happiest time
of her life, she declares, 'mais comment en jouir au milieu des
combats intérieurs que ma faiblesse ne pouvait soutenir et qui
absorbait ma vie tout entière?'

Hortense returned to Paris where Flahaut, now a colonel, was
one of the ornaments of her salon.   'Je n'avais plus d'esprit
quand il était là; je ne trouvais plus un mot; il fallait, je le sentais
bien, lui adresser la parole comme aux autres, mais c'était sans le
regarder et d'une voix qui n'était plus naturelle.   S'il parlait je
n'avais l'air de l'entendre, et cependant rien de ce qu'il disait
n'était perdu pour moi.'   He often wrote, and in her replies she
confesses that she no longer sought to hide her feelings.   'Loin
de lui il me semblait que je l'aimais mille fois davantage.'   Unfortunately no letters of the lovers have survived.   She longed for
his visits, but she could never be sure of the constancy of a man
'plus animé du désir de plaire que pénétré du besoin d'être aimé.
Beaucoup des dames semblaient s'occuper de M. de Flahaut.   Je
m'en apercevais.   Vainement il m'assurait qu'il ne pourrait
jamais en aimer une autre, qu'il était trop difficile de rencontrer
une personne comme moi, que la première je lui avais fait croire
au bien, que je le rendais meilleur, qu'il n'aurait pas le courage de
me tromper.   Cependant malgré toutes ces protestations, j'avais
toujours à lui arracher l'aveu de quelque faiblesse, et le présent
comme l'avenir en était troublé.   Je sentais trop avec ce caractère
qu'il fallait m'habituer à n'être plus aimée un jour.'   For her he
was everything: for him she was one of a crowd.

On October 21, 1811, Hortense gave birth to a son, destined to
fame as the Duc de Morny.   How had one of the leading figures
at Court and in society been able to conceal her condition?   Or
was no concealment possible?   It is astonishing that no reference
to it has been discovered in the voluminous memoirs and correspondence of the time.   On the other hand, it is impossible to
believe that nobody knew.   She was unwell at a dinner at the
Tuileries on February 1, 1811, and in the sixth month she appeared
at the festivities in celebration of the birth of the Roi de Rome.
Her latest biographer, Pierre de Lacretelle, suggests that the
Emperor deliberately closed his eyes and that, in consequence,
everyone followed his example.   The hypothesis is unconvincing,
for in a scandal-loving country tongues and pens were always busy

with the private lives of the great. The problem seems insoluble, and even Frédéric Masson gives it up.

Hortense had spent August at Aix, but her subsequent movements are not fully known. She left Aix with her secretary, Mlle Cochelet, on August 31, furnished with passports in another name, for a house near Geneva which she had acquired four months earlier. On September 14 she informed the governess of her children that she was hoping to meet her brother in the Borromean Isles and that it was useless to write to her during the journey. She was back in Paris on October 9 or 10, and Mme Campan, the oldest of her friends, wrote to the wife of Marshal Ney: 'Ce qu'on me dit de sa maladie m'inquiète beaucoup; pauvre martir au physique comme au moral, mon cœur saigne de la voir dans cet état.' In a letter to Eugène on September 25 Josephine seems to believe that they were together in Italy. So effective was the smoke-screen of a grave illness that we cannot be sure where the child was born. It was registered on October 22 in the third *arrondissement* of Paris as Charles Auguste Louis Joseph Demorny, born on the previous day to Emilie Coralie Fleury, wife of Auguste Jean Hyacinthe Demorny, propriétaire à Saint-Dominique, a shadowy and perhaps a fictitious personage. Flahaut hoped that Hortense would be able to dissolve her marriage and marry him, but a divorce was impracticable. So well was the secret kept that Napoleon III only learned it after her death.

During the next three years the lovers appear to have seen less of each other, for Flahaut, now a general and aide-de-camp to the Emperor, accompanied him to the Russian campaign, fought in the battles of 1813–14, and was present at Waterloo. He was employed to discuss his master's departure with the Provisional Government. When the fallen dictator left Malmaison for the coast Hortense went once more to Aix, where Flahaut unexpectedly appeared. He had handed over the command of his division and had obtained six months' leave. He had come, he declared, to consecrate his life to her. She replied that her political past might compromise him, just as his presence might compromise her until the time should come when she could again receive her friends. He realised the necessity of the sacrifice, she writes. This was not the whole truth, for after three days he was asked by the Prefect to leave Aix. The parting was more painful than ever, for Hortense felt a presentiment of trouble which was soon to be fulfilled. Letters arrived for him, but she feared that to forward them to Lyons, where he was staying, might do him harm. On the other hand they might contain things of importance for him to know. 'J'avais sa confiance; je les ouvrais sans me croire coupable d'indiscrétion; que devins-je, grand Dieu! en lisant les expressions passionnées d'une femme qui paraissait liée avec lui et qui se flattait de posséder son amour! Au même instant toute autre douleur disparut à mes yeux. Ma patrie, mes amis, mes craintes, mes dangers, tout fit place à une seule idée: j'ai été trompée. Mon premier mouvement fut de lui envoyer un éternel adieu; le second de penser qu'il était malheureux.' The lady in question, though her name is not revealed in the *Memoirs*, was Mlle Mars, the popular Paris actress. Hortense wrote Flahaut a letter of mingled recrimination and pity, urging him to rejoin the woman whose love must be very precious to him since he had sacrificed to it such an affection as her own. She promised to remain his friend on the sole condition of his telling her the truth. After this painful effort she collapsed. 'Ce courage, que les événements n'avaient pu abattre, succombait. J'était frappée au cœur.' Mlle Cochelet tells us in her *Memoirs* that she had several heart attacks every day and was unable to eat. At this agonising moment an agent of Louis Bonaparte came to remove her eldest son in accordance with the decision of a court of law.

A letter from Flahaut to his mother, from whom he had no secrets, reveals that he was to some extent aware what he had done. 'I am very unhappy about my cousin [her name was never mentioned in the correspondence]. Some old letters came for me to Aix, and she opened them. Among them was one from Mlle M., which upset her terribly and threw her into a nervous fever.' To Hortense he replied that he regretted not to have met his death at Waterloo; he wished to come and explain and ask forgiveness. Fearing the tumult of emotions, she refused. She still loved him, but she had learned at last that he was false. 'Sa douleur me faisait pitié; il me jurait dans les termes les plus touchants que son cœur n'avait jamais cessé d'être à moi, mais rien ne me satisfaisait. J'avais été trompée; je voulais bien pardonner, mais je ne pouvais oublier.' Yet a further letter bringing the familiar assurance that she was his only interest in life swung her round again. 'Je l'aimais trop; j'avais trop besoin de me reposer sur quelque idée consolante pour ne pas le croire, et je me rattachai de nouveau à l'affection, moi qui avait juré, peu de temps avant, de ne plus m'y fier.'

Flahaut continued to write from England, where he settled after resigning his commission, and she consoled herself in exile at Constance with the hope of reunion. 'Il ne pensait qu'aux moyens de se rapprocher à moi,' writes the credulous Hortense. Without actually expecting him, she used to walk in the direction from which he might arrive. If she saw a man approaching in the distance her heart began to beat. Yet chilly reason occasionally intervened. What would the world say of their reunion? Would it not have the right to reproach her? And what happiness could she offer a man who linked his fate to her misfortunes? 'Il est fait pour la société, me disais-je; il l'aime; il y obtient du succès; me suivre maintenant, ce serait y renoncer pour se vouer à l'infortune, et l'affection la plus profonde peut seule tenir lieu de tout. Dois je croire à celle que j'inspire après ce qu'est arrivé?' At this moment a letter from her husband invited her to join him in begging the Pope to dissolve the marriage on the ground that it had been forced. It was a tempting prospect to be able to marry the only man she ever loved, but she declined on the ground that it was untrue and that it would injure the interests of her sons.

We are now near the end of our journey. One day a letter arrived which brought the unsubstantial fabric of her dreams crashing to the ground. 'Il avait plu à une jeune personne riche, indépendante, remplie de qualités et de talents. Il était touché de l'intérêt qu'elle lui montrait, mais ne songeait qu'à venir me rejoindre et sollicitait son passeport.' He did not say that he was engaged or even in love, but it was easy to read between the lines. 'Il pouvait être heureux loin de moi, faire un mariage avantageux, et je devenais un obstacle à son bonheur.' She bade him follow his feelings and consult his interests. His next letter referred to passport difficulties and contained a phrase which she correctly interpreted as the *coup de grâce*: 'Mes amis ici croient que j'aurais grand tort de m'éloigner dans ce moment.' The final renunciation cost her terrible pangs, for she was still desperately in love. 'La passion dont mon cœur était plein semblait s'accroître au milieu des efforts que je faisais pour l'étouffer. J'étais sans cesse forcée d'en mesurer l'étendue et je m'effrayais de tout ce que j'y découvrais. Qui m'aidera, qui me soutiendra dans cette-lutte contre moi-même?'

The only solution, she decided, was to ask God's help. In October 1816 she followed the pilgrims' path to Einsiedeln and poured out her heart in the confessional. Yet the cure was far from complete. Though she wrote to Flahaut, telling him of the torments her love for him had caused and begging him to put aside all thought of rejoining her, her pen outran the promptings of her heart. 'O faiblesse humaine! En traçant cette résolution, j'espérais encore qu'il ne me croirait pas, qu'il viendrait peut-être me forcer à la retracter.' It was too late. In June 1817 Flahaut married Margaret Elphinstone, daughter of Lord Keith, and their daughter was to become the wife of the third Lord Lansdowne. He continued to write letters breathing the most tender friendship and esteem. 'Il se trouvait heureux et son bonheur m'était cher, puisqu'il était un peu mon ouvrage.' Though Hortense was to visit England many years later, and Flahaut was later to return to France, there is no solid evidence that they met again. She had happy moments at Arenenberg, her home in Switzerland, where she settled after years of wandering, and in Rome where she often spent the winter. There was no lack of friends and visitors. She continued to enjoy her painting and her music, and she read with critical eyes the books on the Napoleonic period which were beginning to appear. The future Emperor was an affectionate son, though his political escapades were a sore trial. Yet the two decades which followed the battle of Waterloo and the marriage of Flahaut were merely an epilogue to the drama, and a lingering death from cancer in 1837 at the age of fifty-four rounded off a life of disappointment, frustration, and storm.

Bibliographical Note.—The *Mémoires* in three volumes are admirably edited by Jean Hanoteau. *Queen Hortense* by I. Taylor, 2 vols., is a good summary of the material available before their appearance. Turquan, *La Reine Hortense*, and Pierre de Lacretelle, *La Reine Hortense*, are unfriendly. Henri Bordeaux, *Le Cœur de la Reine Hortense*, deals sympathetically with her love for Flahaut. The *Mémoires sur la Reine Hortense et la Famille Impériale*, in four volumes, by Louise Cochelet, the school friend, *lectrice*, secretary, factotum, the faithful companion in good and evil days, were compiled to cover the years 1813–15. There are two abridged editions. Her relations to the Bonapartes must be studied in Frédéric Masson's monumental work, *Napoléon et sa Famille*, 13 vols. The latest authoritative survey of Napoleon's career is by Madelin, *The Consulate and the Empire*, 2 vols. Five volumes of Madelin's biography have appeared, and seven more are to come. The best sketch of Flahaut is in *The Secret of the Coup d'État*, edited by the Earl of Kerry. Some correspondence relating to Hortense between Flahaut and his mother is published in *The First Napoleon*, edited by the Earl of Kerry.

CHAPTER XXIII

CAULAINCOURT, NAPOLEON, AND ALEXANDER

THE publication of the *Memoirs* of Caulaincourt, soldier and diplomatist, in 1933, is the latest outstanding event in the history of Napoleonic studies. Thiers and Vandal had been allowed to see them, but their interest, like those of Hortense, surpassed all expectations. They cover only a short period; yet the Grand Écuyer, the Ambassador to Russia, and the Foreign Minister, saw and heard so much that we could hardly spare a page of the three substantial volumes. He was well aware of the interest of the drama in which he played an active part, and his detailed reports of the dictator's conversations are unique. 'Mes notes ont été prises partout, dans le Cabinet, au bivouac, chaque jour, à chaque instant, elles sont l'œuvre de tous les moments. Je n'ai rien fardé, rien déguisé, parce que si l'homme se montrait quelquefois, on reconnaissait encore plus souvent le demi-dieu.' Though the journal, written under the eyes of his master, might of course have fallen into his hands, he tells us that he suppressed nothing. This circumstance, he adds, disproves the statements that no one dared to think, talk, and write freely while Napoleon was on the throne. That it diminished his friendliness was true enough, but he could bear *bona fide* criticism. 'I felt confident that my notes, which faithfully reproduced what I had said to him, would only be resented if they were published as a reproach to his policy and his glory.' Though Caulaincourt's public career ended after Waterloo, it was not till 1822 that he began to put his papers into shape, for he was ailing and depressed. When his old rival Maret, Duc de Bassano, returned to France in 1820 and attempted to justify himself by supplying documents to various writers, Caulaincourt felt that he, too, must tell his tale. His task was finished in 1825 and he died of cancer in 1827, at the age of fifty-three.

Caulaincourt belonged to one of the oldest families in Picardy. His father was a general who became a Senator and a Count under the Empire. His mother, after being in the service of the wife of the Comte d'Artois, later Charles X, became *dame d'honneur* to Hortense, for the elder Caulaincourt had been a friend of Alexandre de Beauharnais. The son, born in 1773, followed his father's footsteps, entering the army at the age of fourteen, seeing service in the Rhineland, and finding himself with Moreau at Hohenlinden. Josephine never forgot her early friends, and in 1801 he was sent to St Petersburg with a letter from the First Consul, congratulating Alexander I on his accession. On his way back he received the unexpected news that he had been appointed an aide-de-camp, and in 1803 he became a General of Brigade.

Caulaincourt, like the Rémusats, was happy enough at the outset, but, like them, he was shocked by the execution of the Duc d'Enghien. The tragedy darkened his life, for he never quite succeeded in destroying the legend that he had shared in the crime. When appointed to the Embassy at St Petersburg in 1807 he found the society of the capital so chilly that he submitted to the Tsar the documents disproving the 'odious calumny.' Alexander examined them and declared that they disproved his complicity in 'that horrible affair.' His will, dated 1821, reveals the undying bitterness in his heart. 'Je jure que je n'ai été pour rien dans l'arrestation du Duc d'Enghien. Amèrement calomnié la posterité me rendra justice.' Two days before his death he solemnly reiterated his innocence. The Duke had been kidnapped at Ettenheim in Baden by General Ordener, not, as was widely believed, by Caulaincourt. The latter had been ordered to Offenburg to arrest a certain Baronne de Reich and some British agents. When the Duke was brought to Strasbourg he received an order to send him to Paris. He made the necessary arrangements, and instructed the officer and the two gendarmes to show the captive every consideration. He never saw him, had no notion of the fate that awaited him, and only heard of the tragedy of Vincennes on reaching Malmaison.

Though Caulaincourt found it difficult to forgive his master for having exposed him to cruel misrepresentation, he accepted the honours heaped upon him, and his fidelity was beyond reproach. The establishment of the Empire was followed by a shower of decorative titles. Fesch became Grand Almoner, Talleyrand Grand Chamberlain, Duroc Grand Marshal of the Palace, Berthier Master of the Hunt, Ségur Master of Ceremonies. Caulaincourt, now promoted to General of Division, became Grand Écuyer. For nearly a year he had been Inspector-General of the Stables, and henceforth it was his duty to look after the couriers, organise journeys, accompany the Emperor to the army, shield him from harm. Though he was too reserved to be generally popular, he was extremely efficient and was most highly appreciated by those who knew him best. 'C'est l'homme que j'estime le plus,' remarked the Tsar Alexander to Mme Junot; 'il y a du chevaleresque dans l'âme. Oui, c'est un honnête homme.' Still higher was the praise from the fallen Emperor of Maret and Caulaincourt—'deux hommes de cœur et de droiture.'

From the proclamation of the Empire in 1804 to the closing scenes in June 1815 Caulaincourt formed one of the innermost circle. He accompanied his master on the dazzling campaigns of 1805–7, and after the return of peace he was selected as Ambassador to St Petersburg. It is at this point that the *Memoirs* begin. He was received by the Tsar as an old friend, was tacitly assigned the

first place in the diplomatic corps, and became Duke of Vicenza.
He felt Alexander's charm and trusted him rather more than he
deserved. 'Words and actions alike,' he reported on the eve of
the Tsar's departure for the Congress of Erfurt, 'prove to me that
Your Majesty can count on this Court whatever the course of
events.' He never ceased to stress the need of co-operation, and
it was not his fault that Napoleon made the greatest mistake of his
life.

Caulaincourt was present at the Congress of Erfurt, and, though
he took no direct part in the negotiations, he freely exchanged
ideas with his master. A year's experience as a diplomatist had
enabled him to feel the pulse of Europe, and he spoke plainly of
the apprehensions which were widely entertained. Austria was
almost openly hostile, the occupation of Spain had left a bad
impression, and the presence of French garrisons in Germany
created alarm. Everyone, he declared, felt himself threatened.

N. Quel projet me croit-on donc?

C. De dominer seul.

N. Mais la France est assez grande. Que puis-je désirer?
N'ai-je pas assez de mes affaires d'Espagne, de la guerre contre
l'Angleterre?

C. Il y en aurait, sans doute, plus qu'il n'en faudrait pour
occuper tout autre que Votre Majesté; mais la présence de ses
troupes en Allemagne, sa détermination de garder ses positions sur
l'Oder, tout porte à croire, comme pour mon compte, je l'avoue à
Votre Majesté, j'en suis convaincu, qu'elle a d'autres projets et
que son ambition n'est pas satisfaite.

The Emperor, while laughing at these apprehensions, asked
Caulaincourt how he would propose to remove them. First of all,
replied the Ambassador, Prussia should recover her independence.
'Retirez vos troupes d'Allemagne, Sire, ne gardez qu'une place
comme garantie de vos contributions, et le monde restera en paix.'
Calming the fears of Europe would be worth more to him than an
army of 100,000 men or ten strongholds on the Oder. That,
retorted the dictator, was a policy of weakness. It would destroy
the fruits of all his sacrifices for the reduction of England, which
necessitated the closing of Continental ports to her commerce.
The system of commercial restriction, interjected Caulaincourt,
could continue without the presence of troops. 'Vous n'entendez
rien aux affaires,' observed his master with a smile; yet a few
hours later he sent Duroc to offer his outspoken critic the Foreign
Office. The post was declined, but the Emperor continued his
efforts to vindicate his policy. 'Votre Emperor Alexandre est
têtu comme une mule. Il fait le sourd pour les choses qu'il ne
veut pas entendre. Ces diables d'affaires d'Espagne me coûtent
cher.' Despite his dissatisfaction he sounded the Tsar through

Caulaincourt and Talleyrand about a possible divorce and re-marriage. The reply was friendly but non-committal. Though the Congress appeared to the world to be a brilliant success, the two Emperors trusted each other even less at the close than at the start, and the Ambassador returned to St Petersburg more apprehensive than ever. Talleyrand, the leader of the malcontents, claims in his *Memoirs* that he agreed with him on everything. That they both wished to preserve peace is true enough; but while the one leaned towards Austria, the other placed his hopes in the Tsar.

Caulaincourt's later years in St Petersburg were unhappy, for dark clouds were gathering in the sky. Alexander, though remaining friendly, became less expansive, and Napoleon henceforth sent instructions through the Foreign Minister instead of direct. The Ambassador, who was suffering from the climate, resolved to resign if his reiterated request for his recall continued to be ignored. The end came in the spring of 1811, and he was coldly received at Saint-Cloud, when the conversation lasted five hours. Alexander, declared the Emperor, was false, and he proceeded to pour out a torrent of complaints. Caulaincourt stood up to him, maintaining the accuracy of his reports, and expressing his readiness to lay his head on the block if his successor and subsequent events did not confirm them. This appeared to make an impression, for the Emperor walked up and down the room in silence for a quarter of an hour.

N. Then you believe that Russia does not want war and would remain in the alliance and support the Continental System if I satisfied her about Poland?

C. It is no longer merely a question of Poland. But I am sure they would be very satisfied if Your Majesty withdrew from Danzig and Prussia at any rate the larger part of the forces which they regard as directed against Russia.

N. Then the Russians are afraid?

C. No, Sire, but, being reasonable people, they prefer open war to an unreal peace.

N. They want to dictate to me?

C. No, Sire.

N. But it is dictating to demand that I evacuate Danzig.

C. The Emperor Alexander avoids threats, but he feels that Your Majesty's armies on the Russian frontier have not come to maintain the alliance. I have seen what caused him anxiety, so I can tell Your Majesty what would reassure him.

N. The Russians wish to force me to evacuate Danzig. I am not Louis XV. The French people would not swallow such a humiliation. You wish to humiliate me?

C. Neither Your Majesty nor France. I am asked how to preserve the alliance and I do so.

N. Do you advise this humiliation?

C. I wish to restore the position after Erfurt. That is no humiliation. But if Your Majesty contemplates the restoration of Poland, which is incompatible with the alliance, my observations are superfluous.

N. I told you I did not desire to restore Poland.

C. Then I do not understand what makes Your Majesty sacrifice the alliance.

N. It is Russia who has broken it because she dislikes the Continental System. You are in love with Alexander?

C. No, Sire, I am in love with peace.

N. You are always talking of peace. Peace only has a meaning when it is lasting and honourable. Confess that Alexander desires war.

C. No, Sire, I stake my head that he will not fire the first shot.

N. Then we are agreed, for I desire neither war nor the restoration of Poland.

C. Then, Sire, the presence of Your Majesty's armies in Danzig and the north of Prussia requires explanation.

That the Emperor had made up his mind was revealed by his next observation. In the event of war, he declared, the Russian grandees would tremble for their palaces, and after a good battle they would force Alexander to make peace. 'Your Majesty is in error,' replied Caulaincourt, who recalled his final conversations with the Tsar. If Napoleon made war, he had declared, the invader would probably win battles, but that would not secure peace. The Spaniards, though often beaten, were unvanquished, and they had neither the climate nor the resources of Russia, who possessed a good army as well as room to manœuvre. If things went badly the Tsar would rather retire to Kamschatka than cede provinces and sign a treaty which would be merely a truce. The winter was on his side. Napoleon appeared to be impressed, but a moment later he repeated that 'une bonne bataille' would do the trick. Soon afterwards he complained to the Russian Ambassador at a crowded reception that Caulaincourt had become Russian and that Alexander had talked him over.

N. (*turning to* CAULAINCOURT). N'est-ce pas que vous êtes devenu Russe?

C. Je suis un très bon Français, Sire, et le temps prouvera à Votre Majesté que je lui ai dit la vérité comme un fidèle serviteur.

N. Je sais bien que vous êtes un brave homme, mais les cajoleries de l'Empereur Alexandre vous ont tourné la tête et vous êtes devenu Russe.

Early in 1812 the Grand Écuyer had further political conversations. The coming war, he remarked, would not be merely on account of Poland; it would be to eliminate all rivals in Europe and to have only vassals. The ruler of France had not collected so many troops in the north nor spent so much on preparations without intending to use them to satisfy his darling passion.

N. Quelle est cette passion?

C. La guerre, Sire.

The dictator protested feebly, but his good humour encouraged further home truths. The pursuit of hegemony in Europe, he was told, would provoke hostility which would sooner or later be fatal. The time for universal monarchies was past. France was already too big. His possessions beyond the Rhine would lead to war. If he could force England to make peace, rejoined the Emperor, that would be the end of the war-like ambition with which he was reproached. Caulaincourt knew his master too well to be impressed, but he pays unstinted tribute to his conversational arts. 'When he liked he had in his voice, his expression, and his manners something seductive and persuasive which gave him no less advantage over his interlocutor than the superiority and flexibility of his mind. To resist him it was necessary to have had experience, as I had, of all the political errors concealed behind this art. No woman ever displayed more skill in getting her way. He did everything with passion.'

The Grand Écuyer accompanied the gambler when he sallied forth in May 1812 to cross swords with the Tsar. A fall from his horse on the banks of the Niemen was widely regarded as an evil omen, and the Emperor himself was momentarily upset; but his confidence quickly returned. Within two months, he declared, Russia would ask for peace. Caulaincourt's eloquent silence annoyed him, for even dictators like to have their optimism confirmed. When pressed to speak he recalled the Tsar's striking utterances which he had quoted on his return to Paris. Napoleon listened quietly but made no response. On entering Vilna without a battle he cheerfully remarked that the Russians would be at his feet within a month. 'Je suis venu pour en finir une bonne fois avec le colosse des barbares du nord. Il faut les refouler dans leur glaces afin que, de vingt-cinq ans, ils ne viennent pas se mêler des affaires de l'Europe civilisée.' What happened in Germany was no concern of theirs. It was an ordeal for Caulaincourt when the Emperor, in the presence of a Russian envoy, revived the old charge of having been turned into a Russian by the Tsar's cajoleries. He was a good Frenchman, was the reply, better than those who advocated war. He had always told his master the truth, while others hoped to please him with fairy tales. He could bear such pleasantries before his compatriots, who knew and esteemed him, but not in the presence of a foreigner. He was proud of being against the war and having done his best to prevent it. Having for some time noticed that his services were no longer agreeable,

he begged leave to resign; and since he could not honourably go
home while there was a war, he begged for a command in Spain.

Napoleon took the outburst calmly. 'Who doubts your fidelity?
I was only chaffing. You know I esteem you.' Caulaincourt was
too worked up to be pacified, and was about to burst forth again
when two of his friends pulled his coat and implored him to keep
silence. The Emperor withdrew, and the injured official made
arrangements for his departure. Next day, after mediators had
intervened in vain, Napoleon sent a direct command to appear,
and greeted him with the words: 'Êtes vous fou de vouloir me
quitter? Je vous estime, et n'ai point voulu vous blesser.' After
this it was impossible to resign, though his master still spoke of
'Your friend Alexander whose cajoleries have turned your head.'

While condemning the Russian campaign Caulaincourt retained
his admiration for his master's genius and his gratitude for his
services to France. The Emperor, he testifies, had changed the
character of his countrymen. They had become serious, and
every one would have blushed to be found wanting in patriotism.
His entourage made it a point of honour not to flatter him, and
their criticisms never quenched their zeal and devotion. 'Les
détracteurs de cette grande époque diront ce qu'ils voudront:
jamais souverain n'a été entouré de plus d'hommes capables, gens
de bien avant tout et nullement courtisans quels que fussent
l'admiration et l'attachement pour le Grand Homme. La gloire,
soit qu'on en fût rassassié, soit que la raison portât à se méfier de
ses prestiges, n'avait énivré personne. On était resté modéré et
bon Français avant tout.' This handsome tribute to the civil
courage of Napoleonic France was written when the dictator was
in his tomb.

When the arrogant invader marched into Moscow, after his
costly victory at Borodino, he ordered the Grand Écuyer to report
the event in letters dated from the Russian capital; yet his disappointment at the sight of empty streets and houses was stamped
plainly on his face. Not a soul was in the Kremlin when the
Emperor took up his quarters in the royal apartments. The fires
in different quarters of the city were at first attributed to negligence,
but their scale and the capture of incendiaries quickly proved that
they were planned. Most ominous of all was the silence of the
Tsar. The Emperor avoided political conversation, contenting
himself with occasional pin-pricks. The early autumn of 1812 was
so warm that he contrasted it favourably with the climate at
Fontainebleau. 'Voilà un échantillon de ce terrible hiver de
Russie dont M. de Caulaincourt fait peur aux enfants.' When,
however, October was reached without any prospect of a settlement, he asked his fearless counsellor if he thought the Tsar would
respond to overtures for peace. The sacrifice of Moscow, was the

reply, did not suggest it, and the approaching winter favoured the Russian cause. 'Voulez-vous aller à Petersbourg? Vous verrez l'Empereur Alexandre. Je vous chargerai d'une lettre et vous ferez la paix.' The Tsar, answered Caulaincourt, would not receive him. 'You do not know what you are saying,' rejoined the Emperor. The Tsar would be all the more eager to seize the chance of negotiations since the nobility, ruined by the war and the burning of Moscow, desired peace. Caulaincourt declined the mission on the ground that it had no chance of success. 'Eh bien! j'enverrai Lauriston; il aura l'honneur d'avoir fait la paix et de sauver la couronne à votre ami Alexandre.'

Instead of receiving the desired response the Emperor learned that Cossacks were astride the road to Smolensk. When Caulaincourt felt it his duty to point out the dangers of campaigning in winter, his master listened without annoyance, though he remarked to Duroc and Berthier, 'Caulaincourt se croit déjà gélé.' He was already half-converted, but he found it difficult to swallow his pride. 'The Emperor Alexander is obstinate and he will regret it. He will never again get such good conditions as I was prepared to offer.' When Caulaincourt suggested that the Tsar was aware of his own advantages and the invader's embarrassment, Napoleon asked in an angry tone what he meant. He quickly regained self-control, but his emotion was unconcealed.

N. Vous croyez donc que je quitte Moscou?

C. Oui, Sire.

N. Cela n'est pas sûr. Nulle part je ne serai mieux qu'à Moscou. Nous aurons encore beaucoup de bons jours avant l'hiver.

C. Ne vous y fiez pas, Sire. L'hiver arrivera comme une bombe et vous ne sauriez trop le redouter dans l'état où est l'armée.

These emphatic warnings were confirmed by events, and at last the terrible retreat began. 'Ceci devient grave,' remarked the Emperor. 'Je bats toujours les Russes, mais cela ne termine rien.' The celebrated 29th bulletin told the world that the gamble had failed, and there was nothing left but to hurry back to Paris, where the Malet conspiracy had revealed the shaky foundations of the Empire. Caulaincourt was chosen as his sole travelling companion, and his notes were written up when they stopped for the night. The Emperor travelled incognito as M. de Rayneval, secretary to the Duc de Vicence. On crossing the Niemen and finding himself safe in the Grand Duchy of Warsaw he regained his spirits. The army at Vilna, he declared, could easily hold up the Russians who were at least as exhausted as the invaders. Shutting his eyes to the immensity of his losses, he remarked that the attitude of Austria and Prussia was his only anxiety. The disasters would make a great sensation in France, but his return to Paris would restore the tone of the country. If the Poles wished to be a nation again, they would rise *en masse* and he would arm them. Austria's assent could be purchased by the cessions she desired. If, on the other hand, the Poles did not play up, there would be no need to consider them, and a settlement with Russia would be easy to secure. Every Cabinet in Europe was interested in keeping the Cossacks beyond the Niemen. The war against Russia was in the interest of civilisation. The Emperor Francis mistrusted the Tsar and his projects in Turkey, and the reverses suffered by France would remove the apprehensions aroused by her power. 'On ne doit plus voir qu'un ennemi en Europe. Cet ennemi, c'est le colosse russe.'

These illusions were challenged with even more than the accustomed freedom. 'It is Your Majesty whom people fear so much that they are blind to other dangers. It is the universal monarchy of which the cabinets are afraid. It is the fiscal system adopted three years ago which injures German interests. It is the political inquisition established in Germany by some tactless agents which outrages national sentiment and pride. It is the military régime imposed on Germany by Davout which has exasperated the peoples even more than the cabinets.' The dictator was now in such good humour that he listened quietly and patted his companion on the cheek. There might have been some administrative abuses, he admitted, but the foundations were liberal and enlightened, well adapted to the ideas of the century and to the real needs of the peoples. Instead of being treated like conquered countries, they were administered like French Departments. The commercial restrictions were naturally resented, but only peace with England could end them. People must be patient. The English Government would fall within two years. 'On le forcera à la paix et à une paix dans l'intérêt des droits commerciaux de toutes les nations. Chacun oubliera alors la gêne dont il se plaint, et la prospérité qui en résultera, ainsi que l'état de choses qui s'établira, donneront largement les moyens de réparer promptement toutes les pertes.' What Caulaincourt called the colossus of French power was in the interest of all Europe, for it was the only means of abating England's excessive pretensions. She had forced him to do all he had done. If she had not broken the Treaty of Amiens, if she had made peace after Austerlitz or Tilsit, he would have stayed quietly at home. 'Je ne suis pas un Don Quichotte qui a besoin des aventures. Je suis un être de raison qui ne fait que ce qu'il croit utile. La seule différence entre moi et les autres souverains c'est que les difficultés les arrêtent et que j'aime à les surmonter quand il m'est démontré que le but est grand, noble, digne de moi et de la nation que je gouverne.' He even toyed with the idea of attacking England in India.

At intervals during the long journey the Emperor asked his companion whether he thought Russia would make peace. Caulaincourt replied that French reverses were not calculated to induce a pacific mood in the Tsar.

N. Vous le croyez donc bien fier?

C. Je le crois opiniâtre. Il pourrait être fier d'avoir un peu prévu ce qui est arrivé et de ne pas avoir voulu écouter des propositions à Moscou.

The Emperor confessed that he would have been wise to finish the war in Spain before attacking Russia and that he stayed too long in the capital. If he had retired four days after he entered, as he had thought of doing when he saw the fires, Russia would have been beaten. He would have offered generous terms from Vilna, and 'votre cher Empereur' would have accepted them. The game, however, was by no means lost, and by the following summer the situation would be very different. The Poles had been unskilfully handled. He wished for peace and it was England who kept up the war. 'On se trompe; je ne suis pas ambitieux. Les veilles, la fatigue, la guerre, ne sont plus de mon âge. J'aime plus que personne mon lit et le repos, mais je veux finir mon ouvrage. Dans ce monde il n'y a que deux alternatives: commander ou obéir. Je veux profiter de l'occasion pour vider cette vieille querelle du continent avec l'Angleterre.' He returned to the subject again and again, for England dominated his thoughts. The main object of the Russian campaign was to prevent England from securing a powerful ally.

When peace returned, continued the Emperor in an expansive mood, he would be the good fairy. He would spend four months every year travelling about 'cette belle France,' especially in the Departments where roads, canals, and industry needed encouragement. In ten years people would bless him as much as they hated him to-day. He spoke so frequently and with such affection of the Empress and his son, particularly of the former, that Caulaincourt was surprised and touched. 'Je me fais plus méchant que je ne suis. On me croit sévère, même dur. Tant mieux; cela me dispose de l'être. Allez, Caulaincourt, je suis homme. J'ai aussi, quoiqu'en disent certaines personnes, des entrailles, un cœur, mais c'est un cœur de souverain. Je ne m'apitoie pas sur les larmes d'une duchesse, mais je suis touché des maux des peuples. Je les veux heureux et les Français le seront. L'aisance sera partout si je vis dix ans. Croyez-vous donc que je n'aime pas aussi à faire plaisir? Un visage content me fait du bien à voir, mais je suis obligé de me défendre de cette disposition naturelle, car on en abuserait.' He had learned that with Josephine, whose tears had extracted concessions which would have been better refused.

Never had Caulaincourt felt so drawn towards his master. 'I wished all Europe could have heard him, and I should have liked the conversation, of which I did not lose a word, to continue indefinitely.' A letter from the Empress containing news of his son was handed over with the words: 'N'est ce pas que j'ai là une bonne femme?' At this moment he was merely the best of husbands, the tenderest father. 'Je ne puis exprimer le plaisir que j'avais à le contempler dans ces instants. Sa joie, son bonheur, empreints sur tous ses traits, m'allaient au cœur.' On crossing the Prussian frontier the Emperor gaily suggested that they might be kidnapped and handed over to the English.

N. Vous figurez-vous, Caulaincourt, la mine que vous feriez dans une cage de fer, sur la place de Londres?

C. Si c'était pour partager votre sort, Sire, je ne me plaindrais pas.

The idea made the Emperor laugh more heartily than his companion had ever seen, and for some time they were joking like schoolboys without a care in the world. When they drove up to the Tuileries late at night on December 18 Caulaincourt felt immense relief. The superman for whose welfare he had felt responsible during the rapid and perilous winter journey across Europe was safe and sound. Physically it had been an ordeal, for he had rarely slept, and the cold was intense. Intellectually it was a delight, for no one could talk like Napoleon, and no one had such chances of listening to him till the eagle with broken wings was locked in his cage at St Helena. While the Emperor pretended to believe that personal interest and ambition were the only motives of mankind, he recognised Caulaincourt's unchanging fidelity and thanked him for his vigilant care.

CHAPTER XXIV

CAULAINCOURT AND THE FALL OF THE EMPIRE

THE Emperor's return to Paris at the end of December 1812 steadied French nerves, which had been badly shaken by the publication in the *Moniteur* of the 29th bulletin. He was in excellent spirits and as full of illusions as ever. Caulaincourt, on the other hand, who saw the situation as it was, urged his master to use the good offices of Austria for the restoration of peace. Once again his advice was ignored, for the incorrigible warmonger refused to take the Austrian danger seriously and hurried on preparations for a fresh campaign. Despite the disasters his prestige still stood high. He was off again on April 15, 1813, and three weeks later won the battle of Lutzen.

Caulaincourt was now in high favour, and on the death of Duroc in battle he was appointed Grand Marshal, while retaining his position as Grand Écuyer. He represented the Emperor at the Congress of Prague, though he desired to make greater sacrifices for peace than his master approved. He urged the acceptance of Metternich's demands before it was too late; but before a reply was received Austria declared war. He was with his master on the stricken field at Leipzig and after the disaster succeeded Maret as Foreign Minister, surrendering the post of Grand Marshal to General Bertrand. Talleyrand had refused to return to the office where he had won renown, nominally because he resented certain conditions attached to the offer, but in reality owing to his conviction that the Emperor was *un homme fini*. Caulaincourt doubtless thought the same, but he was not the man to leave the sinking ship. Maret had been dismissed because he was widely believed to be intransigent, and his successor was chosen for tactical reasons as a friend of peace. The change made no practical difference, for policy was determined by the Emperor alone. Unfortunately the *Memoirs* omit almost the whole of the eventful year 1813, and the narrative is only resumed at the opening of 1814 when the Foreign Minister started for the Congress of Châtillon.

The failure of the Congress, declares Caulaincourt, was inevitable; for the best cards were now in the enemy's hands. The Great Powers had at last learned the lesson that only by joining forces could they deliver Europe from the perpetual menace of war, and the battle of Leipzig was correctly interpreted as the beginning of the end. His master, however, still believed in his star. A military success, he declared, would keep the enemy away from the capital, and the courage of French citizens would drive him back across

the frontier. He refused to admit that the sovereigns and govern-
ments of Europe were fighting no longer against France but against
himself, and that the interests of the French people demanded his
defeat. Caulaincourt emphasised the intransigence of the Coali-
tion, but in vain. 'Dangers from every quarter surrounded him,
but he believed he could escape from them and even hide them
from others by shutting his eyes. Even if his genius could triumph
at one point, he could not save his subordinates from defeat elsewhere, for his resources were everywhere insufficient. Everyone
admitted it, at Headquarters as well as in Paris. Discouragement
was general, not from fear of danger from day to day, but because
no one could see the way out.' The Emperor knew what his
entourage was thinking, though he avoided painful conversations. His policy was to play for time, trusting that something
would turn up. 'Sans doute c'était demander un miracle à
la fortune; mais son génie et son audace avaient tant obtenu
d'elle qu'il pouvait moins qu'un autre désespérer de ses
faveurs.'

The task of the Foreign Minister at Châtillon, possessing as he
did responsibility without power, was painful in the extreme.
The Emperor, annoyed by the cruel truths in his dispatches, did
not mince his words, and Caulaincourt came in for most of the
kicks. One day he would be charged with dishonouring his
master, while the next he would receive a message of gratitude and
confidence. That he was not a mere tool Napoleon knew from
long experience. 'Il est dur, Caulaincourt; toujours le Grand
Écuyer, le fouet à la main; je suis le postillon.' Another time he
remarked that he no longer read the Foreign Minister's letters,
which bored him. Whether he read them or not, he did not
always reply, or at any rate did not reply in time. Maret, the late
Foreign Minister, now Secretary of State, whose influence Caulaincourt particularly deplored, censured him for demanding decisions.
'Mon dévouement, ma franchise étaient presque érigés en trahison.'
Yet Maret's motives were honourable enough, for he was one of
the few people who really cared for his master and longed to spare
him the bitterness of consenting to cruel sacrifices. 'Il faut des
sacrifices,' wrote the Foreign Secretary; 'il faut les faire à temps.'
The Emperor and Maret, he complains, failed to realise that
decisions had often to be made within twenty-four hours. A
letter from Maret dated February 5, 1814, had given him [full
powers on paper. 'L'Empereur me charge de vous faire con-
nâitre que Sa Majesté vous donne carte blanche pour conduire
les négociations à une heureuse issue, sauver la capitale et
éviter une bataille où sont les dernières espérances de la nation.'
Only twelve days later this power was withdrawn by the
Emperor on the ground that the position was known to himself

alone. To accept conditions which his master would decline to ratify was useless, but to refuse concessions was to seal the doom of Paris and France.

The dictator, trusting to his star, took the failure of the Congress calmly. They tried to impose on him a peace which would have been only a truce, he remarked in their first conversation, for no one signed a dishonourable treaty in good faith. That is why he refused: he could not stoop to such deceit. 'Ce que veulent les ennemis, c'est de nous humilier, mais plutôt mourir. Je suis un trop vieux soldat pour tenir à la vie; jamais je ne signerais la honte de la France. Vous avez bien fait de ne pas souscrire aux conditions; je vous aurais désavoué à Paris.' The military situation, he continued, was by no means hopeless, and the enemy was not in Paris. 'I alone know the French people: depression will give way to indignation. You will see what happens within a week. The whole population will be armed. We shall have to rescue the invaders from popular excesses, for everybody who looks like a foreigner will be killed. We will fight, Caulaincourt. If the nation supports me, the enemy is nearer ruin than I, for the exasperation is extreme. I shall cut their communications. They have numbers but lack bases. I shall rally part of my garrisons. I shall destroy one of their corps, and the slightest reverse may have far-reaching results.' Negotiations, he added, were a waste of time, for the Allies were out to dismember France. 'I know Metternich and the Russians. If you yield to-day on one point, you will have to sacrifice something else to-morrow.' The Foreign Minister continued his efforts to save something from the wreck, but in vain.

The Emperor's belief that the Allies would hesitate to march on the capital while he was campaigning in Eastern France proved as false as his other political and military calculations. The news of the capitulation of Paris, whither he at last decided to return, was a terrible shock. 'Quelle lâcheté! Capituler! Joseph a tout perdu. Si je fusse arrivé quatre heures plus tôt, tout était sauvé.' The mood of despair passed quickly, and he was once more full of plans. 'Four hours have compromised everything, but in a few hours the courage and devotion of my good Parisians can save the situation. My carriage, Caulaincourt! We will go to Paris. I will put myself at the head of the National Guard and the troops. We'll put things straight.' None of the party responded, and they set out for the capital in deep depression. The Emperor's mood changed from hour to hour. At one moment he was denouncing his brother and exclaiming that all was lost. 'Joseph m'a perdu l'Espagne; il me perd Paris.' The next he was declaring that in three days he could dispose of troops sufficient to smite the invaders hip and thigh. 'We'll fight, Caulaincourt. Better to die with arms in our hands than to grovel before foreigners.' The professing realist had lost his sense of realities.

The dictator finally decided to send his Foreign Minister to Paris. 'Go and save France and your Emperor. Do what you can. They will insist on hard conditions, but I trust to your honour as a Frenchman and to your tried fidelity.' No precise instructions were given. He was unwilling to put into writing sacrifices which in conversation he recognised to be inevitable, for he wished to be able to disavow his envoy in case of need. Caulaincourt could not help admiring the pride and force of character which made him prefer the loss of his throne to what he called the disgrace of certain surrenders. Neither master nor servant had much expectation of success. 'You will arrive too late. The authorities in Paris, fearing to compromise the inhabitants, will refuse to listen to you, for the enemy has other projects than those hitherto announced. At any rate, you will judge what we can hope for, and so your report will be of value. If you find that salvation is to be sought in our courage alone, we will fight and die gloriously.' Even now he could not realise that the victors were no longer in the mood to negotiate. Caulaincourt's request that Berthier should share the heavy responsibility was declined on the ground that he could not be spared.

The envoy reached Paris early on March 31 and joined the delegation which was starting out to meet the Russians at the city boundary. His chilly reception from the delegates froze his heart, for it indicated that the cause of the Emperor was lost. Nesselrode's first words removed any lingering doubt. 'Your mission is useless,' began the Russian Foreign Minister. 'The time to treat was at Châtillon. The Emperor Napoleon has always refused to make peace. To-day the sovereigns decline to deal with him. Nothing can prevent us from entering Paris. The capitulation has been arranged. The city authorities know that the Allied troops come as friends, and that the object of this war was peace, which we have always desired.' An hour later Caulaincourt was received by the Tsar with his accustomed benevolence, though with a delicate reminder of his status. 'C'est le Duc de Vicence que je revois toujours avec grand plaisir et comme ami.' The envoy's plea for negotiations was rejected on the ground that a settlement with his master could not last. France, added Alexander, was doubtless as sick of him as Europe. When Schwarzenberg proved less friendly than Alexander, and equally intransigent, the envoy resolved, if possible, to save the throne for the King of Rome.

On returning to Paris, after these depressing interviews, Caulaincourt called on Talleyrand.

·T. The Emperor ruined us by not letting you make peace at Châtillon.

C. Can we count on you in our misfortune?

T. You will hear that I did my best two days ago to save his throne, to retain the Empress and his son, but the Emperor gives secret orders which spoil everything. He distrusts everyone. The fear of displeasing and disobeying him is paralysing. He has ruined himself and France. None of us can save them to-day. Why did he let things come to this pass? Why did he prefer the advice of flatterers, like Maret, to that of men devoted to his glory and to France?

C. This is not the moment to talk of his mistakes. He has sent me to the Emperor Alexander to defend him and to sign the peace which everyone wants. Will you help me? Will you abandon him in his misfortune? Will you sacrifice the Empress, the King of Rome, the true interests of France?

T. At the last Council I tried hard to save them, to prevent them from leaving. However unjustly the Emperor has treated me, I have fought almost alone for him and them, but without success since he gave secret orders. He has ruined everything, right up to the Council of Regency. You will know that I have done my duty.

While this conversation was in progress, the Allies were marching into Paris, and in the evening Caulaincourt had a second interview with the Tsar. The opinion of the capital, began Alexander, seemed very hostile to Napoleon. This verdict was challenged by the envoy, who argued that the Bourbons were unpopular, that the army was loyal to its old chief, that the deposition of the dynasty might mean the renewal of hostilities, and that Talleyrand did not speak for France. The Tsar listened patiently but his mind was made up. On the following day Caulaincourt discovered that his master had few friends. Some senators declined to see him, and those with whom he talked were hostile. Some appeared favourable to a Regency, but the fear of the Emperor's return and the hope of winning the favour of the new Government prevailed. 'Lâches fonctionnaires! Mauvais citoyens! Français ingrats! Ils souriaient déjà au soleil levant, oubliant leur gloire, le sang qu'ils avaient versé pour la patrie.' The Tsar's benevolent assurances, he adds, had turned their heads. 'These old senators were bewitched; their infatuation or their fear was almost frenzied.' Even more dangerous was Talleyrand, who appears as the wicked uncle in these pages. That Caulaincourt's zeal and devotion waxed with his master's growing misfortunes is a tribute to his nobility of soul. When the sun had shone brightly he was the outspoken critic: now he was the champion and the friend.

The second interview with Schwarzenberg was as chilly as the first. France, argued the envoy, did not want the Bourbons, and the attempt to restore them would renew the war. 'Our object,' retorted the Generalissimo, 'is to assure a long spell of peace for our children and tranquillity for the world. The Emperor Napoleon has proved too often in recent years that he had no wish for these things. There is no security for Europe while he is there.' A second interview with the Tsar was more genial, for, while ruling out Napoleon, he declared that the Allies had not yet decided on his successor. A second interview with Talleyrand made it clear that he was working, though without enthusiasm, for the Bourbons. A Regency appeared to him impossible, for Napoleon would always be listening at the door. The only ray of light during this unhappy day was the Tsar's statement that a final decision had not been reached. A third interview was still more cordial, for the ruler seemed touched by the envoy's emotion and took both his hands affectionately in his. 'Brave homme, calmez vous.' Not a bitter word was said about the past. 'I have admired him too much not to pity him in his misfortune.' We cannot imagine the Emperor Francis or Frederick William III using such chivalrous language about their terrible foe.

Napoleon had arrived at Fontainebleau on March 31, and late in the evening of April 2 Caulaincourt reported on his mission. He found his master surprisingly impassive. 'I do not cling to the throne. Born a soldier, I can become a citizen again without complaining. I have wished to see France great and powerful; I wish her above all happy. I would rather abdicate than sign a dishonourable peace. I am glad they declined your conditions, for I should have had to ratify them, and history would have reproached this act of weakness. Only a Bourbon can accept a peace dictated by the Cossacks.' Despite the machinations of Metternich, 'a rascal bought by the English,' the Emperor Francis, he believed, did not desire the dethronement of his daughter and grandson—an opinion which Caulaincourt promptly challenged. Though the Senate had announced the deposition of the Emperor and his family, he still spoke of victory in a final battle. 'I shall fight, not for a crown, for I no longer cling to mine, but for the honour of France and to prove that Frenchmen are not made to obey Cossack demands.' His brief address to the soldiers massed outside the palace—'Jurons de vaincre ou de mourir'—evoked a storm of cheers as in the days of his power. It was a satisfaction to Caulaincourt that now, at last, his master admitted his error in the Russian campaign. 'Vous m'avez dit la vérité.' Maret and Berthier, he continued, loved him. Duroc was devoted, but did not love him. 'Vous, vous m'avez dit la vérité, mais vous ne m'aimez pas. Vous m'êtes fidèle, parce que vous êtes un homme d'honneur: aussi je vous estime.'

Caulaincourt was ordered to reopen negotiations on the basis of a Regency, which his master continued to believe would be accepted by the Emperor Francis. He could not refuse, but he insisted that Marshals Ney and Macdonald should accompany him. After telling Schwarzenberg the object of their mission, the envoys were received by the Tsar, who learned with satisfaction that the ruler of France had abdicated in favour of his son. It would be difficult, he declared, to go back on the decision of the Senate, but he was very friendly and promised a reply after consulting his allies. The only chance of success, in Caulaincourt's opinion, was to make the invaders believe that the army stood solidly behind its old chief; but this slender rampart was swept away when the troops under Marmont, whom the Emperor had implicitly trusted, declared for the Bourbons. The news reached the Tsar during a conversation with the envoys and sealed the fate of the dynasty. When they left Caulaincourt was called back for private talk. The Tsar sympathised with his patriotic emotion, promising to defend the fallen dictator against assassination and to ameliorate his lot. The place of his detention was discussed and the envoy suggested Elba.

Returning to Fontainebleau at two in the morning, Caulaincourt was received by his master who, while denouncing the treachery of Marmont, realised that the game was up. His conditional abdication was made absolute. The envoy brought the document to the Tsar, who again promised to do his best both for Napoleon and for France. The King of Prussia spoke bitterly of the fallen ruler, but added that he did not wish to exploit his misfortunes. Now the throne was lost the most vital question for Napoleon was the future of his family. He still believed that the Emperor Francis would think it wrong to break up his home, but Metternich convinced the envoy that it was a false hope. The Empress, declared the Austrian Chancellor, would be regarded merely as an Archduchess or Princess, and the King of Rome as a Prince. Castlereagh was frank and friendly but unyielding. The signing of the treaty on April 11 stirred Caulaincourt to poignant reflections. 'The Emperor Napoleon, who had chained up anarchy, who had given France the best institutions and the best administration in Europe, who had carried the glory of the French name almost all over the world, established our credit, created our industry, against whom the fatherland can doubtless bring certain reproaches but to whom it owed so much glory and the germs of prosperity, abandoned by this nation, exiled from its soil and from the Continent filled with his immortal renown: these reflections overwhelmed me. What a destiny! What a spectacle for a Frenchman to see this King of Kings who, less than a year before, was the arbiter of Europe, this man whom the world and France had regarded as a demigod, to be reduced to owing the only consideration he could henceforth expect to the magnanimity of a foreign prince!'

The terms of the agreement of April 11 appeared to satisfy Napoleon, though he doubted whether all its provisions would be carried out and feared that he might be assassinated on the way to Elba. He was quiet and resigned, but deeply depressed. 'Ah! mon pauvre Caulaincourt, quelle destinée! Pauvre France! Quand je pense à la situation actuelle, à l'humiliation que lui imposeront les étrangers, la vie m'est insupportable.' The last words he repeated again and again with deep sighs and between long silences. The idea of suicide had already crossed his mind, though the faithful friend did not know it. For the first time in their decade of intimate collaboration the superman showed genuine tenderness. '"Embrassez-moi," et il me serra contre son cœur avec émotion.' Caulaincourt was deeply moved and his tears fell on his master's cheeks and hands. Of all the brilliant throng who had surrounded him only Caulaincourt and Maret remained to the end: even Berthier and Ney had left. He found a certain consolation in talking of his achievements, and at Elba he looked forward to writing the history of his campaigns. But the decision that his wife and son were not to join him was a bitter blow.

When Caulaincourt discovered to his horror that his master had taken the opium which he had carried about since the Russian campaign, he attempted to call for help, but was overruled. 'Je ne veux que vous, Caulaincourt.' His death, he added, would perhaps be the salvation of France and his family, and the past fortnight had been far more painful than the final scene. He complained of the slow operation of the poison, but his companion, who describes the vomiting and other phases of the agony, expected every moment to be the last. The dose, which was said to be sufficient to kill two men, was too weak for its purpose, but this record proves that the attempt at suicide was seriously meant. A few days later the fallen dictator left Fontainebleau for Elba. The *Memoirs* end at this point, and the closing sentence is a summary of the whole book: 'J'ose croire que j'ai toujours justifié sa confiance, et l'Empereur Napoléon a dit encore plus d'une fois dans son adversité: Caulaincourt est un homme d'honneur.'

Declining a friendly invitation to live in Russia, the General withdrew to the family estate in Picardy in the belief that his career was over. But he had never believed that France wished for the Bourbons, and the return of the eagle from Elba revealed the weakness of their position. He hurried to meet his old master, though he never expected the *coup* to succeed. Once again he reluctantly accepted the post of Foreign Minister and was made a peer, but there was little he could do. 'Ni paix, ni trêve, plus de réconciliation avec cet homme,' wrote the Tsar to Hortense, and he kept his vow. Caulaincourt wished to accompany his master to the front, but he was bidden to remain in the capital to keep an eye on the Emperor's brothers, Fouché, and other uncertain elements. After Waterloo the clear-sighted realist advised Napoleon to abdicate in favour of his son and to escape from France before it was too late. For a brief space he co-operated with Fouché and Carnot in a provisional government, but Fouché's secret support of the Bourbons decided the issue. The Tsar was a changed man, refusing for the first time to receive his old friend. This time it was really the end of his career. He resigned from the army, and the impenitent Bonapartist was excluded from the Chamber of Peers. The closing years were lonely and sorrowful. Yet never for a moment did he regret or apologise for his services to the demigod of whose faults and errors he was well aware, but whom in the days of misfortune he had at last almost learned to love.

Bibliographical Note.—Caulaincourt is fortunate in his editor, Jean Hanoteau, whose Introduction fills half the first volume. The General's account of Franco-Russian relations should be compared with Vandal's masterpiece, *Napoléon et Alexandre*; Sorel, *L'Europe et la Révolution Française*, vols. 7 and 8; and Tarlé, *Napoleon's Invasion of Russia, 1812*. The story of the fall of the Empire is told with great spirit by Houssaye in *1814*, *1815*, and *Waterloo*.

CHAPTER XXV

MME ADAM AND GAMBETTA

JULIETTE ADAM, *La Grande Française,* stands out from the throng of clever women who adorned the Third Republic. Every French salon, literary and political, has its lion, and in her brilliant circle Gambetta for a few golden years played the part of Chateaubriand in the enchanted world of Mme Recamier. How the beautiful and precocious girl captured literary Paris during the Second Empire, encouraged the Republican Opposition, endured the horrors of the siege and the Commune, taught the eloquent young *méridional* how to behave in cultivated society, fought his battles, applauded his triumphs, and broke with him when he abandoned the *Revanche,* is recorded in the seven volumes of her sparkling *Souvenirs,* published between 1902 and 1910. The student of France in the second half of the nineteenth century can neglect them as little as the Journals of Horace de Viel-Castel and the de Goncourt brothers.

Born in Picardy in 1836 Juliette Lambert grew up in the ideology of her father, an unworldly Jacobin doctor to whom *Liberté, Égalité, Fraternité,* was a religion, not a mere phrase. The men of 1848, she explains, were apostles and saints—not politicians, but souls in love with the ideal. So intense was his sympathy with the underdog that he dreamed of marrying her to a working man—a project which made no appeal to the ambitious and fastidious girl. His final choice was little better, for at sixteen she was forced into a loveless match with a lawyer of Italian descent twice her age. After the birth of Alice, her only child, they separated, and Mme Lamessine settled in Paris at the age of nineteen, determined to make her own career. Her attempts at poetry were frustrated by the judicious counsel of the veteran Béranger: "My child, you will never be a poet, but you may one day be a writer." Her first book, published at the age of twenty-two, *Idées anti-Proudhoniennes sur l'amour, la femme et le mariage,* a reply to Proudhon's attacks on George Sand and Daniel Stern (Mme d'Agoult), won her the devoted friendship of the former and opened the door to literary circles in the capital.

Literature was not enough for this ardent soul, who was soon in touch with the republican foes of the Second Empire. In 1864 she opened a salon which was frequented by Challemel-Lacour, Henri Martin, Gaston Paris and other celebrities, among them Edmond Adam, a wealthy and respected banker, twenty years her senior, whom she married in 1868 on the death of the odious Lamessine. All the opposition parties, even the Orleanists, were welcome in this republican circle. The first task was to overthrow the Man of December, whom they hated and despised, and to restore constitutional liberty to France. The hostess, a rigid *abstentioniste*, frowned on the *sermentistes* who, like Grévy, took the oath to the Empire in order to attack it from within. It was a shock when, in 1869, her husband announced his intention of standing for a constituency.

JULIETTE. Et tu préterez serment, toi?

ADAM. Out. J'y ai longuement réfléchi. Quelque objection que tu soulèves, je l'ai soulevée et rejetée.

An abyss seemed to open under her feet as he started for the campaign, but she was not the woman to surrender without a fight. Her love, she argued, was nourished by her respect, and to forfeit the latter was the worst of infidelities. Adam's letters seemed to indicate a certain hesitation, and when a telegram arrived with the single word *Viens* her hopes revived. She was greeted with the words: "Es-tu devenue moins sectaire, moins absolue, Juliette?" Honour, she replied, was honour. It was in vain that he cited the example of other stalwart republicans, and on the very day that he was to take the candidate's oath she induced him to withdraw. He explained to the astonished electors that he had changed his mind, and the happy couple returned to Paris, Juliette prouder than ever to bear his name.

The outstanding event in the history of the Adam salon was the arrival in 1868 of Gambetta, the youngest and most formidable recruit to the ranks of the Republican opposition.

JULIETTE. Il faut le faire connaître à notre milieu, me l'amener.

ADAM. C'est qu'il a des façons bien étudiant, qu'il ne se gêne en rien, ni en paroles, ni comme tenue. Il a un accent impossible, discute avec insolence, et je ne tiens pas à ce que tu l'entendes juger les hommes de 1848.

JULIETTE. Bref, est-il extraordinaire, a-t-il une grande valeur, oui ou non?

ADAM. Il est extraordinaire, il a une valeur. Mais il est bohème, vulgaire, brutal, vivant comme personne, le type de l'homme des foules, un Danton, plus retors, et s'emparant avec autorité de la parole où qu'il soit.

JULIETTE. Invitons-le.

Before taking the plunge the hostess made further inquiries. "Is he invitable?" she asked one of the pillars of her salon. "No, impossible," was the reply. Alphonse Daudet, he added, described him as a noisy Gascon, a sort of commercial traveller in politics, provincial to his finger-tips, ill-dressed and blind in one eye. This realistic snapshot made Mme Adam hesitate, for a salon can be ruined by the introduction of a discordant element. Her husband found the verdict too severe, for his talk, though fiery, was never mere fireworks.

The young lawyer, of whom Paris was beginning to talk, was invited to dinner to meet Jules Ferry, Challemel-Lacour, and a few other intimates. One of them, the Marquis de Lasteyrie, a grandson of Lafayette, arrived early and remarked to the hostess, "I shall tell Thiers about this dinner, for I know he is greatly intrigued by the *jeune monstre.*" A moment later Gambetta was announced. Believing that he was the guest of a blue-stocking he turned up in an ill-fitting suit, a cross between an overcoat and a frock-coat, with a flannel shirt peeping behind the waistcoat. Seeing everyone else in evening dress he excused himself. The only way to rehabilitate him, the hostess decided, was for him to take her in to dinner, instead of the Marquis, as had been arranged. Adam could hardly believe his eyes, but Juliette had done the right thing and Gambetta understood. "Madame," he whispered, "je n'oublierai jamais une leçon donnée ainsi." Henceforth the place of honour was his by right of genius. The conversation that night turned on the burning issue of abstentionism, of which the hostess was an ardent champion.

GAMBETTA. L'abstentionisme est une naiveté. Si l'on veut forcer l'ennemi il faut suivre la trace de ses pas.

JULIETTE. A moins qu'on ne puisse le viser de haut et l'abattre d'un coup.

GAMBETTA. Nous sommes sous l'Empire. Combattons l'Empire avec les procédés de l'Empire. Inutiles de chausser des escarpins (pumps) pour entrer dans les égouts. Mettons des bottes d'égoutiers.

Shortly afterwards the *jeune monstre* leapt into fame by a speech at a political trial in which he denounced the Second Empire in ringing tones. Adam was in Court, and Juliette's father, the old crusader of 1848, expressed a longing to kiss the tribune's shoes. With one accord the fighting republicans exclaimed *Nous avons un chef!* The storm of eloquence, it was said, had shaken the imperial tree. The veteran Thiers, a friend of Adam though not yet of Juliette, admitted that the affair had gone better than he expected, but he distrusted the orator's Italian blood. The Italian rulers of France, Mazarin and Bonaparte, he declared, had done her no good. Gambetta was carried away by his own eloquence, though sincere in his sonorous formulas, a blend of Rienzi and Mirabeau. His anti-clericalism was deplorable. "Je deviens l'ennemi de vos amis, Adam. Votre Gambetta est un danger politique et social. Gambetta, même avant son succès, désagrégeait déjà l'opposition constitutionelle. Que sera-ce aujourd'hui avec l'autorité qu'il vient d'acquerir?" Adam remained unshaken by what seemed to him merely an old man's jealousy of a younger rival.

The Empire had lost its glamour, and to eager eyes the Third Republic, free, generous, and pacific, seemed to be in sight. Gambetta, now a member of the Corps Législatif, sketched a programme in his first great constructive speech at Belleville. Neither the man nor his message, however, was to everybody's taste. Jules Simon denounced him as a fanatical atheist; George Sand declared bluntly: "Thiers est le seul homme politique parmi vous tous, croyez-moi." Gambetta had a boundless belief in himself, and when someone spoke apprehensively of the spectre of anarchy, he laughed. No member of the Adam circle took the Liberal Empire seriously, and Juliette despised Ollivier as nothing but an accomplished phrasemaker. The only Imperialist to enjoy her friendship was Mérimée, whose charm and wit outweighed his political heresies.

While Gambetta and his friends were absorbed in their fight against Napoleon III, Bismarck was preparing his knock-out blow. For Juliette and her husband the Prussian spectre only began to take shape in 1869 when their friend Nino Bixio, the comrade of Garibaldi, met them in Genoa. "I have just paid a visit to France and Germany by order of the King, who wished to know the condition of the French and German armies, since he is convinced that Bismarck is meditating war against France. I share this conviction. Within a year you will be attacked, and, since you are unprepared, you will be smashed." Adam turned pale. "Taisez-vous, Nino, ou je vous jette à la mer. La France battue par les Prussiens! Jamais, entendez-vous, jamais!" "Ah! mon pauvre Adam," rejoined the General quietly, "que la France est aveugle!" On returning from his holiday Adam informed Thiers, who remarked that the conversation confirmed his own fears; but in Juliette's salon the warning fell on deaf ears. A year later, when the Adam family were staying with George Sand in her country home, the news of the declaration of war arrived. *Vive la France!* cried Maurice Sand, the gifted son of the hostess. They all repeated the words with trembling lips, and the two women burst into tears. That Ollivier accepted the responsibility for the declaration of war *d'un cœur léger* filled them with fury, and Juliette, a good hater, never forgave him the unlucky slip.

When the news of Sedan reached Paris Mme Adam made her first public speech to the crowd outside the Chamber of Deputies. "The Republic," she cried, "is not decreed, it is made, it is your own child. *Vive la République!*" It was music to the ears of this implacable foe of the Empire to hear thousands of voices echo the cry. The bitterness of the initial defeats was partially assuaged by the dawn of a great hope. Her friends were in the Provisional Government, Gambetta Minister of the Interior, Jules Simon at the Education Office, Adam for a few weeks Prefect of Police.

20*

That she would share the perils of the siege, sustain the courage of her neighbours, work in the hospitals, and join the ranks of "*les à l'Outrance*," went without saying, for her flaming patriotism enabled her to endure to the end. When the horrors of bombardment were added to the miseries of cold and hunger, the end was near and Paris surrendered on January 28, 1871. Soon afterwards her journal of the siege, kept for her absent daughter, was published at the wish of Victor Hugo.

The monarchical majority elected to the National Assembly in February was a shock. Adam was returned for a Paris constituency and voted in the minority (107 to 546) against the conclusion of peace. His sharp-tongued wife denounced the *capitulards* who, as she saw it, played Bismarck's game. Intransigent by nature her patriotism became a consuming passion. Now that the Empire had gone, a vitriolic hatred of Germany filled her heart. Her head felt as if it would burst, and she could no longer weep. When a Prussian official touched her hand in returning her pass she shuddered as if he were a poisonous animal. The war was the supreme event of her life, for the iron of defeat had entered her soul. Henceforth she lived for *la revanche*. Starting her career as a writer and a hostess, she had become a politician in spite of herself. Reopening her salon she dedicated herself to France.

Gambetta had proved his worth in the days of trial, but to Thiers as to many of his countrymen he was *le fou furieux* who had prolonged resistance beyond all reasonable limits. When Dumas scornfully remarked that his supporters were of no account, Juliette rejoined: 'Tant pis pour moi et pour Adam, qui avons en lui une foi absolue et ne connaissons pas d'autre chef.' His speech at Bordeaux on June 26, 1871, was balm to their bleeding hearts. He was the man of the Left Centre, the only Leader who could heal his country's wounds. His watchword, declared Adam, was: 'Instruire et armer la France pour la rendre digne de la liberté.' At his next appearance in the salon they congratulated him on the pronouncement. Thiers had praised its wisdom, remarked Adam, and might begin to regard him as a rival. Thiers, replied Gambetta, knew very well that he had nothing to fear. 'Did I not yield him the place at Bordeaux which I could have kept for myself? Not to the others, but to him, to the old man who, unable to fight, toured Europe in search of aid for France while Jules Favre refused even to cross the Channel.' As they talked Juliette admired the readiness of her husband, a man of ripe experience, to accept the leadership of their young guest.

'You need a great daily,' remarked Adam. The money could easily be found, and the collaborators were at hand—Challemel, Spuller, Ranc, Paul Bert and other knights of the Round Table. *L'Avenir National*, which he had helped to finance, was dead;

a fresh start was needed. That was Challemel's opinion too, rejoined Gambetta, who added that they had already chosen the title: *La République Française*. Admirable! exclaimed the host and hostess. 'Notre salon, notre maison, notre dévouement, nos relations,' she adds with legitimate pride, 'devinrent fort utiles à Gambetta. Il voyait chez nous des artistes qu'il charmait, des financiers qu'il rassurait, des adversaires politiques qu'il enrôlait.' It was to be 'my Athenian Republic,' very different from the unhappy models of 1849 and 1793. Thiers stood aloof, but Adam remained in close touch with the old campaigner whose counsel was needed in the conflict with the Right.

THIERS. Obtenez de vos amis, mon cher Adam, la difficile sagesse; sinon votre République vous échappera.

ADAM. Nous sommes résolus à la patience, et je la prêche.

THIERS. Faites-la aussi prêcher par votre femme, qui ne l'aime guère.

ADAM. Vous vous trompez, M. le Président. Ma femme aussi prêche la patience.

Both leaders were needed for the convalescence of France, and men with a foot in both camps, such as Adam and Freycinet, strove to bridge the gulf between them. 'Le petit grand homme,' the embodiment of the conservative republic, was the man of the moment, for he alone seemed able to save the country from the Royalists; but the time of the young *méridional*, less than half his age, would surely come. It was a delight to these ardent souls to watch him growing in stature and authority. 'Notre enthusiasme pour Gambetta va croissant. Il s'est surpassé dans le discours de Saint-Quentin. Voilà bien le langage d'un chef. Et quel patriotisme! J'avais mis dans le culte voué à Gambetta tout mon cœur de Française.' Juliette felt proud to be not merely the follower but the friend and colleague of the chief ornament of her salon. Sardou's caricature in *Rabagas* filled her with angry disgust. She made friends with the Gambetta family on the Riviera, where she had a villa, and drank in the stories of his penniless youth. Shortly before his birth a fortune-teller had told his mother that she would bear a man who would rule over France. When he made one of his resonant speeches in the provinces the friends would say: 'C'est la voix de la France,' and read aloud the purple passages again and again. Victor Hugo's *L'Année Terrible* and Déroulède's *Chants du Soldat* were music to their ears. 'Tous vos fils, ô Français, ne sont pas aux tombeaux,' chanted Juliette and Alice again and again.

Mme. Adam admired Renan, but she had no use for his pregnant aphorism: 'La vérité est dans les nuances.' There were no half tones in her pictures. Her friend Sarcey, the dramatic critic, told her that she had always been 'une emballée pour ou contre,' and that she was only bearable because she was ready to confess her mistakes. She divided Frenchmen into friends and foes of *La Revanche*. 'Si la France était assez oublieuse et impie pour ne pas avoir constamment sous les yeux cette image de votre Alsace sanglante et mutilée,' declared Gambetta in thanking some Alsatians for a *plaque*, 'alors vous auriez le droit de désespérer.' This was too strong meat for Thiers, who remarked: 'Qu'il attende, qu'il attende pour dire ces choses!' Such caution was not to the taste of the Adam salon. It was a shock to hear George Sand, so justly admired and beloved, denouncing the young tribune as a windbag.

GEORGE SAND. Il n'y a rien en lui, mais rien, rien, je vous le répète.

JULIETTE. Ma grande amie, de grâce, vous ne pouvez imaginer ce que vous nous faites souffrir, Adam et moi. Nous n'avons pas d'autre espoir, pas d'autre culte que Gambetta. Il est pour nous la personification même de la France.

GEORGE SAND. Mes pauvres enfants, le siège vous a rendus fous. C'est vous avec votre imagination qui égarez Adam. Vous êtes seule responsable de cet engouement.

ADAM. C'est moi plutôt que vous pourriez accuser d'avoir influencé Juliette; car j'ai connu Gambetta avant elle. C'est le seul médecin qui saura panser nos blessures.

GEORGE SAND. Et que penses-tu de tout ce que nous disons, Alice?

ALICE. Je pense de M. Gambetta comme mon père et ma mère. Vous ne l'avez entendu, vous ne le connaissez pas, vous l'aimeriez, car il est vivant et gai, comme vous aimez qu'on le soit.

GEORGE SAND. Singulier ensorceleur!

The bubbling enthusiasm in these volumes helps us to visualise the *rôle* of Gambetta in the moral recovery of France. Every speech increased the gratitude and devotion of his followers and friends. When the Adams read that he had broken down in an address to a deputation from Alsace-Lorraine—'les nobles provinces, toujours dévouées à la France, toujours regardant son drapeau'—they too shed tears. 'Nous pensons en même temps: la politique, les partis, qu'est ce que cela? Nous nous disons que nous n'aurons plus qu'un idéal, qu'une religion, qu'un but, qu'un pourquoi à notre vie: incarner plus encore notre dévouement à la patrie dans l'homme de la défense nationale, l'homme de la revanche.' While Thiers, the President, and Charles de Rémusat, the Foreign Minister, privately complained of these emotional utterances, the disciples of Gambetta rejoiced that there was at any rate one resonant voice, free from the trammels of office, who could express the yearnings in every French heart.

The overthrow of Thiers in 1873 by a combination of Legitimists,

Orleanists and Bonapartists under the leadership of the Duc de Broglie was a milestone in the history of the Third Republic. The triumph of the Right was naturally distasteful to the Adams, but there were compensations. The reactionaries, though numerically strong, were deeply divided. The famous aphorism of Thiers— La République, c'est ce qui nous divise le moins—was the literal truth, and the Monarchists knew it. The Left felt sure that its time would come, and Gambetta's friends experienced a certain feeling of relief when his only rival, full of years and honours, left office. Mme. Adam attended the more important debates at Versailles and rejoiced when her husband was elected a Life Senator. Gambetta had shown that he could act, but he also knew how to wait. France, he believed, was looking forward, not backward. She would soon tire of the Right, and then power would fall into his hands like ripe fruit. Meanwhile his task was to restore the self-confidence of the nation and to avoid factious attacks on the Government. If they had enough rope, he reflected, they would hang themselves. MacMahon, the new President, was a brave soldier, but, politically speaking, a light weight.

Gambetta was not only the political chief but the delightful correspondent, travelling companion and guest both at Paris and in the Adam villa near Cannes. *Beau mangeur, beau buveur, fin gourmet*, this exuberant son of the south warmed both hands before the fire of life. The faithful Spuller, his unselfish secretary and friend, was also good company, for, like the Chief, he was well read. There were sufficient differences of emphasis among these ardent democrats to give savour to their talk. Spuller, a theist, regretted the anti-clericalism of his leader and Paul Bert. Juliette pleaded for what Gambetta called her aristocratic or Athenian republic, an *élite* superior to anything monarchies could produce. 'We must raise the whole mass,' rejoined Gambetta. 'To pick and choose is favouritism. Quality will always emerge.' They had become such friends that he talked to her of his love for Leonie Léon, who was always to be seen in the Assembly when he was due to speak.

The gulf between Thiers and Gambetta was never completely bridged, though they often fought on the same side. 'Sait-il écrire et parler aux femmes?' inquired the old man sarcastically. 'En France tout est là.' Juliette replied that he was soaked in French literature and history and was a judge of art.

THIERS. Quoi, il plait aux dames? je dis aux dames.

JULIETTE. Si je suis dame, il me plait à moi. Il est ami délicat, conteur et causeur charmant; ses lettres ont du mouvement, de l'intérêt, souvent de la hauteur de pensée.

She could speak with authority of his letters, many of which adorn her pages. In the middle seventies this historic friendship was at its height.   She admired the generous soul in which rancour found no place, and he was grateful for her encouragement.   It was a happy time for both.   France was showing her usual resilience.   The Republic was taking root, and the leader was preparing for his task.   No one dreamed of the sorrows which lay close ahead.   The first blow was the death of Adam, one of the most unselfish members of the old Republican guard.   The second was the ideological breach between the Chief and his hostess.   The third was the failure of *Le Grand Ministère*, quickly followed by the death of the great tribune at the age of forty-four.   But there were still many battles to be fought and victories to be won before the curtain fell.

CHAPTER XXVI

MME ADAM AND THE *REVANCHE*

THE seventh and last volume of the *Souvenirs*, entitled *Après l'abandon de la Revanche*, is the most valuable of them all and made the most stir. That the hero of the National Defence, the chief architect of the national revival, the one Frenchman who seemed able to stand up to Bismarck, the author of the famous formula *Pensez y toujours, n'en parlez jamais*, should consent to sheathe his sword and trust to 'immanent justice' for redress of a great wrong seemed almost beyond belief. His most intimate friends were aware of the change, but his conversion remained a secret till his old hostess told her story a quarter of a century after his death. In these passionate pages he is depicted as the lost leader, sinning against the light.

Adam's death occurred in 1877 on the eve of the final defeat of the Royalists, when Marshal MacMahon dismissed the Jules Simon Ministry, recalled the Duc de Broglie to power, and, backed by the Senate, appealed to the country. Juliette worked hard to win over moderate conservatives for whom the Presidential *coup d'état* of May 16 had gone too far. Under Gambetta's dynamic leadership the French people saved the Republic from its enemies, who, owing to their incurable divisions, could never have provided a stable regime. The reactionary old Marshal was only a pawn, but he had willingly played the Royalist game. 'Quand la France aura fait entendre sa voix souveraine, il faudra se soumettre ou se démettre,' cried Gambetta, adopting a slogan invented by Freycinet. The Marshal resigned and Grévy, a veteran lawyer, was installed at the Élysée. At last the world was convinced that the Republic had come to stay.

Realising that mutilated France could never recover the Rhine provinces without allies, Juliette turned her longing eyes to Russia. Gambetta, on the other hand, to her horror and surprise, got in touch with agents of Bismarck and the Prince of Wales. He described with gusto his first interview with 'Son Altesse Impériale,' whom his hostess regarded with deep suspicion. France, she felt, should avoid complicated combinations, and should continue to cherish the patriotic passion which saved her from the cowardly acceptance of defeat. 'I know my adored country. I know that when it is no longer directed by some great national idea, it goes astray or yields to self-indulgence.' Gambetta, she complained, was so obsessed by his struggle with the men of May 16 that the ardent memories of the past were beginning to fade. 'Ma chère amie,' he protested, 'continuez à me croire aussi patriote que

vous, et gardez-moi jalousement toute votre confiance, j'en ai
besoin.' They were still great friends and he turned to her for
help in his private affairs. When his mother suddenly appeared
in Paris he asked Juliette to tell her gently that she had better
return. 'Pauvre maman! Je lui dis le plus doucement du monde
qu'il ne faut pas trop s'attarder. Elle comprend, elle devine que
son adoré fils désire son départ. Elle éclate en sanglots.'

Mme Adam was not the only person to worry about German
propaganda and German plans. Bismarck's unconcealed preference for the Republic moved her to fury. As if the Republicans
had less fighting spirit than the Royalists! Thiers, now in his
eightieth year but still full of vigour, asked her to visit him before
leaving Paris for her summer holiday. He was anxious about
Count Henckel von Donnersmarck, the notorious financier who had
fished in the muddy waters of the Second Empire, had been
Governor of Metz during the war, and had now returned to Paris
to make more mischief. Thiers had spoken to the Duc Decazes,
who complained that the Chancellor was taking too much interest
in French affairs. The ex-President recognised that Gambetta
had become the bulwark of the Republic and wished to preserve
his prestige. Juliette agreed, adding that 'the dauphin' must
be guarded from the wiles not only of Henckel but of the Prince of
Wales.

THIERS. Il faut que vos amis l'entourent chez vous comme
lorsque Adam vivait. Il faut recommencer à les réunir tous, à
jour fixe, dès votre retour.

JULIETTE. Je n'en aurai pas la force encore.

THIERS. La force, non peut-être, mais le courage, vous l'aurez.

It was their last meeting, for a few days later 'le petit bourgeois'
was dead. He had hoped to return to the Élysée after the
expected eviction of MacMahon and then to make full use of 'the
dauphin.' 'C'est moi qui présentera Gambetta à l'Europe,' he
had confided to Juliette. 'J'en ferai mon Ministre des Affaires
Étrangères, Président du Conseil.' His colleagues would include
Ferry at the Interior and Léon Say at the Treasury. A combination of the Left under Gambetta and the Left Centre under Thiers
would give France the stable and progressive Government she
needed and deserved. Juliette had learned to admire and trust
the vivacious old patriot who had been her husband's friend, and,
like the majority of French citizens, she mourned his loss.

When Gambetta was leading the Republican hosts to victory in
the elections of October 1877 a dark shadow fell across his path.
The *Figaro* hinted that a bomb was about to burst under his feet,
and Mme Adam asked Spuller what was wrong. An ex-mistress,
was the reply, possessed compromising documents and was bent
on revenge. More precise information was supplied by Émile de

Girardin, the veteran journalist. Dazzled by the young orator's leap into fame, the lady, known in the world of gallantry as Comtesse de Sainte-M——, had sought his acquaintance, and the relationship had continued till 1876. She had never forgiven him for transferring his affections, and she was now about to sell her treasures to Rouher, the Bonapartist chief. 'Stop it, buy the documents!' cried Juliette. He had tried in vain, replied Girardin, and a friend of the lady had also failed. There was not a moment to lose, for she was going to Rouher on the following day. There was one ray of hope: before parting with the high explosive she had expressed a wish to see Mme Adam. 'Il faut, je vous le demande au nom du parti tout entier, que vous les achetiez, bien entendu pour notre compte à tous.'

The first task was to summon the incautious Chief.

GAMBETTA. De quoi s'agit-il, grands dieux?

JULIETTE. De vous seul, et de façon bien désagréable.

When she told him what she had heard from Girardin, he was greatly upset. 'Yes, this woman was my mistress for several years. She was with me at Bordeaux and Saint-Sebastian. She has stolen some of my state papers and a woman's letters. Among other things she has a photo of me on which, with a lover's madness, I wrote some words which would produce a storm if they reached Rouher's hands. I have sent one or two friends to her. Perhaps you can save me.' Early next morning the interview took place, and the lady confessed that Rouher was ready to buy the *dossier* on the following day.

JULIETTE. Vous allez livrer ces papiers au plus cruel ennemi de celui dont vous avez partagé la vie?

MME DE SAINTE-M. Je me venge. Moi, la compagne des premiers et des mauvais jours, j'ai été chassée comme une servante.

JULIETTE. Vous avez aimé M. Gambetta?

MME DE SAINTE-M. Avec toute ma passion, tout mon dévouement.

After further conversation she agreed to hand over her treasures for 6000 francs. There was the photo, with the words which would have echoed round the world: *A ma petite Reine, que j'aime plus que la France.* When Juliette read them, her eyes filled with tears. The same evening the Chief came and burned the whole *dossier*. 'C'est l'un de vos miracles,' he exclaimed in gratitude and relief.

Gambetta was saved, but a few days later his rescuer had another and a greater shock. On October 18, 1877, Spuller arrived with the shattering news that the Chief had paid several visits to Henckel von Donnersmarck in his luxurious home in the Champs Élysées, and had actually spent an evening with Prince Hohenlohe at the German Embassy. Spuller had dined with his leader at

Henckel's house and listened to the host's cynical talk. He boasted, for instance, that by spreading rumours of war in the German press he had engineered the Chancellor's support for the Republicans in the recent decisive elections. After that, exclaimed Mme Adam, the man of *La Revanche*, the hero of the National Defence, might be negotiating with Bismarck—unless he was under the hallucination that he might recover the lost provinces through Bismarck's hands. No, replied Spuller, the Chief had made up his mind: politics had triumphed over patriotism. He was resolved to rescue the Republic from its internal foes, no matter what the price. 'Bismarck desires the republic in France'— Spuller had heard his leader use those very words. The Prussian statesman believed that modern republics meant peace abroad and dissension at home. Spuller, the ardent patriot, feeling unable to bear alone the burden of this distressing secret, confided it to Juliette, with the strict injunction not to talk about it, not even to Gambetta himself.

What could the *patriote farouche*, as she calls herself, say to her hero when next they met? The Russo-Turkish War was in progress, and she reiterated her well-known interest in Russia, 'our only possible ally.' 'Cosaque,' was his smiling comment— an old joke, for their disagreement on this point was not of yesterday. There was nothing to be done with Russia, he argued: victor or vanquished in the Turkish war, defeat awaited her. Gorchakoff was too old, Alexander II too hesitant. As Germany grew, Russia declined. So as Germany waxed stronger, retorted the indignant hostess, her strength was to be increased by France's submission to her aims! The situation was even worse than she had thought, and Spuller was almost in despair. Gambetta had said things which his friend had not the courage to repeat. The Chancellor enjoined secrecy on the ground that the Republican leader would lose the support of the patriots, who had been his earliest followers, if he avowed his abandonment of *La Revanche*, and he could not find equivalent support elsewhere. It was anti-clericalism, added Spuller, which had brought the old antagonists together.

Juliette felt an abyss opening under her feet. 'If the Republic becomes the ally of the Prussians; if the defender of our cause makes an arrangement with the man whose claws have torn out Alsace-Lorraine, our national heart, there is nothing more for me to do among my friends, and I will bury myself at Bruyères with my memories of the dead.' 'Les rancunes de Mme Adam,' observed Gambetta with a smile, 'sont poussées jusqu'à la férocité.' His letters ceased, a sign that he was pursuing his Bismarckian policy. Nothing, she felt, could interrupt the fraternity of heart, but their minds were becoming estranged. 'Moi, plus Française que lui, je sens que ce que le vaincu peut toujours défendre contre la vainqueur c'est la dignité.' No political rapprochement with the hated foe! No social relations! Should she write to him? No! It would be too painful and her reprimands would be useless. She could not change his Italian blood. His opportunism, she reflected, was the *combinazione* dear to politicians of his father's land.

In the closing days of 1877 a letter from Spuller confirmed the worst fears. The contact with Henckel had become ever closer, and the latter had dared to say: 'Il vous reste maintenant, mon cher Gambetta, à aller à Varzin.' 'Pourquoi pas?' was the reply. Spuller had not been present, but the words were repeated to him by the Chief himself. 'Ah! madame, je le sais, vous avez des larmes dans les yeux et vous pouvez pleurer. Moi, il m'a fallu une force au delà de ce que je croyais possible pour entendre de telles paroles d'une telle bouche.' Henckel had added that it would require more than one conversation to restore confidence between the two countries on the base of a common policy against the Papacy. Spuller's next meeting with his leader was stormy.

GAMBETTA (*roughly*). Tu as aujourd'hui une figure d'enterrement.

SPULLER. C'est qu'aussi tu enterres quelque chose.

GAMBETTA. En tout cas pas la République.

SPULLER. Oh! non.

A few days later, at the opening of 1878, after a brief visit to Rome, Gambetta visited his friend in her Riviera home and they had their first heart-to-heart talk about his new course. Forced to choose between two evils, effacement and participation in the game of European diplomacy, he had chosen the latter because it would help his domestic policy. Bismarck, she rejoined, was already tired of the *Kulturkampf*. A French *Kulturkampf* would merely strengthen the anti-clericals who pretended to be his friends, but would be quite ready to break him in due course.

GAMBETTA. Vous me croyez donc bismarckien parce que je suis anti-clérical?

JULIETTE. Certaines de vos restrictions, votre changement de langage à propos de nos provinces perdues, m'ont angoissée.

GAMBETTA. Ma chère amie, vous savez bien que nous ne pouvons sans folie songer à reprendre l'Alsace-Lorraine.

JULIETTE. A cette heure, je le sais, mais plus tard. . . . Ah! mon grand ami, comment vous peindre mon chagrin de vous deviner de plus en plus engagé avec l'Allemagne! Pardon, pardon du mot cruel, mais je le dis: Vous trahissez votre destinée. Mais je vous blesse.

GAMBETTA. Vous ne pouvez me blesser, ma chère amie.

JULIETTE. Vous êtes Prussien! Je reste Cosaque. J'essaierai de vous barrer le chemin chaque fois que vous vous approcherez de Bismarck.

GAMBETTA. Vous êtes d'accord avec vos sentiments, moi avec ma raison. Allons donc chacun notre chemin.

JULIETTE. Mon chemin à moi, c'est la route nationale, tracée par le grand, le fier passé de ma race; le vôtre est une *combinazione* et un casse-cou.

GAMBETTA. Quels que soient nos combats, promettons-nous de rester fidèles à notre amitié.

JULIETTE. J'en fais le serment.

On her return to Paris early in 1878 Juliette resumed her weekly political dinners, and Gambetta occupied the usual place of honour at her right hand. His change of attitude was unknown to the public, but the secret would be difficult to keep, for Henckel boasted that he would himself take Gambetta to Berlin. Only God could prevent the crime, exclaimed Spuller, trembling with emotion. What could his friends do? Nothing, replied Juliette. France must know that she was being deceived. She could not shake hands after he had taken the blood-stained hand of the foe. Despite her earlier resolve to let things take their course, she consented, at the wish of a Lorrainer, who had somehow learned the secret, to make a direct appeal. An urgent message brought the Chief, and with tears in their eyes the two friends implored him, in the name of Alsace-Lorraine, to give up the visit. He replied with emotion that he had given it up. The joyful news was promptly communicated to Spuller, who wept like a child and, like the author of the Memoirs, kept repeating the words *Il n'ira pas.*

Open scandal had been averted, but there was no change in his attitude. Instead of talking bluntly of *La Revanche,* he spoke of the diplomatic recovery of France, the necessity of regaining her position as a Great Power. He was increasingly nfluenced by Jules Ferry, Camille Barrère and Ranc, none of them good *Revanchards* in the critical eyes of Juliette. To this school of thought it was the duty of France to take her place and pull her weight in the Congress of Berlin. To Juliette it was a humiliation to accept an invitation from her mortal foe. Moreover, why should France join in setting limits to Russian influence in Eastern Europe? It would be rightly interpreted as the official renunciation of her claims. That France should be represented by her Foreign Minister, Waddington, 'un Anglais anglophile et germanophile,' was an added grief. The more she considered participation, the stronger became her conviction that it meant the side-tracking of *La Revanche.* 'Why do you go to a Congress at Berlin?' inquired her friend, the Italian Ambassador, General Cialdini. 'You compel us to go, too. Believe me, Bismarck will lay a trap for one of us, perhaps for both.'

Juliette repeated the words to Gambetta, whose annoyance was reflected in the loud tones of his voice. 'Are you having a quarrel?'

asked some of the guests. 'It is about the Congress of Berlin,' he replied. 'I keep telling our friends that France cannot remain aloof from a European consultation without risking the loss of her position as a Great Power.' Europe, retorted Juliette, had not troubled about France in 1870–71, and France need not trouble about Europe now. 'Si vous me disiez qu'il sera parlé à Berlin de l'Alsace-Lorraine d'une façon quelconque qui créât un précédent de protestation ou de réserve, je comprendrais.' Her grief was increased by the fact that not only Gambetta but Freycinet and other valued friends approved participation. How could France stand aside, they asked, while the treaties of 1856 and 1871, which bore her signature, were discussed and revised? Her apprehensions were confirmed when France, with the foreknowledge of Bismarck and Salisbury, seized Tunis and thereby drove Italy into the arms of the Central Powers. Colonial expansion made no appeal to Madame l'Amazone, as a friend called her, not only because it diverted attention from *La Revanche*, but because it involved compromising accommodations with France's enemies, Germany and England.

At their first meeting after the Congress Juliette made a frontal attack on her lost leader.

JULIETTE. Vous êtes satisfait, mon cher ami, de votre homme de confiance, de M. Waddington? Vous trouvez qu'il a fait à Berlin une figure digne de la France, amputée de l'Alsace-Lorraine?

GAMBETTA. Il a suivi à la lettre mes instructions sans jamais s'en écarter.

JULIETTE. En y mêlant quelques inspirations de Disraeli, enguirlandées par Salisbury et le tout parachevé par la traîtrise bismarckienne.

GAMBETTA. Vous ne voulez jamais voir que ce que vous voyez, tournant en rond autour de l'Alsace-Lorraine. Ce qu'il faut à la France c'est justement sortir de ce rond tracé par les esprits étroits. Il nous faut avant tout respirer, vivre, il nous faut l'expansion, la marche en avant.

JULIETTE. Je suis pour la marche à la revanche.

The only excuse she could imagine was his Italian blood. His side of the story was revealed in the life of Gambetta by Paul Deschanel, published in 1919, shortly before he succeeded Poincaré as President of the Republic. The conversion was more gradual than she was aware, and the new material proves that her narrative does him injustice. His longing for the recovery of the Rhine provinces was unchanged, but he abandoned the belief that it could only be achieved by the sword. His visits to Germany had impressed him with her enormous strength, and Henckel described him to Bismarck as the only Frenchman who really knew their country. A striking letter to Ranc, dated September 20, 1875, shortly after the war scare of the spring, gives the first hint of the new course. 'If by diplomatic action we can avert the threatened conflict, or at any rate postpone it, or, still better, prevent the shedding of blood which we anticipate, should we not try? The means? Our colonies! With you I can speak frankly. Is it better to preserve for France her distant possessions or her future generations? Let us face this agonising dilemma: either the lives of our French youth or portions of our colonial territory. Ought we not to profit by this tendency to expand, this taste of the Germans for colonies? As they have none they desire them, and we have what they want. Is not that a chance for us? How can we save ourselves from the approaching catastrophe?' The thought that Germany might attack does not seem to have occurred to Juliette, but it was always in his mind.

A few weeks later, on December 1, 1875, a second letter to Ranc reiterates that Bismarck might perhaps be ready for a deal. 'Here is an unlooked-for opportunity! The Chancellor is coming to Paris and wishes to converse with one or two French personages. Ought I to hold aloof? Is it really my duty as a Frenchman?' That Bismarck contemplated a visit to Paris was a myth, but could not they meet elsewhere? Two years later, on October 17, 1877, when the Republicans had routed the Royalists, Henckel reported to Bismarck that he was in close touch with Gambetta, who paid him visits in the country. Herbert Bismarck cautiously replied on behalf of his father that the French statesman must not compromise his prestige by public contact with the Chancellor. It need not be public, rejoined Henckel. 'I undertake to send him to you publicly or privately, whichever you prefer.' Gambetta, repeated Bismarck, must not run risks and must keep his political capital intact. 'Il était trop bon,' declared Spuller later; 'il n'avait pas le sens critique de l'humanité.' Though there was nothing dishonourable about his dream that the provinces might possibly be recovered by a bargain, it was a pure illusion, for even had the Chancellor been willing to negotiate, the soldiers would have intervened.

The announcement of a Congress at Berlin to decide the problems of the Near East filled Gambetta with excitement. 'I have read the monster's speech,' he wrote on February 20, 1878, to Léonie Léon. 'I am enchanted—it is just what I wished and expected. The equilibrium and regrouping of Continental forces is admirably sketched. It is for us to profit by circumstances and rival ambitions, to state plainly our legitimate claims, to found the new order in agreement with him.' Should he see the Chancellor before the Congress met? The question answered itself. Either fight or negotiate, he declared—and France could not fight. On April 4 Henckel proposed a meeting. Bismarck accepted it for April 30, when he would return to Berlin for the opening of the Reichstag. It was not to be, for on April 18 Henckel received a brief note from Gambetta. 'Man proposes, Parliament disposes. When I gladly accepted yesterday, I had not counted with the unforeseen. Large questions relating to the Ministry of War have emerged, and I cannot leave my Parliamentary post.' Bismarck was naturally annoyed, and the project was never revived. That an interview would have led to practical results is improbable. The whole story is a reflection not on Gambetta's patriotism, as Juliette argues, but on his grasp of realities.

A fresh chapter in the life of La Grande Française began in 1879 with the foundation of a successful fortnightly, *La Nouvelle Revue*, which she edited for the next twenty years. It was an old project, for the *Revue des deux Mondes* had no gospel to preach and preferred veteran celebrities to the ardours of youth. The decision to launch the enterprise at this moment was due not only to the conversion of Gambetta but to the growing realisation that the Third Republic was not the Athenian polity of her dreams. Strong in the conviction of her own political wisdom, justly proud of her literary ability, and fortified by promises of support from influential friends, she craved for a platform whence she could trumpet forth the gospel of revenge. 'What are the aims of your review?' asked Gladstone at a dinner at which Gambetta was one of the guests. 'They are three,' was her reply. 'The struggle against Bismarck, the unceasing demand for the recovery of Alsace-Lorraine, the desire to lift the shadow of defeat from the mind of young writers and to give them fame ten years earlier than they could achieve it without my review.'

The Editor reserved for herself the articles on foreign affairs, in which she poured out a lava stream of invective against Bismarck and the Frenchmen who, in her opinion, danced to his tune. That she was a force to be reckoned with was quickly realised on both sides of the Rhine. 'Can nobody silence *cette diablesse de femme?*' exclaimed the Iron Chancellor. It was in vain that Grévy, Gambetta, and Ferry implored her to moderate her tone. To the latter, who needed German support for his colonial schemes, she replied that she would only desist if she were imprisoned. 'And what an honour to be imprisoned for attacking Bismarck!' Realising that France needed an ally to recover her lost children, she proclaimed without ceasing that Russia must be won for the great crusade. Anything which might divert the eyes of Frenchmen from the gap in the Vosges was anathema. Gambetta's readiness to co-operate with the English in the control of Egypt was a fresh ground of complaint, and the seizure of Tunis was interpreted as a triumph for Bismarck's diabolical plan of driving a wedge between Paris and Rome.

Despite the pact that political differences should never destroy their friendship, Gambetta faded out of Juliette's life. For *La Nouvelle Revue* he cared nothing. Would she be as hostile to himself as to his policy? he asked. She would say in the review what she could no longer tell him in her salon, was the reply. 'That is a declaration of war,' he exclaimed. 'No,' she rejoined, 'it is a declaration of independence.' His formula was the more accurate, yet she regretted that her friend had missed the highest political prizes. When the Royalists were routed in 1877 and the reactionary Marshal was evicted, he should have gone to the Élysée instead of contenting himself with the Presidency of the Chamber. Grévy had always distrusted the eloquent *méridional*, and he barred his way to office as long as he could. 'His policy will not suit this country,' he observed to Freycinet, who vainly protested against the veto.

Juliette had known the President for twenty years and had never liked him, but they found a point of contact in their detestation of Gambetta's new course. To her complaint that he had not summoned him to office, he replied that his *combinazioni* were too dangerous for France. Power, added to his immense prestige, would enable him to bring about the official entente with Bismarck. 'Il a été un grand chef d'opposition, il ne sera jamais un homme de gouvernement. D'ailleurs, ma chère amie, vous le pensez vous-même. Croyez-moi, Gambetta n'a pas notre vieux sang français dans les veines. Son patriotisme n'a été qu'un patriotisme de tête, ajoutons-y, pour vous plaire, aussi de cœur, mais pas du sang.' When at last he called the Chief to office *Le Grand Ministère*, which the leading politicians declined to enter, lasted only two months. A year later the broken statesman, prematurely aged and weary of the fray, was in his grave.

Mme Adam rings down the curtain in 1880, before the final eclipse of her old leader, and in later life she was reluctant to talk of his closing years. There is no indication of her feelings on this phase in the delightful biography by her friend Winifred Stephens, to which we must turn for the second half of her career. In any case, her course was set. *La forteresse de l'idée française*, as Léon Daudet called her, would never capitulate. She rejoiced at the Russian alliance, of which she had been one of the chief architects. She distrusted England till we fought side by side in 1914. Worshipping the army and desiring to uphold the prestige of the military caste, she was a violent anti-Dreyfusard, and her salon, though by that time more literary than political, was purged of its more liberal elements. When Germany surrendered in 1918 and the lost provinces were restored, the indomitable octogenarian, like the Empress Eugénie, could sing her *Nunc dimittis*. Clemenceau sent a military car to take her to the Hall of Mirrors where she witnessed the signing of the Treaty of Versailles. 'To be defeated and never to despair, that is victory.' Pilsudski's noble aphorism may serve as the epitaph of Juliette Adam. The indomitable old warrior lived till 1936, only missing her century by a few weeks.

Bibliographical Note.—The *Life of Mme Adam* by her English friend Winifred Stephens, published during her lifetime, is supplemented by the same writer's obituary article in the *Contemporary Review*, October 1936. Spuller, *Figures Disparues*, contains a notice of his friend Edmond Adam. The best biography of Gambetta is by Paul Deschanel. The early years of the Third Republic should be studied in Hanotaux, *Histoire de la France Contemporaine*, 4 vols., which ends in 1882; Daniel Halévy, *La Fin des Notables*, 2 vols., which ends in 1879; Freycinet, *Souvenirs*, 2 vols., which ends in 1893; and Brogan, *The Third Republic*. The survey of Franco-German relations, 1871–1914, in Gooch, *Studies in Diplomacy and Statecraft*, contains a brief bibliography of the subject which formed the dominant interest of Juliette Adam's long life.

PRINTED IN GREAT BRITAIN BY NEILL AND CO., LTD., EDINBURGH.